# The Reservoir War

# The Reservoir War

A History of
Ohio's Forgotten Riot
in America's Gilded Age,
1874-1888

Jerett W. Godeke

ISBN: 9798853195578 (paperback)
ISBN: 9798853289529 (hardcover)

Cover designed by Jerett W. Godeke and Amelia Myers
Book designed and published by Jerett W. Godeke

FIRST EDITION

For rights, permissions, and other inquiries, please email:
jerett.godeke@gmail.com

I want to dedicate this book to (and extend an eternal sense of gratitude toward) my high school history teacher, Tony Unverferth. The man who inspired me to enter the history profession, for which this book was able to exist because of that inspiration.

At midnight along the towpath to the reservoir will be embalmed in song and story in the distant future when the history of the Paulding County rebellion comes to be written.[1]

---

1 "War on the Wabash," *Cincinnati Commercial Gazette*, April 28, 1887, 1.

# -Table of Contents-

# -Acknowledgements-

The task of writing about the history of Six Mile Reservoir and Paulding County's Reservoir War turned out to be a far more arduous undertaking than initially anticipated in 2020. Though the bulk of the research was completed without much outside assistance, this book would not have been possible without the encouragement of my peers and a little guidance here and there to find some materials.

I must first thank the History Department at Bowling Green State University for admitting me into the graduate program in 2020, especially considering this book started as my roughly chronological notes for a class paper or two and my public history capstone project. If I had not been admitted, I would likely never have pursued this research.

I would also like to thank the Paulding County Carnegie Library for having many of the local newspaper volumes digitized and made available online. While I did have to skim those hundreds if not thousands of pages because the OCR was not perfect, being able to search for keywords to catch most of the information, rather than mindlessly scrolling through thousands of pages of newspapers on microfilm, undoubtedly saved countless hours of my sadly finite life.

Kim Sutton, then president of the John Paulding Historical Society in Paulding, Ohio, provided generous assistance with the initial research in 2020 and provided a few anecdotes that sent me searching the newspapers to find more primary sources. She also served on my committee for the capstone project and has been my biggest cheerleader during this entire process as she eagerly anticipated reading the final product(s). Kim, I cannot thank you enough for your continued support.

Jane Nice graciously helped find the sources that went into making the first chapter of this book and has been one of the biggest supporters of the project, repeatedly telling me how excited she was that I was doing this research. The last source she gave me, which she received from Judge Michael Wehrkamp, was monumental in filling in the missing pieces of the military occupation of Paulding County and how much it cost the State of Ohio. Jane, I hope this book goes a long way in shaping future iterations of your Reservoir War play, *No Compromise!*

Jane Nice and Melinda Krick gave my very first draft a once-over in 2022, and their willingness to take the time to do so was greatly appreciated. Their help put this book on a path toward being far more readable, especially because I tend to struggle with sentence fragments. That said, the draft they read and edited, quite thoroughly I may add, has changed somewhat drastically since they last saw it a year ago. Any errors in grammar, spelling, and punctuation that persisted into the final product are ultimately my fault as the final editor of this book.

Walter Lang consistently helped me find those specific locations throughout Paulding County that help place the locations in our modern context. He also assisted in finding information on specific individuals and some newspaper clippings I may have overlooked.

The staff at the Paulding County Clerk of Courts were immensely accommodating in helping me track down the court records for the Stambaugh lawsuits in the 1870s. Those few documents were more than sufficient to discuss the premise behind the cases, which had remained an enigma in the newspapers.

My parents (Dawn & Ken), my brother (Jasper), and Amelia Myers (who helped design the book's cover) always had some time to listen to my probably incoherent rambling in private as I found one new fact after another for almost two years. You all deserve some of the highest praises after dealing with me so wrapped around this research for so long. Thank you for always supporting me.

Rebecca Rollings, a former coworker, and friend of mine was gracious enough to take some time from her lunch break to wander over to the Genealogy Center of the Allen County Public Library to have a look at a last-minute source for me. That source was rather eye-opening. Thank you for your time in helping make this project as comprehensive as it could be.

The staff at the Andrew L. Tuttle Memorial Museum in Defiance, Ohio were immensely helpful in helping me find a couple of locations that have long since disappeared from Defiance's streets. The staff at that museum was also very helpful in providing information for my previous research topic before the Reservoir War research came to the forefront.

Ohio National Guard Historian SFC Joshua D. Mann was very helpful in providing me with information about the guns that the

Ohio National Guard were using at the time of the Reservoir War. Though our correspondence was brief, and my reasoning for the research request was vague, he was still able to determine that I was researching what the Ohio National Guard refers to as the Paulding Reservoir mission.

If anybody went unacknowledged and therefore unthanked, I owe you my sincerest apologies and probably a lunch or dinner at your favorite restaurant. If I got anything wrong or forgot something in my recollections about who did what, that was entirely my fault, and I apologize.

# -Author's Note-

This project was started amid the COVID-19 pandemic in September 2020, and during my first semester of graduate school. Due to travel restrictions, among other concerns, a different research topic from my original choice was advisable. About that time, I recalled a short conversation with Terry Zartman that occurred while practicing driving in driver's ed. This conversation happened in 2012 or 2013 when I was fifteen, and I am not entirely sure why I remembered it.

Nevertheless, it seemed like a good topic for a graduate-level local history course at Bowling Green State University. It quickly became clear that the Reservoir War was far beyond the scope of a term paper, and that term paper turned into a brief history of leisure on the banks of Six Mile Reservoir. Considering there is a book in your hands now, suffice it to say that a great deal of information was found that would not have allowed me to adhere to that requirement of only writing about twenty-pages.

I would like to first clarify that the usage of the word 'war' was, likely, for dramatic effect; especially when considering the term did not see major usage until after there was a military response by the state. The event of study was more often referred to (and rightfully so) as a riot by contemporary newspapers. Much like any riot or unrest of exceptional scale and volatility, it too saw some sort of authority force deployed to quell it. The word 'war' was hyperbolic, but to some extent used in a similar way to other largely bloodless conflicts like the Toledo War in 1835-36, Aroostook War in 1838-1839, and the Pig War in 1859. In all these cases, there was little to no direct engagement between belligerents that would traditionally define a war, but nevertheless there were still casualties and in some cases loss of life.

The work of my predecessors, particularly that of Henry Howe, Everett A. Budd, and Otto E. Ehrhart, was ultimately short and parochial in nature because of brevity or technological limitations of their time (or both). This book was able to be as exhaustive as it is because, among other helpful resources at my disposal, I had the means of looking through thousands of pages of newspapers and state records via the Internet with minimal need to travel and the ability to keyword search; something my predecessors could have only dreamed of being able to do. Nevertheless, their work served as the foundation of my research, and I am eternally grateful that they wrote *something* down for future generations of historians to find and build upon. While I am not the first to write a history of the Reservoir War, this book is the first comprehensive history of the event.

To provide a better understanding of what came together to cause the Reservoir War, what happened during the 'war,' and what happened in the following year and a half. This book will synthesize contemporary newspaper articles and legislative reports, with some exceptions for better context on certain aspects of the past, to weave together the many scattered and sometimes conflicting sources into one coherent book. Because some assumptions needed to be made based on logical interpretation of the evidence, this book does its best to present multiple interpretations of historical events where there is no single "official" explanation.

It is not necessarily my intention currently to overtly apply any of the information in this book to the broader trends of history. All the reader needs to know going forward is that America's Gilded Age, in general, was a time of great upheaval and unrest socially, politically, and economically. Some of America's most notable riots occurred at this time in history, namely those of the Great Railroad Strike of 1877, the Haymarket Affair in 1886, and the Pullman Strike in 1894. Though the Reservoir War stands as yet another example (albeit a minor one) of the discontent indicative of America's Gilded Age, it was largely inconsequential outside of its localized concerns. It caused a brief stir amongst national newspapers, that much is true. However, it did not achieve the same long-lasting notoriety as other notable events with further reaching implications that happened about the same time.

That said, just because it was practically inconsequential to the rest of America's history, does not make it any less important to those it did affect at the local level. It may be possible that other events that happened around the same time partially inspired the locals. For instance, I have taken the liberty to note for future scholars instances where one of the local papers at the time, the *Antwerp Argus*, and local citizens implied on multiple occasions that dynamiters from Chicago were the 'real' culprits of the destruction. However, I have found no conclusive reason for why they did this other than possibly trying to use the recent Haymarket Affair in Chicago as a scapegoat for their actions.

While the Reservoir War has largely been forgotten, even by many of those who reside in Paulding County, it is still commemorated and talked about by local historians and those just interested in the county's history. Paulding County's motto is "No Compromise!" in reference to part of the inscription on the Dynamiters' black flag. An Ohio historical marker for the Reservoir War was also erected in 2021 (delayed from 2020 due to COVID-19) at the corner of County Road 180 and Township Road 77. It is a silent sentinel, briefly and succinctly telling curious travelers of what happened at such an innocuous location.

Lastly, it should be noted that all quotes in this book are kept in their original prose and spelling, or as close as possible, to preserve the phrasing intended. Care has also been taken to make sure names are accurate. However, there is no guarantee that the records were accurate for some names. When there was a discrepancy in spelling, I elected to fall back on the name they were remembered by on their headstone, or if no grave could be found, based on often limited genealogical records.

Footnote Key:

¶ = Additional Historical Information/Context

§ = Author's Comment

@ = Location Information

(Doubled symbols indicate a successive note of same type)

# -Historical Context-

## The Canal and Six Mile Reservoir

### (1826-1868)

Two canals were constructed through Paulding County, Ohio; the Miami & Erie Canal and the Wabash & Erie Canal. Surveying for the Wabash & Erie Canal began in 1826, and was completed in the fall of 1828.[1] In 1827, the State of Indiana received a federal land grant to build a canal between "the mouth of the Tippecanoe River on the Wabash to the mouth of the Auglaize River on the Maumee."[2] That land grant the State of Indiana received also included the portion of the canal to be built in the State of Ohio, thus the land would need to be transferred before work could begin.[3]

The State of Ohio received its own federal land grant in 1828 to build an extension of the Miami & Erie Canal north from Dayton, Ohio, to Lake Erie.[4] That said, the extension of the Miami & Erie Canal was not authorized until 1831, two years after the completion of the Miami & Erie Canal between Cincinnati, Ohio, and Dayton in 1829. However, construction of this extension would not begin until 1833.[5]

The State of Ohio had, in 1829, "pledged to complete the Wabash & Erie Canal as far eastward as surveys would indicate this to be necessary."[6] However, that agreement was not ratified by the Ohio Legislature until 1834.[7] Even after this agreement was ratified, construction contracts were not awarded until 1836,[8] and actual construction on the Wabash & Erie Canal between Defiance, Ohio (the mouth of the Auglaize River on the Maumee River), and Fort Wayne, Indiana, did not begin until October 25, 1837.[9]

A significant reason for the delay, and presumably why the State of Ohio had neglected to ratify the agreement to complete a portion of the Wabash & Erie Canal in their border as surveyed, was caused by the State of Indiana. Despite beginning construction on its portion of the canal in 1832, the State of Indiana had neglected to transfer, to the State of Ohio, the canal land located in Ohio that the State of Indiana had received from the federal land grant. Therefore, the State of Ohio was unable to begin construction on the portion of the Wabash & Erie Canal between Defiance and Fort Wayne until this transfer was made in 1834.[10]

Other reasons for the delay include a "scarcity of funds" to build the canal, "the sparse settlement of northwestern Ohio," as well as a "fear that the Wabash & Erie Canal would serve the interests of northern Indiana much more than it would serve Ohio."[11] The most significant issue for the State of Ohio, however, was the unsettled border dispute with the Michigan Territory that became known as the Toledo War (1835–1836).[12] This border dispute was caused in no small part by the State of Ohio's plans to build the two canals and the local debate over where the northern terminus of the combined canals would be located near Lake Erie on the Maumee River.[13]

After the border dispute was settled, the State of Ohio was able to begin construction on the Wabash & Erie Canal and the Miami & Erie Canal. The latter of the two had already been "theoretically completed as far as the Maumee River… but it was not in condition to use" in 1836.[14] Due to the nature of the Great Black Swamp the canals were built through, a proverbial "howling wilderness,"[15] and the Financial Panic of 1837,[16] the Wabash & Erie Canal did not open until May 1843.[17] The cost to construct the Wabash & Erie Canal from Junction, Ohio to the State Line, a distance of roughly eighteen miles, was $450,000 (~$18,000,000 in 2023).[18]

At the time of their construction in the early 1840s, (when the young[¶] Paulding County's population was only around 1,034 total residents[19]) the locals considered the opening of the canals as "one of the most important events" of the county's history.[20] The construction of the canals was reportedly "hailed with delight," and the canals themselves would be "held in high esteem by the people along their banks" due to their overall improvement of transporting goods and people in the region compared to previous methods.[21]

The canal's completion allowed "the entire produce of the Wabash Valley" in Indiana to "pass through [Fort Wayne] and be shipped on Lake Erie."[22] This greatly benefitted those producers as the canal replaced the need to ship bulk goods overland about one hundred miles to Michigan City, Indiana or Chicago, Illinois.

---

¶ Paulding County was formed on April 1, 1820, but was not formally organized until March 18, 1839.
(Henry Howe, *Historical Collections of Ohio in Three Volumes*, Volume III, 30; State of Ohio, *Acts of a General Nature, Passed by the Thirty-Seventh General Assembly of Ohio*, Volume XXXVII, 385-86.)

There, the bulk goods would be loaded on to a ship which would need to travel around the Michigan peninsula to reach Lake Erie and points east.[23] The canal's completion would also greatly expedite safe passenger travel across parts of Ohio and Indiana wherein individual's heading to points west could easily and safely get part of the way there at a cost of "but a few dollars."[24]

On July 10, 1842, before the Wabash & Erie Canal was even opened the full length to Toledo, Ohio, the canal boat *Jesse L. Williams*, captained by Samuel Mahon, was the first boat to transit the canal between Fort Wayne and Defiance.[25] The first canal boat was ceremoniously guided into Defiance by the "Defiance Band and a number of the citizens."[26] After the official opening of the Wabash & Erie Canal in 1843, an opening celebration would be held on July 4, 1843.[27]

The canal had formally opened for navigation on May 8, 1843,¶ but the celebration was delayed to coincide with Independence Day.[28] A projected ten to fifteen thousand people from Indiana and Ohio, up and down the route of the canal, and further beyond, reportedly gathered in Fort Wayne to celebrate not only American Independence, but the completion of "the shortest and most eligible route [between] the navigable waters of the northern lakes with those of the Mississippi."[29]

---

¶ Johnny Appleseed reportedly used the newly opened canal to help his nephew Timothy move to the vicinity of Saylor Lock in Allen County, Indiana near the State Line. Timothy became the lockkeeper at the nearby Saylor Lock soon after and was also later a section foreman for the nearby Wabash Railroad. Timothy's home was also reportedly John's 'headquarters' at one time before his death in 1845.
(Mary E. Roebuck, *Genealogy of the Chapman Family*, 5, 21, 23, 29, 31.)

The day's "exercises" would take place on a grove owned by Thomas W. Swinney,@ and boats lined the canal "double tier... the whole length of the city, from the upper to the lower basin."[30] The day's itinerary began at sunrise with a "national salute of 26 guns" that was fired from Old Fort Wayne.[31] At 9 a.m. a "13 gun salute" was performed "in honor of invited guests and strangers."[32] At 10 a.m. "3 minute guns" were fired and the procession was to form at Public Square ready to begin the day's festivities.[33] At 11 a.m. the "immense procession" that had gathered at Public Square began toward the Swinney Farm in the following order: Martial Music; Toledo Guards; Revolutionary soldiers and soldiers of the late war, with national colors; Orator; Reader; Chaplain; President; Vice Presidents; Ladies; Defiance Band; Invited Guests; Committees; Marion Band; Engineer Corps; German Band; Citizens of Ohio and Other States; Miami Warriors; Kekionga Band; Citizens of Indiana.[34]

After arriving at the grove, a prayer was said and the Declaration of Independence was read to the crowd, after which Lewis Cass made his address.[35] Following his address, the crowd proceeded to another part of the grove and "partook of a plenteous cold collation prepared for the occasion."[36] There, the crowd drank to toasts, more speeches were held, and letters were read from those who had been invited to the festivities, but could

---

@ The grove was on the farm of Thomas W. Swinney, which is now East Swinney Park in Fort Wayne.
("Swinney Park," City of Fort Wayne Parks & Recreation, accessed
    August 11, 2022, https://www.fortwayneparks.org/parks/38-
    parks/park-page-links/186-swinney-park.html.)

not attend.[37]¶ When all was done at the grove, the crowd returned to the city in the same order they had processed to the grove.[38]

The Miami & Erie Canal was not completed until June 27, 1845.[39] In total, the roughly 250-mile canal cost $5,920,200.41 (~$231,000,000 in 2023) to build.[40] Prior to its completion, the canal from Junction to Toledo was referred to as the Wabash & Erie Canal. On March 14, 1849, the "shared" portion of the canal between those points was renamed to match the Miami & Erie Canal.[41]

A new town, aptly named Junction, was created in 1842 where the two canals came together.[42] Its economic potential by sitting at the junction of the two canals had some believing the new town could surpass Fort Wayne as the region's economic center.[43] Because of its position, Junction reportedly acted as a "clearing house" for canal traffic going in all directions.[44] At one time, Junction reportedly had "a brewery, a distillery, five warehouses, grist mill, nearly a dozen stores" among other things that made a community in those days like a post office, hotels, churches, schools, and saloons.[45] The record for the most boats docked in Junction at one time was reportedly sixty-five.[46] Junction's population peaked at 300 individuals, and it never quite lived up to the hype that was envisioned about it.[47]

While the Miami & Erie Canal would seemingly prosper with towns popping up every few miles, the Wabash & Erie Canal did

---

¶ Among those invited to the festivities but did not attend were former Michigan Governor William Woodbridge, former President Martin Van Buren, General Winfield Scott, former Speaker of the House Henry Clay, and former Secretary of State Daniel Webster.
(Allen County Public Library, *Canal Celebrations in Old Fort Wayne*, 93, 104-106, 108.)

not share that distinction, despite predating the Miami & Erie Canal by two years. Reportedly, this was due to talks of railroads as early as the canal's construction and a general lack of materials to ship abroad from the area, as the timber was locally manufactured into finished goods.[48] That said, two iron furnaces were set up along the Wabash & Erie Canal in Antwerp and south of Cecil around 1865.[49] This was not because there was any iron ore in Paulding County, but because the process of smelting the iron at the time used charcoal (made from burning wood) rather than coal or other resources. [50] To make things more cost-effective, the iron ore was shipped by boat from the iron ranges around Lake Superior to places like Paulding County, where the wood was plentiful.[51] The smelted iron ore was then exported by boat to mills in the east to be processed into a finished product.[52]

Tate's Landing@ was the first settlement west of Junction, situated at the second lock upbound on the canal. There is admittedly not much known about Tate's Landing. What is known is that Tate's Landing was named after Lyle Tate, a canal worker who wished to seek his fortune by acquiring land near Sharp's Lock (later known as Tate's Lock), where a small settlement started that would come to have a general store, post office, taverns, and a church among other small buildings and dwellings. The post office was named after Captain Robert M. Reid, and thus, the location also came to be known as Reid's Post Office.[53]

---

@ Tate's Landing was located where Emerald Road (Road 115) meets State Route 111 in Paulding County.
(*Map of Paulding County, Ohio*. Drawn and Compiled by W. A. Strong. Paulding, Ohio. 1878.)

Furnace was the next settlement up the canal from Tate's Landing and was home to the Paulding Furnace.@ Henry Howe described the Paulding Furnace as a "huge brown building, and on the plateau beside it, and in contrast with it, lines of structures shaped like beehives... twenty-three in number and being white as snow."[54] These snow-white structures were kilns for the creation of charcoal by burning the plethora of wood found in this region in the nineteenth century.[55] The Paulding Furnace was not the only structure at this location, as there existed a blacksmith shop, a store, and dwellings with enough residents living at Furnace to require Miss Mary Schaffer to begin teaching sometime around May 1887.[56]

The next and final settlement upbound on the canal, and the focal point of this book, is Antwerp. Platted in 1841 and incorporated on August 6, 1864.[57] By the time Henry Howe visited in 1888, Antwerp was home to "2 large stave factories, one of which combines with it the manufacture of dressed and rough lumber; 2 factories for tobacco, candy, and jelly pails and cannicans—small, wooden cans—axle grease boxes, 1 patent hoop manufacturer, flouring mill, etc."[58]

Antwerp was also an excellent market for grains and livestock alongside the industries already present. Antwerp was also exporting commodities such as poultry and any other wild game that local hunters had taken down. Howe notes that these

---

@ Furnace, and by proxy the Paulding Furnace, were located along the north side of County Road 180 on the east side of the former Cincinnati Northern tracks south of Cecil. As of 2023, there are still remnants of one of the furnace's kilns hidden in the woods and brush just east of the aggregate company's property.
(*Map of Paulding County, Ohio*. Drawn and Compiled by W. A. Strong. Paulding, Ohio. 1878.)

included animals like "wild turkeys, ducks, quail, partridges, etc."[59] As mentioned above, prior to Henry Howe's visit, an iron furnace was also present in Antwerp, as were the usual accommodations that were befitting of a large rural community in Gilded Age Northwest Ohio, as we shall see.

Despite the low number of settlements along the Wabash & Erie Canal in Ohio, the canal was significant to the few settlements along its banks; such was the case with Antwerp. In comparison, it was not quite like the nearby town of Junction, which was poised to reap the rewards of being platted at the confluence of the two canals. Antwerp's canal significance came in its sprawling industrial base, and a much larger presence on the southeastern edge of town.

Keeping a canal at a consistent water level was crucial for it to be a viable transportation thoroughfare; this necessitated building a feeder reservoir. The State of Ohio designated the land just southeast of Antwerp for this purpose as early as 1826, but work would not commence until 1840.[60] Work on Six Mile Reservoir was supervised by Alexander S. Latty.[61] Such a reservoir would necessitate a large tract of land to be helpful. What land was already owned by the residents of Paulding County at that time was "cheerfully" given to the State of Ohio for the "'common cause'—the canal interest."[62] Despite making the land useless for any other purpose,[63] the canal infrastructure was "regarded as a public necessity and the citizens acquiesced in the desolation which it wrought."[64] This perception remained as long as the canal infrastructure was still considered useful to the people of Paulding County, when it was no longer considered useful, it would be perceived as a "curse to the county."[65]

The work to build the canal and reservoir was arduous. Despite beliefs among some contractors that "no man in the use of liquors should have employment at their hands" when constructing other parts of the canal, [66] during Six Mile Reservoir's construction, workers were given "jiggers."[67] These were small 12oz. bottles of whiskey given before each meal and at about 9:30 a.m. and 4:30 p.m. while the men were at work.[68] This allowed the workers to drink something despite "the character of the water" in Paulding County.[69] Six Mile Reservoir was completed in the fall of 1842.[70] The total cost of construction was $172,000 (~$6,250,941 in 2023).[71]

The Wabash & Erie Canal's prism in Ohio was originally planned to have a dimension of forty feet in width at the surface of the water and was only to be four feet deep.[72] However, the section of canal from Junction to the State Line was enlarged to be fifty feet in width at the surface of the water and five feet deep.[73] Confusingly, the rest of the Wabash & Erie Canal from Junction to Manhattan (Toledo) was built to a dimension of sixty feet in width at the surface of the water and five feet deep;[74] "substantially increasing water requirements" of the canal, according to historian Harry N. Scheiber.[75] Despite this change, the St. Joseph Feeder Canal in Fort Wayne could typically supply the water needed for the canal in Ohio.[76] However, an additional feeder reservoir was deemed necessary east of Antwerp to more consistently supply water to the canal in the dry seasons.[77]

To keep Six Mile Reservoir as full as possible, especially when water from the winter and "rainy spring season" flowed through the St. Joseph Feeder Canal and down the Wabash & Erie Canal, any excess water from the canal would escape into the reservoir through a side cut and over a tumble wall next to Banks Lock on the reservoir's northwest corner.[78] The St. Joseph River could purportedly supply upwards of "five thousand cubic feet [of water] per minute."[79] The namesake Six Mile Creek, a "small stream with a very poorly defined channel,"[80] also helped supply the reservoir with the "drainage of the county for fifteen miles to the west, and an average of four miles to the south" that flowed into that creek and then into the reservoir.[81]

In "ordinary seasons," Six Mile Creek was expected to be able to supply the reservoir alone.[82] Combined, the two water sources amply supplied Six Mile Reservoir for the dry season in the summer and fall.[83] The St. Joseph River being the "only" feeder for the reservoir in the dry seasons.[84] However, this arrangement made five miles of the canal in the State of Ohio above Banks Lock (and Six Mile Reservoir) dependent on the St. Joseph River in Fort Wayne.[85] This left this section of canal vulnerable to water supply issues should anything happen in Indiana. The rest of the canal from Banks Lock to Junction, however, was always able to be fed by the reservoir and was therefore safe from this vulnerability.[86]

The construction of Six Mile Reservoir used two-inch thick oak planking, laid edgewise, encased in clay to form its embankments,[87] a practice known as sheet piling.[88] These plank walls were built to be as tall as the reservoir's waterline.[89] The benefit of doing this was the prevention of animals from burrowing through the embankment and weakening the earthwork by allowing water through the burrow.[90]

Workers then soaked the clay in water and allowed it to harden to create a wall that was resistant to water seeping through it.[91] Oxen were reportedly walked back and forth across the hardening clay to further compact it, similar to modern steam rollers. [92] The practice strengthened the earthen bank against the immense pressure of the water, and made the banks "watertight." [93] The clay used in building the reservoir was wheelbarrowed from nearby to the embankment locations, mostly by Irish laborers. [94] Those embankments were built to varying heights between five and fourteen feet; [95] the northeastern walls were the tallest.¶

When it was all said and done, Six Mile Reservoir was no small reservoir. According to the *Sixth Annual Report of the Board of Public Works*, published in 1843, "this reservoir covers an area of two thousand five hundred acres of land." [96] Modern Google Earth software backs this up, as tracing the reservoir on a modern aerial map, the land taken up comes out to roughly four square miles or approximately 2,500 acres. This original size does not factor in how much land was reportedly flooded by the reservoir at peak/over-capacity. That number ranges from 10,000 acres to 20,000 acres. [97] This much more significant number is only made real by a large amount of rainfall, and so its number varies depending on how much rain the area got at any given time.[98]

After their construction, a few issues would plague the Wabash & Erie Canal and Six Mile Reservoir for the first thirty years. A little over a decade after their construction, in 1855, the newly completed Toledo & Illinois Railroad in Ohio and Lake

---

¶ Legend has it that some of those Irish laborers were entombed in the eastern bank after dying in a cholera epidemic.
[see "Tour Directions To Old Six Mile Reservoir," in Bibliography]

Erie, Wabash & St. Louis Railroad in Indiana (henceforth referred to as their better-known successor Wabash Railroad) had not only been built in direct competition to the canal,[99] but it became apparent that the water supply to Six Mile Reservoir from Six Mile Creek was interfered with by the railroad's construction.[100]

About "one half" of the water supply from the fifteen miles to the west of Six Mile Reservoir was cut off when the railroads constructed ditches along its right of way, and it was "conveyed under the canal" through a culvert near Antwerp.[101] The State of Ohio recognized that this had drastically cut off "a very important channel for the supply of the reservoir." Stating that the "resort would inevitably have to be made to the St. Joseph River, by the way of the Indiana canal, in order to supply the deficiency created in the loss resulting from this railroad cut-off."[102] From approximately 1855 onwards, Six Mile Reservoir would be fed predominantly by the St. Joseph River in Indiana, though the state would explore other unexplained methods of feeding the reservoir so it could be sufficiently filled for the dry seasons.[103]

By 1858, the State of Ohio became aware of a flooding issue (especially during the spring and fall) to the south of the canal between the Wabash Railroad and the canal. The cost of building a culvert sufficient in size to better drain the land was estimated at $1,800 (~$65,417 in 2023).[104] Also occurring by 1858, in spite of the fact that the reservoir was cleared of timber except "a belt of a few rods width" left near the banks specifically to protect them from 'wave action.'[105] "Two miles of the north, and half a mile of the east embankment" of Six Mile Reservoir had been eroded, by as much as one-third of the original height, by what can only be presumed to be wave action.[106] This 'wave action' was reportedly caused by "floods and high winds."[107]

There was now a concern that a high enough water level in the future could cause a complete failure of the rest of the embankment, not unlike a dam failure caused by the water overtopping the dam.[108] Understandably, the northern bank of the reservoir (which was also the southern bank of the canal) was deemed to be in "bad condition" and "unsafe."[109] Believing the cost to repair the embankments would only amount to $3,000 (~$109,028 in 2023), work commenced in the summer and fall of 1858 to make the repairs.[110] As the season was short, only half of the northern bank was repaired and protected with a "stone slope wall" at the cost of $1,100 (~$39,977 in 2023).[111] The rebuilding efforts would continue in spring of 1859.

In 1859, "over seven thousand cubic yards of earth" and "one thousand cubic yards of stone" were transported and deposited along the banks. [112] That 7,000+ cubic yards of earth were transported from a mile away, by boat, at the cost of $3,500 (~$125,667 in 2023). The 1,000 cubic yards of stone were also transported by boat, twelve to eighteen miles from the Blue Creek Quarries near Junction, at the cost of $2,600 (~$93,353 in 2023).[113] That was not enough material to sufficiently repair the banks, as the east bank had to be "temporarily protected with plank, to prevent the waves from washing over the bank until earth and stone can be procured" to repair the bank completely.[114]

The rebuilding project was already costing more than expected. Going into 1860, as much as "one thousand cubic yards of protection stone, and five thousand cubic yards of embankment" was still needed to repair the east bank completely. That would cost the state a further $5,100 (~$183,115 in 2023).[115] That all said, the cost paled in comparison to the losses expected if Six Mile Reservoir failed. Had Six Mile Reservoir failed, it would have caused the canal to lose an estimated $25,000 to $30,000 (~$897,620 and ~$1,077,145 in 2023) annually until it could be repaired.[116]

It was presumably repaired, as it would not be until 1867 that Six Mile Reservoir and the Wabash & Erie Canal were scrutinized again. Representative William D. Hill presented a resolution in the 1867 Ohio General Assembly to acknowledge the flooding issues that were noted as early as 1858.[117] At that time, Mr. Hill "presented the petition of J. C. Banks and 64 other citizens" that asked the Ohio Legislature to "require the Board of Public Works to construct and repair culverts" in Paulding County.[118] Mr. Hill also introduced House Joint Resolution 136, which stated:

> Whereas, in the construction of the Wabash & Erie Canal through the county of Paulding, in the State of Ohio, her officers and agents caused said canal to be so constructed that the water level in the same is, for many miles between the villages of Junction and Antwerp, in said county, several feet higher that the natural surface of the country through which said canal passes, thereby causing the lands adjacent and along the line of said canal, to be partially overflowed a great portion of the year, by reason of leakage through the embankments and levees on said canal; and Whereas, on account of said leakage and inefficient drainage, many farms in said county are greatly damaged, and the roads and highways leading to and along the line of said canal are thereby rendered difficult of travel in many places; therefore, resolved, That the committee on Public Works be and are hereby instructed to report, by bill or otherwise, what action, if any, is necessary to be taken by this General

Assembly to require the Board of Public Works to construct drains and ditches along said canal, so as to remedy the evils herein set forth.[119]

This bill passed sixty-one to two on March 18, 1867.[120] A few days prior, on March 13, 1867, the Ohio Senate had referred a resolution to the Public Works committee that directed the Board of Public Works to "view" and make an "assessment of the damages sustained... by William Slough, by the vacation and removal of Lock No. 13 (Doering Lock), in the Wabash & Erie Canal."[121@] In all, $22,000 (~$442,988 in 2023) was reportedly appropriated for this purpose, but it seems that little, if anything, was done to remedy the situation in Paulding County.[122] The *Antwerp Gazette* asserted that had this work been adequately done, "the evils which beset the people of Paulding County and along the line of the canal between this place and Defiance, would have been greatly alleviated."[123]

A meeting was held at the Paulding Furnace on May 20, 1867, to discuss this matter related to the Wabash & Erie Canal.[124] Those at the meeting reiterated what Joint Resolution 136 expressed. Asserting that "in consequence of the improper construction of the Wabash and Erie Canal through the county of Paulding, and the reservoir connected therewith; great injury has been done to the inhabitants thereof...."[125] The locals further expressed discontent that water was not allowed to flow from the south side of the canal to the Maumee River, thus flooding the land.[126]

---

@ Doering Lock was just west of the Wabash Railroad's bridge over the canal west of Antwerp. It is not entirely certain when it was vacated. (Bill Oeters et. al., *Taming the Swamp*, 32.)

Furthermore, the water feeding into the reservoir was greater than the canal needed, thus overflowing the reservoir via the waste weir and flooding more land east of Six Mile Reservoir.[127] Not helping the matter was that the drainage ditches east of the reservoir were impeded by debris and timber, further causing flooding.[128] The locals claimed all of this flooding only hindered the region's settlement, notably by impeding travel and causing miasma in the area. The locals believed that because the State of Ohio caused the issues, the state should fix the mess by building the necessary culverts to abate the problem.[129]

Those attending the meeting took positive notice of the Ohio General Assembly's request for the Board of Public Works to look into citizens' complaints earlier in the year.[130] Those at the meeting also stated that the locals would warmly welcome a committee from the Board of Public Works upon their arrival in the area to examine the works.[131] A welcoming committee was formed consisting of James F. Latimore, A. H. Rodgers, George McCormick, John Hardesty, Robert M. Reid, Alonzo H. Seldon, Lewis S. Gordon, Henry Oswalt, Dr. Daniel W. Hixson, and T. J. Merchant.[132] William M. Crane was appointed secretary of the committee, and Nathan Evans, Richard Short, and George McCormick were appointed to manage expenses.[133]

The *Defiance Democrat* reported on February 15, 1868, that more work had been done on Six Mile Reservoir, at least according to the *Annual Report of the Board of Public Works for 1867*. This time, Six Mile Reservoir's western bank was damaged by wave action. That repair was completed by constructing a "wharf of counter-hewed timber, 1,165 feet long, and containing over 5,000 feet of timber."[134] The report also stated that the issue of flooding, noted earlier, was investigated, and it was made clear there were two areas that the Board of Public Works did determine needed work.

The first tract of land that was investigated for being prone to flooding was one and a half miles west of Antwerp, on the west side of where the Wabash Railroad crossed the canal. Here, a large tract of land to the south of the canal was constantly flooded as there was no proper drainage to the Maumee River or Six Mile Creek, as the land existed between the elevated Wabash Railroad and Wabash & Erie Canal. There was a culvert under the canal, but it was inadequate for the volume of water. A new culvert with a capacity equal to 40 square feet would be necessary to remedy this complaint, and a "semi-circular culvert of 8 feet span, on abutments of 2 feet high" was proposed at the cost of $3,500 (~$70,475 in 2023),[135] higher than the expected cost of $1,800 (~$65,417 in 2023) from 1858.[136]

The second was located roughly six and a quarter mile west of Junction in Section 24 in Emerald Township. Here, another tract of land was flooded for a similar reason as the first. The canal was in the way of the natural drainage into Six Mile Creek, and an insufficiently sized culvert was built. It was technically possible to drain this land, particularly via the Big and Little Flat Rock Creeks, but an aqueduct was recommended otherwise to replace the culvert. This aqueduct would need to be 24 feet in span, allowing for a waterway of 100 sq. feet to pass under it. This proposal would cost $4,000 (~$80,543 in 2023). Furthermore, a ditch would need to be dug from the aqueduct to meet with Six Mile Creek. This ditch would need to be 58 chains (3,828 feet) long, 12 feet wide at its bottom, and roughly 9 feet deep. This ditch would cost $10,500 (~$211,426 in 2023) for an estimated total of $14,500 (~$291,969 in 2023).[137]

The Board denied any claims that the canal was directly leaking into citizens' lands except for William Slough's land, which confirmed his complaint; that land was on the west side of Antwerp, directly east of the Wabash bridge over the canal, on the north side of the canal.[138] Even still, the board of Public Works reported that the volume of water was negligible and could be remedied by a small drainage ditch along the towpath. A two-inch diameter pipe could reportedly handle the volume of water present during the committee's visit to Mr. Slough's land.[139] William Slough was awarded $500 (~$11,400 in 2023) in 1870 for "damages... sustained by the removal of lock No. 13, on the Wabash and Erie canal."[140]

At least some of the work was presumably completed by placing an aqueduct six and a quarter mile west of Junction. An aqueduct is mentioned in later newspapers as being in roughly that location. That aqueduct becomes relevant in the Reservoir War matters later in this book. Therefore, it is not much of a stretch to say that the rest of the work was also completed—this is aided by the fact that complaints directly related to Joint Resolution 136 ceased after 1867.

During this time between 1840 and 1870, Paulding County's population had increased dramatically from a few over 1,000 people to 8,544,[141] thus, as more settlers wanted land in the county, proper drainage of the land for cultivation and other uses by those settlers would become more of an issue as the population grew.

## Historical Context Notes

1 Everett A. Budd, "Brief History of Paulding County, Ohio," in
    *Historical Atlas of Paulding County, Ohio, 1892*, 24.

2 Paul Fatout, *Indiana Canals*, 39; Alvin F. Harlow, *Old Towpaths: The
    Story of the American Canal Era*, 249.

3 Carolyn I. Schmidt et al, *Gateway to the East*, 15; Alvin F. Harlow, *Old
    Towpaths: The Story of the American Canal Era*, 249.

4 Carolyn I. Schmidt et al, *Gateway to the East*, 15; Alvin F. Harlow, *Old
    Towpaths: The Story of the American Canal Era*, 249.

5 Alvin F. Harlow, *Old Towpaths: The Story of the American Canal Era*,
    250, 252.

6 Charles R. Poinsatte, *Fort Wayne During the Canal Era 1828–1855*, 68.

7 Charles R. Poinsatte, *Fort Wayne During the Canal Era 1828–1855*, 68.

8 Charles R. Poinsatte, *Fort Wayne During the Canal Era 1828–1855*, 68.

9 Carolyn I. Schmidt et al, *Gateway to the East*, 21.

10 Carolyn I. Schmidt et al, *Gateway to the East*, 15.

11 Charles R. Poinsatte, *Fort Wayne During the Canal Era 1828–1855*, 68.

12 Charles R. Poinsatte, *Fort Wayne During the Canal Era 1828–1855*, 68.

13 Don Faber, *The Toledo War: The First Michigan–Ohio Rivalry*, 27, 38–
    40; Carolyn I. Schmidt et al, *Gateway to the East*, 15–16.

14 Alvin F. Harlow, *Old Towpaths: The Story of the American Canal Era*,
    252.

15 "The Facts in the Case," *Paulding County Gazette*, May 5, 1887, 4.

16 Carolyn I. Schmidt et al, *Gateway to the East*, 21; Charles R. Poinsatte,
    *Fort Wayne During the Canal Era 1828–1855*, 70.

17 Carolyn I. Schmidt et al, *Gateway to the East*, 21; Alvin F. Harlow, *Old
    Towpaths: The Story of the American Canal Era*, 257.

18 State of Ohio, *Executive Documents: Annual Reports for 1888, Made to
    the Sixty-Eighth General Assembly*, Part II, 1085.

19 U.S. Census Bureau, *1840 Census: Compendium of the Enumeration of
    the Inhabitants and Statistics of the United States*, Ohio, 78.

20 Everett A. Budd, "Brief History of Paulding County, Ohio," in
    *Historical Atlas of Paulding County, Ohio, 1892*, 24.

21 "The Facts in the Case," *Paulding County Gazette*, May 5, 1887, 4.

22 "Canal Celebration at Defiance," *Fort Wayne Sentinel*, July 16, 1842,
    3.

23 "Canal Celebration at Defiance," *Fort Wayne Sentinel*, July 16, 1842,
    3.

24 "Canal Celebration at Defiance," *Fort Wayne Sentinel*, July 16, 1842,
    3.

25 "Canal Celebration at Defiance," *Fort Wayne Sentinel*, July 16, 1842,
    3.

26 "Canal Celebration at Defiance," *Fort Wayne Sentinel*, July 16, 1842,
    3.

27 "Canal Celebration," *Fort Wayne Sentinel*, May 13, 1843, 3.

28 Nevin O. Winter, *A History of Northwest Ohio*, 252; Allen County Public Library, *Canal Celebrations in Old Fort Wayne*, 48.

29 Allen County Public Library, *Canal Celebrations in Old Fort Wayne*, 48, 80.

30 Allen County Public Library, *Canal Celebrations in Old Fort Wayne*, 50-51.

31 "Wabash & Erie Canal Celebration on the Anniversary of American Independence," *Fort Wayne Sentinel*, July 1, 1843, 8.

32 "Wabash & Erie Canal Celebration on the Anniversary of American Independence," *Fort Wayne Sentinel*, July 1, 1843, 8.

33 "Wabash & Erie Canal Celebration on the Anniversary of American Independence," *Fort Wayne Sentinel*, July 1, 1843, 8.

34 "Wabash & Erie Canal Celebration on the Anniversary of American Independence," *Fort Wayne Sentinel*, July 1, 1843, 8; Allen County Public Library, *Canal Celebrations in Old Fort Wayne*, 51-52.

35 Allen County Public Library, *Canal Celebrations in Old Fort Wayne*, 52.

36 Allen County Public Library, *Canal Celebrations in Old Fort Wayne*, 80.

37 Allen County Public Library, *Canal Celebrations in Old Fort Wayne*, 80.

38 Allen County Public Library, *Canal Celebrations in Old Fort Wayne*, 80.

39 Carolyn I. Schmidt et al, *Gateway to the East*, 22.

40 State of Ohio, *Executive Documents: Annual Reports for 1888, Made to the Sixty-Eighth General Assembly*, Part II, 1085.

41 Carolyn I. Schmidt et al, *Gateway to the East*, 22.

42 Dorothy M. Yenser and Peter Wilhelm, *The "Junction" of the Canals*, 1988, 5.

43 Alvin F. Harlow, *Old Towpaths: The Story of the American Canal Era*, 258-259; Dorothy M. Yenser and Peter Wilhelm, *The "Junction" of the Canals*, 1988, 5-6.

44 "Canal Towns Were Numerous," *Paulding County Republican*, January 12, 1922, 3.

45 "Canal Towns Were Numerous," *Paulding County Republican*, January 12, 1922, 3; Dorothy M. Yenser and Peter Wilhelm, *The "Junction" of the Canals*, 1988, 5-8.

46 "Canal Towns Were Numerous," *Paulding County Republican*, January 12, 1922, 3.

47 Dorothy M. Yenser and Peter Wilhelm, *The "Junction" of the Canals*, 1988, 8.

48 "Canal Towns Were Numerous," *Paulding County Republican*, January 19, 1922, 7.

49 "Canal Towns Were Numerous," *Paulding County Republican*, January 19, 1922, 7; Everett A. Budd, "Brief History of Paulding County, Ohio," in *Historical Atlas of Paulding County, Ohio, 1892*, 23.

50 "Canal Towns Were Numerous," *Paulding County Republican*, January 19, 1922, 7; Everett A. Budd, "Brief History of Paulding County, Ohio," in *Historical Atlas of Paulding County, Ohio, 1892*, 23.

51 "Canal Towns Were Numerous," *Paulding County Republican*, January 19, 1922, 7; Everett A. Budd, "Brief History of Paulding County, Ohio," in *Historical Atlas of Paulding County, Ohio, 1892*, 23.

52 "Canal Towns Were Numerous," *Paulding County Republican*, January 19, 1922, 7.

53 "Tate's Landing (Reids) (Sharp's Lock) — Emerald Township," Paulding County, Ohio Ghost Town Exploration Co., accessed November 22, 2020, https://ohioghosttowns.org/paulding-county/; *Map of Paulding County, Ohio, 1878*, https://pauldingcountyengineer.com/wp-content/uploads/2019/03/COUNTY-MAP.pdf; "Canal Towns Were Numerous," *Paulding County Republican*, January 19, 1922, 7.

54 Henry Howe, *Historical Collections of Ohio in Three Volumes: An Encyclopedia of the State*, Vol. III, 34.

55 Henry Howe, *Historical Collections of Ohio in Three Volumes: An Encyclopedia of the State*, Vol. III, 34.

56 Kim Sutton, "Railroads & their forgotten towns: Cincinnati Northern," *Paulding Progress*, May 15, 2020, https://progressnewspaper.org/Content/Social/Social/Article/Railroads-their-forgotten-towns-Cincinnati-Northern/-2/-2/200728.

57 Otto E. Ehrhart, "A Brief History of Antwerp," in *A Century of Progress: Antwerp, Ohio*, 6; Dale L. Ehrhart, "Municipal History of Antwerp," in *A Century of Progress: Antwerp, Ohio*, 29.

58 Henry Howe, *Historical Collections of Ohio in Three Volumes: An Encyclopedia of the State*, Vol. III, 39.

59 Henry Howe, *Historical Collections of Ohio in Three Volumes: An Encyclopedia of the State*, Vol. III, 39.

60 Otto E. Ehrhart, "Six Mile Reservoir," in *A Century of Progress: Antwerp, Ohio*, 22.

61 "Death of Judge Latty," *Democratic Northwest and Henry County News* (Napoleon, Ohio), June 6, 1895, 1.

62 "The Facts in the Case," *Paulding County Gazette*, May 5, 1887, 4.

63 "The Facts in the Case," *Paulding County Gazette*, May 5, 1887, 4; William S. Hardesty, *Representative Citizens of Paulding County*, 107.

64 William S. Hardesty, *Representative Citizens of Paulding County*, 107.

65 "The Facts in the Case," *Paulding County Gazette*, May 5, 1887, 4.

66 Nevin O. Winter, *A History of Northwest Ohio*, 252.

67 Nevin O. Winter, *A History of Northwest Ohio*, 252.

68 Nevin O. Winter, *A History of Northwest Ohio*, 252.

69 Nevin O. Winter, *A History of Northwest Ohio*, 252.

70 State of Ohio, *Message and Reports Made to the General Assembly and Governor of the State of Ohio for the Year 1858*, Part II, 113.

71 State of Ohio, *Executive Documents: Annual Reports for 1888, Made to the Sixty-Eighth General Assembly*, Part II, 1086.

72 Harry N. Scheiber, *Ohio Canal Era: A Case Study of Government and the Economy, 1820–1861*, 123.

73 State of Ohio, *Sixth Annual Report of the Board of Public Works, of the State of Ohio, to the Forty-First General Assembly*, 19.

74 Harry N. Scheiber, *Ohio Canal Era: A Case Study of Government and the Economy, 1820–1861*, 123; State of Ohio, *Sixth Annual Report of the Board of Public Works, of the State of Ohio, to the Forty-First General Assembly*, 19.

75 Harry N. Scheiber, *Ohio Canal Era: A Case Study of Government and the Economy, 1820–1861*, 123.

76 Carolyn I. Schmidt et al, *Canalabration*, 98; State of Ohio, *Message and Reports Made to the General Assembly and Governor of the State of Ohio for the Year 1858*, Part II, 113.

77 Carolyn I. Schmidt et al, *Canalabration*, 98; State of Ohio, *Message and Reports Made to the General Assembly and Governor of the State of Ohio for the Year 1858*, Part II, 114.

78 State of Ohio, *Annual Reports, Made to the Governor of the State of Ohio for the Year 1859*, Part I, 575; State of Ohio, *Message and Reports made to the General Assembly and Governor of the State of Ohio for the Year 1858*, Part II, 113; Carolyn I. Schmidt et al, *Canalabration*, 98; State of Ohio, *Sixth Annual Report of the Board of Public Works, of the State of Ohio, to the Forty-First General Assembly*, 19; "The First Gun!," *Defiance Democrat*, October 13, 1887, 2.

79 State of Ohio, *Sixth Annual Report of the Board of Public Works, of the State of Ohio, to the Forty-First General Assembly*, 19.

80 "The First Gun!," *Defiance Democrat*, October 13, 1887, 2.

81 State of Ohio, *Message and Reports made to the General Assembly and Governor of the State of Ohio for the Year 1858*, Part II, 113; State of Ohio, *Sixth Annual Report of the Board of Public Works, of the State of Ohio, to the Forty-First General Assembly*, 19.

82 State of Ohio, *Sixth Annual Report of the Board of Public Works, of the State of Ohio, to the Forty-First General Assembly*, 19.

83 Carolyn I. Schmidt et al, *Canalabration*, 98; "The First Gun!," *Defiance Democrat*, October 13, 1887, 2; State of Ohio, *Message and Reports made to the General Assembly and Governor of the State of Ohio for the Year 1858*, Part II, 113.

84 "The First Gun!," *Defiance Democrat*, October 13, 1887, 2.

85 State of Ohio, *Annual Reports, Made to the Governor of the State of Ohio for the Year 1859*, Part I, 575; "The First Gun!," *Defiance Democrat*, October 13, 1887, 2.

86 State of Ohio, *Annual Reports, Made to the Governor of the State of Ohio for the Year 1859*, Part I, 575.

87 State of Ohio, *Sixth Annual Report of the Board of Public Works, of the State of Ohio, to the Forty-First General Assembly*, 18; Otto E. Ehrhart, "Six Mile Reservoir," in *A Century of Progress: Antwerp, Ohio*, 22; Carolyn I. Schmidt et al, *Canalabration*, 98.

88 Carolyn I. Schmidt et al, *Canalabration*, 98.

89 State of Ohio, *Sixth Annual Report of the Board of Public Works, of the State of Ohio, to the Forty-First General Assembly*, 18- 19.

90 State of Ohio, *Sixth Annual Report of the Board of Public Works, of the State of Ohio, to the Forty-First General Assembly*, 18; Otto E. Ehrhart, "Six Mile Reservoir," in *A Century of Progress: Antwerp, Ohio*, 22; Carolyn I. Schmidt et al, *Canalabration*, 98.

91 Otto E. Ehrhart, "Six Mile Reservoir," in *A Century of Progress: Antwerp, Ohio*, 22; Carolyn I. Schmidt et al, *Canalabration*, 98.

92 Otto E. Ehrhart, "Six Mile Reservoir," in *A Century of Progress: Antwerp, Ohio*, 22; Carolyn I. Schmidt et al, *Canalabration*, 98.

93 Otto E. Ehrhart, "Six Mile Reservoir," in *A Century of Progress: Antwerp, Ohio*, 22; Carolyn I. Schmidt et al, *Canalabration*, 98.

94 "Tour Directions To Old Six Mile Reservoir," Document Found Within Wabash-Erie Canal — Antwerp Folder, Folder Found within Box File 0031 / Contents: Canal History at the John Paulding Historical Society.

95 State of Ohio, *Sixth Annual Report of the Board of Public Works, of the State of Ohio, to the Forty-First General Assembly*, 18.

96 State of Ohio, *Sixth Annual Report of the Board of Public Works, of the State of Ohio, to the Forty-First General Assembly*, 18.

97 "Canal and Reservoir," *Paulding Democrat*, January 20, 1887, 4; *Paulding Democrat*, January 20, 1887, 8; "An Adverse Report," *Antwerp Argus*, February 10, 1887, 2; William S. Hardesty, *Representative Citizens of Paulding County*, 107.

98 "An Adverse Report," *Antwerp Argus*, February 10, 1887, 2.

99 H. Roger Grant, *"Follow the Flag": A History of the Wabash Railroad Company*, 15, 17-18; State of Ohio, *Annual Reports, Made to the Governor of the State of Ohio for the Year 1859*, Part I, 573; State of Ohio, *Message and Reports made to the General Assembly and Governor of the State of Ohio for the Year 1858*, Part II, 113.

100 State of Ohio, *Message and Reports Made to the General Assembly and Governor of the State of Ohio for the Year 1858*, Part II, 113-114.

101 State of Ohio, *Message and Reports Made to the General Assembly and Governor of the State of Ohio for the Year 1858*, Part II, 114.

102 State of Ohio, *Message and Reports Made to the General Assembly and Governor of the State of Ohio for the Year 1858*, Part II, 114.

103 State of Ohio, *Message and Reports Made to the General Assembly and Governor of the State of Ohio for the Year 1858*, Part II, 114.

104 State of Ohio, *Annual Reports, Made to the Governor of the State of Ohio for the Year 1859*, Part I, 574.

105 State of Ohio, *Sixth Annual Report of the Board of Public Works, of the State of Ohio, to the Forty-First General Assembly*, 18.

106 State of Ohio, *Annual Reports, Made to the Governor of the State of Ohio for the Year 1859*, Part I, 574.

107 State of Ohio, *Annual Reports, Made to the Governor of the State of Ohio for the Year 1859*, Part I, 574.

108 State of Ohio, *Annual Reports, Made to the Governor of the State of Ohio for the Year 1859*, Part I, 574.

109 State of Ohio, *Message and Reports made to the General Assembly and Governor of the State of Ohio for the Year 1858*, Part II, 113; State of Ohio, *Annual Reports, Made to the Governor of the State of Ohio for the Year 1859*, Part I, 574.

110 State of Ohio, *Message and Reports Made to the General Assembly and Governor of the State of Ohio for the Year 1858*, Part II, 113; State of Ohio, *Annual Reports, Made to the Governor of the State of Ohio for the Year 1859*, Part I, 574.

111 State of Ohio, *Message and Reports Made to the General Assembly and Governor of the State of Ohio for the Year 1858*, Part II, 113; State of Ohio, *Annual Reports, Made to the Governor of the State of Ohio for the Year 1859*, Part I, 574.

112 State of Ohio, *Annual Reports, Made to the Governor of the State of Ohio for the Year 1859*, Part I, 574.

113 State of Ohio, *Annual Reports, Made to the Governor of the State of Ohio for the Year 1859*, Part I, 574.

114 State of Ohio, *Annual Reports, Made to the Governor of the State of Ohio for the Year 1859*, Part I, 574-575.

115 State of Ohio, *Annual Reports, Made to the Governor of the State of Ohio for the Year 1859*, Part I, 575.

116 State of Ohio, *Annual Reports, Made to the Governor of the State of Ohio for the Year 1859*, Part I, 575.

117 "The Canal Question," *Antwerp Gazette*, March 7, 1878, 2.

118 State of Ohio, *Journal of the House of Representatives of the State of Ohio, for the Adjourned Session of the Fifty-Seventh General Assembly*, Volume LXIII, 242.

119 State of Ohio, *Journal of the House of Representatives of the State of Ohio, for the Adjourned Session of the Fifty-Seventh General Assembly*, Volume LXIII, 430; "The Canal Question," *Antwerp Gazette*, March 7, 1878, 2.

120 State of Ohio, *Journal of the House of Representatives of the State of Ohio, for the Adjourned Session of the Fifty-Seventh General Assembly*, Volume LXIII, 430.

121 State of Ohio, *Journal of the Senate of the State of Ohio, for the Adjourned Session of the Fifty-Seventh General Assembly*, Volume LXIII, 323.

122 "The Canal Question," *Antwerp Gazette*, March 7, 1878, 2.

123 "The Canal Question," *Antwerp Gazette*, March 7, 1878, 2.

124 "Public Meeting in Paulding," *Defiance Democrat*, June 1, 1867, 2.

125 "Public Meeting in Paulding," *Defiance Democrat*, June 1, 1867, 2.

126 "Public Meeting in Paulding," *Defiance Democrat*, June 1, 1867, 2.

127 "Public Meeting in Paulding," *Defiance Democrat*, June 1, 1867, 2.

128 "Public Meeting in Paulding," *Defiance Democrat*, June 1, 1867, 2.

129 "Public Meeting in Paulding," *Defiance Democrat*, June 1, 1867, 2.

130 "Public Meeting in Paulding," *Defiance Democrat*, June 1, 1867, 2.

131 "Public Meeting in Paulding," *Defiance Democrat*, June 1, 1867, 2.

132 "Public Meeting in Paulding," *Defiance Democrat*, June 1, 1867, 2.

133 "Public Meeting in Paulding," *Defiance Democrat*, June 1, 1867, 2.

134 "Canal Ditches and Culverts," *Defiance Democrat*, February 15, 1868, 2.

135 "Canal Ditches and Culverts," *Defiance Democrat*, February 15, 1868, 2; State of Ohio, *Annual Reports, Made to the Governor of the State of Ohio for the Year 1859*, Part I, 574.

136 State of Ohio, *Annual Reports, Made to the Governor of the State of Ohio for the Year 1859*, Part I, 574.

137 "Canal Ditches and Culverts," *Defiance Democrat*, February 15, 1868, 2.

138 "Canal Ditches and Culverts," *Defiance Democrat*, February 15, 1868, 2; *Map of Paulding County, Ohio*, 1878, https://pauldingcountyengineer.com/wp-content/uploads/2019/03/COUNTY-MAP.pdf.

139 "Canal Ditches and Culverts," *Defiance Democrat*, February 15, 1868, 2.

140 State of Ohio, *General and Local Laws, and Joint Resolutions, Passed by the Fifty-Ninth General Assembly*, Volume LXVII, 67; State of Ohio, *Journal of the House of Representatives of the State of Ohio for the Regular Session of the Fifty-Ninth General Assembly*, Volume LXVI, 674.

141 U.S. Census Bureau, *1880 Census: Population of Each State and Territory by Counties, in the Aggregate, at the Censuses*, Table II, Ohio, 75.

# -1-

# Dr. Stambaugh Makes His Case

## (November 1874 – May 1878)

On November 20, 1874,[1] Dr. Solomon Schultz Stambaugh, a dealer in lands for the Toledo, Ohio law firm of Lockwood & Everett,[2] was granted land by the United States Federal Government at the General Land Office in Chillicothe, Ohio.[3] This land deeded to him amounted to 656 acres in Paulding County, Ohio, the overwhelming majority in Crane Township and all within Six Mile Reservoir.[4]

On December 21, 1874, Dr. Stambaugh's attorneys (Toledo lawyers William F. Lockwood and Clayton W. Everett) filed suit in the Paulding County Court of Common Pleas on behalf of their client, against the "members of the Board of Public Works and the lessees."[5] The grounds of the lawsuit were that "the [Board of Public Works and lessees]... unlawfully keep [Dr. Stambaugh] out of the possession of said premise" by:

> Unlawfully using said lands in connection with said surrounding lands for the reservoir purposes... and [Dr. Stambaugh] therefore says that [the Board of Public Works and lessees] are thus keeping and maintaining a nuisance which deprives [Dr. Stambaugh] of the possession of his said lands-and which ought to be abated.[6]

The reasoning behind this was, in his argument, that the defendants had constructed and maintained the banks of the reservoir. Thus, blocking the land's natural drainage, thereby flooding the land he possessed and making them practically worthless for anything but fishing and boating. [7] In Dr. Stambaugh's belief, if the walls were removed and the water was allowed to drain properly, the land he possessed would "be of great value to him for agricultural and other purposes."[8]

The Attorney General of Ohio, John Little, informed Governor William Allen that Dr. Stambaugh had been able to acquire the land in Six Mile Reservoir after he "ascertained that the State of Ohio had no title, according to the land records at Washington."[9] AG Little then hypothesized that the state had once held the title to the land. However, any record of this was likely lost in a fire at the State and United States land offices in Defiance in 1851.[10] AG Little then asserted to Governor Allen that Dr. Stambaugh had to have known the reservoir existed when he acquired title to the land, as the reservoir had existed for about thirty years at the time of the lawsuit.[11]

On February 4, 1875, the canal lessees filed an answer to Dr. Stambaugh's lawsuit.[12] In their response, the lessees, pointing to their lease, denied that "they or either of them keep [Dr. Stambaugh] out of the possession of said premises in the petition described."[13] They also denied that any of them had "caused to be built the artificial walls in said petition mentioned or that they or either keep and maintain said walls or any part thereof except as [explained in their lease]."[14]

The lessees also denied that they were "unlawfully using, or is unlawfully using, or in any way using the lands in said petition described as belonging to [Dr. Stambaugh]." [15] The lessees explained that they had leased the Miami & Erie Canal and "all of its feeders, reservoirs, locks, houses, collectors of fees, weirs, and all leases of surplus water connected to it" from 1871 to 1881.[16] This lease included Six Mile Reservoir, which the lessees asserted was constructed thirty years prior to Dr. Stambaugh coming into possession of the land and was used to supply water to the Miami & Erie Canal.[17§]

The lessees then elaborated on their logic for the denial. They only maintained the reservoir as obligated by the Board of Public Works or an engineer appointed by that body. The lessees also stated that they did so for no other reason than to maintain navigation on the canal, not to keep Dr. Stambaugh out of his land.[18] The lessees also asserted that they had no authority to remove the embankments and explained that it was made a crime to do so, punishable by jail for between three and seven years, and the payment of the cost to repair such damage.[19]

The lessees also asserted that Dr. Stambaugh had no case because he entered the land when it was already a reservoir, had been for three decades, and there was no way, they believed, he could not have known this. Furthermore, no repairs had been made to the reservoir banks since Dr. Stambaugh took possession of the land; therefore, no effort was made to maintain the walls just to keep Dr. Stambaugh out of the land.[20] Lastly, the lessees asserted that the land had no value even before the reservoir was built. In their argument, removing the

---

§ Readers may be confused why the lessees asserted Six Mile Reservoir fed the Miami & Erie Canal, when it was previously stated as feeding the Wabash & Erie Canal. Keep reading, and all will be explained.

reservoir would not increase the value of that land but instead "destroy said reservoir and said public works connected."[21]

AG Little (on behalf of the Board of Public Works and its lessees) filed a motion to have the case dismissed "on the ground that the plaintiff had no authority to sue them."[22] When presented with the demand to vacate the reservoir, AG Little stated:

> Under these circumstances, the state, however much it might deplore the untillable condition of Mr. Stambaugh's alleged farm, or any hindrance to his agricultural pursuits, could not consent, as it seemed to me, to the destruction of so valuable a part of the public works, not to enter into litigation with one of its citizens concerning the same.[23]

The AG's motion to dismiss the case was granted, and the lawsuit of Stambaugh vs. Herznig et al. was dismissed.[24] However, Dr. Stambaugh (or Lockwood & Everett on his behalf) would not concede and filed suit against *just* the lessees of the canal.[25] Unsurprisingly, the lessees requested that the "State and said Board, on their own motion, become parties defendant, and take such steps as may be necessary to prevent the injury to the public works threatened thereby."[26] Had this motion been made, it likely would have just made the second lawsuit a repeat of the first.

That said, AG Little did not see it as "advisable that the State become a party" and did not file a motion for the State to do as they were requested.[27] He instead urged the Governor to "make more rigorous the provisions of law respecting injury to the embankments of the public reservoirs, in view of the 'threatened damage'" they might sustain.[28] AG Little also warned that

"Speculators" had also done similar actions to Dr. Stambaugh in claiming titles from the United States Federal Government at other locations along the Ohio canal system.[29]

AG Little recommended that the state needed to do something about the ownership of these parcels of land post-haste to prevent further litigation. AG Little also wanted to prevent an instance in the future where the correct information is lost to history and a "generously disposed and well-lobbied legislature will pay" the demands of the people who acquired title to those lands, quite possibly in error.[30] Interestingly, AG Little did state that if Dr. Stambaugh's claim to the land was accurate and was legally acquired, he "had no objection to the State's consenting that he enter the reservoir and construct a levee around his premise sufficient to shut out the waters of the lake, should he desire to do so."[31] AG Little even noted that such a farm would "in all probability never lack the ready means for abundant irrigation."[32]

Efforts to abandon the reservoir would not resurface until January 4, 1877, when a report hit the *Paulding Democrat* of a petition circulating in Paulding County. [33] The petition was circulated by Francis B. DeWitt of Paulding, Ohio. The immediate benefits of abandoning the works, according to Mr. DeWitt, were increased drainage of the land around Six Mile Reservoir. He proposed that the canal be turned into a "ditch or watercourse," and some 4,000+ acres regularly occupied by the reservoir would be drained of water and opened to cultivation.[34]

Mr. DeWitt's position was not unlike what Dr. Stambaugh had first asked for a few years prior. While the *Paulding Democrat* seemed ecstatic about the proposition, the *Antwerp Gazette* urged caution in proceeding with the matter after the latter paper talked to Mr. DeWitt regarding the circulation of his petition on January 17, 1877.[35] An individual going by the initials 'R. B. D.' wrote to the *Antwerp Gazette* that they were concerned over whether abandoning the works was in the county's best interests, namely, the county's timber industry. At the time of the 'call,' Mr. DeWitt's petition had already received several signatures from area citizens.[36]

Meanwhile, citizens of Defiance, Ohio, were circulating their own petition to prevent the abandonment. [37] The *Defiance Democrat* called it "a huge swindle" put up by a "land-jobbing ring."[38] The *Antwerp Gazette* agreed in calling it a scheme devised by 'land sharks,' and asserted that the attempt to abandon the canal and reservoir was related to parties from Toledo, Ohio having "become possessors of from five hundred to one thousand acres of land, now lying in the reservoir."[39] Directly referring to Dr. Stambaugh and the attempt to have the reservoir vacated. The *Antwerp Gazette* further lamented that many had not heeded their warning and signed the petition, "not at the time considering what they were doing."[40]

The *Defiance Democrat* reported to their readers that Dr. Stambaugh was able to acquire the land due to an oversight in the "title of the reservoir land."[41] As stated before, this oversight was hypothesized as being caused by records having been lost to fire. However, the *Defiance Democrat* asserted that the State of Ohio had not properly acquired the land used for Six Mile Reservoir from the United States Federal Government. The real reason for this records mix-up is lost to history.

The *Defiance Democrat* correctly stated that Dr. Stambaugh was able to use this oversight to acquire three sections of land now occupied by Six Mile Reservoir in 1874.[42] Dr. Stambaugh now had to wait for his lawsuit against the lessees in the Paulding County Court of Common Pleas to be heard, which would take some time. To speed up his intentions, possibly because he might lose the lawsuit, the *Defiance Democrat* reported that he wished to influence the locals into abandoning the canal and reservoir under the pretense that it would benefit the county.[43] Given the petition by Mr. DeWitt, a local of Paulding County, their suspicions were not unfounded.

The scheme, presumably, was to purchase the inundated land within the reservoir at a relatively low price, influence the locals to petition for the abandonment of the reservoir and canal, and then sell the land at a higher price than purchased for. The *Antwerp Gazette* encouraged locals to denounce the petitions as the abandonment of the canal works in the area would bring "great disaster for those interested in the freights, rafting of timber, etc."[44] The *Defiance Democrat* voiced similar sentiments but also asserted that Six Mile Reservoir was a feeder reservoir for the Miami & Erie Canal a few miles downstream. Losing the reservoir, they believed, would cause their end of the canal to "suffer materially."[45]

Rafting timber on the canal was a prevalent practice in Paulding County due to the abundance of trees in the former Great Black Swamp that was harvested from cheap land. Settlers wishing to set up farms in the area considered the abundance of trees a "nuisance," so they were "eager to dispose of it as easily as possible."[46] Individuals such as Fred W. LeSuer moved to the region to meet that need to remove the timber, and established their timber business in nearby Defiance, reportedly paying about $175,000 (~$5,500,000 in 2023) annually for the timber that was removed by his business.[47]

Timber that was not taken to the iron furnaces at Antwerp and south of Cecil, or used by local manufacturers, was rafted and shipped abroad for various manufacturing needs.[48] Locally, some of these early uses of the timber included making hoop poles, barrel staves, and railroad ties; as far away as the United Kingdom, the timber was used to build ships, but by 1892, the timber was used abroad for the manufacturing of "streetcars, furniture, coffins, and other articles requiring first-class timber."[49]

The *Antwerp Gazette* reported on April 19, 1877, that "millions of feet of ship timber, taken from the big woods of Paulding County, is floating down the Maumee River and Canal for Toledo, this week."[50] A few years later, in 1881, the timber industry was so productive that "the canals banks will be lined heavier than they were two years ago, while the amount of timber on the railroad and at the factories here will already greatly exceed that ever before delivered at this point in one season." Moreover, that record amount of timber was still predicted to almost double in quantity.[51]

During the timeframe this book is predominantly covering, from about 1870 until 1890, the heavy deforestation of Paulding County would take place in earnest. By 1870, only 21,443 acres of the 220,000 acres of Paulding County were under cultivation. By 1880, that number would increase to 47,199. By 1890, almost 100,000 acres, or half of Paulding County's land, was under cultivation. It would not be until 1910 that "virtually all [of the land] had been improved" and opened to cultivation.[52]

Because of the backlash, the *Defiance Democrat* reported that "The scheme to have the Antwerp reservoir abandoned is not meeting with the success that the ring would desire."[53] While Dr. Stambaugh's case was on hold for the foreseeable future in Paulding County, he and the 'land sharks' would be back again later. While that happened, disaster would strike the Wabash & Erie Canal. Despite the recent rebuilding of the St. Joseph Feeder Dam the previous summer at the cost of $10,000 (~$283,819 in 2023),[54] on the night of February 20, 1877, a break opened in the dam northeast of Fort Wayne, Indiana. When initially discovered on the morning of February 21, 1877, the breach was only eight feet wide but progressed to fifty feet wide by noon.[55]

By the time the *Fort Wayne Weekly Sentinel* went to print, the break had increased to 70 feet.[56] The water level in the Wabash & Erie Canal from Fort Wayne to Banks Lock east of Antwerp began to fall due to the dam's failure. When the water would return to the canal, and when the dam would be repaired was not certain. The *Fort Wayne Weekly Sentinel* only reported, "it will be some time before the break can be repaired."[57] While the water was low in the St. Joseph Feeder Canal, a rather gruesome discovery was made before any work could commence to repair the dam. Some local children found the body of an infant not long after the dam failed, and the water dried up. The body was described as having "been in the canal some time."[58]

While the dam was being rebuilt, the water in the canal would, understandably, remain low east of Fort Wayne to Antwerp. As early as April, the *Antwerp Gazette* became concerned that there would not be enough water in the canal to suppress a serious fire in town, calling for "good cisterns" to be placed around town.[59]

Navigation on the Ohio canals would officially open by April 26, 1877, but not on the Wabash & Erie Canal.[60] On May 24, 1877, the Antwerp Hub & Spoke Company would have to employ someone to pump water from another source than the canal because of its low level.[61] Despite the low water on the canal through Antwerp, the canal below Banks Lock and Six Mile Reservoir was not adversely affected, as "millions of feet of ship timber" were still being rafted down either the Maumee River or the Wabash & Erie Canal in mid-April.[62]

Making matters worse for the locals who favored the Wabash & Erie Canal, trouble was on the horizon for the canal and reservoir that would decide the canal's fate in a decade. On March 1, 1877, the *Antwerp Gazette* reported that a rumor had reached them of possible abandonment of the canal between Antwerp (State Line) and the City of Fort Wayne. The *Antwerp Gazette* showed contempt for such a possibility. Fort Wayne still received "an immense amount of wood, timber, etc.," from Paulding County, and the rumors were blamed on parties in Fort Wayne that cared more about the city's own waterworks than they did any other benefit for others.[63] Unknown to the *Antwerp Gazette*, the rumors would come to pass, but it would be a few years before parties in Indiana moved forward with their plans.

On the same day that news hit Antwerp about possible abandonment in Indiana, the *Defiance Democrat* reported that the 'land sharks' had come close to success in an attempt to have the Lewistown Reservoir (present-day Indian Lake) abandoned.[64] The *Defiance Democrat* then rested the concerns of its readers in stating, "they will fail, however, in that matter, just as they will in their contemplated grab of the Antwerp Reservoir."[65] Interestingly, the *Wapakoneta Democrat*, reported by the *Defiance Democrat,* denounced the attempted abandonment of the Lewistown Reservoir for a different reason than what had been given in the matter of Six Mile Reservoir. Those in Wapakoneta were concerned with losing the fishing and hunting carried out on the banks of Lewistown Reservoir. A sentiment heretofore unstated by parties in Defiance.[66]

While silence would befall on the canal and reservoir matters in Paulding County,[67] they would be replaced by those in Logan County, Ohio.[68] In November, reports returned that the 'land sharks' were again interested in having Six Mile Reservoir abandoned.[69] At the same time, interest was renewed in building a ship canal between Lake Michigan and Lake Erie. This proposal was nothing new, as reports of a similar project dated back to 1857.[70] The most recent at that time was in 1874.[71] The *Defiance Democrat* asserted that "if the Government ever orders a survey with a view of connecting the two lakes, the Maumee and St. Joe River project should be included in the survey," believing it to be the best route for the proposed project.[72]

On December 13, 1877, the canal and reservoir matter in Paulding County, returned to the forefront of the locale's attention when the *Antwerp Gazette* noted that "the canals may have seen their palmy days, but they must not be allowed to go down."[73] Dr. Stambaugh was reportedly back again to press the issue on the right to his land within Six Mile Reservoir that he had acquired.[74]

The *Defiance Democrat* warned its readers, reiterating previous talking points, that if Dr. Stambaugh and the 'land sharks' were successful, the Miami & Erie Canal and the manufacturing and timber interests in Defiance and Paulding County would suffer greatly. [75] The *Defiance Democrat* then reported it was still uncertain how Dr. Stambaugh was able to acquire the land within the reservoir. They reasoned that land was supposed to be reserved by the United States Federal Government for the canal purposes of the State, not for private interests. The *Defiance Democrat* asserted it was likely acquired by "a species of robbery," and if this were the case, the land ought to "be restored for the benefit of the canal."[76]

Worse still, the *Defiance Democrat* reported that the canal lessees "have taken no steps to contest the suit of Stambaugh, to recover lands in the Paulding Reservoir."[77] The Board of Public Works also reportedly took "no interest in Stambaugh's suit,"[78] and Senator James B. Steedman favored abandonment. [79] By 1878, the State still had not done what the AG suggested, and on January 7, 1878, AG Little sent the biennial report to Governor Thomas L. Young.[80] In that report, AG Little reiterated that the state needed to mitigate future issues regarding these kinds of claims to land used for canal purposes. He also informed the Governor that Dr. Stambaugh's case was still pending in the Paulding County Court of Common Pleas and that other such cases could possibly be filed to vacate parts of the "Mercer County, Licking County, and Loramie Reservoirs."[81@]

---

@ Today known as Grand Lake St. Marys, Buckeye Lake, and Lake Loramie respectively.

As the canal and reservoir question continued to heat up, The *Defiance Democrat* continued to assert that the bid to abandon the Wabash & Erie Canal and Six Mile Reservoir in Paulding County was an attack on not only the Miami & Erie Canal, but the entire canal system of Ohio.[82] Others asserted that the canal was the only serious competitor to the railroad in transporting logs and heavy freight down the Maumee River to Toledo and Defiance. The canal could reliably provide navigation, while the river's ability to sustain navigation was considered unreliable in comparison.[83]

On January 3, 1878, the *Paulding Democrat* objected to their assertions that Six Mile Reservoir was vital to the survival of the Miami & Erie Canal. The *Paulding Democrat* asserted that "very little water reaches them from that source [the Wabash & Erie Canal and Six Mile Reservoir]."[84] That paper's logic being the water did not make its way to the Miami & Erie Canal at Junction because the algae build-up in the canal was unbroken by any water movement,[85] further asserting that the Defiance manufacturers would do just fine without the canal and reservoir.[86] Because this was a primary concern for the Defiance parties, the *Defiance Democrat* claimed the *Paulding Democrat* was "probably subsidized on the canal question" or at the very least was "ignorant of the great benefit derived in Paulding County from the Canal."[87]

The *Defiance Democrat* went on to assert that, for the most part, the benefits from the canal came in the form of the timber industry, which they reported paid $12,000 (~$357,612 in 2023) to $15,000 (~$447,015 in 2023) to area residents.[88] Furthermore, the *Defiance Democrat* asserted that two new factories had recently opened in Defiance that would "use annually from five to ten million feet of Elm logs. Two-thirds of this amount will naturally come from Paulding County, and must come down the canal."[89] The *Defiance Democrat* asked again how this could not be of great benefit to Paulding County and declared that the interests of Paulding County and Defiance manufacturers were intertwined.[90]

The *Paulding Democrat* objected to the *Defiance Democrat*'s assertions, declaring the canal works a "curse" that the people of Paulding County should not suffer so a few capitalists could reap the county's resources. The *Paulding Democrat* asserted that the money from the timber industry was mostly paid to non-residents, speculators, or the 'land sharks.'[91] The correspondent for the *Paulding Democrat* from Antwerp toed the line with that paper, further stating that the canal should be turned into a drainage canal.[92] He also asserted that if the local canal works were abandoned, as much as 2,200 acres could be turned into farmland and further aid in the area's food supply and general livelihood.[93]

There was also a belief that draining the works would eliminate the area's malaria problem. The locals believed the bodies of water were generating "malaria" that was "poisoning for miles around the atmosphere."[94] The concern of malaria had been voiced before, typically when the waters of the canal and reservoir had become low.[95] Readers might be confused about the disease concern; malaria is caused by a parasite transmitted by mosquitoes, not something poisoning the air.[96]

Those living in Antwerp and Paulding County at the time did not know this. Malaria was believed to be caused by "miasmas" (a term for a foul stench that was believed to make people ill), but the term malaria also literally means "bad air."[97] Because of this, the terms were seemingly used somewhat interchangeably by the locals. Whatever the term, this 'bad air' was viewed as the cause of diseases such as "autumnal fever, intermittent fever, or fever and ague."[98] Such miasmatic/malarial diseases were also generally believed to have been "embedded in the landscape," particularly swamps, and permeated from "stagnant water, putrefying vegetation, and animal remains."[99]

Unknown individuals from Defiance then reportedly hassled the ice farmers of Antwerp by telling them they would have to pay them for the privilege of taking ice from the canal.[100] After this transgression, the *Antwerp Gazette* insulted the Defiance men's intelligence, saying they had "less brains than a mosquito." [101] Furthermore, the *Antwerp Gazette*, which had previously been cautious on abandonment, stated that the canal was "nothing more than a filthy, disease bearing ditch." Telling those at Defiance to come and take their canal "out of the cold."[102] However, they also shut down some of the points the *Paulding Democrat* was making in conjunction with the *Port Clinton News*. The *Antwerp Gazette* believed the two papers to be subsidized by the 'land sharks' for their positions and asserting the *Paulding Democrat* only hated the canal because it was "beneficial to Defiance."[103]

The *Defiance Democrat* responded to the *Antwerp Gazette*'s remarks about the canal with a snide remark toward the editor of the *Antwerp Gazette*.[104] The *Antwerp Gazette* responded, stating either party had not bought them in the matter of the abandonment question. Editor William E. Osborn of the *Antwerp Gazette* just believed that they in Antwerp:

> Feel ourselves at liberty to say what we please on the subject, especially when our citizens are compelled to pay a walking beer keg from Defiance four or five dollars for the privilege of taking a few loads of ice from a ditch that has been of very little benefit to our citizens for the past two or three years. Indiana waters have been very uncertain for some time past, and until we have the assurance that the canal will be kept up, we don't propose to work for a shoddy concern that is of no benefit to us.[105]

The crux of the issue was now exposed, that being the unease regarding rumors that Indiana's end of the Wabash & Erie Canal would be abandoned. The *Paulding Democrat* concurred with the *Antwerp Gazette*, believing that:

> If the Indiana portion of the canal is not to be kept up, of what earthly use will the small portion in this state be to anyone, except a few who happen to own a water power in the vicinity of Defiance, and would it be right to flood 40,000 acres of our best land for their special benefit?[106]

The *Paulding Democrat* also implied that it would be a possible compromise to keep the canal and reservoir if only the canal in Indiana was preserved, although the *Paulding Democrat* did not believe this was a possible scenario, believing that because, in their opinion, the "canal is dead we are in favor of doing away with the corpse."[107]

The *Defiance Democrat* was quick to jump on the inconsistency of the *Paulding Democrat* when they stated that they wanted the reservoir gone because it floods a lot of land but would be okay with the land still being flooded so long as the canal was kept up in Indiana. [108] As mentioned earlier, the locals were indeed willing to put up with the negative aspects of the canal infrastructure to some extent as long as they had some ability to benefit from it.

On January 31, 1878, the *Defiance Democrat* asked the editors of the *Paulding Democrat* if they intended to "antagonize the Democrats of Paulding with the businessmen of Defiance?"[109] A week later, the *Paulding Democrat* responded by saying it was not their intent "as far as business is concerned." Their goal had nothing to do with political affiliation but to fight back against what they believed were "a few businessmen of Defiance [who] propose to keep the best of our land underwater, for their private interests to the detriment of the many of our county then we say to them—kick, and if the wrath of the businessmen of Defiance is to follow, let it come."[110]

Around this time, another point was made by a local of Paulding County. This individual going by '*A Farmer*' asserted that all parties were not considering specific consequences of Six Mile Reservoir. The first was the weather. As a large body of water, he argued that Six Mile Reservoir "naturally draws rain, and hence, Paulding County is a frog pond the whole year-round." In his mind, this would explain why the area experienced frequent flooding.¶ His second point was that Six Mile Reservoir attracted "idle vagrants" to the locale to do some

---

¶ According to Joshua Steiner, a Ph.D. student of Atmospheric Science at The Ohio State University and a longtime friend of the author, given the size of Six Mile Reservoir, it would "almost certainly affect the local climate and probably helped create microclimates surrounding it too." However, it "would not necessarily influence rainfall patterns" as *A Farmer* asserts. Mr. Steiner, however, could not be entirely sure of any of his hypotheses without data which does not likely exist.

hunting and fishing and, in his observation, often illegally kill the wild game and use "unlawful nets" to catch their fish. He asserted they even killed area livestock in the absence of any other game. In his mind, these two issues, alongside others already noted by Paulding County newspapers, were more than enough reason to view the canal and reservoir and nuisances.[111]

During all this debate, Dr. Stambaugh's lawsuit had come up at the courthouse in Paulding, Ohio, on January 9, 1878.[112] Unfortunately for Dr. Stambaugh, and likely why it did not generate more press, the case went nowhere. The hearing was "continued" until a further date, and the matter was not yet settled.[113] Despite this continuance, and the *Defiance Democrat* declaring that "Stambaugh didn't win,"[114] Dr. Stambaugh reportedly remained optimistic that he would win the suit but would have to wait for the next term of the Paulding County Court of Common Pleas to bring the matter up and try again.[115] One little detail left out is that Dr. Stambaugh no longer worked for Lockwood & Everett and did not even live in Ohio by 1878; he had moved back to California to open a medical practice.[116]

Despite having moved away from the land interests, Dr. Stambaugh's lawsuit against the lessees of the canal would be decided on May 7, 1878.[117] The court's judgment was in favor of Dr. Stambaugh, by default of defense, and he "was granted an order for vacation of the Reservoir."[118] As such, Dr. Stambaugh had won, and the reservoir was ordered to be vacated, and the reservoir would be abandoned at the very least.

Parties in Defiance watched on with great interest as the months carried on. There were still questions about whether he could drain the reservoir because the State of Ohio indeed owned the banks, and it would be a crime to disturb them.[119] There were ulterior motives attributed to Charles Parrott and the canal lessees, namely that they did not "care a fig about the State's interest." [120] Worse yet, they were accused by the *Defiance Democrat* of actively helping Dr. Stambaugh abandon the reservoir for their private gain, or helping him and the 'land sharks' to "capture the legislature."[121]

The likely reason for the default of defense, however, was that the canal lessees were no longer the ones in charge of the canal works by the time a judge decided on Dr. Stambaugh's case. As noted previously, Dr. Stambaugh's second lawsuit was *only* against "Charles Parrott et al.," the canal lessees, [122] having elected not to include the Board of Public Works, unlike the first lawsuit that was dismissed.

On June 30, 1877, the *Defiance Democrat* reported that the canal lessees intended to end their contracted lease of the Ohio Public Works in December of that year.[123] The lessee's decision to back out of their lease was precipitated by the Ohio Legislature's decision to allow the City of Hamilton, Ohio to "fill up part of a basin."[124] As such, the lessees felt that they had been evicted by the State "from an important and material part of the premises leased to use by the state," and refused to continue paying their rent unless the basin was left alone.[125]

When that apparently did not occur, the canal lessees abandoned the canal works to the State, as promised, on December 1, 1877.[126] When questioned where the lease payment was by the Auditor of the State on December 5th, Charles Parrott responded on December 8th that the lessees denied owing the State any money regarding the lease agreement and "declined to pay." [127] Thus the canal lessees defaulted on their annual payment of $20,075 (~$567,450 in 2023).[128] However, the lease was apparently paid in six-month intervals, and they had only owed $10,037.50 (~$283,725 in 2023.)[129]

The State of Ohio, understandably, sued the canal lessees over their apparent breach of the lease, but lost. Therefore, the canal lessees were "released from all responsibility to the State."[130] By May 16, 1878, the State of Ohio had "again resumed the control of her Public Works."[131] While the State of Ohio regained control of the canals, the canal lessees, no longer having anything to do with the Public Works and previously asserting that they had nothing to do with what they were being sued for; likely elected not to put up a defense in court.

The *Defiance County Express* conceded that, while Dr. Stambaugh owned "a part of the Paulding Reservoir," the water in the canal would continue to flow freely. [132] The *Defiance Democrat* had called Dr. Stambaugh a "figure head" for the 'land sharks' in their December 27, 1877 paper.[133] Dr. Stambaugh had no prior history of dealing with lands prior to working with Lockwood & Everett. He was a medical professional in between lines of work and was not even present in Ohio at the time the lawsuit in his name was decided.[134]

The claim that he was a figurehead seems a likely assertion. Despite Dr. Stambaugh's victory, the *Defiance Democrat* reported on May 16, 1878, that Dr. Stambaugh had "yet to cut the reservoir bank."[135] A week later, on May 23, 1878, the *Defiance Democrat* reported that "Stambaugh will want the State to pay him a big price for his land in the center of the Paulding reservoir... And still, the reservoir furnishes water for this end of the canal."[136]

On May 16, 1878, the *Defiance Democrat* also cheerfully reported that "the canal business will improve in this section under the management of the Public Works."[137]

## Chapter 1 Notes

1 John Little, *Biennial Report of the Attorney General to the Governor of the State of Ohio, for the Years 1874-1875*, 7; U.S. Department of the Interior, United States of America Bureau of Land Management, General Land Office Records: BLM Certificate 210117, 210118, and 210119, dated November 20, 1874.

2 *The Bay of San Francisco: The Metropolis of the Pacific Coast and its Suburban Cities: A History*, Volume I, 656; Ancestry.com, *Toledo, OH City Directories for 1875, 1876, and 1877.*

3 U.S. Department of the Interior, United States of America Bureau of Land Management, General Land Office Records: BLM Certificate 210117, 210118, and 210119, dated November 20, 1874.

4 U.S. Department of the Interior, United States of America Bureau of Land Management, General Land Office Records: BLM Certificate 210117, 210118, and 210119, dated November 20, 1874; *Map of Paulding County, Ohio*, 1878, https://pauldingcountyengineer.com/wp-content/uploads/2019/03/COUNTY-MAP.pdf.

5 John Little, *Biennial Report of the Attorney General to the Governor of the State of Ohio, for the Years 1874-1875*, 7; Stambaugh vs. Herznig et al., filed December 21, 1874, case number 1050.

6 Stambaugh vs. Herznig et al., filed December 21, 1874, case number 1050.

7 Stambaugh vs. Herznig et al., filed December 21, 1874, case number 1050.

8 Stambaugh vs. Herznig et al., filed December 21, 1874, case number 1050.

9 John Little, *Biennial Report of the Attorney General to the Governor of the State of Ohio, for the Years 1874-1875*, 7.

10 John Little, *Biennial Report of the Attorney General to the Governor of the State of Ohio, for the Years 1874-1875*, 7-8.

11 John Little, *Biennial Report of the Attorney General to the Governor of the State of Ohio, for the Years 1874-1875*, 7.

12 Stambaugh vs. Herznig et al., Answer of the Lessees of the Public Works, filed February 4, 1875, case number 1050.

13 Stambaugh vs. Herznig et al., Answer of the Lessees of the Public Works, filed February 4, 1875, case number 1050.

14 Stambaugh vs. Herznig et al., Answer of the Lessees of the Public Works, filed February 4, 1875, case number 1050.

15 Stambaugh vs Herznig et al, Answer of the Lessees of the Public Works, filed February 4, 1875, case number 1050.

16 Stambaugh vs. Herznig et al., Answer of the Lessees of the Public Works, filed February 4, 1875, case number 1050.

17 Stambaugh vs. Herznig et al., Answer of the Lessees of the Public Works, filed February 4, 1875, case number 1050.

18 Stambaugh vs. Herznig et al., Answer of the Lessees of the Public
    Works, filed February 4, 1875, case number 1050.
19 Stambaugh vs. Herznig et al., Answer of the Lessees of the Public
    Works, filed February 4, 1875, case number 1050.
20 Stambaugh vs. Herznig et al., Answer of the Lessees of the Public
    Works, filed February 4, 1875, case number 1050.
21 Stambaugh vs. Herznig et al., Answer of the Lessees of the Public
    Works, filed February 4, 1875, case number 1050.
22 John Little, *Biennial Report of the Attorney General to the Governor of
    the State of Ohio, for the Years 1874-1875*, 8.
23 John Little, *Biennial Report of the Attorney General to the Governor of
    the State of Ohio, for the Years 1874-1875*, 8.
24 John Little, *Biennial Report of the Attorney General to the Governor of
    the State of Ohio, for the Years 1874-1875*, 8, 14.
25 John Little, *Biennial Report of the Attorney General to the Governor of
    the State of Ohio, for the Years 1874-1875*, 8.
26 John Little, *Biennial Report of the Attorney General to the Governor of
    the State of Ohio, for the Years 1874-1875*, 8.
27 John Little, *Biennial Report of the Attorney General to the Governor of
    the State of Ohio, for the Years 1874-1875*, 8.
28 John Little, *Biennial Report of the Attorney General to the Governor of
    the State of Ohio, for the Years 1874-1875*, 8.
29 John Little, *Biennial Report of the Attorney General to the Governor of
    the State of Ohio, for the Years 1874-1875*, 8.
30 John Little, *Biennial Report of the Attorney General to the Governor of
    the State of Ohio, for the Years 1874-1875*, 8.
31 John Little, *Biennial Report of the Attorney General to the Governor of
    the State of Ohio, for the Years 1874-1875*, 8.
32 John Little, *Biennial Report of the Attorney General to the Governor of
    the State of Ohio, for the Years 1874-1875*, 8.
33 "Local and Miscellaneous," *Paulding Democrat*, January 4, 1877, 3.
34 "Improvement," *Paulding Democrat*, January 11, 1877, 3.
35 "Home Matters," *Antwerp Gazette*, January 18, 1877, 3.
36 "Junction, O., Jan 24th, 1877, Editor Gazette." *Antwerp Gazette*,
    February 1, 1877, 2.
37 "Chit Chat," *Defiance Democrat*, January 25, 1877, 3.
38 "A Huge Swindle," *Defiance Democrat*, January 25, 1877, 3.
39 "Home Matters," *Antwerp Gazette*, February 8, 1877, 3.
40 "Home Matters," *Antwerp Gazette*, February 8, 1877, 3.
41 "A Huge Swindle," *Defiance Democrat*, January 25, 1877, 3.
42 "A Huge Swindle," *Defiance Democrat*, January 25, 1877, 3.
43 "A Huge Swindle," *Defiance Democrat*, January 25, 1877, 3.
44 "Home Matters," *Antwerp Gazette*, February 8, 1877, 3.
45 "A Huge Swindle," *Defiance Democrat*, January 25, 1877, 3.
46 *History of Crane Township Paulding County*, unknown publisher,
    1941.
47 Everett A. Budd, "Brief History of Paulding County, Ohio," in
    *Historical Atlas of Paulding County, Ohio, 1892*, 23.

48 Everett A. Budd, "Brief History of Paulding County, Ohio," in *Historical Atlas of Paulding County, Ohio, 1892*, 23; Melinda Krick, "Timber Era Brought Workers, Growth, Wealth," *The West Bend News* (Antwerp), July 6, 2020, https://www.westbendnews.net/autonews/2020/07/06/timber-era-brought-workers-growth-wealth/.

49 Everett A. Budd, "Brief History of Paulding County, Ohio," in *Historical Atlas of Paulding County, Ohio, 1892*, 23; Melinda Krick, "Timber Era Brought Workers, Growth, Wealth," *The West Bend News* (Antwerp), July 06, 2020, https://www.westbendnews.net/autonews/2020/07/06/timber-era-brought-workers-growth-wealth/.

50 "Home Matters," *Antwerp Gazette*, April 19, 1877, 3.

51 "Brief Local," *Paulding Democrat*, January 13, 1881, 3.

52 Melinda Krick, "Timber Era Brought Workers, Growth, Wealth," *The West Bend News* (Antwerp), July 06, 2020, https://www.westbendnews.net/autonews/2020/07/06/timber-era-brought-workers-growth-wealth/.

53 "Chit Chat," *Defiance Democrat*, February 8, 1877, 3.

54 *Fort Wayne Weekly Sentinel*, February 21, 1877, 3.

55 *Fort Wayne Weekly Sentinel*, February 21, 1877, 3.

56 "City Chat," *Fort Wayne Weekly Sentinel*, February 21, 1877, 3.

57 *Fort Wayne Weekly Sentinel*, February 21, 1877, 3.

58 "City Chat," *Fort Wayne Weekly Sentinel*, February 28, 1877, 6.

59 "Additional Locals," *Antwerp Gazette*, April 19, 1877, 2.

60 "Home Matters," *Antwerp Gazette*, April 26, 1877, 3.

61 "Home Matters," *Antwerp Gazette*, May 24, 1877, 3.

62 "Home Matters," *Antwerp Gazette*, April 19, 1877, 3.

63 "Home Matters," *Antwerp Gazette*, March 1, 1877, 3.

64 "Chit Chat," *Defiance Democrat*, March 1, 1877, 4.

65 "Chit Chat," *Defiance Democrat*, March 1, 1877, 4.

66 "Chit Chat," *Defiance Democrat*, March 8, 1877, 4.

67 "Chit Chat," *Defiance Democrat*, March 15, 1877, 4.

68 "The Lewistown Reservoir," *Defiance Democrat*, March 8, 1877, 1; "Chit Chat," *Defiance Democrat*, March 15, 1877, 4; "Local and Miscellaneous: Lewistown Reservoir," *Defiance Democrat*, March 15, 1877, 5; "Chit Chat," *Defiance Democrat*, March 22, 1877, 4; "Chit Chat," *Defiance Democrat*, March 29, 1877, 4; "Chit Chat," *Defiance Democrat*, April 5, 1877, 4.

69 "Local and Miscellaneous," *Defiance Democrat*, November 15, 1877, 5.

70 "Lake Michigan and Erie Ship Canal," *Fort Wayne Sentinel*, June 20, 1857, 2.

71 "Home Matters," *Antwerp Gazette*, June 25, 1874, 3.

72 "Ship Canal," *Defiance Democrat*, November 8, 1877, 4; "The Ship Canal Project," *Defiance Democrat*, November 29, 1877, 4; "Ship Canal," *Defiance Democrat*, December 20, 1877, 4.

73 "Home Matters," *Antwerp Gazette*, December 13, 1877, 3.

74 "The Land Sharks Again," *Defiance Democrat*, December 20, 1877, 4.

75 "The Land Sharks Again," *Defiance Democrat*, December 20, 1877, 4; *Defiance Democrat*, December 27, 1877, 4.

76 "The Land Sharks Again," *Defiance Democrat*, December 20, 1877, 4.

77 *Defiance Democrat*, December 27, 1877, 4.

78 *Defiance Democrat*, January 3, 1878, 4.

79 *Defiance Democrat*, January 10, 1878, 4.

80 State of Ohio, *Executive Documents: Annual Reports for 1877, Made to the Sixty-Third General Assembly*, Part II, 1131.

81 State of Ohio, *Executive Documents: Annual Reports for 1877, Made to the Sixty-Third General Assembly*, Part II, 1144.

82 "Chit Chat," *Defiance Democrat*, February 7, 1878, 4.

83 "Home Matters," *Antwerp Gazette*, February 28, 1878, 3.

84 "Local and Miscellaneous," *Paulding Democrat*, January 3, 1878, 3.

85 "Local and Miscellaneous," *Paulding Democrat*, January 3, 1878, 3.

86 "Local and Miscellaneous," *Paulding Democrat*, January 3, 1878, 3.

87 *Defiance Democrat*, January 10, 1878, 4; "Subsidized, or What?," *Defiance Democrat*, January 10, 1878, 4.

88 "Subsidized, or What?," *Defiance Democrat*, January 10, 1878, 4.

89 "Subsidized, or What?," *Defiance Democrat*, January 10, 1878, 4.

90 "Subsidized, or What?," *Defiance Democrat*, January 10, 1878, 4.

91 "Subsidized, or What?," *Paulding Democrat*, January 17, 1878, 2.

92 "From Antwerp," *Paulding Democrat*, January 17, 1878, 7.

93 "From Antwerp," *Paulding Democrat*, January 17, 1878, 7.

94 "From Antwerp," *Paulding Democrat*, January 17, 1878, 7.

95 "Home Matters," *Antwerp Gazette*, August 30, 1877, 3.

96 Center for Disease Control and Prevention, *Malaria*, accessed March 17, 2022, https://www.cdc.gov/parasites/malaria/index.html.

97 Sonia Shah, *The Fever: How Malaria Has Ruled Humankind for 500,000 Years*, 43; Peter C. Baldwin, "How Night Air Became Good Air," 413, https://www.jstor.org/stable/3986202.

98 Peter C. Baldwin, "How Night Air Became Good Air," 413, https://www.jstor.org/stable/3986202.

99 Sonia Shah, *The Fever: How Malaria Has Ruled Humankind for 500,000 Years*, 43, 143; Peter C. Baldwin, "How Night Air Became Good Air," 413, https://www.jstor.org/stable/3986202.

100 "Home Matters," *Antwerp Gazette*, January 24, 1878, 3.

101 "Home Matters," *Antwerp Gazette*, January 24, 1878, 3.

102 "Home Matters," *Antwerp Gazette*, January 24, 1878, 3.

103 *Antwerp Gazette*, January 31, 1878, 2.

104 "Home Matters," *Antwerp Gazette*, February 7, 1878, 3.

105 "Home Matters," *Antwerp Gazette*, February 7, 1878, 3.

106 "Local and Miscellaneous," *Paulding Democrat*, February 14, 1878, 7.

107 "Local and Miscellaneous," *Paulding Democrat*, February 14, 1878, 7.

108 *Defiance Democrat*, February 21, 1878, 4.

109 *Defiance Democrat*, January 31, 1878, 4.

110 *Paulding Democrat*, February 7, 1878, 3.

111 "That Reservoir," *Paulding Democrat*, March 14, 1878, 7.

112 *Defiance Democrat*, January 10, 1878, 4.

113 *Defiance Democrat*, January 10, 1878, 4.

114 "Chit Chat," *Defiance Democrat*, January 10, 1878, 4.

115 "Chit Chat," *Defiance Democrat*, January 10, 1878, 4; "Chit Chat," *Defiance Democrat*, January 31, 1878, 4.

116 *The Bay of San Francisco: The Metropolis of the Pacific Coast and its Suburban Cities: A History*, Volume I, 656.

117 "Stambaugh Wins," *Defiance Democrat*, May 9, 1878, 4.

118 "Court Proceedings," *Paulding Democrat*, May 16, 1878, 1; "Stambaugh Wins," *Defiance Democrat*, May 9, 1878, 4.

119 "Stambaugh Wins," *Defiance Democrat*, May 9, 1878, 4; "A Huge Swindle," *Defiance Democrat*, January 25, 1877, 3.

120 *Defiance Democrat*, December 27, 1877, 4.

121 "A Big Game," *Defiance Democrat*, December 20, 1877, 4; *Defiance Democrat*, December 27, 1877, 4; *Defiance Democrat*, February 14, 1878, 4.

122 "Court Proceedings," *Paulding Democrat*, May 16, 1878, 1.

123 *Defiance Democrat*, June 30, 1877, 4.

124 *Defiance Democrat*, June 30, 1877, 4.; "The Lessees Propose to Surrender the Public Works," *Defiance Democrat*, July 5, 1877, 1; "The Canals," *Defiance Democrat*, December 6, 1877, 4; "Governor's Message," *Defiance Democrat*, January 10, 1878, 6; Alvin F. Harlow, *Old Towpaths: The Story of the American Canal Era*, 260-261; State of Ohio, *Executive Documents: Annual Reports for 1877, Made to the Sixty-Third General Assembly*, Part II, 1140.

125 "The Lessees Propose to Surrender the Public Works," *Defiance Democrat*, July 5, 1877, 1; State of Ohio, *Executive Documents: Annual Reports for 1877, Made to the Sixty-Third General Assembly*, Part II, 1140.

126 "The Canals," *Defiance Democrat*, December 6, 1877, 4; State of Ohio, *Executive Documents: Annual Reports for 1877, Made to the Sixty-Third General Assembly*, Part II, 1140.

127 *Defiance Democrat*, December 13, 1877, 8.

128 Bill Oeters and Nancy Gulick, *Images of America: Miami and Erie Canal*, 109.

129 *Defiance Democrat*, December 13, 1877, 8; "Governor's Message," *Defiance Democrat*, January 10, 1878, 6; State of Ohio, *Executive Documents: Annual Reports for 1877, Made to the Sixty-Third General Assembly*, Part II, 1140.

130 "Governor's Message," *Defiance Democrat*, January 10, 1878, 6; State of Ohio, *Executive Documents: Annual Reports for 1877, Made to the Sixty-Third General Assembly*, Part II, 1141; "The Canals," *Defiance Democrat*, April 18, 1878, 4; *Defiance Democrat*, April 18, 1878, 4; *Defiance Democrat*, April 25, 1878, 4.

131 "Ohio Canals," *Defiance Democrat*, May 16, 1878, 3.

132 *Defiance County Express*, May 17, 1878, 5-6.
133 *Defiance Democrat*, December 27, 1877, 4.
134 *The Bay of San Francisco: The Metropolis of the Pacific Coast and its Suburban Cities: A History*, Volume I, 656.
135 "Chit Chat," *Defiance Democrat*, May 16, 1878, 4.
136 "Chit Chat," *Defiance Democrat*, May 23, 1878, 4.
137 "Chit Chat," *Defiance Democrat*, May 16, 1878, 4.

# -2-

# Détente

### (May 1878 – January 1884)

The canals had been returned to the State of Ohio in "miserable shape," and were described as a "disgrace to the State." [1] Due to their condition, the canal lessees were accused of having "skinned the public works" by not spending any money to maintain the canal infrastructure in order to make a tidy profit for themselves. [2] The lessees reportedly had $160,000 (~$4,635,700 in 2023) in reserve funds,[3] and to put the canals back into "good repair" would have reportedly taken a majority of that money to complete, which the canal lessees were accused of being opposed to doing in order to make as much money as possible.[4]

Throughout the summer of 1878, consistent rainfall, and the water it brought, continued to be a significant problem for Paulding County (at least to some of its citizens). At the same time, the St. Mary's Reservoir in Mercer County was reported to be at a historically low level, resulting in the near suspension of operations on the Miami & Erie Canal downstream of it.[5] The *Paulding Democrat* asked the *Delphos Courant* to send their reservoir up to Paulding County, as it would probably be filled within the next two days.[6]

'*Alcinous*' of Antwerp wrote to the *Paulding Democrat* in July 1878 to further call for the abandonment of the canal and reservoir.[7] He asserted that the reservoir was a "large twenty-two hundred acre-shallow, stagnant pool of water, decaying timber—a very cesspool of disease, and another added source of our heavy rainfall."[8] Believing the canal should be turned into a drainage ditch to help facilitate the draining of the land in the county. Doing so, he also believed, would stop attracting rain to the already "wet, forested state" of Paulding County.[9]

If the flood conditions were not enough to deal with, tragedy would occur during preparations to repair Banks Lock east of Antwerp. Willoughby H. Doering, the brother of Phaon P. Doering, and a prominent citizen of Antwerp who was one of the owning members of the Antwerp Hub & Spoke Company, drowned in the canal on the morning of July 1, 1878. W. H. Doering and a few others, including Mr. Foncannon, the head sawyer at the Hub & Spoke Factory, were in the progress of building a dam in the canal just west of Banks Lock when the incident occurred. While both W. H. Doering and Mr. Foncannon were in the water between the lock and the new dam, the lock wickets (the gate that lets water in from the upper level) was opened to drain the water.[10]

Unfortunately for the two, when the wickets were opened, the dam they had just built failed, sending water and debris into the two men and washing them toward the lock. Mr. Foncannon had the great fortune of being washed through a wicket (a roughly 16x16 inch hole) and into the lock chamber, where he could be rescued. Tragically, W. H. Doering became caught in one of the wickets. Trapped below the water's surface by debris, and therefore unable to resurface; he drowned.[11]

Later, in November 1878, a meeting was called for those interested in maintaining the Wabash & Erie Canal to meet at the Crosby Hotel in Defiance, Ohio, on November 25, 1878.[12] @ Nothing of note happened at this meeting, according to the *Defiance Democrat.* The basic premise of the meeting was to advocate for the maintenance of the Ohio canal system.[13] In a way, those advocations were answered when the winter had passed. On April 24, 1879, it was announced that "the canal locks between Junction and the Indiana State line will be rebuilt during the coming summer."[14]

This news came with a report that a couple of petitions had been circulating in Paulding County "praying for the widening and deepening of the Wabash & Erie Canal" that was to be sent to Congress.[15] Work on the Wabash & Erie Canal by the State of Ohio was to commence sometime around the middle of May 1879.[16] While that did not happen, further good news graced the *Fort Wayne Weekly Sentinel* on July 23, 1879. That paper, quoting the *Antwerp Banner*, reported that Ohio and Indiana had agreed to "build new locks between Fort Wayne, Indiana and Junction, Ohio, and clean out and put the canal in a navigable condition."[17] This work was to occur when the shipping season ended the forthcoming winter, and the locks would be "repaired sufficiently" until then.[18]

---

@ The Crosby Hotel was located on the northwest corner of 3rd Street and Wayne Street in Defiance.
(*Sanborn Fire Insurance Map from Defiance, Defiance County, Ohio,* August 1888.)

The canal would need some serious work, as it was described as being in a dilapidated state between Fort Wayne and Antwerp. "[The] canal is still there, but the towpath is overgrown and fallen trees obstruct passage to a greater or less extent." [19] Despite the poor condition of the canal, at least one boat was able to make it to Fort Wayne from Antwerp. This report was likely one of the last revenue canal boats from Antwerp to Fort Wayne. Carrying a load of kindling, the boat arrived in Fort Wayne on November 5, 1879. [20]

Interestingly, in November 1879, it seemed there was an attempt by the State of Ohio to break the ice on a canal in Paulding County during the winter. [21] Such practice was not unheard of for canals; the Chesapeake & Ohio Canal used a "scow, loaded with pig iron" as an icebreaker during the winters. [22] Such practice on that canal required "as many as 40 mules from the boats in the procession" to be tied to the icebreaker. [23] The mules would drag the scow up on the ice, and the weight of the scow would break up the ice, [24] not too dissimilar to how icebreaking is done on the Great Lakes today.

This was seemingly only accomplished with any success on the C&O Canal when a relatively sizeable convoy of boats needed to pass through the canal in the winter. Besides a large number of animals, a large number of men were often needed to help "pump water out of a barge if the ice broke a hole in it" and "hack at the ice with their axes if necessary." [25] Icebreakers on the canal in Paulding County were very rarely mentioned. The winter of 1879 is the only known newspaper mention of their existence that was found. The herculean effort it took to break the ice on other canals at this time, as well as economic reasons, may have contributed to a lack of interest in regularly maintaining navigation in the winter season.

On November 27, 1879, it became evident that no money had been appropriated for the canal repairs proposed earlier in the year. Representative Benjamin Patton made it clear to his constituents in Paulding County that

> I am, and always have been in favor of keeping up the canals, and think the state should expend any amount of money that is necessary to put and keep them in good condition and to develop the full measure of their usefulness. They are people highways, and about the only remaining barrier left against the power and exaction of the railroad monopolies.[26]

His insistence in the Ohio General Assembly paid off, and by April 14, 1880, the State of Ohio had passed a bill to appropriate $10,000 (~$292,167 in 2023) in order to "rebuild the locks and make other necessary repairs on the canal from Junction to the Indiana State Line."[27]

To overcome opposition, a few amendments were agreed upon that saved the bill from failure. The first was that a

> bond or other security in $10,000 from the owners of the Indiana part of the canal, that, barring casualties and accidents, they will keep their part of the canal in navigable order, and will continue to furnish the usual supply of water from the feeder at Fort Wayne.[28]

The second was adjusting the terms of when the appropriated money could be used. Rather than being able to outright use the money coming from the State Treasury, it would first come from tolls and other funds from the Public Works themselves (totaling about $13,000 (~$379,817 in 2023)). Then they could use the

$10,000 appropriated to them.[29] With that agreed upon, it was believed that should Indiana make that guarantee, the measure would be "fully secured, and its friends may feel assured to have the work done."[30]

Nothing would be done to repair the canal in 1880, despite the appropriations set aside. The *Defiance Democrat* joked that "Judge Patton will have to get after somebody with a sharp stick" because of it.[31] It was then rumored in early 1881 that the canal would "be put in good navigable condition next summer." [32] While the States of Ohio and Indiana seemed intent on doing their work at some point, there was another attempt to revitalize the Wabash & Erie Canal, and it had to do with the ship canal proposals mentioned earlier. At some point, the topic of building a ship canal between Lake Erie and the Mississippi River was also proposed.

Because the proposed ship canal would utilize the right of way of the already present Wabash & Erie Canal, it was believed that widening and deepening the canal would not incur a great expense.[33] There was also a belief that, despite the Wabash & Erie Canal not being utilized by much canal traffic by 1879, the United States Federal Government had "considered this connection by the canal a great public necessity as early as 1827;"[34] therefore the canal should be preserved in some form as direct competition to the railroads.[35]

A meeting was held in Huntington, Indiana, on May 31, 1879, to discuss this matter.[36] Among those present was the Mayor of Defiance, Ohio, William C. Holgate, among other Defiance representatives. [37] Representatives from Toledo, Napoleon, Florida, Texas, and Antwerp in Ohio and Wabash, Lagro,

Antioch, Roanoke, and Huntington in Indiana were also present at the meeting. [38] Captain Arthur Reuben Wynne of St. Catherines, Ontario, was also present.[39]

After some orating by those most interested in the matter, the meeting adjourned after creating a permanent organization that would ensure that "cheap transportation and water navigation... is secured."[40] The organization would be called the Wabash & Erie Canal Enlargement Company.[41] Those appointed to oversee this organization were Alfred Moore of Huntington, Indiana, James Long of Antioch, Indiana, Phaon P. Doering of Antwerp, Ohio, James B. Kenner of Huntington, Indiana, and a Captain Wilhelm of Defiance, Ohio.[42]

Things were looking favorable for their proposition, seeing that it was reported from Tate's Landing that a "petition for the rebuilding and enlargement of the canal" was well signed by citizens of Paulding County. [43] 'Old Wash.' of Tate's Landing concluded that "we presume our citizens are not yet disgusted with the old ditch."[44] This source does not mention *which* canal the petition was referring to, but on January 17, 1880, the answer to that mystery became clear. Representative William D. Hill presented the petition to the United States Congress, "signed by over twelve hundred people," [45] to conduct a survey between Toledo, Ohio, and Cincinnati, Ohio, for a ship canal via the Miami & Erie Canal.[46]

As it was introduced, the joint resolution implored the Secretary of War to oversee the creation of the survey for all the reasons mentioned in previous ship canal proposals.[47] Later, the Wabash & Erie Canal would be surveyed between Toledo, Ohio and Lafayette, Indiana, at the request of the U.S. Government, for a similar purpose, and the survey report was sent to the United States War Department.[48]

Despite making no strong appeal for war purposes, Congress appropriated $10,000 (~$292,167 in 2023) to survey the Miami & Erie Canal between Cincinnati, Ohio, and Junction, Ohio.[49] CPT William S. Williams was appointed as the superintendent of the survey by the Army Corps of Engineers. While he could not provide particulars on the specifications of the canal, CPT Williams believed it would be a similar specification to the Erie Canal, seventy feet wide and seven feet deep.[50] Interestingly enough, Great Lakes vessels would not be the intended vessel for the project; the boats would be larger canal boats with single-screw steam propulsion that was "capable of carrying 240 tons."[51] The Wabash & Erie Canal survey between Toledo and Lafayette was overseen by Chief Engineer William H. Goshorn.[52] Congress had appropriated $15,000 (~$438,250 in 2023) to survey that canal.[53]

The Wabash & Erie Canal's specification was proposed to be slightly different. It would be the same size dimensionally, seventy feet wide at surface level, fifty-two and a half feet wide at the base of the canal, and seven feet deep, accommodating 250-ton vessels "capable of carrying 8,000 bushels of grain, the amount transported by a train of twenty ordinary freight cars."[54] Locks on these two proposals would be built to permit the passage of two vessels simultaneously (double locks) with a dimension of 110 feet in length, eighteen feet wide, and a minimum depth of seven feet.[55]

Despite the belief that the cost to widen and deepen the canal could be kept low by using the old right of way, the price tag for such a project was monumental. The Wabash & Erie Canal would require $24,236,135.17 (~$708,099,083 in 2023) to rebuild into a ship canal. The Miami & Erie would cost more, totaling $28,557,173.13 (~$834,345,408 in 2023).[56] The Wabash & Erie Canal alone would require sixty-five new double locks, 163 iron bridges, 129 masonry culverts, nine masonry aqueducts, and twenty new masonry waste ways.[57] This was *just* for the reconstruction of the Wabash & Erie Canal. Metrics were not given on what the Miami & Erie Canal needed. This was a tremendous amount of money, not only by today's standards but even more so by that time's standards. It seemed that the only saving grace was that it would employ an incredible amount of people to construct it.[58]

Despite this, the residents of Paulding County, which had grown to a population of 13,485 people by 1880,[59] still had high hopes that the Wabash & Erie Canal (and the Miami & Erie Canal by proxy) would be revitalized one way or another. Whether by the work of the State of Ohio or the work of the United States Federal Government. Indiana also seemed to be playing along with the possibilities. Some believed that the ship canal was a "dead certainty;" The only thing that could stand in its way and stop it was the railroad interests that would likely lose traffic from its construction.[60] Indeed, and before any work could commence on the Wabash & Erie Canal, news broke on February 24, 1881, that a portion of the Wabash & Erie Canal in Indiana had been sold to the New York, Chicago & St. Louis Railroad (henceforth referred to as the Nickel Plate Road) for $137,000 (~$4,002,683 in 2023).[61]

As the State of Ohio was trying to make a deal with the State of Indiana to maintain their part of the canal, by 1880, the State of Indiana had already abandoned and sold off portions of the Wabash & Erie Canal in their state.[62] One such portion was the northern division between the Ohio State Line and Lafayette, Indiana, which had been sold to William Fleming and other industrialists.[63] Men who did not have the canal's interest in mind.

Besides the profits he made from selling parts of the canal,[64] William Fleming was deeply involved with the Nickel Plate Road as a "large stockholder and director," as well as a prominent Fort Wayne businessman being the president of the First National Bank of Fort Wayne.[65] Nickel Plate Road historian Taylor Hampton states that "Fort Wayne was deeply indebted to William Fleming... for the building of the road through the city."[66] This is due to the fact that the Nickel Plate Road was originally surveyed to pass north of Fort Wayne. However, at the insistence of Mr. Fleming and his offering to sell the canal right of way through the city, the railroad acquired the canal.[67]

With this acquisition, the Nickel Plate Road now had access to an unimpeded right of way that was "250 feet wide through the heart of the City of Fort Wayne."[68] After draining the water and grading the towpath for their right of way,[69] the Nickel Plate Road's first passenger trains between Chicago, Illinois, and Cleveland, Ohio, passed through Fort Wayne on October 23, 1882.[70]

This single event, the Nickel Plate Road filling in the canal in Fort Wayne, spelled doom for Six Mile Reservoir. As a result of this, the water supply for the Wabash & Erie Canal east of Fort

Wayne and the "principle feeder" of Six Mile Reservoir was cut off.[71] As established earlier, Six Mile Creek was already woefully incapable of filling the reservoir alone, especially after the construction of the Wabash Railroad cut off half of the water supply in the 1850s. Never mind the fact that this left no water supply for the few miles of canal west of the reservoir and left Six Mile Reservoir as the sole feeder for the Wabash & Erie Canal east of the reservoir to Junction.

To make matters even worse, at an unknown point in time, the Commissioners of Allen County, Indiana constructed a new drainage ditch "about a mile and a half west of the State Line" in Maumee Township.[72] By distance from the State Line, this likely referred to the Edgerton Ditch (now called Marsh Ditch), but confusingly, a purported 1870s ditch map of Maumee Township shows that the Edgerton-State Line Ditch (now called Viland Ditch) was also present between the State Line and Edgerton Ditch by the 1870s. [73] Furthermore, it is claimed that the "'Edgerton State Line Ditch,' dredged along the state line, which was the first to be surveyed; and others, tributary to it or separate, followed."[74]

However, Otto E. Ehrhart states in his brief memoir that they did not begin digging the Edgerton-State Line Ditch until probably sometime around 1900.[75] Mr. Ehrhart himself actually rode a short distance on the dredge, and stated that the construction of said ditch began "several years" after he and his family arrived in America in 1893.[76] It is possible the '1870s' map had been updated as the years progressed and does not *just* show the ditches that were present in the 1870s. Whatever the case may be, the result was the same, and the water supply for Six

Mile Creek in Ohio was further cut off because all of the run-off water from Indiana now drained to the Maumee River before reaching Ohio.[77]

From this point onward, Six Mile Reservoir was only furnished with water from an area that was "four or five miles long and from one to two miles in width," which was understandably described as "insufficient."[78] The State of Ohio then built a dam across the canal somewhere between Antwerp and the State Line,[79] presumably to keep the water in the canal from escaping into Indiana's ditch(es).

A month after the news broke of the acquisition of the canal in Indiana by the Nickel Plate Road, Representative Patton, who had previously championed expending money on rebuilding the Wabash & Erie Canal, introduced a bill to the Ohio Legislature that would repeal the $10,000 in appropriations made to repair the canal.[80] The legislation passed likely under a very strong presumption that Indiana would not be able to uphold their end of the requirement for the appropriations. Following the repeal, concern grew about the future of the ship canal proposal, to which the *Paulding County Gazette* placated concerns by telling its readers that:

> The recent sale of the Wabash and Erie Canal will not prevent its enlargement to a ship canal should the project prove feasible, and Congress appropriates the necessary means to carry it out, which will probably be done at some time in the not distant future.[81]

Whether it was for the cost, or the government was unwilling to exercise eminent domain over the former canal lands, the proposal was effectively dead upon the acquisition of the

Wabash & Erie Canal by the Nickel Plate Road. Few to no mentions of the proposal came up again after 1881.

Likely considering the railroad's acquisition and the repeal of appropriations, Ohio's Board of Public Works, in June 1881, was on the verge of allowing the Wabash & Erie Canal to fall into disrepair. [82] Before that could happen, timber interests in Defiance sent John R. Wilhelm and Sumner P. Shelly to Columbus, Ohio to meet with the Board of Public Works. Their goal was to convince the Board that the Wabash & Erie Canal was "largely used by the timber interest, and was important to Defiance manufacturers." [83] Upon this assertion by Defiance timber interests, and despite the ever-growing problem of feeding the canal and reservoir with enough water, the Board of Public Works agreed to repair three locks on the canal between Junction and Six Mile Reservoir, not the State Line like the repealed 1880 appropriations. [84] This work was scheduled to begin in the following winter, [85] but first, another round of appropriations would be necessary.

Senator Elmer White introduced the bill to the Ohio Senate for the needed appropriations on January 6, 1882.[86] Again, this bill would appropriate $10,000 (~$292,167 in 2023) to put the Wabash & Erie Canal in "good order for navigation" between Junction and the west line of Antwerp (Payne Lock@), this time leaving out repairs to the State Line.[87] Representative Lewis S. Gordon, a Paulding County native, was reportedly also "in favor

---

@ Payne Lock was roughly located just northwest of T-29 (Shaffer Road) where the road turns south, on the west side of the ditch west of Antwerp.
(Bill Oeters et. al., *Taming the Swamp*, 32.)

of keeping up the canals," and it was not much of a stretch to think he would support the appropriations bill in the House.[88]

New appropriations came as good news to the residents of Paulding County, who, by the winter of 1882, had become fed up with the condition and uselessness of the canal for one reason or another, and petitions began to circulate to either repair the canal and reservoir or abandon them.[89] Peculiarly, H. H. Vocke & Bros. and 79 others from Henry County, Ohio signed a petition that supported "an appropriation to rebuild locks and to repair that portion of the Miami & Erie Canal between Junction and the village of Antwerp."[90]

Many "leading citizens" of Antwerp continued to favor abandonment unless the canal was rebuilt and would only ever agree to the maintaining of the canal if it was repaired and dredged to Antwerp so the community could again benefit from the canal's existence.[91] Despite his alleged favorable position to maintaining the canal, Lewis S. Gordon presented a petition to the Ohio Legislature that was signed by Wilson H. Snook and two hundred and ninety-three citizens of Paulding County "praying for the abandonment of part of the Miami & Erie Canal,§ between the Ohio and Indiana State Line and Junction, in Paulding County, also for abandonment of reservoir on said canal."[92] However, with news of the bill to appropriate $10,000 to repair the canal, many of those who had favored abandonment changed their opinions in favor of the repairs.[93]

---

§ The Ohio portion of the Wabash & Erie Canal was occasionally referred to as a branch of the Miami & Erie Canal. For simplicity, this book refers to the canal between Junction, Ohio and the Indiana-Ohio State Line as the Wabash & Erie Canal.

Meanwhile, according to the *Defiance Democrat*, the Toledo 'land sharks' lead by Dr. Solomon S. Stambaugh, as well as John Cummings, and Clayton W. Everett, were "still after the land in Paulding reservoir" four years later.[94] When Senator White's bill passed both houses sometime around March 2, 1882,[95] some residents of Paulding County were "jubilant," [96] and an individual correspondent for the *Paulding County Gazette* going by the name '*Rex-Y*' voiced his opinion that:

> We are hardly ready to abandon the canal. Let it run, say ten years longer, and by that time, a large amount of our surplus timber will have floated to market, down its 'briny' waters. Then we will be prepared in this section of the country to begin to talk about farming.[97]

The bill was not without serious scrutiny, as it required three readings by the House.[98] The opposition passed a bill that would establish an inquiry with the Board of Public Works to determine whether the Board believed the repairs were necessary and worthy of money being appropriated.[99]

As planned, the Board of Public Works was promptly scrutinized about the project. The House asked the Board whether the repairs would be "in the financial interest of the State of Ohio," whether it would be "in the best interest of the State to abandon said improvement," whether the reservoir was a feeder to any other canal, and most importantly, whether the Board of Public Works had the funds to make such repairs. The Board answered the questions succinctly, stating that they believed maintaining the Wabash & Erie Canal was in the financial interests of the State of Ohio, namely because of the timber industry that used the canal to ship the timber, and the canal was needed to compete with the area railroads and their "exorbitant charges."[100]

The Board of Public Works also believed that Six Mile Reservoir was a feeder for the Miami & Erie Canal and would help maintain navigation on said canal north of Junction should something cause issues feeding it from the south. That all said, the Board could not make the necessary repairs to the Wabash & Erie Canal, now "in a poor state of repair" due to the negligence of the canal lessees, without the $10,000 appropriation. The canal fund at the disposal of the Board was deemed insufficient for the task, and to use it without the added funds would put the Board in danger of being unable to make any necessary repairs elsewhere on Ohio's canal system.[101]

In line with the Board of Public Works' assessment in June of 1881, the Board responded with a firm no when asked whether the abandonment of the canal and reservoir would be in the best interest of the State of Ohio. As to what amount of land would be reclaimed, the Board stated that, should the reservoir be maintained and all else abandoned, "water will flow to within one mile and one quarter of the town of Antwerp, consequently the quality of the land to be reclaimed would merely be that one and one quarter mile of canal bed."[102]

What is important to point out is the appropriations bill contradicted what the Board of Public Works intended to accomplish during the meeting with Defiance timber interests in June 1881. This assessment implies that the Board of Public Works knew that, despite Senator White's bill promising repairs would be made to Antwerp, the canal was not viable to Antwerp. They had described to the inquiry that there was "no water" above the reservoir on the canal, given that the feeder had been cut off and the water from Six Mile Reservoir only reached one and one quarter mile east of town. However, the Ohio Legislature passed the bill, and the discrepancy was never acknowledged during the inquiry.[103]

However, before work could commence on the Wabash & Erie Canal, the Board of Public Works had to deal with controversy, particularly from its Clerk, F. W. Newburg, who had embezzled the Board of Public Works fund to the tune of $20,000 ($551,270 in 2023).[104] It was reported that, despite what the Board said about its book-keeping:

> These books were not kept as required by law, nor did the Board at the end of each year add the checks and certificates together, or make comparisons with the books in either the office of the Treasurer or Auditor of State. No such comparisons were ever made by the Board, but their annual reports were made simply to square with the report of the Auditor of State.[105]

Because of the actions of Mr. Newburg and the general mistrust of other members of the Board who, by inaction, allowed this scheme to occur for the better part of three years, James Fullington, who was the next member to be up for reelection, would face considerable odds to remain on the Board. Despite there being no evidence to implicate him in the scheme.[106] It was Charles A. Flickinger, a prominent Defiance businessman, that was named as a possible replacement for Mr. Fullington.[107] That June, Mr. Flickinger was nominated by the Republican Convention for the Board of Public Works "by acclamation," sometime around June 8, 1882.[108] Ultimately, Mr.

Flickinger failed to be elected to the Board of Public Works that November; losing to Democrat Henry Weible by 15,725 votes.[109]

A few weeks after the election, word of work commencing on the canal appeared in the *Defiance Democrat*. Improvements to locks between Junction and Six Mile Reservoir were in order. The *Defiance Democrat* also reported that there were still plans to dredge the canal to Antwerp. This report further contradicted the intents of the Board after the 1881 meeting with timber interests and what was established with the inquiry after the 1882 appropriations bill was passed. Which stated the canal was not viable within one and one quarter mile of Antwerp. Nevertheless, Chief Engineer Gregory told the *Defiance Democrat* that the work would be finished by the following winter.[110]

In January 1883, Chief Engineer Gregory made his way to the area to prepare for the Wabash & Erie Canal's reconstruction.[111] By the end of April 1883, contracts for the work were being bid on. M. R. Langell's bid was reportedly a "straw bid" of $6,500 (~$191,789 in 2023) to rebuild three locks, leaving behind $3,500 (~$103,271 in 2023) for the dredging work.[112] William J. Jackson, a veteran canal engineer from Piqua, Ohio, was the other individual who bid on the work, declaring he would do all of the intended work for the $10,000 allocated to the project.[113]

It was not until August 1, 1883, that the Board of Public Works inspected Six Mile Reservoir regarding the recent proposals.[114] On August 16, 1883, it was reported that work had finally commenced on making repairs to the Wabash & Erie Canal, starting with work "rapidly being pushed on the new canal lock which is being put in at the upper end of the reservoir."[115] Two weeks later, water had been taken out of the canal downstream of Six Mile Reservoir through Furnace, leading to a prediction of increased malaria patients for local physicians.[116] All lumber was in place by September 6, 1883, to repair those three canal locks between Junction and Six Mile Reservoir.[117] On that same date, the *Antwerp Argus* noted that the only lock being worked on was at "the lower end of the reservoir" (Hutchins Lock). Indicating that work had begun on repairing the three remaining locks.[118]

There was no mention of replacing the fourth lock at the upper end of the reservoir (Banks Lock) in the bidding process. The reason why it was replaced becomes evident when looking back at what has already been established. During the 1882 Ohio General Assembly's session, when the Board of Public Works were pressed on the proposed repairs, the Board noted that water would only flow within one and one quarter mile of Antwerp from Six Mile Reservoir. The Board's 1881 meeting with timber interests from Defiance further proved the Board never intended to repair the canal to Antwerp. The approximate location of Banks Lock was almost precisely one and one quarter mile east of Antwerp.

Six Mile Reservoir could not furnish Antwerp with water, not only because it was incapable of doing so because of physics,¶ but now there was also a recently refurbished lock as far as the water could reliably be furnished to sufficient levels. Despite this, area

---

¶ If it was not already apparent why this was the case, a gradient profile of the Wabash & Erie Canal clearly shows that Six Mile Reservoir was downbound from the summit in Fort Wayne. This is why water from the St. Joseph River was capable of furnishing water to the canal and reservoir in Paulding County; the water quite literally flowed downhill from Fort Wayne. Because of physics, Six Mile Reservoir was incapable of feeding water above its own level back up the hill toward Fort Wayne. (*Profile of the Wabash & Erie Canal*, Drawn by Thomas Meek with assistance from Julia Meek.)

newspapers still claimed that the canal would be dredged to Antwerp, reportedly beginning sometime in the spring.[119] Hope for such dredging flourished when reports came that the steam-powered dredge was on the way in December 1883.[120] The dredge appeared sometime between then and January 1884, but it could not begin work until winter ended.[121]

## Chapter 2 Notes

1 "The Canals," *Defiance Democrat*, December 6, 1877, 4.
2 "The Canal Fight," *Defiance Democrat*, February 14, 1878, 4; ; "The Canal Rats," *Defiance Democrat*, December 20, 1877, 8; "The Canals," *Defiance Democrat*, December 6, 1877, 4.
3 "The Canal Fight," *Defiance Democrat*, February 14, 1878, 4; "The Canal Rats," *Defiance Democrat*, December 20, 1877, 8
4 "The Canal Fight," *Defiance Democrat*, February 14, 1878, 4.
5 "Neighborhood News," *Paulding Democrat*, July 4, 1878, 1; "Local Splinters," *Paulding Democrat*, May 9, 1878, 5.
6 "Local Splinters," *Paulding Democrat*, May 9, 1878, 5.
7 "Local Correspondence: Drain the County," *Paulding Democrat*, July 18, 1878, 1.
8 "Local Correspondence: Drain the County," *Paulding Democrat*, July 18, 1878, 1.
9 "Local Correspondence: Drain the County," *Paulding Democrat*, July 18, 1878, 1.
10 "Terrible Calamity," *Antwerp Gazette*, July 4, 1878, 3.
11 "Terrible Calamity," *Antwerp Gazette*, July 4, 1878, 3.
12 "Wabash Canal," *Antwerp Gazette*, November 21, 1878, 3.
13 "The Canal Meeting," *Defiance Democrat*, December 5, 1878, 3.
14 "Brief Local," *Paulding Democrat*, April 24, 1879, 3.
15 "Local News," *Paulding County Gazette*, April 24, 1879, 3.
16 "Fresh and Newsy," *Defiance Democrat*, May 8, 1879, 3; "Brief Local," *Paulding Democrat*, May 1, 1879, 3.
17 *Fort Wayne Weekly Sentinel*, July 23, 1879, 6.
18 *Fort Wayne Weekly Sentinel*, July 23, 1879, 6.
19 "Antwerp's Sensation," *Fort Wayne Weekly Sentinel*, August 13, 1879, 13.
20 "The City," *Fort Wayne Sentinel*, November 5, 1879, 6.
21 "Brief Local," *Paulding Democrat*, November 27, 1879, 3.
22 Harlan D. Unrau, *Historic Resource Study: Chesapeake & Ohio Canal*, Hagerstown: National Park Service, 2007, https://www.nps.gov/parkhistory/online_books/choh/unrau_hrs.pdf, 820.
23 Harlan D. Unrau, *Historic Resource Study: Chesapeake & Ohio Canal*, https://www.nps.gov/parkhistory/online_books/choh/unrau_hrs.pdf, 820.
24 Harlan D. Unrau, *Historic Resource Study: Chesapeake & Ohio Canal*, https://www.nps.gov/parkhistory/online_books/choh/unrau_hrs.pdf, 820.
25 Harlan D. Unrau, *Historic Resource Study: Chesapeake & Ohio Canal*, https://www.nps.gov/parkhistory/online_books/choh/unrau_hrs.pdf, 820.
26 "Attention Citizens of Paulding County," *Paulding Democrat*, November 27, 1879, 2.

27 "Letter from Judge Patton," *Paulding Democrat*, April 22, 1880, 2.

28 "Letter from Judge Patton," *Paulding Democrat*, April 22, 1880, 2.

29 "Letter from Judge Patton," *Paulding Democrat*, April 22, 1880, 2.

30 "Letter from Judge Patton," *Paulding Democrat*, April 22, 1880, 2.

31 "Chat," *Defiance Democrat*, December 30, 1880, 3.

32 "Brief Local," *Paulding Democrat*, February 3, 1881, 3.

33 "Wabash & Erie Canal," *Paulding County Gazette*, March 20, 1879, 2.

34 "Wabash & Erie Canal," *Paulding County Gazette*, March 20, 1879, 2.

35 "Wabash & Erie Canal," *Paulding County Gazette*, March 20, 1879, 2;
    "Ship Canal," *Paulding County Gazette*, March 27, 1879, 2;
    "Ship Canal," *Paulding Democrat*, December 11, 1879, 3.

36 "Canal Convention," *Fort Wayne Sentinel*, June 3, 1879, 4; "Wabash
    & Erie Canal Convention," *Paulding County Gazette*, May 22,
    1879, 3; "Canal Question," *Paulding County Gazette*, May 29,
    1879, 2.

37 "Canal Question," *Paulding County Gazette*, May 29, 1879, 2.

38 "Canal Convention," *Fort Wayne Sentinel*, June 3, 1879, 4; "Wabash
    & Erie Canal Convention," *Paulding County Gazette*, May 22,
    1879, 3; "Canal Question," *Paulding County Gazette*, May 29,
    1879, 2.

39 "Ship Canal," *Paulding Democrat*, December 11, 1879, 3; "Canal
    Convention," *Fort Wayne Sentinel*, June 3, 1879, 4.

40 "Canal Convention," *Fort Wayne Sentinel*, June 3, 1879, 4.

41 "Ship Canal," *Paulding Democrat*, December 11, 1879, 3.

42 "Canal Convention," *Fort Wayne Sentinel*, June 3, 1879, 4.

43 "Tate's Landing, Ohio," *Paulding Democrat*, January 1, 1880, 3.

44 "Tate's Landing, Ohio," *Paulding Democrat*, January 1, 1880, 3.

45 "Local News," *Paulding County Gazette*, February 5, 1880, 3.

46 "The Ship Canal Project," *Paulding County Gazette*, January 29,
    1880, 2; "Proposed Ship Canal from Cincinnati to Toledo,"
    *Paulding Democrat*, October 14, 1880, 3; "Local News,"
    *Paulding County Gazette*, February 5, 1880, 3.

47 "The Ship Canal Project," *Paulding County Gazette*, January 29,
    1880, 2.

48 "Enlarged Wabash and Erie Canal," *Paulding County Gazette*,
    February 17, 1881, 2.

49 "Proposed Ship Canal from Cincinnati to Toledo," *Paulding
    Democrat*, October 14, 1880, 3.

50 "Proposed Ship Canal from Cincinnati to Toledo," *Paulding
    Democrat*, October 14, 1880, 3.

51 "Proposed Ship Canal from Cincinnati to Toledo," *Paulding
    Democrat*, October 14, 1880, 3.

52 "Ship Canal," *Paulding County Gazette*, November 18, 1880, 2.

53 "Ship Canal," *Paulding County Gazette*, November 18, 1880, 2.

54 "Lake Erie and Ohio River Ship Canal," *Paulding Democrat*, May 19,
    1881, 3.

55 "Lake Erie and Ohio River Ship Canal," *Paulding Democrat*, May 19,
    1881, 3.

56 "Lake Erie and Ohio River Ship Canal," *Paulding Democrat*, May 19, 1881, 3.

57 "Enlarged Wabash and Erie Canal," *Paulding County Gazette*, February 17, 1881, 2.

58 "Enlarged Wabash and Erie Canal," *Paulding County Gazette*, February 17, 1881, 2.

59 U.S. Census Bureau, *1880 Census: Population of Each State and Territory by Counties, in the Aggregate, at the Censuses*, Table II, Ohio, 75.

60 "Ship Canal," *Paulding County Gazette*, November 25, 1880, 3.

61 "Purchase of the Wabash & Erie Canal by the Continental Railroad Co.," *Paulding Democrat*, February 24, 1881, 3; Taylor Hampton, *The Nickel Plate Road: The History of a Great Railroad*, 113.

62 "The Wabash & Erie Canal," in *Towpaths: A Collection of Articles from the Quarterly Publication of the Canal Society of Ohio*, 60; Alvin F. Harlow, *Old Towpaths: The Story of the American Canal Era*, 278; Paul Fatout, *Indiana Canals*, 174, 176.

63 Thomas E. Castaldi, "The Wabash & Erie Canal," in *History of Fort Wayne & Allen County, Indiana*, Volume I, 163; Taylor Hampton, *The Nickel Plate Road: The History of a Great Railroad*, 125-126.

64 Taylor Hampton, *The Nickel Plate Road: The History of a Great Railroad*, 125-126.

65 Taylor Hampton, *The Nickel Plate Road: The History of a Great Railroad*, 45, 113.

66 Taylor Hampton, *The Nickel Plate Road: The History of a Great Railroad*, 45, 113.

67 Taylor Hampton, *The Nickel Plate Road: The History of a Great Railroad*, 45, 113-114.

68 Taylor Hampton, *The Nickel Plate Road: The History of a Great Railroad*, 112.

69 Thomas E. Castaldi, "The Wabash & Erie Canal," in *History of Fort Wayne & Allen County, Indiana*, Volume I, 163.

70 Taylor Hampton, *The Nickel Plate Road: The History of a Great Railroad*, 143.

71 "The First Gun!," *Defiance Democrat*, October 13, 1887, 2.

72 "A Useless Water Supply," *Paulding County Gazette*, August 12, 1886, 1; "The Canal and Reservoir," *Antwerp Argus*, January 20, 1887, 2; "The First Gun!," *Defiance Democrat*, October 13, 1887, 2.

73 Maumee Township Ditch Map, 1870s, Allen Co., https://www.acgsi.org/maps/maumee.1870s.pdf.

74 *Home Community U. S. A.: Woodburn, Indiana*, 1955, 24.

75 Otto E. Ehrhart, *Memories*, Unknown Date, transcribed by Kim K. Sutton.

76 Otto E. Ehrhart, *Memories*, Unknown Date, transcribed by Kim K. Sutton.

77 "The Canal and Reservoir," *Antwerp Argus*, January 20, 1887, 2;
"The First Gun!," *Defiance Democrat*, October 13, 1887, 2;
Maumee Township Ditch Map, 1870s, Allen Co.,
https://www.acgsi.org/maps/maumee.1870s.pdf.

78 State of Ohio, *Executive Documents: Annual Reports for 1887, Made to
the Sixty-Eighth General Assembly*, Part I, 1294.

79 Charles E. Slocum, *History of the Maumee River Basin*, 610; Albert F.
Celley and Daniel F. Perch, "The Junction of Two Historic
Waterways in the Early History of Ohio and Indiana," 259.

80 "Relief," *Cincinnati Enquirer*, March 25, 1881, 1; "The Acts,"
*Cincinnati Commercial*, April 25, 1881, 3.

81 "Local News," *Paulding County Gazette*, March 24, 1881, 3.

82 *Defiance Democrat*, June 9, 1881, 3.

83 *Defiance Democrat*, June 9, 1881, 3; "Neighborhood News: Defiance,"
*Paulding County Gazette*, June 16, 1881, 3.

84 *Defiance Democrat*, June 9, 1881, 3; "Neighborhood News:
Defiance," *Paulding County Gazette*, June 16, 1881, 3.

85 *Defiance Democrat*, June 9, 1881, 3; "Neighborhood News: Defiance,"
*Paulding County Gazette*, June 16, 1881, 3.

86 "Columbus Notes," *Defiance Democrat*, January 12, 1882, 2.

87 "Proposed Improvement of the Canal from Junction to Antwerp,"
*Defiance Democrat*, January 19, 1882, 3.

88 "Local News," *Paulding County Gazette*, October 27, 1881, 3.

89 "Antwerp Items," *Paulding County Gazette*, January 12, 1882, 3.

90 State of Ohio, *Journal of the House of Representatives of the State of
Ohio, for the Adjourned Session of the Sixty-Fifth General
Assembly*, Volume LXXVIII, 209.

91 "Antwerp Items," *Paulding County Gazette*, January 12, 1882, 3.

92 State of Ohio, *Journal of the House of Representatives of the State of
Ohio, for the Adjourned Session of the Sixty-Fifth General
Assembly*, Volume LXXVIII, 209.

93 "Antwerp Items," *Paulding County Gazette*, February 9, 1882, 2.

94 *Defiance Democrat*, February 16, 1882, 2.

95 "Brief Local, *Paulding Democrat*, March 2, 1882, 3.

96 "Antwerp Items," *Paulding County Gazette*, February 23, 1882, 2.

97 "Antwerp Items," *Paulding County Gazette*, February 23, 1882, 2.

98 "Antwerp Items," *Paulding County Gazette*, February 9, 1882, 2.

99 "What the Board of Public Works Think About the Paulding End of
the Canal," *Defiance Democrat*, March 2, 1882, 3.

100 "What the Board of Public Works Think About the Paulding End of
the Canal," *Defiance Democrat*, March 2, 1882, 3.

101 "What the Board of Public Works Think About the Paulding End of
the Canal," *Defiance Democrat*, March 2, 1882, 3.

102 "What the Board of Public Works Think About the Paulding End of
the Canal," *Defiance Democrat*, March 2, 1882, 3.

103 "What the Board of Public Works Think About the Paulding End of
the Canal," *Defiance Democrat*, March 2, 1882, 3.

104 "The Public Works Board," *Defiance County Express*, April 20, 1882, 7.

105 "The Public Works Board," *Defiance County Express*, April 20, 1882, 7.

106 "The Public Works Board," *Defiance County Express*, April 20, 1882, 7.

107 "The Public Works Board," *Defiance County Express*, April 20, 1882, 7.

108 "Our State Ticket," *Defiance County Express*, June 15, 1882, 3; "Republican Ticket," *Defiance County Express*, June 8, 1882, 4.

109 Joseph P. Smith, *History of the Republican Party in Ohio*, Volume I, 460.

110 "The Canal Improvement," *Defiance Democrat*, November 23, 1882, 3.

111 "Columbus Notes," *Defiance Democrat*, January 11, 1883, 2.

112 "Local and Miscellaneous," *Defiance Democrat*, April 26, 1883, 3.

113 "Local and Miscellaneous," *Defiance Democrat*, April 26, 1883, 3.

114 "Local and Miscellaneous," *Defiance Democrat*, August 2, 1883, 3; "Our Home Corner," *Antwerp Argus*, August 2, 1883, 3.

115 "Our Home Corner," *Antwerp Argus*, August 16, 1883, 3.

116 "Furnace Flashes," *Antwerp Argus*, August 30, 1883, 3.

117 "Our Home Corner," *Antwerp Argus*, September 6, 1883, 3.

118 "Our Home Corner," *Antwerp Argus*, September 6, 1883, 3.

119 "Chat," *Defiance Democrat*, October 25, 1883, 3; "Our Home Corner," *Antwerp Argus*, November 1, 1883, 3; "Chat," *Defiance Democrat*, November 8, 1883, 3; "Our Home Corner," *Antwerp Argus*, November 15, 1883, 3.

120 "Our Home Corner, *Antwerp Argus*, December 20, 1883, 3.

121 "Our Home Corner, *Antwerp Argus*, January 24, 1884, 3.

# -3-

# Dissension

## (April 1884 – November 1886)

When navigation on the canal reopened after the winter around April 10, 1884,[1] dredging commenced on the Wabash & Erie Canal from Six Mile Reservoir to Antwerp.[2] This continued right up until the end of April,[3] when the dredge, which "after dredging a short distance in the canal... pulled up stakes and floated away."[4] The reason given to the *Antwerp Argus* was a lack of funds to finish the work, and no further funds had been appropriated in the 1884 Ohio legislative session.[5] That seemed like a convenient excuse to give the local newspaper, especially considering that it would later come out that approximately $3,800 (~$115,555 in 2023) remained for the job to be completed.[6]

The reality of the situation is that the Board of Public Works never planned to have the work done to Antwerp at all. Instead of using the remaining funds to repair the canal to Antwerp, the Board instead only took measures to maintain the water in the canal east of Six Mile Reservoir by rebuilding and dredging to Banks Lock, where they knew water from the reservoir could reliably get to. Despite holding hope for years that the canal to (or through) Antwerp would be rebuilt in some form, the

*Antwerp Argus* would later lament that "the citizens of our county who were the most interested, and labored the hardest for this appropriation, were not benefited one iota by the improvements made, or the money thus expended."[7]

Because of this perceived betrayal by the Board of Public Works and the State of Ohio, the locals surrounding Six Mile Reservoir began to voice their discontent increasingly. The residents had complained before about the pungent smell and the possibility of the canal works producing disease. Those assertions had previously come from times when the water was abnormally low, and a fish die-off occurred.[8] However, as early as 1881, some unnamed factories in Antwerp dammed up the canal to better maintain the water supply of the canal for their factories after the primary water supply from Indiana was permanently cut off.[9] These dams were perceived as a culprit for the stagnant water that was alleged to breed miasma and disease from the canal.[10] This arrangement of local factories damming the canal had not changed by 1884.[11]

In June 1884, almost two months after the dredge had left, the locals, again, began to complain about a "smell to heaven" emanating from the canal.[12] The canal had developed algae upon it, and the local paper joked that a "bull-frog broke his leg trying to get through" because it had become so thick.[13] There was so much algae in the stagnant water that it reportedly gave the illusion that the canal was dry, despite two feet of water being present.[14] This time, not only did the locals blame the factory dams for it, but they also began to blame Defiance for it.

In July 1884, the locals began to call for abandonment, resurrecting old talking points. They attacked Defiance for "reaping the benefits of water furnished from the reservoir at this place, and Antwerp has the stink."[15] More worrisome to the locals was that they believed the canal works would "breed a pestilence in our midst, and before it is too late, a large portion of our community will be stricken down with some loathsome disease."[16] Furthermore, the *Antwerp Argus* asserted that:

> We should hardly feel willing to furnish our friends below with water, and get nothing in return for our accommodation, but stink, from a pestilent breeding, stench emitting, scum covered canal bed. We kick, and the sooner our neighbors at Defiance, and the State Board of Public Works know it, the better.[17]

Some even argued that the health of citizens in Defiance could benefit from abandonment. One local reportedly observed that, while "they are capturing water from our reservoir," it was arriving in Defiance "just as green as green can be!"[18] This, according to the *Antwerp Argus*, had become a sanitary issue for Defiance which could "make them sick of their bargain before the season was over."[19] If Six Mile Reservoir and the Wabash & Erie Canal were abandoned, others believed that the immediate area would be able to "bid defiance to all epidemic diseases."[20]

In December 1884, residents planned to petition the State of Ohio to abandon the canal works unless the originally promised work to repair the canal to Antwerp was completed.[21] The *Antwerp Argus* also demanded that the factories, which had dammed up the canal for their private purposes, remove those dams and replace them with two above the furthest west factory and one below the furthest east factory.[22] Doing so, they believed, would allow the water to "be more pure," thus leading to fewer complaints about any smell from the canal. [23] The *Antwerp Argus* acknowledged this as a possible compromise to finishing the canal's repairs to town, [24] but they also believed abandonment was "only a question of time." [25]

The *Cleveland Plain Dealer*, being reported by the *Defiance Democrat*, made a few remarks on the situation as it unfolded in August 1884. They perceived the situation to be of great detriment to the manufacturers of Antwerp, and its citizens by proxy (who numbered about 1,300 in the 1880s [26]) who were "dependent on these factories." [27] The *Cleveland Plain Dealer* also believed the fault of the "treachery" fell on the State of Indiana, which abandoned and subsequently sold their portion of the Wabash & Erie Canal without considering how it may affect their citizens, and citizens in Ohio. [28] The *Cleveland Plain Dealer* also acknowledged the approximately 5,000 acres of land that was "made useless by the reservoir" [29] and lamented to its readers that

> this stricken population are robbed of their canal, and yet forced to submit to the loss of the land, for which loss the canal was the sole compensation. The loss of both canal and the use of 5,000 acres of land, which might, before now, be occupied by tax-paying farmers and profitable patrons of Antwerp's trade, is beyond the pale of human endurance or just exaction... Why shall we be surprised to her threats of cutting the banks of the reservoir and rumors of a disposition to vote for a member of the Board of Public Works who does not live in a rival town or in a city which experiences benefits rather than resentment at the situation of the victim of treachery and corruption of lawmakers in another state. It is but natural for these victims of wrong doing to seek an impartial juror to sit in judgement upon their appeal for redress and not one whose town and kindred prosper upon the woes of a stricken rival. [30]

The *Cleveland Plain Dealer* had their finger precisely on the core issue almost three years before the climax of the Reservoir War.

That member of the Board of Public Works mentioned by the *Cleveland Plain Dealer* was Charles A. Flickinger, who had once again been nominated for a position on the Board of Public Works, and this time defeated Democrat John H. Benfer by 17,283 votes in the 1884 election.[31] Mr. Flickinger's position on the Ohio canals was that the canals could be "made self-sustaining if properly conducted," that is if they were run like "any private business is."[32] However, Mr. Flickinger opposed abandoning any part of the established canal system in Ohio under the auspice of his belief they could be made self-sustaining and were "of vital importance to the people of the state."[33]

In 1885, the question of whether the Wabash & Erie Canal and Six Mile Reservoir would be abandoned had gained renewed publicity, as the planned petition mentioned earlier had been circulating around the area. [34] The *Antwerp Argus*, however, argued that Antwerp's factories and their canal interests were of greater importance to the town than the "canal or reservoir is a damage." [35] Despite these petitions, the *Defiance Democrat* assured its readers that there was "no immediate danger of the reservoir being abandoned."[36]

That said, the *Defiance Democrat* (and to a more subtle extent, the *Defiance County Express*) warned its readers that this renewed effort was, yet again, the work of Dr. Solomon S. Stambaugh and "the land grabbers." [37] This was in spite of the fact that Dr. Stambaugh, during the year of 1885, would start another medical practice in California after making a "disastrous investment" in the "pine timber lands of Alabama and Mississippi."[38]

Governor George Hoadly seemed to also denounce the actions of the 'land sharks' as he believed:

> The State acquired the land by purchase or gift, owns it, built, and has maintained the canals, is not called on to give it away, or lose its investment, and ought not part with it for private use, except for full compensation. If these lands can be converted to other and better public uses, well and good, provided they are free to all, or the payment for their use is to the State... but if private persons or corporations are to be directly or indirectly the beneficiaries of State property, such persons or corporations ought to pay its full value.[39]

Governor Hoadly seemed to imply that the State of Ohio, while it had no intentions of abandoning the canal and reservoir, it would possibly be willing to get rid of the property if there was no longer any possible good public use for it; and the state was adequately compensated for the land by the private beneficiaries of it.

A salient question in 1885 was whether "appropriations be made annually to sustain parts [of the Ohio canal system] that do not pay expenses, or shall these non-supporting parts be abandoned and only those parts preserved that do pay expenses?"[40] On February 10, 1885, a meeting was held at "George's hall" in Antwerp to discuss whether abandonment was a feasible option for the community.[41] A few petitions had been circulated in the weeks prior to the meeting and were "pretty generally signed by our citizens, and it seems to be the determination to either have the canal dredged to west line of Antwerp, in accordance with the appropriation made, or force its abandonment."[42] Phaon P. Doering, John H. Chester, and Wilson H. Snook were chosen to "raise by subscription the necessary funds for all expenses incurred."[43] The results of this meeting were never established, implying that the petition had fallen on deaf ears at Columbus.

The only other major news regarding the future of the canal during 1885 was that the Van Wert & Michigan Railroad (a predecessor of the Cincinnati, Jackson & Mackinaw Railroad and Cincinnati Northern Railroad) announced that it wished to cross the Wabash & Erie Canal at the Paulding Furnace using a fixed bridge rather than the swing bridge in place for canal traffic to pass through. [44] The *Defiance Democrat* did not favor this arrangement, as installing a fixed bridge at that location would "destroy canal navigation from that point to the reservoir."[45] Interestingly, the *Defiance Democrat* also acknowledged that the State of Ohio did not do what was expected from the 1882 appropriations bill. By May 1885, the canal to Antwerp had still not been dredged, and the *Defiance Democrat* stated, "dredging could and should be done this summer." [46] No dredging took place that summer.

1886 would begin with the *Defiance County Express* proudly declaring that the canals were not in danger.[47] This came from an interview with Mr. Flickinger, the Board of Public Works member elected in 1884.[48] His reasoning for such an assertion was that "there are too many interests bound up in it, too many millions have been spent upon it... such a course would remove a very valuable check upon railroad extortion in the matter of freight rates." [49] Nevertheless, the *Paulding Democrat* ran an article from the *Defiance Democrat* stating that something had to be done to alleviate some of the financial strain on taxpayers' and the profitable parts of the canal. Especially considering the "majority of the canals are not productive."[50] The idea presented in that article was to compartmentalize the canal revenue. Therefore, each canal would have to maintain a sufficient operating ratio to generate enough revenue to pay for its own upkeep, or it would likely face abandonment.[51]

The *Defiance Democrat* had maintained this opinion for almost a decade. In December 1877, when discussing the abandonment of the Muskingum Improvement, they stated that they were "in favor of keeping up all the Public Works of the State which are self-supporting, and not in favor of taxing the people of the State to maintaining unprofitable works."[52] The cost to maintain the Muskingum Improvement reportedly exceeded the revenue it generated by a "considerable amount each year."[53]

There was little concern about the Miami & Erie Canal, as it was claimed to be a profitable canal brought down by the expenditures of the other unprofitable canals.[54] The article from the *Defiance Democrat* likely meant the main canal was profitable, but that is not made clear and is left ambiguous. The reason this is important is that, in Governor Joseph B. Foraker's message to the Ohio Legislature in 1886, the Miami & Erie Canal was reported to have expended more money ($101,444.42 (~$3,216,112 in 2023)) than it took in from tolls ($79,156.21 (~$2,509,504 in 2023)).[55] However, the report does not differentiate the Wabash & Erie Canal from the Miami & Erie Canal at this date,[56] and the former's losses could have skewed the Miami & Erie Canal's losses.

According to Governor Foraker, in his first address to the Ohio General Assembly, the canals had not turned a profit since the State of Ohio took back the canals from the lessees.[57] Between 1880 and 1885, the Ohio canal system had taken in $1,001,763.54 (~$31,727,398 in 2023) in tolls but had expended $1,474,268.45 (~$46,739,015 in 2023) in the same amount of time. Over these six years, the canals were in the red by $472,781.70 (~$14,988,689 in 2023).[58]

The hardship for the Ohio canals, according to Governor Foraker, was due to a couple of factors. The first was a series of floods in 1882, 1883, and 1884 that damaged the canals throughout the state and required more money to be expended than what may have been typical to make the repairs. The second and most important was the increased competition from the railroad industry. Because more tonnage was being shipped by rail due to its speed, the State of Ohio had no choice but to lower the tolls on the canal to try and compete.[59]

Unfortunately, the railroads also had an advantage in this matter over canals. The railroads could lower their rates and make up for the reduced rate by running longer trains that logically carried more freight. The canals could not compensate for the lower toll with higher tonnage because the canals, by their design, limited the dimensions of the boats, which limited their carrying capacity. The only option was to run more boats at a reduced rate, which was not happening.[60]

On February 19, 1886, a meeting was held at the Smith Hotel@ in Antwerp to discuss matters relating to the abandonment of the canal works and, oddly enough, the construction of Paulding County's new courthouse.[61] Francis B. DeWitt and William E. Osborn oversaw the meeting. Lewis S. Gordon, Phaon P. Doering, and Wilson H. Snook favored the abandonment of the canal works.[62] On the other hand, they were not in favor of levying any new taxes to build a new courthouse. They reasoned that the "burden of taxation was already more than many of us could bear."[63] That said, if the county citizens still wished to proceed with building the new courthouse, they would relent in their position despite the costs.[64]

As for the canal question, according to this meeting, there was about $4,000 (~$127,306 in 2023) that was left from the canal repairs that was to be used "for dredging purposes."[65] This aligns with the earlier report of $3,800 remaining, but that money had since reverted to the State Treasury, and the "work which was of the most vital interest to our county, and more especially Antwerp, was never finished."[66]

Those attending the meeting further asserted that the canal works, "in their present condition,"[67] were not in the county's interests, as they occupied "many thousand acres of land that would soon become valuable."[68] Echoing similar sentiments from almost a decade prior when Dr. Solomon S. Stambaugh filed

---

@ I am not certain of the location of the Smith Hotel in Antwerp, but based on a couple sources, it was likely in the middle of Railroad Street between Cleveland Street and Main Street on the south side of the road. ("Our Home Corner, *Antwerp Argus*, November 24, 1887, 3; *Antwerp Argus*, February 28, 1889, 2; *Sanborn Fire Insurance Map from Antwerp, Paulding County, Ohio*, August 1893.)

his lawsuit. Those attending the meeting also made the following statement on the matter: "we hardly feel willing to still continue as the tail end of the Defiance kite... if we are owned, body and soul, and controlled by Defiance interests, the quicker we battle for our rights the better."[69]

It was then announced at the meeting that a delegation from the Ohio Legislature, interested in the canal matter, were coming to Paulding County. A reception committee was created to greet these legislators, consisting of Lewis S. Gordon, Phaon P. Doering, Antwerp Mayor William F. Fleck,[¶] William E. Osborn, John B. Zuber, Wilson H. Snook, William D. Wilson, Franz J. Zuber, Francis B. DeWitt, and James P. Gasser. These same men would visit Paulding to view the "present deplorable condition of the courthouse." According to the *Antwerp Argus*, others present at this meeting were Dr. Hiram M. Ayres, Kenton E. Shuster, Madison C. Powell, Oscar F. Kraner, and Peter Kemler.[70]

The Ohio Supreme Court then decided on July 4, 1886, that "ownership of canal beds, when canals have been abandoned, reverts to the owners of the abutting real estate."[71] This decision seemingly paved the way for ownership of abandoned canal lands to end up in the hands of local citizens instead of 'land sharks.'[72] A month later, Francis B. DeWitt would return to Antwerp to talk up the abandonment of Six Mile Reservoir again, as he had done for most of the last decade. The *Antwerp Argus* reported that petitions would circulate again.[73]

---

¶ Antwerp's mayor between April 1886 and April 1888, and November 1888 and April 1889.
(Dale L. Ehrhart, "Municipal History of Antwerp," in *A Century of Progress: Antwerp, Ohio*, 33.)

It is important to mention that the reservoir's water level had become very low, almost dry, earlier in March 1886. The reservoir continued to be low through August when it was declared "the lowest this season ever known in its history." The water level was so low that the reservoir was described as "nothing but one vast stretch of dry land dotted with fields of flag and innumerable stumps."[74] The only parts of the reservoir bottoms that still had water were the original course of Six Mile Creek and the "excavations made to procure dirt for the building of the bank."[75] The reservoir becoming dry was not a new issue, dating back to at least 1872 and as far as there are newspaper records in Paulding County. Back then, the reservoir also got so low that the *Antwerp Gazette* reported the reservoir would:

> Send forth deadly malaria during the sultry months of July and August, as it is strewn with thousands of dead fish which were caught in the tangled grass and water flag, when the water receded, and the stench arising from the decomposing mass can easily be recognized when the wind blows... although the 'pond' lies nearly a mile and a half from the village.[76]

The *Paulding County Gazette* exclaimed the dry weather "virtually kills the usefulness of this vast artificial lake."[77] That paper also believed the only thing left to convince the Board of Public Works was to "show them its utter uselessness as a canal feeder, secure its abandonment from its present use, and have it turned over to the tillers of the soil."[78] The *Paulding County Gazette* further asserted that the reservoir lands were fertile and valuable farmland, and if used as such, would "prove a source of revenue to the county and enhance the healthfulness of the locality."[79]

That assertion would seemingly be proven by E. O. Johnston of Antwerp, who, in an attempt to grow potatoes within the reservoir and on his land abutting Six Mile Reservoir, succeeded in growing potatoes as large as two pounds, two and one-half ounces. He grew the potatoes within the reservoir due to it being perpetually dried up on the western end where his farm was.[80] The *Antwerp Argus* described the potatoes as being "solid color through... had not grown so rank as to become hollow as many of our large potatoes show, but nice, smooth, and solid." The *Antwerp Argus* also noted that the other potatoes Mr. Johnston brought were "not far behind" that one. For some, this was all the proof they needed that some of the "finest soil in the state lies in Paulding County and the draining of the reservoir and its cultivation will give abundance of wealth to the farming community unthought of years ago."[81]

Another plant had been harvested from Six Mile Reservoir for years prior to Mr. Johnston planting his potato crop within the reservoir walls. Flag, more commonly known as cattails, were typically harvested from Six Mile Reservoir during the late summer and fall months.[82] These cattails were shipped abroad, often filling several canal boats with nothing but cattails during the harvest season.[83] One instance was in 1883 when the harvest was shipped to Cincinnati, Ohio.[84] The cattails were harvested for use in the making of barrels and buckets.[85] If a barrel or bucket leaked after production or with age due to drying out of the staves or headboards, the reeds from cattails (most commonly *Typha latifolia*) could be used as a "gasket material" to fill the gap and stop the leak.[86]

By October 1886, the fierce discontent of the locals reached a boiling point, enough so that the *Antwerp Argus* exclaimed, "the Antwerp reservoir must go, so says our citizens."[87] A meeting was advertised to take place on October 11, 1886, at the Grand Army of the Republic (G. A. R.) Hall in Antwerp.[@] The *Antwerp Argus* then declared that "our citizens mean business, and it will be hardly safe to oppose the abandonment of the reservoir."[88] Placards exclaiming "Shoulder Arms!" were distributed across Paulding County ahead of the upcoming meeting.[89] The *Antwerp Argus* exclaimed that the local citizens needed to cut themselves from the "Defiance kite" and "assert our right to such an extent that we cannot fail to receive justice and recognition."[90]

The *Antwerp Argus* further asserted that one of the benefits of abandoning Six Mile Reservoir was that the land contained within the banks of Six Mile Reservoir was some of the "best land in Ohio." If the declared 7,000 acres could be drained, it would make for the "most tillable and profitable farms" and further aid those with farms already present near the reservoir that had otherwise failed due to excess water from Six Mile Reservoir.[91] The *Antwerp Argus* called upon its readers to work toward "abating this nuisance," stating that "the time has come to strike." The canal works were no longer perceived as a benefit to those within the county and were only a benefit to those outside Paulding County, particularly those in Defiance County whom

---

@ I am not certain where the G. A. R. Hall was in Antwerp. What I do know is that it was on Main Street near River Street. It is possible that it was the room above Oliver S. Applegate's store, which is noted later. ("100th Reunion, *Antwerp Argus*, August 28, 1884, 4; "The Fourth in Antwerp," *Antwerp Argus*, July 9, 1885, 3.)

they asserted were "growing rich from the mossbacks of Paulding County."[92]

A large crowd gathered at the October 11, 1886 meeting, which only had one goal; to show the citizens of Paulding County how they could benefit from the abandonment of Six Mile Reservoir and how it could be removed.[93] Those attending the meeting declared the reservoir a "pestilent breeding, execrable nuisance" that needed to be eliminated.[94] Antwerp's mayor, William F. Fleck, and other citizens of Paulding County declared that "forbearance has, at last, ceased to be a virtue and if we, with our five thousand votes and twenty thousand population, can receive no recognition, it is time we met for ourselves."[95] They further declared that:

> Our citizens are aroused on this subject and will now stop short of nothing but the abandonment of this nuisance — which it now surely is — and by its abandonment a large scope of land can be reclaimed and made to produce crops not equaled by any other part of the State.[96]

The previous June, the *Antwerp Argus* pointed out that Representative John L. Geyer, the representative for both Defiance and Paulding County, had seemingly failed to bring up the canal question to the Ohio Legislature in the 1886 session.[97] At the October meeting, Representative Geyer was chastised for his "lack of energy" by failing to "bring the matter properly before that body."[98] However, this assertion by those at the meeting was not entirely true. Representative Geyer had presented the petition of Franz J. Zuber and 880 other signatures to the Ohio Legislature on May 4, 1886, "asking for the vacation of the Paulding Reservoir and Wabash Canal," which was subsequently accepted and referred to the Committee on Public Works.[99] Representative Geyer did not, however, introduce a bill to force the issue of abandonment as the locals wished he would in conjunction with the petition.

Despite their fiery language, those who attended the meeting resolved to draft more petitions and have them circulated throughout the county, electing John S. Snook, Mayor Fleck, and John H. Chester to oversee this.[100] At the motion of Antwerp's mayor, those at the meeting appointed a committee consisting of George Henshaw, Frank Long,[¶] Jacob Saylor,[¶¶] and Zachariah A. Graves to circulate "subscription paper" and determine the cost of constructing a ditch "through the Village of Antwerp." This ditch would connect South Six Mile Creek and the Maumee River. The committees were then instructed to prepare their assessments for the October 19, 1886 meeting, and the meeting adjourned.[101]

Something oddly ominous occurred the Sunday prior to the next meeting; fire was seen in the direction of Six Mile Reservoir, the fire coming from cattails burning in the reservoir.[102] The next meeting about abandonment did not occur until October 20, 1886, and attendance was lower than expected at this meeting. Nevertheless, the meeting proceeded as planned, but the only matter on the agenda, which was the proposed ditch to drain Six

---

¶ Antwerp's mayor between April 1883 and April 1886, and April 1889 and April 1890, and January 1898 and May 1898.
(Dale L. Ehrhart, "Municipal History of Antwerp," in *A Century of Progress: Antwerp, Ohio*, 33, 37.)

¶¶ Antwerp's mayor between April 1882 and March 1883.
(Dale L. Ehrhart, "Municipal History of Antwerp," in *A Century of Progress: Antwerp, Ohio*, 32.)

Mile Reservoir by cutting it off from its source. The proposed plan was to petition the County Commissioners to create a road and ditch that ran on the line of sections 23 and 24 of Carryall Township and sections 3 and 4 of Harrison Township. Upon reaching the canal, the ditch would be dug east "for a short distance" and then north to connect with the Maumee River.[103]

Nothing about the routing makes much sense except the proposal on the line of sections 3 and 4 in Harrison Township for the most part, as it would also require running down the line of sections 9 and 10 to meet South Six Mile Creek.[104] Sections 23 and 24 in Carryall Township would have been feasible to meet the Maumee River,[105] but the *Antwerp Argus* does not imply this, as it refers to the ditch on that line *before* running the ditch north to the river after running a short distance east.[106] The *Antwerp Argus* could have meant sections 33 and 34 in Carryall Township, which would make sense.[107] At least to run the ditch to the canal, run the water east through the canal, and then north to the river down the line of sections 25 and 26 as well as 23 and 24. Despite the published plan not making sense on a map, the plan was deemed possible and economically feasible by those attending the meeting. Plans were then put forth to make it a reality.[108]

A few weeks later, the petitions drafted at the first meeting at the G. A. R. Hall were being circulated, and were also available to sign during the election at voting precincts throughout the county.[109] Almost 600 citizens signed the petition in Carryall Township,[110] and nearly three-quarters of the voters in Paulding County signed the petitions.[111] Those petitions would be given to Representative Geyer to present along with a bill to the Ohio Legislature in January.[112]

Hopes were high that 1887 would be the year the canal works would finally be abandoned. The *Paulding Democrat* joked to its readers on November 11, 1886, that "if anyone has any pet fish in the big frog pond it is our opinion that he had better make preparations to remove them." [113] The *Antwerp Argus* again declared it to be "dangerous for those desiring favors from the voters in [Paulding County] to oppose [abandoning the reservoir]." [114] The *Antwerp Argus* then issued a foreboding exclamation a couple of weeks later. "Watch out, there is something going to drop."[115]

## Chapter 3 Notes

1 "Our Home Corner," *Antwerp Argus*, April 10, 1884, 4.

2 "Dredging," *Antwerp Argus*, April 10, 1884, 4.

3 "Our Home Corner," *Antwerp Argus*, April 24, 1884, 3.

4 "Floated Away," *Antwerp Argus*, May 1, 1884, 3.

5 "Floated Away," *Antwerp Argus*, May 1, 1884, 3.

6 "The Canal and Reservoir," *Antwerp Argus*, January 20, 1887, 2.

7 "The Canal and Reservoir," *Antwerp Argus*, January 20, 1887, 2.

8 "Drying Up!" *Antwerp Gazette*, May 30, 1872, 3.

9 "Antwerp Items," *Paulding County Gazette*, September 1, 1881, 3.

10 "Antwerp Items," *Paulding County Gazette*, September 1, 1881, 3.

11 "The Old Canal," *Antwerp Argus*, December 18, 1884, 3.

12 "A Heavenward Stench," *Antwerp Argus*, June 26, 1884, 3.

13 "A Heavenward Stench," *Antwerp Argus*, June 26, 1884, 3.

14 "Our Home Corner," *Antwerp Argus*, July 24, 1884, 3.

15 "The Old Canal," *Antwerp Argus*, July 24, 1884, 3.

16 "The Old Canal," *Antwerp Argus*, July 24, 1884, 3.

17 "The Old Canal," *Antwerp Argus*, July 24, 1884, 3.

18 "The Old Canal," *Antwerp Argus*, July 24, 1884, 3.

19 "Our Neighbors," *Antwerp Argus*, July 31, 1884, 3.

20 "Our Home Corner," *Antwerp Argus*, July 31, 1884, 3.

21 "Will Petition," *Antwerp Argus*, December 11, 1884, 3.

22 "The Old Canal," *Antwerp Argus,* December 18, 1884, 3.

23 "The Old Canal," *Antwerp Argus,* December 18, 1884, 3.

24 "The Old Canal," *Antwerp Argus,* December 18, 1884, 3.

25 "The Old Canal," *Antwerp Argus,* December 18, 1884, 3.

26 U.S. Census Bureau. *1890 Census: Report on Population of the United States*. Minor Civil Divisions - Table 5. Ohio. 278.

27 "An Abandoned Canal," *Defiance Democrat*, August 7, 1884, 4.

28 "An Abandoned Canal," *Defiance Democrat*, August 7, 1884, 4.

29 "An Abandoned Canal," *Defiance Democrat*, August 7, 1884, 4.

30 "An Abandoned Canal," *Defiance Democrat*, August 7, 1884, 4.

31 Joseph P. Smith, *History of the Republican Party in Ohio*, Volume I, 498.

32 *Defiance County Express*, April 2, 1885, 4.

33 *Defiance County Express*, April 2, 1885, 4; "To the Defiance Express," *Defiance County Express*, April 9, 1886, 5.

34 "Our Home Corner," *Antwerp Argus*, January 1, 1885, 3.

35 "Our Home Corner," *Antwerp Argus*, January 1, 1885, 3.

36 *Defiance Democrat*, January 15, 1885, 2.

37 *Defiance Democrat*, January 15, 1885, 2; *Defiance County* Express, January 8, 1885, 3.

38 *The Bay of San Francisco: The Metropolis of the Pacific Coast and its Suburban Cities: A History*, Volume I, 656.

39 "Hoadly's Message," *Paulding County Gazette*, January 15, 1885, 1.

40 "Our Home Corner," *Antwerp Argus*, April 23, 1885, 3.

41 "Canal and Reservoir," *Antwerp Argus*, February 12, 1885, 3.
42 "Canal and Reservoir," *Antwerp Argus*, February 12, 1885, 3.
43 "Canal and Reservoir," *Antwerp Argus*, February 12, 1885, 3.
44 "Chat," *Defiance Democrat*, May 14, 1885, 3.
45 "Chat," *Defiance Democrat*, May 14, 1885, 3.
46 "Chat," *Defiance Democrat*, May 14, 1885, 3.
47 "The Canals Not in Danger," *Defiance County Express*, January 7, 1886, 5.
48 "The Canals Not in Danger," *Defiance County Express*, January 7, 1886, 5; Joseph P. Smith, *History of the Republican Party in Ohio*, Volume I, 498.
49 "The Canals Not in Danger," *Defiance County Express*, January 7, 1886, 5.
50 "Local Gossip," *Paulding Democrat*, January 14, 1886, 3.
51 "Local Gossip," *Paulding Democrat*, January 14, 1886, 3.
52 "The Canal Rats," *Defiance Democrat*, December 20, 1877, 8.
53 "The Canal Rats," *Defiance Democrat*, December 20, 1877, 8.
54 "Local Gossip," *Paulding Democrat*, January 14, 1886, 3.
55 "Governor's Message," *Paulding Democrat*, January 14, 1886, 4.
56 "Governor's Message," *Paulding Democrat*, January 14, 1886, 4.
57 "Governor's Message," *Paulding Democrat*, January 14, 1886, 4.
58 "Governor's Message," *Paulding Democrat*, January 14, 1886, 4.
59 "Governor's Message," *Paulding Democrat*, January 14, 1886, 4.
60 "Governor's Message," *Paulding Democrat*, January 14, 1886, 4.
61 "Courthouse and Canal," *Antwerp Argus*, February 25, 1886, 2.
62 "Courthouse and Canal," *Antwerp Argus*, February 25, 1886, 2.
63 "Courthouse and Canal," *Antwerp Argus*, February 25, 1886, 2.
64 "Courthouse and Canal," *Antwerp Argus*, February 25, 1886, 2.
65 "Courthouse and Canal," *Antwerp Argus*, February 25, 1886, 2.
66 "Courthouse and Canal," *Antwerp Argus*, February 25, 1886, 2.
67 "Courthouse and Canal," *Antwerp Argus*, February 25, 1886, 2.
68 "Courthouse and Canal," *Antwerp Argus*, February 25, 1886, 2.
69 "Courthouse and Canal," *Antwerp Argus*, February 25, 1886, 2.
70 "Courthouse and Canal," *Antwerp Argus*, February 25, 1886, 2; "Notes About People," *Antwerp Argus*, February 25, 1886, 3.
71 "The Canals Are Safe," *Paulding County Gazette*, July 8, 1886, 4.
72 "The Canals Are Safe," *Paulding County Gazette*, July 8, 1886, 4.
73 "Personal Mention," *Antwerp Argus*, August 12, 1886, 3.
74 "Chat," *Defiance Democrat*, March 18, 1886, 3; "A Useless Water Supply," *Paulding County Gazette*, August 12, 1886, 1.
75 "A Useless Water Supply," *Paulding County Gazette*, August 12, 1886, 1.
76 "Drying Up!" *Antwerp Gazette*, May 30, 1872, 3.
77 "A Useless Water Supply," *Paulding County Gazette*, August 12, 1886, 1.
78 "A Useless Water Supply," *Paulding County Gazette*, August 12, 1886, 1.

79 "A Useless Water Supply," *Paulding County Gazette*, August 12, 1886, 1.

80 "Round About—Antwerp," *Paulding County Gazette*, September 16, 1886, 5; "Large Potatoes in the Reservoir." *Antwerp Argus*, September 16, 1886, 3.

81 "Large Potatoes in the Reservoir." *Antwerp Argus*, September 16, 1886, 3.

82 "Home Matters," *Antwerp Gazette*, August 10, 1876, 3; "Our Home Corner," *Antwerp Argus*, August 16, 1883, 3; "Our Home Corner," *Antwerp Argus*, October 11, 1883, 3.

83 "Our Home Corner," *Antwerp Argus*, August 16, 1883, 3.

84 "Our Home Corner," *Antwerp Argus*, August 16, 1883, 3.

85 Otto E. Ehrhart, "Wabash-Erie Canal," in *A Century of Progress: Antwerp, Ohio*, 16.

86 *Barrel Maintenance and Repair Manual,* Barrel Builders, Inc., 24, https://barrelbuilders.com/wp-content/uploads/2015/02/Barrel-Maintenance-Repair-Manual.pdf.

87 "Our Home Corner," *Antwerp Argus*, October 7, 1886, 3.

88 "Our Home Corner," *Antwerp Argus*, October 14, 1886, 3.

89 "Round About—Antwerp," *Paulding County Gazette,* October 14, 1886, 5.

90 "The Reservoir," *Antwerp Argus*, October 14, 1886, 3.

91 "The Reservoir," *Antwerp Argus*, October 14, 1886, 3.

92 "The Reservoir," *Antwerp Argus*, October 14, 1886, 3.

93 "The People Aroused and Say in Thunder Tones, That Our County's Past, the Antwerp Reservoir Must Go!," *Antwerp Argus*, October 14, 1886, 3; "Round About—Antwerp," *Paulding County Gazette*, October 14, 1886, 5.

94 "The People Aroused and Say in Thunder Tones, That Our County's Past, the Antwerp Reservoir Must Go!," *Antwerp Argus*, October 14, 1886, 3.

95 "The People Aroused and Say in Thunder Tones, That Our County's Past, the Antwerp Reservoir Must Go!," *Antwerp Argus*, October 14, 1886, 3.

96 "Round About—Antwerp," *Paulding County Gazette*, October 14, 1886, 5.

97 "Our Home Corner, *Antwerp Argus*, June 3, 1886, 3.

98 "The People Aroused and Say in Thunder Tones, That Our County's Past, the Antwerp Reservoir Must Go!," *Antwerp Argus*, October 14, 1886, 3.

99 State of Ohio, *Journal of the House of Representatives of the State of Ohio, for the Regular Session of the Sixty-Seventh General Assembly*, Volume LXXXII, 763.

100 "The People Aroused and Say in Thunder Tones, That Our County's Past, the Antwerp Reservoir Must Go!," *Antwerp Argus*, October 14, 1886, 3; "Round About—Antwerp," *Paulding County Gazette*, October 14, 1886, 5; "Our Home Corner," *Antwerp Argus*, October 28, 1886, 3.

101 "The People Aroused and Say in Thunder Tones, That Our County's Past, the Antwerp Reservoir Must Go!," *Antwerp Argus*, October 14, 1886, 3.

102 "Our Home Corner," *Antwerp Argus*, October 21, 1886, 3.

103 "The Canal Meeting," *Antwerp Argus*, October 28, 1886, 3.

104 *Map of Paulding County, Ohio*, 1878, https://pauldingcountyengineer.com/wp-content/uploads/2019/03/COUNTY-MAP.pdf.

105 *Map of Paulding County, Ohio*, 1878, https://pauldingcountyengineer.com/wp-content/uploads/2019/03/COUNTY-MAP.pdf.

106 "The Canal Meeting," *Antwerp Argus*, October 28, 1886, 3.

107 *Map of Paulding County, Ohio*, 1878, https://pauldingcountyengineer.com/wp-content/uploads/2019/03/COUNTY-MAP.pdf.

108 "The Canal Meeting," *Antwerp Argus*, October 28, 1886, 3.

109 "Local Brevities," *Paulding County Gazette*, November 4, 1886, 5; "Local Gossip," *Paulding Democrat*, November 18, 1886, 3.

110 "Reservoir Git!," *Antwerp Argus*, November 4, 1886, 3.

111 "Must Go!," *Antwerp Argus*, November 11, 1886, 3.

112 "Our Home Corner," *Antwerp Argus*, November 18, 1886, 3.

113 "Local Gossip," *Paulding Democrat*, November 11, 1886, 5.

114 "Must Go!," *Antwerp Argus*, November 11, 1886, 3.

115 "Our Home Corner," *Antwerp Argus*, November 18, 1886, 3.

# -4-

## Forbearance Ceased to Be a Virtue

### (November 1886 – February 1887)

On November 21, 1886, at 11 p.m., Six Mile Reservoir's feeder bulkhead and a nearby canal bank were dynamited.[1] The lock near Junction was also reportedly dynamited,[2] but it soon turned out it was the aqueduct east of the Paulding Furnace that had been destroyed.[3] The first volley in the Reservoir War had begun. Charles A. Flickinger, the President of the Board of Public Works, who was from Defiance, placed a $500 reward on behalf of the State of Ohio for information that would result in the "arrest and conviction of the perpetrators."[4] Canal Division Superintendent Homer Meacham made haste to repair the damaged infrastructure, and such repairs would be completed "in a short time."[5]

Though the individuals responsible for the attack were not really known, Mr. Meacham believed he had "sufficient knowledge of the perpetrators of the deed to lead to their arrest."[6] Otto E. Ehrhart would later state that George P. Hardy had been "delegated or hired by Eli M. Munson," and was one the men responsible for this first attack; Mr. Hardy was allegedly tasked with floating a "bucket filled with dynamite with a long fuse attached into the feeder from the reservoir side."[7]

The *Antwerp Argus* condemned the "depredation at the reservoir" and believed those responsible for the attack needed to be apprehended. [8] Condemnations came from not only Antwerp, but from residents of Cecil. [9] The *Antwerp Argus* reported that it had "at all times advocated legal proceedings in this matter of abandonment, and most strenuously opposed 'dynamite threats.'" [10] The *Antwerp Argus* called the attacks "wholly unwarranted, and contrary to our wishes of all law-abiding citizen." [11] The *Antwerp Argus* further worried that the attacks would do nothing else but "injure the prospects of those who intended to bring the question of abandonment properly before the legislature when it assembles in January." [12]

However, the *Antwerp Argus* was still instigating the matter, stating "we mean business and demand to be heard by the legislature in this matter." [13] In contrast, the *Paulding Democrat* stated, "It is supposed that the ardent desire to see broad wheat fields waving in the midst of this artificial lake had something to do with the blowing up of its banks." [14] Reminding its readers that "for two or three years this sentiment has been enlarging in proportions and petitions have been circulated and signed for its abolishment." [15]

The *Antwerp Argus* also scoffed at the need for such a bounty, believing it to be a form of "intimidation" against the people of Paulding County. [16] Locals were encouraged to continue signing the petitions to the Ohio Legislature, and the *Antwerp Argus* asserted that "if our prayer is refused, we must seek redress elsewhere." [17] The *Antwerp Argus* believed that Mr. Flickinger was only acting in the interest of Defiance and was not willing to give the people of Paulding County "satisfaction." [18] Further asserting that the reservoir was, among other things, a "pestilent breeding stink pond" that was no longer beneficial to the people of Antwerp and Paulding County.[19] Furthermore, the locals did not "feel disposed to suffer simply for the benefit of our neighbors in adjoining counties."[20]

The damage to the reservoir was reported as "considerable without attaining any success in emptying the reservoir."[21] Contradictorily, the damage was also reported to have been "light and seemed to not accomplish the desired effect."[22] Mr. Meacham was not wrong in his statement of a quick repair, as the *Paulding County Gazette* reported on November 25, 1886, just a few days after the attack, that Mr. Meacham and his team had successfully repaired the banks enough that only a little bit of water was still escaping from the reservoir. After which, George Hutchins, the lockkeeper for the aptly named Hutchins Lock,[23] was instructed by Mr. Meacham to "watch for further developments."[24]

Detectives were also rumored to be at work seeking those responsible.[25] A week after the attack, nobody had seemingly put forth any information about the $500 bounty.[26] What is likely a reference to the Haymarket Affair,§ still recent memory at this time, the *Antwerp Argus* asserted that the $500 bounty was a "big price to pay for dynamiters. 'Flick' can buy a dozen or more in Chicago for less than half that amount."[27]

Despite the strong condemnations from area papers, an attempt was made on Hutchins Lock on the night of November

---

§ The Haymarket Affair is one of those events in history that cannot be done any justice with a brief explanation in the footnotes of a book tangentially related to it. As such, I highly encourage readers to seek out information on Haymarket.

28, 1886 (morning of November 29, 1886). [28] This second attempt was more daring than the last, as Mr. Meacham's workers were still present on the state boat some thirty feet away from the lock when it happened.[29] The explosion also reportedly damaged George Hutchins' home near the lock and reservoir.[30]

The *Hicksville News* jokingly showed concern over the matter by stating that Paulding County would blow itself into Indiana by getting rid of Six Mile Reservoir the way some were trying.[31] The *Antwerp Argus* rebuked that statement, stating they would not blow themselves into Indiana but, blow the reservoir into Defiance County, as "they seem the only people who have any use for it."[32]

The *Antwerp Argus* also believed sentiments in Defiance were changing on the abandonment matter, and they had become "somewhat troubled about their timber supply."[33] The *Antwerp Argus* called this observation a "clear case of 'the tail wagging the kit,'" and even went so far as to suggest that Defiance industries would be better served by moving their factories to Paulding County and "have everything to your hand." [34] Reminding those in Defiance that the factories in Antwerp and Paulding County were "abundantly able to use all the timber in the county." [35] Moreover, if Defiance insisted on the canal's preservation, the *Antwerp Argus* believed that the people in Paulding County "should enjoy the same advantages of our neighbors, in which case there would be no difficulty in competing with them. The canal has ceased to be of use to us, so we say 'it must go.'"[36]

Mr. Flickinger traveled to Antwerp in the company of an unnamed member of the Board of Public Works and an unnamed detective.[37] His business in town was not entirely known, but it was obviously concerning finding the culprits and assessing damages to the canal infrastructure. The *Antwerp Argus* reported that "[Mr. Flickinger] seems to have an elephant on his hands, being afraid to say but little on the matter for fear of his political chances next year."[38]

This was what the *Antwerp Argus* reported as "the whole matter in a nutshell," believing that Mr. Flickinger could not openly support the abandonment of the canal works in Paulding County for fear "his neighbors of Defiance County would slaughter him when he comes out for the renomination again next fall."[39] The *Antwerp Argus* made the following statement before the 1887 legislative session began in January:

> The canal and reservoir has lost its usefulness in this county, but the city of Defiance wishes it for their own use, and we must suffer to please them, and [Mr. Flickinger] fears to act in the matter, for political reasons only. This being the case, our citizens should seek proper redress before the Legislature, and with a committee of investigation from that body who will make a fair and impartial report, its abandonment seems certain. Our member, John L. Geyer, has given us to understand that he will make this business his principal work during the coming session of the Legislature, and with the assistance of our citizens, we are certain to receive the favorable report asked for. Our citizens are determined in this matter and we feel assured that not a man in Antwerp favors, or has in any way been connected with the destruction of this State property by dynamite. All we ask is justice at the hands of those in authority, and that we propose to have if it takes all winter. This question is not a local affair, but one in which the whole county is interested in, and one they propose to make themselves heard in.[40]

On January 1, 1887, Representative John L. Geyer of Defiance and Paulding County left for Columbus to attend to his duties at the Ohio Legislature. [41] Representative Geyer informed the *Antwerp Argus* that he would "bring the question before that body at the earliest possible moment, and when the proper time comes it will be necessary for our citizens to act, and that promptly, in accordance with his instructions." [42] In the meantime, the *Antwerp Argus* implored its readers to be ready at a moment's notice for news of a meeting regarding the abandonment situation. [43] "No stone will be left unturned on [Representative Geyer's] part, and with proper assistance from our citizens this great nuisance and curse to our town can be legally abandoned."[44]

The *Defiance Democrat* asserted that the people in and around Paulding County should disapprove of the abandonment proposal, believing that abandoning the canal and reservoir would be "detrimental to many important business interests."[45] However, the *Antwerp Argus* declared that "the citizens of our county are a unit on the question of abandoning the canal and reservoir, and unless the Legislature listens to our appeal, through our honored member, J. L. Geyer, we must seek redress elsewhere."[46]

In his message to the Ohio General Assembly, Governor Joseph B. Foraker declared that:

> [The canals] are not to be abandoned or allowed to fall into decay and disuse. They constitute a valuable public property. The State should not dispose of any part of them. On the contrary, it should be made distinctly the policy of the State to improve, and uphold, and maintain them. When this becomes well understood the result will

be that business upon and along them will be revived; new boats will be built, and their great benefits will be made each year more apparent, and at no distant day they should and will become self-sustaining.[47]

Despite Governor Foraker making his position on abandoning any part of the canal system very clear, on January 5, 1887, Representative Geyer "presented the petition of William N. Snook and four hundred and sixty other citizens of Paulding county, praying for the vacation of the six mile reservoir and Wabash Canal."[48] On January 10, 1887, Representative Geyer did as he promised and introduced a bill (H. B. No. 755) to abandon the Wabash & Erie Canal (including Six Mile Reservoir) in Paulding County.[49] On January 18, 1887, Representative Geyer also presented a petition from "Frank A. Pio and 85 other citizens of Paulding county, asking for the abandonment of the six-mile reservoir and Wabash Canal in Paulding County."[50]

The *Toledo Bee* was quick to voice anger at the abandonment bill, calling it a ploy by 'land sharks' to acquire the land within Six Mile Reservoir through "all kind of schemes."[51] One scheme, according to the *Toledo Bee*, was "the most effectual scheme attempted, and really a successful one." The *Toledo Bee* noted that this scheme had been "put in operation a year ago when the Commissioners of Paulding County were induced to construct a large county ditch directly across Six Mile Creek. A stream of water that supplied the reservoir at all seasons of the year."[52]

The *Antwerp Argus* refuted this assertion, stating that the Paulding County Commissioners had never constructed such a ditch, and Indiana was the one to blame for cutting off Six Mile Creek.[53] However, that was not what the *Toledo Bee* was getting after. While the water supply had been cut off in Indiana, the *Toledo Bee* was pointing out the fact that the locals had previously tried to induce the Paulding County Commissioners to create a road and ditch that would have further redirected both Six Mile Creeks to the Maumee River at two October 1886 meetings.[54]

The *Paulding County Gazette* refuted the claims from those calling the abandonment a scheme by 'land sharks,' stating it was only a "blind to divert attention from the real cause lying at the bottom of their opposition." [55] The real reason for their opposition, according to the *Paulding County Gazette*, was that "abandonment would be 'detrimental to many important business interests.'"[56] These business interests, were, of course, the same that rafted timber on the canal out of Paulding County to their factories and mills. Which the *Paulding County Gazette* asserted took "thousands and thousands of dollars out of the county for which we get only a partial return" as all of the timber went to make "lumber, staves, hoops, headings, etc., etc.," outside of the county, rather than "enriching our people and building up home enterprises."[57]

Furthermore, the *Antwerp Argus* pointed out that the Defiance industries "enjoy the luxury of floating timber from this county on the canal, to the very doors of their factory, while we are compelled to haul the same for miles, generally over bad road and through mud and muck, simply because the canal through our village and adjacent to our factories has ceased to exist."[58]

According to the *Paulding County Gazette*, this was one reason the citizens of Paulding County wished to abandon the canal works.[59] However, they asserted the main one was "to reclaim the three thousand acres covered by the reservoir and about ten thousand acres that are kept in a damp and swampy condition by its proximity."[60] The *Paulding County Gazette* also believed that the reservoir was not a primary feeder for the Miami & Erie Canal, notably because they asserted it "furnished only a meager supply of water to feed the main line of the canal and is decreasing in usefulness yearly." [61] Further asserting that the reservoir was mostly dry much of the year, making it useless as a reservoir. [62] All that remained was "a small section of bad smelling, stagnant water, which our Defiance neighbors value so highly they would move heaven and earth to keep the stinkin' things right where it is."[63]

The *Paulding County Gazette* then made it clear that abandoning the canal works would not only be a "benefit to the people of this county."[64] The land that would be reclaimed for farm use would "more than over-balance the selfish interests of Defiance." [65] Declaring that it would be a "matter of simple justice to Paulding County that their petition... for the abandonment of the Six Mile Reservoir and the Wabash & Erie Canal... be granted."[66]

The *Antwerp Argus* also refuted that 'land sharks' had anything to do with the current wave of support for abandonment, calling that assertion "false in every particular."[67] The *Antwerp Argus* asserted that not much of the land "damaged and made worthless" by Six Mile Reservoir's presence was owned by non-locals, so it would not be the 'land sharks' that benefitted from the abandonment, but rather, citizens of Paulding County.[68]

The *Antwerp Argus* also refuted an assertion by the *Toledo Bee* that "half a hundred manufacturing institutions of Defiance pay a water rent to the State."[69] Their exact proof for refuting this was not given, but they argued that "even if true, what is it compared to the amount our county and State would receive in taxes" if the canal works were abandoned?[70] In fact, the *Antwerp Argus* claimed that the taxes for "lands adjoining" the canal and reservoir would "never be paid until [abandonment] is done."[71] Not because of any protest by the landowners, but because they would not make enough money from the crops on their land to pay their taxes.[72]

The *Antwerp Argus* made the logic of its position clear to its readers and those newspapers it had a weekly edition of an argument with. This reasoning partially echoes sentiments that date back to Dr. Solomon S. Stambaugh's original lawsuit in 1874 and the earliest petitions in 1877:

> Since the abandonment of that portion of the canal in Indiana, and the cutting off of the water supply by our neighbors, the reservoir has virtually ceased to be a feeder for the canal... No less than twenty-five thousand acres of land in this county is made perfectly worthless by it, in its present condition, which land would in a few years be under a perfect state of cultivation, and would return in taxes more than... the amount derived from the canal, in its present dilapidated condition.[73]

The *Antwerp Argus* also lamented that this cutting off of the canal in Indiana often left the canal through Antwerp with

> dead, stagnant water, which, during the summer months, sends forth a pestilent breeding stench, one sniff of which, by the members of our legislature would cause them to beat a hasty retreat and be convinced that

our prayers for redress were just and should be immediately answered.[74]

The *Toledo Blade* and the *Antwerp Argus* continued to blame Indiana for the troubles. Those papers believed that "if the Indiana division were still in existence, we would insist upon [the canal and reservoir's] maintenance."[75] However, this was not the case and had not been the case for about six years at this point. This observation led the *Toledo Blade* to state that, with "the abandonment of the Indiana portion by that state, the Ohio division becomes a... waterway leading nowhere, its usefulness being destroyed by the action of the State of Indiana."[76]

Such a dilapidated waterway reportedly did not bring in enough tolls annually, and what it did bring in was "utterly inadequate to keep the repairs of this canal spur, and the State keeps it in condition at a loss."[77] The *Toledo Blade* had this to say in an editorial:

> It is no wise essential or necessary to the Miami & Erie Canal. There is no traffic on it west of the lock at the western end of the reservoir; in fact, we are not certain that the western six miles of the canal are in a navigable condition... Now, as this is the case, and as the additional fact is developed that all the water needed for navigation is furnished by the great Mercer County Reservoir, there is certainly no good reason why this twenty-mile spur, leading nowhere, with an utterly insufficient traffic, should not be sold by the State and the money so accruing be used to put the Miami & Erie Canal... in first class condition... This would enable the State to sell the 2,900 acres of land now covered by water, embraced in the Six Mile Reservoir—and the finest corn land in Ohio—as well as the territory occupied by that channel of the canal itself... Let us lop off the dead branch that the tree may be more vigorous. Let us sell this useless bit of property, and sue the money so obtained in putting the important canal

line between [Toledo] and Cincinnati in first class condition.[78]

That last sentence was reportedly Representative Geyer's position on the matter, as the *Paulding Democrat* stated he wanted to maintain Ohio's canal system, but the best way to do so was to "chop off all short branches connecting unimportant places and offering no competition of freight rates."[79]

House Bill No. 755's (henceforth referred to as the Geyer Bill) only purpose was to "provide for the abandonment and sale of the Wabash & Erie Canal and Six-Mile Reservoir, in Paulding County, Ohio." Section one of the bill made clear that the bill would abandon, for "canal purposes," the Wabash & Erie Canal and Six Mile Reservoir.[80] The land was the obvious thing to be auctioned off. However, the locks and aqueducts, timber, stone, and other material used to build various pieces of canal infrastructure would be auctioned off unless the Board of Public Works "economically" removed them to another canal for use.[81] Section two discusses how the state would "determine the terms of payment" and appraise it by a panel of three individuals who would go to the area personally and appraise the land and facilities in conjunction with appropriate parties.[82]

These individuals could also divvy up the land into parcels they deemed "best suit the convenience of the purchasers... or... for the most money."[83] These three appointed individuals had to "be resident freeholders of the State, and neither officers of the State, or officers or stockholders in any railroad or transportations company, or in any way interested in the sale or purchase of the said property."[84] Section three through six handled the advertising, terms of the auction and sale, and the monetary situations surrounding the payment of the appraisers as well as stating that the profit from the auctioned land was to be sent to the State Treasury "to the credit of the general revenue fund."[85] Section seven reiterated that the bill took effect upon its passage, not at a pre-determined date in the future.[86]

Americus R. Geyer, the brother of Representative Geyer, went to Columbus to attend a Civil Engineers and Surveyors of the State of Ohio meeting on January 13, 1887.[87] Chairman D. W. Pampel recommended "the adoption of a resolution favoring the enactment of a law by the General Assembly abandoning the canals of the State."[88] Unsurprisingly this created quite the debate, and the recommendation was, in the end, dropped from consideration,[89] but not before A. R. Geyer spoke on Six Mile Reservoir and its abandonment question. A. R. Geyer stated that the reservoir in Paulding County was fed

> with water by two streams... and the land between these streams, embracing about ten thousand acres, is rendered worthless by the presence of the reservoir. Back water from the basin floods it during the rainy season and makes an immense swamp from July to December. During the hot months the reservoir goes dry, so that it is really of no account for the greater part of the year.[90]

Regarding repairing after dynamiting, Representative Geyer stated:

> To repair this damage it was estimated that the cost was more than the toll receipts there for the year. If the reservoir was discontinued, Mr. Geyer said, the streams would have a natural outlet, the swamp land be underdrained [sic] and made arable soil, and thus 13,000 acres be added to the wealth producing land in the State.[91]

A. R. Geyer then called on the group to endorse his brother John's bill in the Ohio Legislature, but the society declined, believing it to be "dabbling in political matters."[92] Nevertheless, an "audible smile went round at the story of the work of the dynamiters."[93]

Two weeks after the Geyer Bill was introduced, it had already been "referred to the Committee on Public Works" after its second reading.[94] That week, a meeting was scheduled for the evening of January 27, 1887, at the G. A. R. Hall in Antwerp to "take action on abandonment of canal and reservoir."[95] That action was related to news that a "Legislative Committee" was on its way to the area, due to arrive on January 29, 1887, at 1 p.m.[96] The purpose of the meeting was to create a set of committees for various duties in preparing for the arrival and assistance of those legislators.[97]

The committee to raise funds for any expense and be the welcoming party consisted of John H. Chester, Maroni P. Jacobs, and Parmenas F. Harris.[98] The committee tasked with providing transportation to the reservoir and around the area were John F. Barnett, Charles A. Bissell,¶ Jacob Saylor, and Nicholas O. Harrmann.[99] Francis B. DeWitt and Sheriff David W. Parr were also in attendance, presumably to oversee the meeting.[100] Those attending the meeting publicly praised the editor of the *Toledo Blade* and Abner L. Backus for their "unsolicited... interest they have taken in the welfare of the people of Paulding County."[101] Mr. Backus of Toledo was also invited to the area to meet with the citizens of Paulding County as well as the legislators' during

---

¶ Antwerp's mayor between January 1930 and January 1940.
(Dale L. Ehrhart, "Municipal History of Antwerp," in *A Century of Progress: Antwerp, Ohio*, 39.)

their visit.[102] Those attending the meeting, however, denounced the *Toledo Bee*, which was vehemently against the abandonment of the canal and reservoir.[103] Stating that Paulding County, as a whole, "had no further use for the *Toledo Bee* or any other paper that opposes the welfare of our people."[104]

Around midnight on January 28, 1887 (technically the 29th if it was after midnight), the legislative committee, consisting of fourteen legislators,¶ arrived in Paulding by train on the Cincinnati, Jackson, and Mackinaw Railroad (CJ&M). Among them was Representative Geyer.[105] A "committee" of Paulding citizens greeted them at the railroad station@ and "escorted them to the hotels."[106] The following morning, the legislators were escorted up the Paulding & Cecil Improved Road (U.S. 127 between Paulding and Cecil) and then up the canal's towpath to Six Mile Reservoir.[107] Those from Paulding who received the committee were Alonzo B. Holcombe, Oscar F. Kraner, George Hardesty, Dr. Hiram M. Ayers, Sheriff David W. Parr, Americus R. Geyer, Tom Young, Tom McBride, and Francis B. DeWitt.[108]

On the morning of January 29, 1887, roughly 200 citizens of Antwerp were reported to have traveled to Hutchins Lock at Six Mile Reservoir to welcome the legislative committee. In spite of the morning starting with wind and a possibly overcast winter sky, and the sun had only just appeared in time for the legislators to arrive. There are no details about what happened during much

---

¶ See Appendix D for lists of those who were part of these committees that visited Paulding County.

@ The CJ&M's depot in Paulding was located on the west side of Walnut Street between Jackson Street and Perry Street.
(*Sanborn Fire Insurance Map from Paulding, Paulding County, Ohio,* June 1895.)

of the day of inspection—only reiterating that the locals were quick to show the legislators all the reasons stated before why they wanted the canal and reservoir abandoned in the first place, particularly that it was no longer useful, "a disgrace to our country," and a giant waste of money for the State of Ohio to maintain.[109]

All of that said, the hospitality of the locals was not ignored in the local paper, as that was the most detailed part. After chauffeuring the committee around the area, the welcoming party brought them to the Smith Hotel in Antwerp, where the citizenry treated them with high regard. After indulging in a "bountiful repast," and taking brief comments from the local citizens, (it was of particular note that no long-winded speeches were heard; it seemed to have been discouraged to do so) Representative Leander C. Cole of Stark County thanked the locals for their hospitality and "assured [the locals'] grievances should receive a fair consideration from their hands." [110] The legislators then left for Columbus via an eastbound Wabash train to Cecil at 2:30 p.m. on January 30, 1887. In Cecil, they switched to a CJ&M train and headed south.[111]

On February 4, 1887, the following report showed up in the *Cincinnati Enquirer*, stating the legislative committee had taken a vote. The result was a six to two vote in favor of "indefinitely postponing action" on the Geyer Bill. [112] While this did not immediately dash the prospects of the bill passing, it was nevertheless not a good start. The only two that supported the bill were Representatives James M. Williams of Coshocton County and Leander C. Cole.[113]

The other six men's decision was either influenced by what they saw in Paulding County, or by a delegation of men from Defiance that arrived in Columbus on the afternoon of February 3, 1887. This delegation consisted of Charles A. Flickinger, Fred W. LeSuer, John Crowe, and other Defiance citizens representing business interests, notably the Defiance Machine Works.[114] It is worth mentioning that Mr. Flickinger had been involved with the Defiance Machine Works since at least 1884,[115] and had been elected as a director of that company in 1885 and 1886,[116] and would be again in 1888.[117] The *Paulding County Gazette* later asserted that, in the matter of abandonment, Mr. Flickinger held Defiance's manufacturing interests in higher regard than the interest of the State of Ohio, which they called a "drop in the bucket in comparison."[118]

Francis B. DeWitt, Antwerp Mayor William F. Fleck, John H. Chester, Lewis S. Gordon, and Phaon P. Doering also traveled to Columbus to show their support but were obviously unsuccessful in convincing the committee.[119] Other than the near-unanimous vote against the bill being a sign, the *Defiance County Express* reported that the delegation from Defiance returned the following evening on February 4, 1887, "in good spirits, feeling that their object had been accomplished."[120] The *Defiance Democrat* reported that the gentlemen's "efforts were successful."[121]

The *Antwerp Argus* asserted that such a decision by the committee would not have been possible had it not been for the "influence brought to bear by our neighbors at Defiance, who were before this committee in force, as was also the Miami Canal Association, who are large in numbers and rich in boodle."[122] The

*Antwerp Argus* believing this to be "another clear case of the 'kite wagging the tail.'"[123] Furthermore, the *Antwerp Argus* declared that the groups had done some "tall lying against our interests," but hope was not all lost, as the Geyer Bill still had friends in Columbus who would see it through, despite the seemingly insurmountable odds against its passing.[124]

The *Antwerp Argus* then went on a bit of a tirade, reminding its readers of the situation thus far. Notably, the Wabash & Erie Canal from the reservoir to the State Line had been practically useless since 1881, and the rest of the canal to Junction was rarely utilized outside of floating timber.[125] The *Antwerp Argus* also made it clear that the canal and reservoir were only filled with water for a "few months in the year."[126] In that time, if the water began to overflow the reservoir and canal banks after a large rainfall, the land adjacent to them was flooded to the point that "very often crops are destroyed or the land placed in such a condition that tilling them is out of the question."[127] Because this reportedly took place every year, the *Antwerp Argus* asserted that the canal infrastructure was "seriously retarding the development of our county, and has a depressing effect on the values of real estate."[128]

What the *Antwerp Argus* expected from the State of Ohio was "a fair and impartial investigation of this question" by a committee that would not be

> bulldozed by outside parties, who have no interest at stake in our county other than the use of this little spur to float timber... who, after they have skinned us of our timber, and grown rich from what they are pleased to term the 'swamps of Paulding County,' will soon lose all interest in this little canal branch and the six mile

frog pond, which during the heated term emits a stench to heaven, causing angels to weep."[129]

If this committee were to find that the canal was actually profitable to the State of Ohio, and was actually a feeder to the Miami & Erie Canal, the people of Antwerp, at least according to the *Antwerp Argus*, "will ever after hold our peace," as the canal could be considered useful.[130] However, if the canal and reservoir was deemed to be better off abandoned and sold because it would increase property values and therefore the taxes on that increased land value, then the *Antwerp Argus* asserted it needed to be abandoned, and the money realized from the sale could be used on other more profitable canals in Ohio.[131]

After declaring that the canal was no longer used for freight transportation, was not a feeder to the Miami & Erie Canal, and had become a useless nuisance to the citizens of Paulding County, the *Antwerp Argus* asserted that there was "no reason why the State should be burdened with it longer, and our citizens be compelled to suffer such an unmitigated pestilent-breeding nuisance. "[132]

It should come as no surprise that the citizens of Antwerp were particularly irate about the committee's decision. [133] Enough so that the citizens took to another, more peaceful manner of protest (at least compared to dynamiting things). The citizens of Antwerp boycotted anything from Defiance, particularly any salesman who came from Defiance to Antwerp to sell their goods.[134] Then they put into practice the resolution from a couple of weeks prior to refuse publications that they believed were smearing their cause, particularly the *Toledo Bee*.[135] The *Toledo Bee* wrote a snarky editorial in response to the boycott, sarcastically bemoaning the loss of their patronage in Antwerp.[136]

The *Defiance Democrat* stated that Antwerp should "not only boycott Defiance and the *Toledo Bee*, but the rest of the State," arguing that much of the state did not support Paulding County's efforts to abandon the public works. Especially the efforts of "a class who by dynamite seek to destroy a public institution that does not suit their fancy."[137] Mr. Flickinger believed the boycott was a pointless gesture, stating "'the boycott savors too much of arnica§ [*sic*] to be successful. Paulding people boycott Defiance except one thing, and that is the agricultural works. They can't get along without that.'"[138]

Senator Robert Mehaffey from Allen County reached out to Philip W. Hardesty of Worstville, Ohio, for more information on Representative Geyer's bill in the House. [139] Mr. Hardesty informed him that, while he had been "confined" to his home for the last few weeks, "quite a number of representative men [in Antwerp] could advise and direct in that behalf." [140] Mr. Hardesty nevertheless informed the Senator that his understanding of the Geyer Bill was that it was "intended to transfer the reservoir bed from the State to 'land-grabbing' capitalists."[141]

---

§ This comment seems to be the origin of his nickname 'Arnica Flick.' Whether this was him mispronouncing anarchy, or a misprint by the newspaper, is open to debate. A later speech from Mr. Flickinger has the same misspelling. Oddly enough, this bungling of the word anarchy with arnica is the butt of a joke published by the *Detroit Free Press* in 1876.
("The Man Who Will Make a Speech," *Paulding Democrat*, December 14, 1876, 1.)

Mr. Hardesty believed that the land "ought to be sold in forty acre lots to actual settlers," believing that "they who have so long suffered from the nuisance should have the benefits of its abandonment."[142] Mr. Hardesty also believed that the otherwise "useless" land would make for "good" farmland that would "add one fourth to the business interests of the town and surrounding country; that the amount for which the land would sell is insufficient compared with the general benefits the county and State would receive; that in the near future it would add ten percent to the tax duplicate of the county."[143] The only issue now was whether the bill would even make it to the Ohio Senate for consideration by Senator Mehaffey.

On February 16, 1887, the Ohio Legislature moved to vote on the Geyer Bill. Unfortunately, a second blow to the bill occurred when the result was tallied forty-six yeas, forty-three nays. Despite having a simple majority, the bill was defeated due to needing fifty-six votes in support.[144] Representative Geyer then secured a reconsideration, and the bill went up for a vote again on February 16, 1887.[145] The second time went better than the first time; the bill received fifty-three votes in favor but still fell short of the necessary fifty-six votes.[146]

That should have been the end of it. However, Representative Geyer, against all odds, was successful in getting yet another reconsideration of the bill. According to *The Cincinnati Enquirer*, the Geyer Bill was "twice defeated and the vote has been twice reconsidered." The bill was shaping up to be "one of the most memorable in the history of the House."[147] The Geyer Bill would not die and had secured a third chance to pass.[148]

The *Cincinnati Enquirer* seemed to assert there was a near-unanimous agreement in the chamber that "the portion of the canal the bill proposes to abolish is of no advantage to the state, of no advantage to Paulding County, and no advantage to commerce." The chamber also agreed that "the only advantage it is to anyone at present is to a few men who raft logs down to Defiance, and it was demonstrated that they paid little or no tolls for this privilege." [149] That last bit is an important note, as somewhere in the vicinity of $50 to $150 in tolls on an annual basis were generated in the previous five years. [150] An issue with that was $144 of the tolls went to pay the one employee on the canal. [151] The bigger problem was the *Toledo Bee* asserted that timber amounting to $3000 in tolls was ready to float down the canal to market, which could reportedly maintain the canal for years. [152]

In the observation of the *Paulding Democrat*, the catch was that, compared to previous years, there could not be enough timber to make up the roughly $2,850 difference in expected tolls. If the timbermen were moving that much timber, what seemed like an average amount, why were the tolls not higher in previous years? In the opinion of not only the *Toledo Blade* (and *Antwerp Argus* by proxy of running the article), Representative Geyer, and apparently the House, the timber interests were not paying much if any tolls to raft their timber in the canal. [153]

Representatives Geyer, Cole, Williams, Boston G. Young of Marion County, and David I. Worthington of Fayette County, among others, were also able to prove that the locals considered the canal works, among other things, a nuisance, a "menace," was "stagnant and pestilent breeding," that no canal boat had traveled on it in the last five years, that it was "an Elysium for tadpoles, wigglers, and small frogs in summer and a skating rink for small boys in winter," and "almost to a man [Paulding County citizens] favored its abandonment."[154] These men made it known to the House that the locals had become "so disgusted" that they resorted to blowing up some of the works back in November 1886, and presumably showing the chamber the signed petitions.[155]

Despite all the rhetoric thus far surrounding the canal and reservoir being an unhealthy, pestilent breeding nightmare, the *Antwerp Argus* refuted any claims that Antwerp was "unhealthy, owing to the near proximity of this pestilent breeding cesspool, known as Six Mile Reservoir, to our village."[156] The *Antwerp Argus* claimed that "our town is not unhealthy, as but very few cases of fever and ague have been reported in this vicinity for years."[157] This statement seemingly disregards a significant part of the ongoing rhetoric it and other local papers had built up. Whether this was meant as a joke is debatable, as the same article implies all of Paulding County's "filth" flows down to Defiance.[158]

The Geyer Bill's only significant opposition came from Representatives Daniel J. Ryan of Scioto County (Speaker *pro tem*[159]) and Thomas Armor of Holmes County, who echoed the Governor's speech that all the canals needed to be maintained no matter the sentiment against them, believing that abandoning any part of the system put the future of the rest of it in jeopardy of also being abandoned.[160] The two men also believed the land acquired from the United States Federal Government was only supposed to be used for "canal purposes forever."[161]

They also believed the local outcry was not grass-roots in origin, believing it to be an astroturfing campaign from "land speculators" who would "step in with old United States land warrants and claim the ground" upon its sale. Almost specifically calling out Dr. Solomon S. Stambaugh's efforts a decade prior.[162] While Mr. Ryan, among others, conceded that the canal and reservoir "were no longer of practical use," they still asserted that Six Mile Reservoir was a feeder to the Miami & Erie Canal, "had been for twenty years," and was vitally necessary to maintain.[163] The *Antwerp Argus* maintained that the Mercer County Reservoir sufficiently fed the Miami & Erie Canal to Defiance despite what the legislators said.[164]

Despite the opposition's efforts and "strong influence brought to bear by timber sharks and others wholly unconversant,"[165] the vote to reconsider the Geyer Bill a third time passed on February 17, 1887, with a vote of sixty-five in favor and twenty-eight opposed.[166] The Geyer Bill was then voted upon on the same day, and passed on the third vote in the House with exactly fifty-six votes in favor to forty-one opposed.[167]¶ However, the fight was not over; the Geyer Bill was off to the Ohio Senate, where the *Defiance Democrat* predicted that it would still face stiff opposition.[168]

The opposition was so stiff that the Geyer Bill, upon its first reading in the Senate on February 17, 1887, was immediately met with a motion for "indefinite postponement" by Senator A. Curtis Cable from Miami County. However, that motion was tabled after a motion by Senator Madison Pavey from Fayette

---

¶ See Appendix E for a complete list of how the representatives voted.

County.[169] On February 18, 1887, the Geyer Bill was supposed to be read a second time; however, in attempting to have it reconsidered and sent to the committee, a problem emerged that Senator Mehaffey identified and called a point of order to argue. As it turned out, the second reading of the Geyer Bill was not on the calendar of bills that needed a second reading, in his mind, as it should have been. He reasoned that "the motion by Senator Pavey last evening to table Mr. Cable's motion to indefinitely postpone said bill, did not carry the bill to the table."[170]

After some deliberation, it was agreed that Senator Mehaffey's point of order had merit, and a quote from Cushing's Manual was read to justify the decision to accept it.[171] The *Defiance Democrat* lambasted this decision, asserting no such rule even existed in Cushing's Manual.[172] Nevertheless, the opposition conceded the point under their belief that the bill could not pass anyway, and allowed the bill to be read a second time. On the motion of Senator Cable, the Geyer Bill was referred to the Senate Committee on Public Works.[173]

After some brief jubilation for the Geyer Bill's passage in the House, where citizens of Antwerp fired "anvils, guns, etc." and hung decorative flags throughout the village, the citizens of Antwerp were roused to prepare for a Senate committee's arrival.[174] The *Antwerp Argus* told its readers to attend the upcoming meeting at the G. A. R. Hall to "make arrangements to receive and properly entertain this committee," and to make sure that "no stone is left unturned in convincing this committee of the advantages the removal of this nuisance from our midst will be to our county, our citizens, and the State at large."[175]

They had to prepare on short notice to show the committee their cause ahead of the Ohio Senate's expected vote the following Wednesday.[176] In that short time, the *Antwerp Argus* warned its readers,

> our enemies are at work, and by the use of money and an unbounded amount of lieing [*sic*], are endeavoring to counteract our movements, but they are watched, and by a unit4ed effort on our part, right and justice will most assuredly prevail. Should we fail at this time we can rest assured that little will be done in our behalf on the question for years to come; therefore, let us work with a will and strike while the iron is hot, and show that we are determined and united in this matter.[177]

Unfortunately for the locals trying to keep the momentum of their movement going, the Ohio Senate committee in question was reportedly made up of "friends of the canals."[178] Worse still, twenty-one of thirty-three senators were against the Geyer Bill, of which seven of those opposed to the Geyer Bill made up the entire Senate Committee on Public Works, which did not bode well for its success.[179] Nevertheless, the Ohio Senate committee was expected to first arrive in Defiance on the evening of February 24, 1887, then travel to tour the canal works that same evening.[180]

In preparation for the senator's tour of Paulding County, prominent citizens of Defiance also came together to "consult as to the best steps to be taken against the proposed bill."[181] Those who met at the Defiance Machine Works@ were "unanimous in antagonizing the bill, realizing that its passage would be a great detriment to our manufacturing interests and consequently to our business interests in general."[182] On February 21, 1887, the following men left for Columbus to stand before the Senate committee and inform them of the "disastrous result of the passage of the Geyer Bill to [Defiance.]"[183] Fred W. LeSuer, F. W. Knapp, John Crowe, Charles A. Flickinger, Rudy Ehrhart, and Stephen F. Eagle.[184] Edwin F. Metz and Kidder V. Haymaker would join them on February 23, 1887.[185]

The *Antwerp Argus* chastised the Defiance men's actions, asserting that they had "chartered a palace car" to bring the senators to the area, and from their "free use of money and hospitality hope to capture them in their behalf;" later noting that the senators would reportedly be "banqueted" at the Crosby Hotel.[186] This observation was not without cause, as the *Antwerp Argus* reported, that $1,500 had been "subscribed by the manufacturing interests of Defiance for this purpose."[187] The *Defiance County Express* reported on February 24, 1887, that Mr. Flickinger was "wielding all his influence on behalf of our canal interests, and is doing unceasing work for his city."[188] Fred W. LeSuer, also a staunch opponent of the Geyer Bill, had reportedly

---

@ The Defiance Machine Works, at the time of the Reservoir War, was located on the northwest corner of Perry Street and 4th Street in Defiance.
(*Sanborn Fire Insurance Map from Defiance, Defiance County, Ohio*, August 1888.)

done "effective work at the capitol with a lavish use of time and money on behalf of our cause."[189]

The *Paulding Democrat* chirped that the state's capital should be moved to Defiance because their prominent citizens frequently traveled to Columbus to "manage the law-making bodies."[190] Never mind that prominent Paulding County citizens such as Phaon P. Doering, William F. Fleck, Wilson H. Snook, Lewis S. Gordon (and his wife Margaret), John H. Chester, and Francis B. DeWitt frequently traveled to Columbus as well for much of the same purpose, to look after the interests of the reservoir bill.[191]

While much of this was going on, Paulding County experienced enough heavy rainfall that the Maumee River had reached such a level that a bridge north of Antwerp was swept away, and the water was considered "raging."[192] Worse still, at least two breaks opened on the canal below Hutchins Lock.[193] This, along with the "back-waters from the reservoir," reportedly resulted in "a great portion of Paulding County" being inundated with water.[194] As much as 200 acres, "a large amount of which is seeded to wheat," was flooded two miles west of Junction after one of the two breaks occurred there.[195]

## Chapter 4 Notes

1 "A Peculiar Blow-Up," *Cincinnati Enquirer*, November 23, 1886, 5; "War on the Reservoir," *Cincinnati Enquirer*, November 23, 1886, 2; "Reservoir Dynamiters," *Defiance Democrat*, November 25, 1886, 3; "Round About—Antwerp," *Paulding County Gazette*, November 25, 1886, 5; "Kerbomb!," *Paulding Democrat*, November 25, 1886, 1; "War on the Big Paulding Reservoir," *Fort Wayne Sentinel*, November 23, 1886, 1; "Hell Gate," *Antwerp Argus*, November 25, 1886, 3; "The Reservoir," *Antwerp Argus*, November 25, 1886, 3.

2 "Local Brevities," *Paulding County Gazette*, November 25, 1886, 1.

3 "A Peculiar Blow-Up," *Cincinnati Enquirer*, November 23, 1886, 5; "Kerbomb!," *Paulding Democrat*, November 25, 1886, 1; "Local Gossip," *Paulding Democrat*, December 2, 1886, 5; "The Reservoir," *Antwerp Argus*, November 25, 1886, 3.

4 "Round About—Antwerp," *Paulding County Gazette*, November 25, 1886, 5; "War on the Reservoir," *Cincinnati Enquirer*, November 23, 1886, 2; "That Reward," *Antwerp Argus*, November 25, 1886, 3; "The Reservoir," *Antwerp Argus*, November 25, 1886, 3.

5 "War on the Reservoir," *Cincinnati Enquirer*, November 23, 1886, 2; "Reservoir Dynamiters," *Defiance Democrat*, November 25, 1886, 3; "Round About—Antwerp," *Paulding County Gazette*, November 25, 1886, 5; "War on the Big Paulding Reservoir," *Fort Wayne Sentinel*, November 23, 1886, 1.

6 "Kerbomb!," *Paulding Democrat*, November 25, 1886, 1.

7 Otto E. Ehrhart, "Wabash-Erie Canal," in *A Century of Progress: Antwerp, Ohio*, 18.

8 "That Reward," *Antwerp Argus*, November 25, 1886, 3.

9 "Slashers from Cecil," *Antwerp Argus*, December 2, 1886, 2.

10 "That Reward," *Antwerp Argus*, November 25, 1886, 3.

11 "The Reservoir," *Antwerp Argus*, November 25, 1886, 3.

12 "The Reservoir," *Antwerp Argus*, November 25, 1886, 3.

13 "That Reward," *Antwerp Argus*, November 25, 1886, 3.

14 "Kerbomb!," *Paulding Democrat*, November 25, 1886, 1.

15 "Kerbomb!," *Paulding Democrat*, November 25, 1886, 1.

16 "That Reward," *Antwerp Argus*, November 25, 1886, 3.

17 "Sign the Petition," *Antwerp Argus*, December 2, 1886, 3.

18 "That Reward," *Antwerp Argus*, November 25, 1886, 3.

19 "That Reward," *Antwerp Argus*, November 25, 1886, 3.

20 "That Reward," *Antwerp Argus*, November 25, 1886, 3.

21 "Round About—Antwerp," *Paulding County Gazette*, November 25, 1886, 5.

22 "Hell Gate," *Antwerp Argus*, November 25, 1886, 3.

23 State of Ohio, *Executive Documents: Annual Reports for 1887, Made to the Sixty-Eighth General Assembly*, Part I, 1240.

24 "Round About—Antwerp," *Paulding County Gazette*, November 25, 1886, 5.

25 "Round About—Antwerp," *Paulding County Gazette*, November 25, 1886, 5.

26 "Round About—Antwerp," *Paulding County Gazette*, December 2, 1886, 1.

27 "Our Home Corner," *Antwerp Argus*, December 2, 1886, 3.

28 "Another Blowout," *Antwerp Argus*, December 2, 1886, 3; *Defiance Democrat*, December 2, 1886, 3.

29 "Another Blowout," *Antwerp Argus*, December 2, 1886, 3.

30 "Additional Locals," *Antwerp Argus*, December 9, 1886, 2.

31 "Our Home Corner," *Antwerp Argus*, December 9, 1886, 3.

32 "Our Home Corner," *Antwerp Argus*, December 9, 1886, 3.

33 "Additional Locals," *Antwerp Argus*, December 9, 1886, 2.

34 "Additional Locals," *Antwerp Argus*, December 9, 1886, 2.

35 "What Our Neighbors Have to Say—Defiance Democrat," *Antwerp Argus*, February 24, 1887, 2.

36 "What Our Neighbors Have to Say—Defiance Democrat," *Antwerp Argus*, February 24, 1887, 2.

37 "Canal and Reservoir," *Antwerp Argus*, December 16, 1886, 3; "Personal Mention," *Antwerp Argus*, December 16, 1886, 3; "Local Gossip," *Paulding Democrat*, December 23, 1886, 9.

38 "Personal Mention," *Antwerp Argus*, December 16, 1886, 3.

39 "Canal and Reservoir," *Antwerp Argus*, December 16, 1886, 3.

40 "Canal and Reservoir," *Antwerp Argus*, December 16, 1886, 3.

41 *Paulding Democrat*, January 6, 1887, 5.

42 "Canal and Reservoir," *Antwerp Argus*, January 6, 1887, 3.

43 "Canal and Reservoir," *Antwerp Argus*, January 6, 1887, 3.

44 "Canal and Reservoir," *Antwerp Argus*, January 6, 1887, 3.

45 *Defiance Democrat*, January 13, 1887, 2.

46 *Antwerp Argus*, January 20, 1887, 2.

47 "State of Ohio: Governor Foraker's Message to the General Assembly," *Paulding County Gazette*, January 13, 1887, 6.

48 State of Ohio, *Journal of the House of Representatives of the State of Ohio, for the Adjourned Session of the Sixty-Seventh General Assembly*, Volume LXXXIII, 17.

49 State of Ohio, *Journal of the House of Representatives of the State of Ohio, for the Adjourned Session of the Sixty-Seventh General Assembly*, Volume LXXXIII, 30.

50 State of Ohio, *Journal of the House of Representatives of the State of Ohio, for the Adjourned Session of the Sixty-Seventh General Assembly*, Volume LXXXIII, 80.

51 "The Canal and Reservoir," *Antwerp Argus*, January 20, 1887, 2.

52 "The Canal and Reservoir," *Antwerp Argus*, January 20, 1887, 2.

53 "The Canal and Reservoir," *Antwerp Argus*, January 20, 1887, 2; *Paulding County Gazette*, January 20, 1887, 4.

54 "The Canal and Reservoir," *Antwerp Argus*, January 20, 1887, 2

55 *Paulding County Gazette*, January 20, 1887, 4.

56 *Paulding County Gazette*, January 20, 1887, 4; *Defiance Democrat*, January 13, 1887, 2.
57 *Paulding County Gazette*, January 20, 1887, 4.
58 *Antwerp Argus*, January 20, 1887, 2.
59 *Paulding County Gazette*, January 20, 1887, 4.
60 *Paulding County Gazette*, January 20, 1887, 4.
61 *Paulding County Gazette*, January 20, 1887, 4.
62 *Paulding County Gazette*, January 20, 1887, 4.
63 *Paulding County Gazette*, January 20, 1887, 4.
64 *Paulding County Gazette*, January 20, 1887, 4.
65 *Paulding County Gazette*, January 20, 1887, 4.
66 *Paulding County Gazette*, January 20, 1887, 4.
67 "The Canal and Reservoir," *Antwerp Argus*, January 20, 1887, 2; *Antwerp Argus*, January 20, 1887, 2.
68 "The Canal and Reservoir," *Antwerp Argus*, January 20, 1887, 2; *Antwerp Argus*, January 20, 1887, 2.
69 *Antwerp Argus*, January 20, 1887, 2.
70 *Antwerp Argus*, January 20, 1887, 2.
71 *Antwerp Argus*, January 20, 1887, 2.
72 *Antwerp Argus*, January 20, 1887, 2.
73 "The Canal and Reservoir," *Antwerp Argus*, January 20, 1887, 2.
74 "The Canal and Reservoir," *Antwerp Argus*, January 20, 1887, 2.
75 "The Wabash Division," *Antwerp Argus*, February 10, 1887, 2.
76 "The Wabash Division," *Antwerp Argus*, February 10, 1887, 2.
77 "The Wabash Division," *Antwerp Argus*, February 10, 1887, 2.
78 "The Wabash Division," *Antwerp Argus*, February 10, 1887, 2.
79 "Canal and Reservoir," *Paulding Democrat*, January 20, 1887, 4.
80 "House Bill No. 755," *Paulding County Gazette*, January 27, 1887, 1; "The Reservoir Bill," *Paulding Democrat*, January 27, 1887, 4.
81 "House Bill No. 755," *Paulding County Gazette*, January 27, 1887, 1; "The Reservoir Bill," *Paulding Democrat*, January 27, 1887, 4.
82 "House Bill No. 755," *Paulding County Gazette*, January 27, 1887, 1; "The Reservoir Bill," *Paulding Democrat*, January 27, 1887, 4.
83 "House Bill No. 755," *Paulding County Gazette*, January 27, 1887, 1; "The Reservoir Bill," *Paulding Democrat*, January 27, 1887, 4.
84 "House Bill No. 755," *Paulding County Gazette*, January 27, 1887, 1; "The Reservoir Bill," *Paulding Democrat*, January 27, 1887, 4.
85 "House Bill No. 755," *Paulding County Gazette*, January 27, 1887, 1; "The Reservoir Bill," *Paulding Democrat*, January 27, 1887, 4.
86 "House Bill No. 755," *Paulding County Gazette*, January 27, 1887, 1; "The Reservoir Bill," *Paulding Democrat*, January 27, 1887, 4.
87 *Paulding Democrat*, January 20, 1887, 8.
88 *Paulding Democrat*, January 20, 1887, 8.
89 *Paulding Democrat*, January 20, 1887, 8.
90 *Paulding Democrat*, January 20, 1887, 8.
91 *Paulding Democrat*, January 20, 1887, 8.
92 *Paulding Democrat*, January 20, 1887, 8.
93 *Paulding Democrat*, January 20, 1887, 8.

94 "Our Columbus Letter," *Paulding Democrat*, January 27, 1887, 4.

95 "Canal Meeting," *Antwerp Argus*, January 27, 1887, 3.

96 "Reception," *Antwerp Argus*, February 3, 1887, 3.

97 "Reception," *Antwerp Argus*, February 3, 1887, 3.

98 "Reception," *Antwerp Argus*, February 3, 1887, 3.

99 "Reception," *Antwerp Argus*, February 3, 1887, 3.

100 "Reception," *Antwerp Argus*, February 3, 1887, 3.

101 "Reception," *Antwerp Argus*, February 3, 1887, 3.

102 "Reception," *Antwerp Argus*, February 3, 1887, 3.

103 "Reception," *Antwerp Argus*, February 3, 1887, 3.

104 "Reception," *Antwerp Argus*, February 3, 1887, 3.

105 "The Reservoir Inspected, *Paulding Democrat*, February 3, 1887, 4.

106 "The Reservoir Inspected, *Paulding Democrat*, February 3, 1887, 4.

107 "The Reservoir Inspected, *Paulding Democrat*, February 3, 1887, 4.

108 "The Reservoir Inspected, *Paulding Democrat*, February 3, 1887, 4; "Reception," *Antwerp Argus*, February 3, 1887, 3.

109 "Reception," *Antwerp Argus*, February 3, 1887, 3; "From Kentner's Corner," *Antwerp Argus*, February 3, 1887, 3; "The Reservoir Inspected, *Paulding Democrat*, February 3, 1887, 4.

110 "Reception," *Antwerp Argus*, February 3, 1887, 3; "The Reservoir Inspected, *Paulding Democrat*, February 3, 1887, 4.

111 "The Reservoir Inspected, *Paulding Democrat*, February 3, 1887, 4; "Round About—Antwerp," *Paulding County Gazette*, February 3, 1887, 5.

112 "The Canal in Paulding County," *Cincinnati Enquirer*, February 4, 1887, 4; "Personal," *Defiance Democrat*, February 10, 1887, 3. "An Adverse Report," *Antwerp Argus*, February 10, 1887, 2.

113 "Local and Personal," *Defiance County Express*, February 10, 1887, 10.

114 "Personal," *Defiance Democrat*, February 10, 1887, 3; "Local and Personal," *Defiance County Express*, February 10, 1887, 10; "Local Gossip," *Paulding Democrat*, February 10, 1887, 5; "Our Home Corner," *Antwerp Argus*, February 10, 1887, 3.

115 "Business Mens' Meeting," *Defiance County Express*, March 27, 1884, 16.

116 "Officers Elect," *Defiance County Express*, January 8, 1885, 6; "Defiance Machine Works," *Defiance County Express*, January 21, 1886, 1.

117 *Defiance Democrat*, January 5, 1888, 3.

118 "Local Brevities," *Paulding County Gazette*, February 17, 1887, 8.

119 "Our Home Corner," *Antwerp Argus*, February 10, 1887, 3; "Local Gossip," *Paulding Democrat*, February 10, 1887, 5.

120 "Local and Personal," *Defiance County Express*, February 10, 1887, 10.

121 "Personal," *Defiance Democrat*, February 10, 1887, 3.

122 "An Adverse Report," *Antwerp Argus*, February 10, 1887, 2.

123 "Our Home Corner," *Antwerp Argus*, February 10, 1887, 3

124 "An Adverse Report," *Antwerp Argus*, February 10, 1887, 2.

125 "An Adverse Report," *Antwerp Argus*, February 10, 1887, 2.

126 "An Adverse Report," *Antwerp Argus*, February 10, 1887, 2.

127 "An Adverse Report," *Antwerp Argus*, February 10, 1887, 2.

128 "An Adverse Report," *Antwerp Argus*, February 10, 1887, 2.

129 "An Adverse Report," *Antwerp Argus*, February 10, 1887, 2.

130 "An Adverse Report," *Antwerp Argus*, February 10, 1887, 2.

131 "An Adverse Report," *Antwerp Argus*, February 10, 1887, 2.

132 "An Adverse Report," *Antwerp Argus*, February 10, 1887, 2.

133 *Defiance Democrat*, February 10, 1887, 2; "Our Home Corner," *Antwerp Argus*, February 10, 1887, 3.

134 "Local and Personal," *Defiance County Express*, February 10, 1887, 10; "Local Gossip," *Paulding Democrat*, February 10, 1887, 5; "Sent Back," *Antwerp Argus*, February 10, 1887, 3; "Our Home Corner," *Antwerp Argus*, February 10, 1887, 3; "What 'Our Neighbors' Have to Say—Defiance Call," *Antwerp Argus*, February 17, 1887, 3; "Round About—Antwerp," *Paulding County Gazette*, March 3, 1887, 5.

135 "Sent Back," *Antwerp Argus*, February 10, 1887, 3; "Round About—Antwerp," *Paulding County Gazette*, February 10, 1887, 5; "What 'Our Neighbors' Have to Say—Paulding Democrat," *Antwerp Argus*, February 17, 1887, 3.

136 "Sat Down On By Antwerp," *Defiance Democrat*, February 10, 1887, 2.

137 "Boycotted by Antwerp," *Defiance Democrat*, February 10, 1887, 3.

138 "May be in Error," *Antwerp Argus*, March 24, 1887, 3.

139 "The Canal Question," *Antwerp Argus*, February 17, 1887, 2.

140 "The Canal Question," *Antwerp Argus*, February 17, 1887, 2.

141 "The Canal Question," *Antwerp Argus*, February 17, 1887, 2.

142 "The Canal Question," *Antwerp Argus*, February 17, 1887, 2.

143 "The Canal Question," *Antwerp Argus*, February 17, 1887, 2.

144 "*Defiance Democrat*, February 17, 1887, 2; "Round About—Antwerp," *Paulding County Gazette*, February 17, 1887, 5; "Ohio Legislature," *Paulding Democrat*, February 24, 1887, 3; "The Reservoir Bill," *Paulding County Gazette*, February 24, 1887, 4; "The First Blow," *Cincinnati Enquirer*, February 18, 1887, 5.

145 "*Defiance Democrat*, February 17, 1887, 2; "Round About—Antwerp," *Paulding County Gazette*, February 17, 1887, 5; "Ohio Legislature," *Cincinnati Commercial Gazette*, February 11, 1887, 6.

146 "The First Blow," *Cincinnati Enquirer*, February 18, 1887, 5; State of Ohio, *Journal of the House of Representatives of the State of Ohio, for the Adjourned Session of the Sixty-Seventh General Assembly*, Volume LXXXIII, 319.

147 "The First Blow," *Cincinnati Enquirer*, February 18, 1887, 5.

148 "Ohio Legislature," *Paulding Democrat*, February 24, 1887, 3; "The First Blow," *Cincinnati Enquirer*, February 18, 1887, 5.

149 "The First Blow," *Cincinnati Enquirer*, February 18, 1887, 5.

150 "Canal and Reservoir," *Paulding Democrat*, January 20, 1887, 4; *Paulding Democrat*, February 17, 1887, 4.

151 "Canal and Reservoir," *Paulding Democrat*, January 20, 1887, 4.

152 *Paulding Democrat*, February 17, 1887, 4.

153 *Paulding Democrat*, February 17, 1887, 4; "Passed," *Paulding Democrat*, February 24, 1887, 4.

154 "The First Blow," *Cincinnati Enquirer*, February 18, 1887, 5; "Passed," *Paulding Democrat*, February 24, 1887, 4.

155 "The First Blow," *Cincinnati Enquirer*, February 18, 1887, 5; "Passed," *Paulding Democrat*, February 24, 1887, 4.

156 "We Object," *Antwerp Argus*, February 10, 1887, 3.

157 "We Object," *Antwerp Argus*, February 10, 1887, 3.

158 "We Object," *Antwerp Argus*, February 10, 1887, 3.

159 Joseph P. Smith, *History of the Republican Party in Ohio*, Volume I, 513.

160 "The First Blow," *Cincinnati Enquirer*, February 18, 1887, 5; "Passed," *Paulding Democrat*, February 24, 1887, 4.

161 "The First Blow," *Cincinnati Enquirer*, February 18, 1887, 5; "Passed," *Paulding Democrat*, February 24, 1887, 4.

162 "The First Blow," *Cincinnati Enquirer*, February 18, 1887, 5; "Passed," *Paulding Democrat*, February 24, 1887, 4.

163 "The First Blow," *Cincinnati Enquirer*, February 18, 1887, 5; "Passed," *Paulding Democrat*, February 24, 1887, 4.

164 "The Wabash Division," *Antwerp Argus*, February 10, 1887, 2.

165 "The World 'Do Move,' *Antwerp Argus*, February 24, 1887, 2.

166 "Ohio Legislature," *Paulding Democrat*, February 24, 1887, 3.

167 "The World 'Do Move,' *Antwerp Argus*, February 24, 1887, 2; *Defiance Democrat*, February 24, 1887, 2; "The Reservoir Bill," *Paulding County Gazette*, February 24, 1887, 4; "The First Blow," *Cincinnati Enquirer*, February 18, 1887, 5; "Ohio Legislature," *Paulding Democrat*, February 24, 1887, 3; State of Ohio, *Journal of the House of Representatives of the State of Ohio, for the Adjourned Session of the Sixty-Seventh General Assembly*, Volume LXXXIII, 328.

168 *Defiance Democrat*, February 24, 1887, 2.

169 "Ohio Legislature," *Paulding Democrat*, February 24, 1887, 3; State of Ohio, *Journal of the Senate of the State of Ohio, for the Adjourned Session of the Sixty-Seventh General Assembly*, Volume LXXXIII, 274.

170 "The Reservoir Bill," *Paulding County Gazette*, February 24, 1887, 4; State of Ohio, *Journal of the Senate of the State of Ohio, for the Adjourned Session of the Sixty-Seventh General Assembly*, Volume LXXXIII, 276.

171 "The Reservoir Bill," *Paulding County Gazette*, February 24, 1887, 4; State of Ohio, *Journal of the Senate of the State of Ohio, for the Adjourned Session of the Sixty-Seventh General Assembly*, Volume LXXXIII, 276.

172 *Defiance Democrat*, February 24, 1887, 2.

173 "The Reservoir Bill," *Paulding County Gazette*, February 24, 1887, 4; "Ohio Legislature," *Paulding Democrat*, February 24, 1887, 3; State of Ohio, *Journal of the Senate of the State of Ohio, for the Adjourned Session of the Sixty-Seventh General Assembly*, Volume LXXXIII, 276.

174 "Round About—Antwerp," *Paulding County Gazette*, February 24, 1887, 5; "Our Home Corner," *Antwerp Argus*, February 24, 1887, 3; The World 'Do Move,' *Antwerp Argus*, February 24, 1887, 2.

175 The World 'Do Move,' *Antwerp Argus*, February 24, 1887, 2.

176 The World 'Do Move,' *Antwerp Argus*, February 24, 1887, 2.

177 The World 'Do Move,' *Antwerp Argus*, February 24, 1887, 2.

178 *Defiance Democrat*, February 24, 1887, 2.

179 "The Reservoir Bill," *Paulding County Gazette*, February 24, 1887, 4.

180 "The World 'Do Move,' *Antwerp Argus*, February 24, 1887, 2; "The Senatorial Committee," *Antwerp Argus*, February 24, 1887, 3; "Chat," *Defiance Democrat*, February 24, 1887, 3; "The Reservoir Bill," *Paulding County Gazette*, February 24, 1887, 4.

181 "Canal Interest," *Defiance Democrat*, February 24, 1887, 3.

182 "Canal Interest," *Defiance Democrat*, February 24, 1887, 3.

183 "Canal Interest," *Defiance Democrat*, February 24, 1887, 3.

184 "Canal Interest," *Defiance Democrat*, February 24, 1887, 3.

185 "What Our Neighbors Have to Say—Defiance Call," *Antwerp Argus*, February 24, 1887, 2.

186 "The Senatorial Committee," *Antwerp Argus*, February 24, 1887, 3; "What Our Neighbors Have to Say—Defiance Express," *Antwerp Argus*, March 3, 1887, 3.

187 "What Our Neighbors Have to Say—Defiance Express," *Antwerp Argus*, March 3, 1887, 3.

188 "Notes About Town," *Defiance County Express*, February 24, 1887, 15.

189 "Notes About Town," *Defiance County Express*, February 24, 1887, 15.

190 *Paulding Democrat*, March 3, 1887, 4.

191 "Personal Mention," *Antwerp Argus*, February 24, 1887, 3; "Personal Mention," *Antwerp Argus*, February 17, 1887, 3; "Local Brevities," *Paulding County Gazette*, February 17, 1887, 8; "Round About—Antwerp," *Paulding County Gazette*, February 17, 1887, 5; "Local Gossip," *Paulding Democrat*, February 10, 1887, 5; "Local Gossip," *Paulding Democrat*, March 3, 1887, 5.

192 "Carried Away," *Antwerp Argus*, February 17, 1887, 3; "Our Home Corner," *Antwerp Argus*, February 17, 1887, 3.

193 "Bad Break," *Antwerp Argus*, February 17, 1887, 3.

194 "What Our Neighbors Have to Say—Defiance Call," *Antwerp Argus*, February 24, 1887, 2.

195 "Local Gossip," *Paulding Democrat*, March 3, 1887, 5.

# -5-

# No Compromise! The Reservoir Must Go!

### (February 1887 – April 1887)

S tartling news befell the citizens of Antwerp when Representative John L. Geyer of Defiance and Paulding County informed them that the senators had decided against touring the canal works.[1] All the citizens could do now was "await further developments."[2] On the night of February 25, 1887, an unknown individual raised a black flag on a pole in Antwerp. A fateful phrase was painted on to the fabric in large white lettering: "No Compromise! The Reservoir Must Go!"[3] For the rest of the week, the flag's presence reportedly generated "considerable excitement."[4] The following night, on February 26, 1887, the citizens of Antwerp held another meeting, again in the G. A. R. Hall.[5]

Those attending the meeting appointed Lewis S. Gordon, Phaon P. Doering, Antwerp Mayor William F. Fleck, John F. Barnett, Maroni P. Jacobs, and John H. Chester to travel to Columbus to "represent our interests." Lewis S. Gordon became ill, and Franz J. Zuber presumably took his place before these men left on February 28, 1887.[6] After petitions were again drafted, a committee took these petitions around the county, particularly to the townships of Crane, Carryall, and Harrison,[¶] as well as Hicksville Township in Defiance County. In all, the petitions received upwards of 500 names. [7] However, the *Cincinnati Weekly Enquirer* later stated that 1,300 people signed the petitions.[8]

Affidavits were also procured from area citizens to further aid the cause. [9] Maroni P. Jacobs was tasked with taking these affidavits to Columbus for presentation to the Senate. [10] The meeting ended with an announcement that a delegation from Defiance would "be in Antwerp on Monday for the purpose, if possible, of affecting a compromise of some kind." [11] Those attending the meeting unanimously agreed on one thing:

> there was no compromise on the part of our citizens other than the passage of the Geyer bill now pending, in which case ample time would be given those having timber on the canal bank to move the same, before any move towards draining canal or reservoir."[12]

As expected, the Defiance delegation, consisting of James Oreott, John Crowe, Frank J. Shead, Loring Marshall, Morris Holston, Peter Kuhn, and Charles A. Flickinger, arrived in Antwerp on February 28, 1887.[13] The meeting was held in the office of Charles S. Carpenter.[14] Mr. Carpenter was the Justice of the Peace for Carryall Township, [15] so his office served as a reasonable 'neutral' ground for the meeting. Many citizens of Antwerp "voiced the sentiments of our people, that we had

---

¶ Rufus J. Crabill "canvassed" Harrison Township and Payne "in the interest of the canal and reservoir abandonment." Maroni P. Jacobs and John H. Chester had "visited Cecil and Paulding to look after the canal abandonment question."
("Personal Mention," *Antwerp Argus*, March 3, 1887, 3.)

suffered this curse until forbearance ceased to be a virtue, and were now of but one opinion, 'that the reservoir must go.'"[16]

The Defiance delegation stated they "sympathized" with the people of Antwerp and Paulding County but were not going to change their views on the prospect of abandonment, deeming it "a death blow to the interests of Defiance, and also the Miami & Erie Canal." [17] While the locals were "glad to meet these gentlemen," particularly because it showed them first-hand the animosity that had grown in the community toward their interests and the canal works, they declined any compromise.[18] Zachariah A. Graves uttered the fateful phrase, "There is no compromise; the old skating rink must go."[19] Furthermore, the *Antwerp Argus* had this to say about the situation up to this point:

> For the past dozen years we have patiently waited and depended on promises from the Board of Public Works, to send us relief in some shape, but in every instance they have failed us, and now for these gentlemen to come among us and propose to restore the canal and reservoir, so as to benefit the village and country at large is all buncombe. We need no appropriations for such a purpose, and if they feel disposed to be friendly and assist us, as they say we deserve, let the State relieve us from our surplus water; abandon the reservoir and sell the land to actual settlers, who will put it in a state of cultivation, from the revenues thousands of dollars will be added to our tax duplicate, and the State at large be benefited. There is no reason why a whole county should be ruined, and her people made to suffer, for the benefit of a few outsiders.[20]

On numerous occasions up to this point in 1887, the people of Antwerp had been promised that the issues surrounding the canal and reservoir would be resolved. However, on every occasion that there was hope for change, nothing ever came to fruition. Worst of all, the canal had been repaired to Banks Lock, but Antwerp was left out of the repairs despite the appropriations explicitly stating they would have the canal repaired to their community. Instead, the Board of Public Works unceremoniously stated that it was not possible to do because water could not be fed to the locale.

This, unintentionally, made it so Defiance would still see benefits from the canal and reservoir's existence, but Antwerp would get practically nothing from its existence. Now, those from Defiance and the Board of Public Works again came to Antwerp to tell the people that it was possible to do what the Board previously asserted to the Ohio Legislature was not possible, and the citizens needed to hold tight for more appropriations. It is not hard to see why the citizens of Antwerp were not swayed.

A quick side note here, despite there being a report that the citizens of Antwerp appreciated "the manner in which Paulding has helped us in the reservoir fight," [21] the *Antwerp Argus* reported a "feeling existing in Paulding toward Antwerp that should at once and forever cease." [22] It was reported that some of Paulding's citizens did not support abandonment because "'we opposed the courthouse, and they do not feel disposed to do anything that would benefit Antwerp.'" [23] The *Antwerp Argus* quickly reminded Paulding's citizens why they in Antwerp did not support the new courthouse, that being the burden of increased taxes to build it. It should be noted that the courthouse was already in the process of being built, and Antwerp's citizens held to their word that they would go along with the construction despite their prior opposition. [24]

The first senator to speak against the Geyer Bill in the proceedings of the Senate on March 2, 1887, was Senator William J. Rannells from Vinton County. Senator Rannells opposed the Geyer Bill, citing the "idea that Ohio would someday need a ship [canal] through its territory. New York had done this, and the time would come when the same course would be necessary to Ohio."[25] For this reason, Senator Rannells believed it would be "ill-advised policy to abandon any part of the canals."[26]

Senator James C. Richardson from Hamilton County opposed the Geyer Bill because he believed Six Mile Reservoir supplied water to the Miami & Erie Canal and did so "some months last year, notwithstanding the assertion... that it was nothing but a mud pond" otherwise. [27] Furthermore, Senator Richardson asserted that the State of Ohio had "invested $150,000 (~$4,750,100 in 2023) in the Wabash & Erie Canal and $170,000 (~$5,383,450 in 2023) in the reservoir," and he believed what the Geyer Bill was proposing was tantamount to "giving [the canal] away." If that was agreed to, Senator Richardson believed the "remaining portions might as well be given up."[28]

Senator Levi Meredith from Auglaize County was reportedly conflicted about the Geyer Bill, seeing "right on one side and fraud on the other" but nevertheless believed the legislation should not pass.[29] Senator Meredith then read a resolution the *Defiance County Express* noted had not been openly opposed to by a delegation from Paulding County in February.[30] On the other hand, Senator George H. Ely from Cuyahoga County "vigorously opposed" the Geyer Bill, as he reportedly had for any other attempt to abandon the canals in Ohio. Senator Ely believed that "the policy of abandoning and selling the feeder was ruinous to the canals," and was apparently accounting for their "meager financial returns." [31] Senators Ferdinand H. Eggers from Cuyahoga County, Alonzo D. Fassett from Mahoning County, and Alva Curtis Cable from Miami County, among other senators, also "spoke in opposition" to the Geyer Bill.[32]

Senator William Lawrence from Guernsey County, despite reportedly being a "friend of the Public Works," actually supported the Geyer Bill, believing it to be a "good policy to lop off the non-paying portion."[33] Senator Thomas B. Coulter from Jefferson County reportedly read the affidavits that Maroni P. Jacobs had taken to Columbus, which stated "the country was rendered unhealthy by the canal and reservoir, and that it was of no public utility."[34]

After a "communication from W. F. Fleck, mayor of Antwerp, and P. F. Harris, township clerk, urging the passage of the [bill]" was presented to the chamber, the final vote on the Geyer Bill was taken.[35] The results of that vote was eight in favor against twenty-six opposed.[36]¶ A motion to reconsider followed but still failed with a vote of fourteen in favor against twenty opposed.[37] On March 3, 1887, the *Defiance County Express* reported that the Ohio Senate had voted against the Geyer Bill, and it was officially dead,¶¶ "for this year anyhow."[38] The *Defiance County Express* asserted that "Defiance interests are thus safe for another two years."[39]

---

¶ See Appendix E for a complete list of how the representatives voted.

¶¶ Representative Geyer tried to get the canal and reservoir abandoned as a rider to a bill to do the same to the Walhonding Canal and another canal section. That also failed, with 28 in favor against 47 opposed. ("Another Whirl," *Cincinnati Enquirer*, March 12, 1887, 2.)

The *Defiance County Express* was able to report that news a full week before any of the other area papers, and also presented the reason why the senators never came to tour the canal and reservoir:

> When our people went to Columbus to escort the committee on their tour this way they found that Mr. Flickinger, speaking for the Board of Public Works, had presented the Defiance view of the matter so strongly that the senators said there was no use traveling this way—the Senate would not consent to the proposed encroachment on the general system of water-ways of Ohio.[40]

A joint resolution was later introduced to the Ohio Senate "providing for a commission to examine and report upon the proposed abandonment of various canals in the State."[41] It was believed by those who introduced the resolution that there was not enough information "in such specific and accurate shape as to be valuable for the use of the General Assembly in order to have intelligent legislation on the subject."[42]

Doing this indicated that, rather than take any practical action on the abandonment question (which had hundreds of signatures on petitions as well as affidavits from local citizens favoring it), the Ohio Senate favored more bureaucracy that would report their findings to the Ohio Legislature, even if it ignored the outcries of those being represented. The people appointed to the proposed commission did not even have to be from near those canals they were surveying, just anybody the Governor wished to appoint that were Ohio citizens and had no financial interest in the upkeep or abandonment of the canals.[43]

The *Paulding Democrat* asserted that the reason for the State of Ohio's "declining to do justice to Paulding County" was strictly a political issue; claiming that those senators

> outside of this district, especially the Republicans, who opposed us, justify themselves on the ground that the State administration—Governor Foraker and his party backers and advisors—forbade it. Thus, it will be seen that it has been done to curry and abet political sentiment. A number of them have been forced to admit that the bill was possessed of the elements of right but were afraid to record themselves in favor of it for the reasons above stated.[44]

When the news was reported in the *Antwerp Argus* a week later, and it became clear how badly the bill failed, the *Antwerp Argus* had this to say on the matter:

> Let them jollify, and while they are doing so, let our citizens, one and all, register a solemn vow to ever after remember those who took an active part in the scheme to retard the growth of Paulding County, for their own selfish desires. These water-ways have long passed their usefulness, as every member of the Board of Public Works; every State Senator, and every 'timber shark' in Defiance knows. Put their names on the black list boys, and at every opportunity offered, pay them back tenfold.[45]

Much to the indignation of the *Paulding Democrat*, Paulding County's representation in the Ohio Senate had reportedly been corrupted and "openly avowed that they cared not for the ill-will of all Paulding County so long as they were supported by a few politicians in each of the other six which compose their Senatorial district." [46] The *Paulding Democrat* insinuated that their representatives had sold out for political gains.[47]

The *Paulding Democrat* claimed that both Senator Meredith and Senator Robert Mehaffey from Allen County had voted against the "proposition to reconsider the vote of the Senate by which the reservoir bill was lost."[48] While they were correct that Senator Meredith had voted against reconsideration, Senator Mehaffey had actually voted in favor of reconsideration.[49] That said, both senators still voted against the Geyer Bill when it was initially voted on.[50]

Senator Mehaffey was further criticized for reportedly introducing legislation that "provides that no assessments greater than 33 per cent of the tax valuation can be placed upon lands for ditch purposes."[51] The *Paulding Democrat* asserted that "as the territory which is hoped will be benefitted by such law lies in close proximity to the Six-mile reservoir, it will be seen that it could hardly be taxed at all, the valuation on the tax duplicate being nearly nominal for the reason that the reservoir deteriorates its worth."[52] The *Paulding Democrat* viewed this legislation as catering to the interests of "foreign real estate owners," and lambasted Senator Mehaffey as a hypocrite for stating that Representative Geyer was "in league with public land thieves," yet would introduce legislation in the "interest of monopoly."[53]

Senator Meredith was also quick to catch criticism, but his vote was nevertheless expected. Senator Meredith had been nominated and elected to the Ohio Senate during a special election in February (after the death of Senator John P. Schmeider from Auglaize County[54]) and was favorable to opposing the abandonment of the canal and reservoir.[55] The *Defiance County Express* reported that Senator Meredith "read the resolutions adopted at the convention in Van Wert, where he was nominated... The resolutions opposed the abandonment of the canals." As mentioned, peculiarly, the delegation from Paulding County reportedly "offered no opposition" to his reading of those resolutions in February.[56]

The *Antwerp Argus* declared that Senator Meredith, and Senator Mehaffey were "wholly responsible" for the Geyer Bill's defeat. [57] Furthermore, the *Antwerp Argus* believed the two senators were "wholly unfit" to be in their positions. [58] Particularly because the *Antwerp Argus* reported that Senator Meredith had made a speech that, in effect, stated "the words of these two senators should count more than affidavits of citizens."[59]

Moreover, "[The senators] denounced the bill as a steal and a land grab, and claimed that they were pledged to their constituents to use their every endeavor to defeat it." [60] The *Antwerp Argus* asserted that the two senators knew "nothing about this canal or reservoir, having never been here to post themselves on their uselessness,"[61] making their positions even more baffling. Mr. Flickinger did not escape further criticism from the *Antwerp Argus*, who called him "wholly unfit" for his office as well.[62]

The *Paulding Democrat* also called out Representatives John C. Entrekin of Ross County (Speaker[63]) and Daniel J. Ryan of Scioto County (Speaker *pro tem*[64]) for their own hypocrisy in the matter. The *Paulding Democrat* asserted that, despite being "great friends of the canal system," they had worked to pass a bill that would have authorized the Board of Public Works to "lease a canal water basin in the city of Chillicothe to a railroad company." This was a problem because Representative Entrekin reportedly owned "a tract of ten acres of land in close proximity to this part of the public works desired to be vacated, which would have been laid out in town lots and its value increased tenfold."[65] That bill failed abysmally with only fourteen votes, but the *Paulding Democrat* had shown its readers that some of those who "pose as the saviors of the canals" had their own ulterior motives when it came to their own interests.[66]

It is worth noting that on May 1, 1879, the Board of Public Works had been authorized to "lease to, or permit the Paulding & Antwerp Railroad Company (P&A) to use and occupy the south bank of the six-mile reservoir... for a road-bed, and also... to cross the southwest corner of said reservoir with its railroad."[67] This situation differed because Six Mile Reservoir would have still existed and functioned as it had before the railroad was built, unlike the basin in Chillicothe which would have presumably been filled in for railroad purposes. The P&A was expected to use "trestle work or piling" to cross the reservoir, and the P&A was also expected to be

> responsible for and pay all damages caused by overflow of water, or otherwise resulting from the construction of the bed of said railroad, and also for all damages which may result from the flowing of water across the track of said railroad on said premises, to forever keep the same in good repair for reservoir purposes.[68]

That all said, the P&A's proposed routing had moved just before the authorization was granted, going one and a half miles further south to transit a "better scope of the country."[69] Even before the Board of Public Works had been authorized to permit such use of the southern bank and the crossing of Six Mile Reservoir, the Antwerp Furnace's railroad to Section Two of Harrison Township[70] had already built a bridge across the canal "some time" before June 1878, but after March 28, 1878, and across the reservoir around December 1878.[71]

The Antwerp Furnace's railroad did business as the Antwerp & Paulding Railroad (A&P),[72] and officially began operations to Section Two of Harrison Township on September 1, 1879.[73] By the spring of 1880, the citizens of Antwerp were encouraging the A&P to extend its railroad to Paulding.[74] In the end, however, no railroad was ever built that directly connected Antwerp and Paulding. It is not entirely clear when the A&P ceased operations, but it was torn up by June 17, 1886.[75]

On March 7, 1887, the black flag that had been flying near the railroad tracks in Antwerp was "floated down the Maumee, flying from the masthead of a raft." This was explicitly done to show their dissatisfaction to the citizens of Defiance downriver of them.[76] However, the only newspaper in Defiance to pick up on it was the *Defiance Call* when it passed through town the next day on March 8, 1887.[77]

On March 17, 1887, the *Antwerp Argus* printed the following:

> If we must wade water and mud another season, for the benefit of a few 'timber sharks' in adjoining counties, let there be a feeling down deep in our hearts that we have friends to reward and enemies to punish, and that our labors will never cease until all these debts have been paid. The honor of our citizens has been maligned, our rights trampled upon, and the justice demanded from our servants has been denied us. Let this insult and unjust legislation be ever remembered.[78]

On that same day, a thinly veiled threat was printed in the *Antwerp Argus*, stating, "the war veterans are looking for scalps this year."[79] The *Toledo Blade* even suggested that "Antwerp citizens will 'get even' with those who insist on keeping a lot of muddy water in Paulding County."[80] The *Antwerp Argus* did not deny this, asserting, "you can bet your last nickel on this and win every time."[81] However, the *Antwerp Argus* denied that Antwerp's citizens alone would be the ones who may act, as the "whole county is united and will stand firm to the bitter end."[82] The *Antwerp Argus*, however, made it abundantly clear to its readers that they did not support "any man who temporizes with Anarchy."[83]

Hicksville, Ohio's John M. Ainsworth had circulated the petition for abandonment in Hicksville Township, and "a large number of signers it received indicates that Hicksville is heartily in sympathy with Paulding County." [84] The *Defiance Call* denounced the citizens of Hicksville's support of Paulding County's cause, asserting that the two locale's "interests are not identical, and with the county seat they are, or should be," warning that the citizens of Hicksville would "feed on husks for her prodigal acts." [85] Meanwhile, the *Hicksville Independent*, understanding the deteriorating situation and what was to come, jokingly promised that the citizens of Hicksville would "form in line and march to the spot where the reservoir once was to view the wreck the day following the explosion."[86]

A mere two weeks later, on the night of March 19, 1887, a gang of masked men were seen on a Wabash train in Antwerp. [87] According to Otto E. Ehrhart, the men had boarded the train at the Wabash Railroad's depot@ in Antwerp with the help of the station agent, a man named John L. Pocock. [88] While Otto E. Ehrhart's retelling states it was John who was station agent, this was in all likelihood a misremembering by his interviewee(s).

The reality is that it was more likely John's brother Emmet E. Pocock who greeted the masked men at the depot, as he was the night operator for the Wabash Railroad at Antwerp at the time, and had been since May 1882.[89] John had been the day operator from May 1874 until May 1882 when he resigned the position and John S. Berne (the then night operator) took his place.[90] As far as the historical record has shown, John had no affiliation with the Wabash Railroad by this time in 1887. John was implicated, possibly erroneously, by Mr. Ehrhart and those he interviewed as being involved with the masked men, at least in this way.

Nevertheless, the fact of the matter is that an employee of the Wabash Railroad at Antwerp was reportedly a man in on what the masked men were planning. His task was to inform the train's conductor to "pay no attention to [the masked men]—just collect their tickets and put them off at their destination." [91] Understandably, the passengers must have thought a robbery was occurring on the train, and they too had to be coaxed by the conductor to pay the masked men no attention. After all, these masked men were heavily armed, carrying "shotguns, rifles, and revolvers," and presumably looking for trouble.[92]

---

@ The Wabash's depot in Antwerp was originally located on the north side of the railroad's tracks between Main Street and Cleveland Street. It still stands in 2023, having been moved to the west end of town on River Street.
(*Sanborn Fire Insurance Map from Antwerp, Paulding County, Ohio,*
    August 1893.)

After riding but a few short miles, the train stopped at Knox Station,@ where a group of them detrained and walked south toward Six Mile Reservoir.[93] The rest of them detrained a little further east at Cecil and proceeded south toward the canal.[94] From their destinations, they all seemingly disappeared into the night.[95] Despite nothing else of significance being reported on this evening, a fuse was reportedly found in the lock at Tate's Landing,[96] and "several packages of dynamite" had allegedly been discovered "in the vicinity of the canal and reservoir" on March 20, 1887.[97]

On the following Friday night, March 25, 1887, another attack was made on Six Mile Reservoir and the aqueduct east of the Paulding & Cecil Improved Road.[98] Upon hearing rumors of an impending attack, Bob Bristle, a correspondent to the *Paulding Democrat* from Antwerp, started toward the reservoir to see if there was "any truth in the report."[99] He reported that the night was "clear and cold, the stars were shining brightly while nothing save the clatter of the pony hoofs broke the deep silence."[100]

That was until Mr. Bristle encountered a flame flicker in his path two miles into the journey (roughly where C.R. 180 dead-ends on the west side of U.S. 24); Mr. Bristle had encountered the first sentinel.[101] After quietly dismounting from his horse and exercising "great caution," Mr. Bristle was able to evade not only the first sentinel but two more within a mile of the first. After evading the third sentinel, Mr. Bristle again mounted his horse

---

@ Knox Station (later Knoxdale) was located where T-69 meets the railroad tracks and the current alignment of U.S. 24 in Paulding County. (O. Morrow and F.W. Bashore, *Historical Atlas of Paulding County, Ohio, 1892,* 89-90.)

and made his way east toward lights "plainly discernable in the distance."[102] Mr. Bristle made it to the vicinity of present-day Zuber Cutoff before encountering about thirty men. Roughly twelve of them were carrying lanterns, the rest were "working as if their lives depended upon the amount of dirt they removed with pick and shovel."[103]

Only one person was barking orders, described as having a "gruff voice," but alas, Mr. Bristle could not identify him by his voice alone.[104] Mr. Bristle set off to see what else he could see, determining that there was work possibly being done at Hutchins Lock about a mile further down the canal, and a group on horseback was reportedly progressing east.[105] Unfortunately for him, he did not make it further than about two hundred yards before someone exclaimed, "halt!" Seeing no sense in causing a fuss, Mr. Bristle only inquired "what was wanted." The men who spotted Mr. Bristle from the other side of the canal on the reservoir bank only responded with another question about what business he had being there at that time of night.[106]

Again, not wanting to start anything, Mr. Bristle informed them his business was "in the interest of the press" and only asked how far ahead those men on horseback were. The unknown men informed Mr. Bristle that the horsemen were already four miles distant and that he would not "'ketch'em neither.'" Not wanting to get himself hurt, and understanding that chasing after the horsemen was futile, Mr. Bristle returned to Antwerp via a "circuitous route" to avoid more trouble.[107]

Upon reaching home, Mr. Bristle heard two thunderous roars, one at about 2:20 a.m. and the other at around 2:50 a.m., so loud as to reportedly be heard ten miles away and allegedly as far away as Defiance.[108] Apparent successive attacks in the following days cut a fifteen to twenty-five-foot gap in the wall near the reservoir's waste weir and damaged a portion of the bank near the bulkhead, rapidly letting the water out of the reservoir in a torrent.[109] Many citizens of Antwerp and Paulding set off to see the damage done to the reservoir in the days following the chaos.[110]

The damage to the aqueduct was "considerable," and to such an extent that it was thought to be irreparable, thus requiring a new structure.[111] Destroying the aqueduct had also reportedly stranded "nearly four thousand saw logs belong to Foreman E. Simpson of [Paulding County], and parties of Defiance, which were ready for rafting."[112] Mr. Simpson and his wife Georgiana would team up with Stephen F. Eagle to put up a $1,300 reward for the "apprehension" of those responsible for the depredations.[113] With a pang of irony, timber rafting would be described as "not good" soon after the attack, specifically on the Wabash & Erie Canal.[114]

Within a day or two of the attacks, state employees, including Canal Division Superintendent Homer Meacham, were quick to arrive to make repairs to the destroyed works. On March 21, 1887, two of those workers were reportedly nearly frozen and drowned in their efforts to repair the reservoir bank. The two workers were in the process of placing a new plank in the bank, but the current from the escaping water failed to allow them to lodge the plank into the ground, throwing the men and the plank into the water.[115]

The *Defiance Democrat* suggested that it "may become necessary to call out the 'milish' [sic] to protect the reservoir."

Mr. Flickinger, most certainly incensed by the depredations, was reported to have already requested Governor Joseph B. Foraker to send in a company of the Ohio National Guard. As some believed, "it will be only a question of time when it will be destroyed."[116] The *Defiance Democrat* warned the depredators that "the State of Ohio allows no man to destroy its property with impunity."[117]

On February 17, 1887, the *Antwerp Argus* had vehemently denied the existence of what a Defiance correspondent to the *Toledo Blade* asserted was "an organization at Antwerp, the sole object of which is to blow up the reservoir with dynamite."[118] Over a month later, at the end of March, the *Antwerp Argus* now believed a secret society was responsible for the depredations that occurred over the weekend,[119] consisting of individuals from Paulding County and adjacent counties "determined, sooner or later, that this more than nuisance 'must go,' feeling as they do, that they have sought justice at the hands of our law-making powers, but in every instance met with defeat."[120]

The *Antwerp Argus* further stated that they did not support "the destruction of this State property by force."[121] They nevertheless understood why those who acted did so. The *Antwerp Argus* would comment:

> That our community suffers a great loss by unjust legislation, no one will attempt to deny, and this, as it would seem, was brought about for the simple aggrandizement of a few who wished to profit from our forests and to float logs to market and to the doors of their factories in adjoining towns and marketplaces.[122]

The *Antwerp Argus* went so far as suggesting that those in Defiance would be the ones who would destroy the canal and reservoir once their use for it was no longer needed. [123] The *Defiance Democrat* echoed the assertions of the *Antwerp Argus* about a secret society, believing them to be so well put together as to have "passwords, grips, and oaths." [124] The *Fort Wayne Sentinel* would later report that they even had a uniform disguise, wearing "calico and masks."[125] In an interview on April 29, 1887, ADJ GEN Henry A. Axline stated that the secret society was so well organized that "the men assigned to do different kinds of work wore different kinds of masks. For instance, the men who handled the dynamite wore red masks."[126]

Unbeknownst to those in Defiance, Fort Wayne, and maybe those in Antwerp too, there was a secret organization, later referred to as the Dynamiters. How long they had been meeting is uncertain. The *Fort Wayne Sentinel* reported they had been "organized for months." [127] What is known is that the Dynamiters were meeting "in the back room of Frank Lamb's barbershop and above the grocery store of Oliver S. Applegate."[128] They were "sworn to secrecy" and did so under a banner made of a "strip of black bunting." One side saying, "No Compromise," the other side exclaiming, "The Reservoir Must Go."[129]@

---

@ Frank Lamb's barbershop was on the west side of Main Street between River Street and the railroad, where the Antwerp Pharmacy was located until 2023. Next door was Oliver S. Applegate's grocery store and was where the Antwerp Village Hardware was located as of 2023.
(Otto E. Ehrhart, "Business History of Antwerp," in *A Century of Progress: Antwerp, Ohio,* 42; *Antwerp Argus,* October 4, 1883, 3; Stan Jordan, "O.S. Applegate 1844 to 1910," *West Bend News,* December 28, 2016, 6; *Antwerp Argus,* May 27, 1886, 3.)

In late March 1887, the *Antwerp Argus* asserted that unless Defiance was so inclined to foot the bill for repairs, the canal was effectively made permanently useless, and once the timber interests removed their logs from the now useless canal, they would "lose all further interest in the Antwerp 'frog pond,' or the now defunct spur of the once Wabash and Erie Canal." [130] Despite this assertion, by April 7, 1887, the reservoir was repaired, and the mortally wounded aqueduct was "about replaced." [131] Nevertheless, word reached Defiance that they would only have ten days to remove their logs from the canal before another attack was made after repairs had been completed; the *Defiance Democrat* claimed that the apparent armistice was for thirty days two weeks later. [132]

Another threat was made in a "secret letter" sent to Mr. Flickinger, informing him that the reservoir would be blown up again on April 9, 1887. [133] In response to this, on April 8, 1887, Governor Foraker received a petition from Mr. Flickinger and other businessmen of Defiance and Paulding County, urging him to send a regiment of the Ohio National Guard to protect the canal works in Paulding County from further destruction. [134]

Governor Foraker, apparently taken aback by such developments "never before having been called upon to deal with a community in a 'state of arnica' [*sic*]," reportedly promised Mr. Flickinger that he would visit Paulding County soon to evaluate the situation. [135] One report indicated it would have been as soon as the following week. [136] That report did not come to pass, as Governor Foraker never turned up, and the *Antwerp Argus* called the reporting a case of April Fools that nobody believed to begin with. [137]

Governor Foraker, likely because Sheriff David W. Parr of Paulding County had not been the one to request the Ohio National Guard, did not send in troops at this date. If Mr. Flickinger wanted a "military display" so badly, the *Antwerp Argus* chirped, "Why not enlist a company yourself, 'Flick,' since the Governor refused you the aid asked for?"[138] It was about this time a total of ten guards were reportedly placed to protect the canal works.[139]

The *Antwerp Argus* seemingly believed Defiance parties were bankrolling the newly placed guards along the canal and reservoir, asserting that "it is claimed by many that they are there by no authority from the State, and are paid only by private subscription." [140] The *Antwerp Argus* then called the guards "intruders," and made it clear that "Paulding County may not continue [to be] a healthy place for them to remain in."[141] The *Paulding Democrat,* on the other hand, referred to them as State guards.[142] The *Defiance Democrat* referred to them as "guards appointed by the governor."[143]

Guarding the reservoir this time of year made the *Antwerp Argus* a tad wary for their wellbeing on one occasion, as they described the "past few nights" as being "rather cold."[144] The *Paulding Democrat* reported that these guards held their post despite a "disagreeable storm" on the night of April 16, 1887.[145] So serious were these guards that a rumor reached the *Paulding Democrat* that one of the guards almost shot another guard after "mistaking his comrade for one of the dynamiters."[146] A report reached the *Cincinnati Enquirer* that Mr. Flickinger, hot on the heels of the recent destruction of canal works, had told citizens of Defiance, "Gentlemen, there is no use trying to conceal a solemn fact. Paulding County is in a State of Arnica [*sic*], and I will see that it is wiped out if it takes the entire militia of the State to do it!"[147]

The correspondent to the *Cincinnati Enquirer* stated that there was, "along two miles of the canal in [Defiance] are more than $200,000 (~$6,333,475 in 2023) invested in manufacturing establishments, giving employment to nearly one thousand men." [148] Defiance business owners the correspondent spoke with shared the same sentiment, "that their future prosperity depends most largely upon the maintenance of the Paulding County Reservoir and its connecting branch of canal."[149]

This was primarily due to the claim that Paulding County was the "great and nearly sole supply of timber to the Defiance mills" and that the Wabash & Erie Canal was a necessary feeder to the canal through Defiance. Allegedly, the Mercer County Reservoir alone was "inadequate to supply the requisite amount of water for the successful operation of the mills at Defiance."[150] Submerging timber preserves it, and it was claimed there would not be enough water from the distant reservoir in Mercer County to allow this preservation beyond "limited quantities" of timber. [151] Should the water level become insufficient in the "cribs and booms" that stored the timber along the canal, especially in the dry summer season, the timber could become unusable if allowed to dry out and rot.[152]

Making things worse was the claim that, if the canal were abandoned, the cost of transporting the timber by land to the mills would be unprofitable to those selling the timber.[153] This would allegedly be a great detriment to those sellers because they reportedly earned a profit "equal to two or three crops" for the sale of timber on their land when transported by water to Defiance; opposed to cutting, burning, and removing the timber at their own expense because the cost to transport the timber overland made the timber, generally speaking, worthless.[154]

Despite the pleas and assertions of those against the abandonment of the Wabash & Erie Canal and Six Mile Reservoir, the *Paulding County Gazette* reported on April 21, 1887, that Antwerp was "on the verge of a boom... A big boom is skirmishing around the confines of our burg and 'something will undoubtedly drop before long. Look out.'"[155]

## Chapter 5 Notes

1 "Our Home Corner," *Antwerp Argus*, March 3, 1887, 3.

2 "Our Home Corner," *Antwerp Argus*, March 3, 1887, 3.

3 "Round About—Antwerp," *Paulding County Gazette*, March 3, 1887, 5; "Antwerp Items," *Paulding Democrat*, March 3, 1887, 5; "No Compromise," *Antwerp Argus*, March 3, 1887, 3.

4 "Round About—Antwerp," *Paulding County Gazette*, March 3, 1887, 5.

5 "Round About—Antwerp," *Paulding County Gazette*, March 3, 1887, 5.

6 "Enthusiastic Meetings," *Antwerp Argus*, March 3, 1887, 3; "Personal Mention," *Antwerp Argus*, March 3, 1887, 3; "Round About—Antwerp," *Paulding County Gazette*, March 3, 1887, 5.

7 "Enthusiastic Meetings," *Antwerp Argus*, March 3, 1887, 3; "Personal Mention," *Antwerp Argus*, March 3, 1887, 3; "Antwerp Items," *Paulding Democrat*, March 3, 1887, 5.

8 "Troops Called For," *Cincinnati Weekly Enquirer*, April 13, 1887, 5.

9 "Good Evidence," *Antwerp Argus*, March 10, 1887, 3.

10 "Personal Mention," *Antwerp Argus*, March 10, 1887, 2; "Good Evidence," *Antwerp Argus*, March 10, 1887, 3.

11 "Enthusiastic Meetings," *Antwerp Argus*, March 3, 1887, 3.

12 "Enthusiastic Meetings," *Antwerp Argus*, March 3, 1887, 3.

13 "A Proposed Compromise," *Antwerp Argus*, March 3, 1887, 2.

14 "A Proposed Compromise," *Antwerp Argus*, March 3, 1887, 2.

15 "Attachment Notice," *Antwerp Argus*, March 31, 1887, 2.

16 "A Proposed Compromise," *Antwerp Argus*, March 3, 1887, 2.

17 "A Proposed Compromise," *Antwerp Argus*, March 3, 1887, 2.

18 "A Proposed Compromise," *Antwerp Argus*, March 3, 1887, 2.

19 "Round About—Antwerp," *Paulding County Gazette*, March 3, 1887, 5.

20 "A Proposed Compromise," *Antwerp Argus*, March 3, 1887, 2.

21 "Antwerp Items," *Paulding Democrat*, March 3, 1887, 5.

22 "Should Forever Cease," *Antwerp Argus*, March 3, 1887, 3.

23 "Should Forever Cease," *Antwerp Argus*, March 3, 1887, 3.

24 "Should Forever Cease," *Antwerp Argus*, March 3, 1887, 3.

25 "Notes About Town," *Defiance County Express*, March 17, 1887, 16.

26 "Notes About Town," *Defiance County Express*, March 17, 1887, 16.

27 "Notes About Town," *Defiance County Express*, March 17, 1887, 16.

28 "Notes About Town," *Defiance County Express*, March 17, 1887, 16.

29 "Notes About Town," *Defiance County Express*, March 17, 1887, 16.

30 "Notes About Town," *Defiance County Express*, March 17, 1887, 16.

31 "Notes About Town," *Defiance County Express*, March 17, 1887, 16.

32 "Notes About Town," *Defiance County Express*, March 17, 1887, 16.

33 "Notes About Town," *Defiance County Express*, March 17, 1887, 16.

34 "Notes About Town," *Defiance County Express*, March 17, 1887, 16.

35 State of Ohio, *Journal of the Senate of the State of Ohio, for the Adjourned Session of the Sixty-Seventh General Assembly*, Volume LXXXIII, 458.

36 "Defeated!," *Antwerp Argus*, March 10, 1887, 2; *Paulding County Gazette*, March 17, 1887, 4; "The Canal is Safe," *Defiance Democrat*, March 10, 1887, 2; "Notes About Town," *Defiance County Express*, March 17, 1887, 16; State of Ohio, *Journal of the Senate of the State of Ohio, for the Adjourned Session of the Sixty-Seventh General Assembly*, Volume LXXXIII, 459.

37 State of Ohio, *Journal of the Senate of the State of Ohio, for the Adjourned Session of the Sixty-Seventh General Assembly*, Volume LXXXIII, 459.

38 "Notes About Town," *Defiance County Express*, March 3, 1887, 16.

39 "Notes About Town," *Defiance County Express*, March 17, 1887, 16.

40 "Notes About Town," *Defiance County Express*, March 3, 1887, 16.

41 "Notes About Town," *Defiance County Express*, March 3, 1887, 16.

42 "Notes About Town," *Defiance County Express*, March 3, 1887, 16.

43 "Notes About Town," *Defiance County Express*, March 3, 1887, 16.

44 "The Reason Why Justice Was Ignored," *Paulding Democrat*, March 17, 1887, 4.

45 "Defeated!," *Antwerp Argus*, March 10, 1887, 2.

46 "The Reason Why Justice Was Ignored," *Paulding Democrat*, March 17, 1887, 4.

47 "The Reason Why Justice Was Ignored," *Paulding Democrat*, March 17, 1887, 4.

48 *Paulding Democrat*, March 17, 1887, 4.

49 State of Ohio, *Journal of the Senate of the State of Ohio, for the Adjourned Session of the Sixty-Seventh General Assembly*, Volume LXXXIII, 459.

50 State of Ohio, *Journal of the Senate of the State of Ohio, for the Adjourned Session of the Sixty-Seventh General Assembly*, Volume LXXXIII, 459.

51 *Paulding Democrat*, March 17, 1887, 4.

52 *Paulding Democrat*, March 17, 1887, 4.

53 *Paulding Democrat*, March 17, 1887, 4.

54 Joseph P. Smith, *History of the Republican Party in Ohio*, Volume I, 513.

55 "The New Senator," *Paulding Democrat*, February 17, 1887, 1; "The Reason Why Justice Was Ignored," *Paulding Democrat*, March 17, 1887, 4; "Notes About Town," *Defiance County Express*, March 17, 1887, 16.

56 "Notes About Town," *Defiance County Express*, March 17, 1887, 16.

57 "Who Are To Blame?," *Antwerp Argus*, March 17, 1887, 2.

58 "Who Are To Blame?," *Antwerp Argus*, March 17, 1887, 2.

59 "Who Are To Blame?," *Antwerp Argus*, March 17, 1887, 2.

60 "Who Are To Blame?," *Antwerp Argus*, March 17, 1887, 2.

61 "Who Are To Blame?," *Antwerp Argus*, March 17, 1887, 2.

62 "Who Are To Blame?," *Antwerp Argus*, March 17, 1887, 2.

63 Joseph P. Smith, *History of the Republican Party in Ohio*, Volume I, 513.

64 Joseph P. Smith, *History of the Republican Party in Ohio*, Volume I, 513.

65 *Paulding Democrat*, March 17, 1887, 4.

66 *Paulding Democrat*, March 17, 1887, 4.

67 State of Ohio, *The Revised Statutes of the State of* Ohio, edited by James M. Williams, Volume III, 489.

68 State of Ohio, *The Revised Statutes of the State of* Ohio, edited by James M. Williams, Volume III, 489.

69 "A. & P. R. R.," *Paulding County Gazette*, April 3, 1879, 2.

70 "Home Matters," *Antwerp Gazette*, March 28, 1878, 3; "The Furnace," *Antwerp Gazette*, October 17, 1878, 3.

71 "Home Matters," *Antwerp Gazette*, June 6, 1878, 3; "Home Matters," *Antwerp Gazette*, March 28, 1878, 3; "From Antwerp," *Paulding Democrat*, November 14, 1878, 1; "The Furnace R. R.," *Antwerp Gazette*, November 14, 1878, 5; "Antwerp Items," *Paulding County Gazette*, December 12, 1878, 2.

72 Henry Varnum Poor, *Manual of the Railroads of the United States: 1882*, Volume 15, 511.

73 Henry Varnum Poor, *Manual of the Railroads of the United States: 1882*, Volume 15, 511.

74 "Antwerp Notes," *Paulding County Gazette*, April 22, 1880, 3; "Antwerp Items," *Paulding County Gazette*, May 6, 1880, 3.

75 "Round—About: Antwerp," *Paulding County Gazette*, June 17, 1886, 1.

76 "Our Home Corner," *Antwerp Argus*, March 10, 1887, 3.

77 "Local Gossip," *Paulding Democrat*, March 17, 1887, 5.

78 "Who Are To Blame?," *Antwerp Argus*, March 17, 1887, 2.

79 "Our Home Corner," *Antwerp Argus*, March 17, 1887, 3.

80 "Our Home Corner," *Antwerp Argus*, March 17, 1887, 3.

81 "Our Home Corner," *Antwerp Argus*, March 17, 1887, 3.

82 "Our Home Corner," *Antwerp Argus*, March 17, 1887, 3.

83 "Our Home Corner," *Antwerp Argus*, March 17, 1887, 3.

84 "What Our Neighbors Have To Say—Hicksville Independent," *Antwerp Argus*, March 10, 1887, 3; "What Our Neighbors Have To Say—Hicksville News," *Antwerp Argus*, March 10, 1887, 3.

85 "Our Home Corner," *Antwerp Argus*, March 17, 1887, 3.

86 "What Our Neighbors Have To Say—Hicksville Independent," *Antwerp Argus*, March 10, 1887, 3.

87 "Who Were They?," *Antwerp Argus*, March 24, 1887, 3.

88 Otto E. Ehrhart, "Wabash-Erie Canal," in *A Century of Progress: Antwerp, Ohio*, 19.

89 "Antwerp Items," *Paulding County Gazette*, June 1, 1882, 3.

90 William S. Hardesty, *Representative Citizens of Paulding County*, 203; "Antwerp Items," *Paulding County Gazette*, June 1, 1882, 3.

91 Otto E. Ehrhart, "Wabash-Erie Canal," in *A Century of Progress: Antwerp, Ohio*, 19, 21.

92 Otto E. Ehrhart, "Wabash-Erie Canal," in *A Century of Progress: Antwerp, Ohio*, 21; "Who Were They?," *Antwerp Argus*, March 24, 1887, 3.

93 Otto E. Ehrhart, "Wabash-Erie Canal," in *A Century of Progress: Antwerp, Ohio*, 19.

94 "Who Were They?," *Antwerp Argus*, March 24, 1887, 3; "Cecil Chimes," *Paulding Democrat*, March 24, 1887, 1.

95 "Who Were They?," *Antwerp Argus*, March 24, 1887, 3.

96 "Cecil Chimes," *Paulding Democrat*, March 24, 1887, 1.

97 "Who Were They?," *Antwerp Argus*, March 24, 1887, 3.

98 "Another Earthquake," *Antwerp Argus*, March 31, 1887, 2; "Dynamiters Daring Deeds," *Paulding Democrat*, March 31, 1887, 5.

99 "Dynamiters Daring Deeds," *Paulding Democrat*, March 31, 1887, 5.

100 "Dynamiters Daring Deeds," *Paulding Democrat*, March 31, 1887, 5.

101 "Dynamiters Daring Deeds," *Paulding Democrat*, March 31, 1887, 5.

102 "Dynamiters Daring Deeds," *Paulding Democrat*, March 31, 1887, 5.

103 "Dynamiters Daring Deeds," *Paulding Democrat*, March 31, 1887, 5.

104 "Dynamiters Daring Deeds," *Paulding Democrat*, March 31, 1887, 5.

105 "Dynamiters Daring Deeds," *Paulding Democrat*, March 31, 1887, 5.

106 "Dynamiters Daring Deeds," *Paulding Democrat*, March 31, 1887, 5.

107 "Dynamiters Daring Deeds," *Paulding Democrat*, March 31, 1887, 5.

108 "Dynamiters Daring Deeds," *Paulding Democrat*, March 31, 1887, 5. "Our Home Corner," *Antwerp Argus*, March 31, 1887, 3; "Dynamiters!" *Paulding County Gazette*, March 31, 1887, 1.

109 "Dynamiters Daring Deeds," *Paulding Democrat*, March 31, 1887, 5; "Dynamiters!" *Paulding County Gazette*, March 31, 1887, 1; "Another Earthquake," *Antwerp Argus*, March 31, 1887, 2.

110 "Our Home Corner," *Antwerp Argus*, March 31, 1887, 3; "Personal Mention," *Antwerp Argus*, March 31, 1887, 3; "Dynamiters!" *Paulding County Gazette*, March 31, 1887, 1; "Round About—Antwerp," *Paulding County Gazette*, March 31, 1887, 5.

111 "Another Earthquake," *Antwerp Argus*, March 31, 1887, 2.

112 "Our Home Corner," *Antwerp Argus*, March 31, 1887, 3; "Dynamiters Daring Deeds," *Paulding Democrat*, March 31, 1887, 5.

113 "Our Home Corner," *Antwerp Argus*, March 31, 1887, 3.

114 "Local Brevities," *Paulding County Gazette*, April 7, 1887, 5.

115 "A Cold Bath," *Antwerp Argus*, March 31, 1887, 3; "Dynamiters," *Paulding County Gazette*, March 31, 1887, 1.

116 "Chat," *Defiance Democrat*, March 31, 1887, 3; "Chat," *Defiance Democrat*, April 7, 1887, 3; "Dynamiters!" *Paulding County Gazette*, March 31, 1887, 1; "Protection Asked," *Antwerp Argus*, April 7, 1887, 3.

117 "Chat," *Defiance Democrat*, April 21, 1887, 2.

118 *Antwerp Argus*, February 17, 1887, 2.

119 "Another Earthquake," *Antwerp Argus*, March 31, 1887, 2.

120 "Another Earthquake," *Antwerp Argus*, March 31, 1887, 2.

121 "Another Earthquake," *Antwerp Argus*, March 31, 1887, 2.
122 "Another Earthquake," *Antwerp Argus*, March 31, 1887, 2.
123 "Another Earthquake," *Antwerp Argus*, March 31, 1887, 2.
124 "Chat," *Defiance Democrat*, April 21, 1887, 2.
125 "States Evidence," *Fort Wayne Sentinel*, April 29, 1887, 2.
126 "The Reservoir Row," *Cincinnati Commercial Gazette*, April 30, 1887, 5.
127 "States Evidence," *Fort Wayne Sentinel*, April 29, 1887, 2.
128 Otto E. Ehrhart, "Wabash-Erie Canal," in *A Century of Progress: Antwerp, Ohio*, 18.
129 Otto E. Ehrhart, "Wabash-Erie Canal," in *A Century of Progress: Antwerp, Ohio*, 18; Everett A. Budd, "Brief History of Paulding County, Ohio," in *Historical Atlas of Paulding County, Ohio, 1892*, 29.
130 "Another Earthquake," *Antwerp Argus*, March 31, 1887, 2.
131 "Local Gossip," *Paulding Democrat*, April 7, 1887, 5.
132 "Local Gossip," *Paulding Democrat*, April 7, 1887, 5; "Damnable Dynamite Deeds," *Defiance Democrat*, April 28, 1887, 3; "Chat," *Defiance Democrat*, April 21, 1887, 2.
133 "Send in the 'Melish'," *Antwerp Argus*, April 14, 1887, 3.
134 "Troops Called For," *Cincinnati Weekly Enquirer*, April 13, 1887, 5; "Send in the 'Melish'," *Antwerp Argus*, April 14, 1887, 3; "The Governor Asked to Send A Regiment to Paulding," *Antwerp Argus*, April 14, 1887, 3.
135 "A State of Arnica," *Defiance Democrat*, April 21, 1887, 2.
136 "Troops Called For," *Cincinnati Weekly Enquirer*, April 13, 1887, 5.
137 "Our Home Corner," *Antwerp Argus*, April 14, 1887, 3.
138 "Send in the 'Melish'," *Antwerp Argus*, April 14, 1887, 3.
139 "War in Paulding County," *Defiance County Express*, April 28, 1887, 10.
140 "Protection Asked," *Antwerp Argus*, April 7, 1887, 3.
141 "Protection Asked," *Antwerp Argus*, April 7, 1887, 3.
142 "Junction Jottings," *Paulding Democrat*, April 14, 1887, 1.
143 "Exciting Times in Ohio," *Defiance Democrat*, May 5, 1887, 1.
144 "Our Home Corner," *Antwerp Argus*, April 7, 1887, 3.
145 "Local Gossip," *Paulding Democrat*, April 21, 1887, 5.
146 "Junction Jottings," *Paulding Democrat*, April 14, 1887, 1.
147 "A State of Arnica," *Defiance Democrat*, April 21, 1887, 2.
148 "A State of Arnica," *Defiance Democrat*, April 21, 1887, 2.
149 "A State of Arnica," *Defiance Democrat*, April 21, 1887, 2.
150 "A State of Arnica," *Defiance Democrat*, April 21, 1887, 2.
151 "A State of Arnica," *Defiance Democrat*, April 21, 1887, 2.
152 "A State of Arnica," *Defiance Democrat*, April 21, 1887, 2.
153 "A State of Arnica," *Defiance Democrat*, April 21, 1887, 2.
154 "A State of Arnica," *Defiance Democrat*, April 21, 1887, 2.
155 "Round About—Antwerp," *Paulding County Gazette*, April 21, 1887, 5.

# −6−

## The Reservoir War
### (April 25, 1887 – May 6, 1887)

Roughly thirty days after the last attack on the canal works, on the evening of April 25, 1887, an alleged 150 to 400 masked individuals left Antwerp,[1§] led by Oliver S. Applegate and Henry W. Sperry.[2] These individuals, later called the Dynamiters, started on foot, horseback, and wagon toward Six Mile Reservoir in another effort to destroy it and other targets along the Wabash & Erie Canal.[3] Upon arriving at the reservoir's waste weir around 10 p.m., four guards were captured unharmed, and subsequently disarmed at this location.[4] Some of the Dynamiters, armed with picks, spades, and dynamite, then began working on cutting the waste weir open again.[5] The rest of the Dynamiters continued down the towpath toward Hutchins Lock.[6]

The Dynamiters quickly worked on Hutchins Lock and the reservoir's bulkhead by destroying them with dynamite charges. [7] Those charges were reportedly "several hundred pounds."[8] Not content with just using dynamite to damage the canal works, the Dynamiters also doused Hutchins Lock with

---

§ This number varies wildly from source to source, but all sources stay within this range provided by the cited source in the *Paulding Democrat*.

kerosene or coal oil[§] and set it ablaze along with the lock keeper's house.[9]

Warner D. Ryel would later state that as many as twenty fifty-pound charges of dynamite were detonated at the same time to destroy the bank of the reservoir after a "12 rod wide" (198 feet) trench was dug to the water line by a group of sixty-eight Dynamiters.[10] Two holes were cut in the reservoir bank nearby to the lock, one hole emptied into the canal, and the other emptied into the ditch on the reservoir's east side.[11] As mentioned, they had cut to "within a few feet of the water" and then placed the dynamite in the cut.[12] Mr. Ryel also stated, "when the explosion occurred the air seemed full of Paulding County mud within an area of five acres."[13]

Mr. Ryel recollected that, at the part of the reservoir bank that was destroyed, the difference in the water level from the canal to the reservoir was about nine feet.[14] When the water was released from Six Mile Reservoir, it was described by Dynamiters later interviewed by Otto E. Ehrhart as being "knee-deep to the horses."[15] North G. Osborn, the son of the *Antwerp Argus'* editor, later claimed that he could "see that huge wall of water pouring through the those big gaps in the bank, and rushing down the old canal, which seemed at times inadequate to hold back the surging rush of the flood... for once that old water artery sure did have an abundance of water."[16]

Mr. Ryel implied in his recollection years later that the torrent of rushing water from the reservoir did not escape from the canal,[17] however, his contemporaries a couple of decades later

---

§ The terms coal oil and kerosene seem to be used interchangeably.

gave Mr. Ehrhart the impression that the escaping water was not entirely contained by the canal, and some water was escaping into the countryside. [18] In relation to this, two newspapers, neither local, reported that a family (presumably with the surname Vermillion[¶]) that was living near the canal was driven from their home due to the whole ordeal.[19]

The *Quincy Daily Journal* of Quincy, Illinois, and the *Decatur Daily Review* of Decatur, Illinois printed the same exact story, which reported the attack "obliged [the family] to hurry to the woods to save their lives. When they returned, their home was flooded with water and everything ruined." [20] The *New York Tribune* reported that "the water surrounded his house" and that his "wife and baby suffered from the cold in the woods until morning."[21] Mr. Ryel corroborates part of this story, stating that a family was indeed "living just north" of the reservoir and that they were "immediately notified to move which they did in a hurry."[22] However, given the conflicting reports about whether water ever escaped from the canal into the countryside, it is hard to deduce whether the home was actually flooded.

While the work was being done at the reservoir, Mr. Applegate and Mr. Sperry led a group further down the canal to Tate's

---

¶ C. M. Vermillion was the lockkeeper at the "Junction" lock, which was One-Mile Lock, and nowhere near the reservoir where this reportedly happened.
(State of Ohio, *Executive Documents: Annual Reports for 1887, Made to the Sixty-Eighth General Assembly*, Part I, 1240.)

Landing.[¶§] At approximately midnight, two fifty-pound dynamite charges were detonated to destroy the gates of Tate's Lock after it was also doused in kerosene or coal oil and burned.[23] As a result of the explosions, several panes of glass were blown out of the windows at the nearby saloon owned by Joseph Reiniche.[24] After the explosion, an unknown citizen, possibly Mr. Reiniche himself (who also happened to be the lockkeeper for the lock that was just destroyed[25]) or possibly more guards, then fired "a couple shots" at the Dynamiters.[26] No Dynamiters were hit, and the Dynamiters reportedly returned two shots, which also missed their mark, and nobody was hurt in the altercation.[27]

---

¶ ADJ GEN Henry A. Axline later stated the Dynamiters had "perfected a system of light signals that extended along the canal for five or six miles." What he probably meant by this was a series of men who stood along the canal towpath with lanterns and conveyed coded messages. Such a system would have probably only extended as far as Tate's Landing from the reservoir by his mileage estimation. However, the existence of such a system is open to debate as this interview in the *Cincinnati Commercial Gazette* is the only time it was ever mentioned. ("The Reservoir Row," *Cincinnati Commercial Gazette*, April 30, 1887, 5.)

§ This note is mostly arguing about semantics as the result in either case was ultimately the same. Depending on what contemporary source is referenced, the Dynamiters either went from the reservoir straight to One-Mile Lock and attacked Tate's Lock on the way back to the reservoir, or they attacked Tate's Lock on the way to One-Mile Lock and made great haste back to the reservoir from there. I find the latter more realistic, because, while coordinated, I find it hard to believe the Dynamiters would have passed up the opportunity to attack Tate's Lock on their way to One-Mile Lock while presumably still having the element of surprise. The timings presented by the *Cincinnati Weekly Enquirer* (which published this timeline) are also realistic given that the approximate time to walk between these locks would be about an hour and a half and about three hours to walk between the reservoir and One-Mile Lock.

After that skirmish, the Dynamiters escaped to the aptly named One-Mile Lock@ one mile west of Junction, where they captured two more guards, who put up no resistance. [28] At roughly 2 a.m.,[29] they dynamited the canal lock after dousing it with kerosene or coal oil and burned it,[30] destroying the gates with another two fifty-pound charges.[31] On their way to that lock, there were reports that the Dynamiters captured some errant timbermen heading back "to their shanties," the Dynamiters instead 'upgraded' their accommodations and "locked them up in an old house."[32]

From One-Mile Lock, the Dynamiters made haste back to the reservoir to regroup with the rest of the rioters. Upon arriving at the reservoir again, they helped cut the reservoir's banks until retreating to their homes around 5 a.m.,[33] releasing the captured guards before escaping. [34] It would only be another thirty minutes before news reached Paulding at about 5:30 a.m. that "the canal locks and State buildings were totally demolished last night by a large force of masked men."[35]

Two guards along the canal reportedly had a less than a stellar experience, one young man reportedly exclaiming seconds before capture, "'Oh! My God, my God, I want to see my ma right away!'" Another guard, in his effort at making a hasty retreat, allegedly suffered palpitations that caused him to faint and fall into the canal, to which the Dynamiters fished him out so he would not drown. There is a distinct possibility he faked the

---

@ One-Mile Lock was roughly located at the southwest corner of the intersection of State Route 111 and State Road 637 in Paulding County. (Bill Oeters et. al., *Taming the Swamp*, 33.)

ordeal as "his agonies ceased at daybreak when he was released."[36]

Later in the morning of April 26, 1887, Charles A. Flickinger reportedly received two "insulting telegrams from Antwerp, signed fictitiously... saying his guards had been killed, the canal wrecked, and he should come on the first train."[37] The report of dead guards was false, but Mr. Flickinger would not have known that at the time. What was true was that the canal was indeed damaged. The following is a flurry of telegrams on the morning and afternoon of April 26, 1887:

9:41 a.m., Governor Joseph B. Foraker received the following telegram from Edward Squire:

> On last night two hundred men marched on the canal in a body, captured the guards and held them in confinement until daylight. Worked all night on front and rear banks of the reservoir, cutting ground enough to let water out, poured coal oil on lock and keeper's house at reservoir and burned all up. One hundred more men went to Tate's and the remaining lock, and blew them up with dynamite. No locks remain on the Wabash canal. The destruction is complete, and mob law reigns supreme. People of Defiance and Paulding counties call on you to protect State property.[38]

9:41 a.m., Governor Foraker received the following telegram from Stephen F. Eagle:

> The mob has again destroyed the reservoir and three locks, besides destroying the lock-keeper's house at reservoir. This is fulfilling the mob's message. What protection can we expect?[39]

9:45 a.m., Governor Foraker received a frantic telegram from Mr. Flickinger:

> Report comes to me this morning that last night (mob) destroyed two locks, burned one and lock tender's home; also blew the banks of reservoir. Will proceed to repair. What can be done? Answer quick.[40]

10:28 a.m., Governor Foraker received the following telegram from Livingston B. Peaslee:

> The condition of affairs in Paulding County is deplorable. The rioting element seems to predominate, and effective measures should be used to preserve the State property and public peace.[41]

11:50 a.m., ADJ GEN Henry A. Axline (who was in Fostoria, Ohio at the time) received the following telegram from Governor Foraker:

> Telegrams from Defiance and Paulding report the aqueduct locks and other public property belonging to the canal destroyed last night by an armed body of rioters, who are reported to be still organized and making trouble and threatening violence. Take one company, whichever may be most convenient, and go immediately to the scene of trouble and there in aid of the civil authorities suppress all such demonstrations. If you need more help you will command it. Report to me promptly here. I will notify Flickinger of the Board of Public Works of your coming.[42]

12:35 p.m., ADJ GEN Axline received the following telegram from Governor Foraker:

> So far as the State property is concerned, protect that. Aid the State authorities in control of it without regard to the civil authorities. Report promptly and fully.[43]

12:39 p.m., Governor Foraker received the following telegram from ADJ GEN Axline:

> Dispatch received. Have ordered company at Toledo to assemble at once and await orders. Will go to Toledo on one-forty-five train and take company to Paulding or where needed. Will report from time to time.[44]

1:20 p.m., MAJ Henry S. Bunker received the following telegram from ADJ GEN Axline:

> Assemble about fifty men from Toledo companies of Sixteenth Regiment as quickly as possible for duty in Paulding County and await further orders. I will arrive at Toledo on three-five Hocking Valley this afternoon. Meet me at train. Acknowledge receipt of this order.[45]

Unknown time, MAJ Bunker acknowledged ADJ GEN Axline's command with the following telegram:

> Order received. Will act at once.[46]

Unknown time, Governor Foraker sent the following telegrams to Mr. Flickinger:

> I have ordered Gen. Axline to go immediately to the scene of trouble with one company of the National Guard, to aid the civil authorities to suppress rioters, protect the property, and preserve the peace. Please have the Sheriff

of Paulding County make formal official demand on me for such help. Proceed immediately to make repairs of the property, and warn all disturbers of the peace that they interfere with you at their peril.[47]

In addition to all else ask for a special grand jury to indict the rioters and demand that the Paulding County officials do their duty and take prompt and vigorous measures to bring the guilty to justice. If any official hesitates to do his duty inform me at once.[48]

Have rioters arrested as fast as you can determine who they are. If Prosecuting Attorney does not willingly serve to employ special counsel and swear out warrants before justice of the peace. Don't do anything else but follow this matter up until the last man is brought to punishment. Spare neither time, money, nor trouble.[49]

Unknown time, Governor Foraker sent the following telegram to Stephen F. Eagle:

I have ordered Gen. Axline to go immediately to the scene of action with one company, and as many others as he may need to suppress the mob, protect the property and preserve the public peace, and have instructed Mr. Flickinger, of the Board of Public Works, to proceed immediately to repair the damage that has been done. The property of the State, and all law-abiding citizens will be fully protected, and every man who acts with or gives aid or comfort to the mob will do so at his peril. The law will be fully enforced to its extremist limit against all such. Keep me fully advised.[50]

2:12 p.m., Governor Foraker received the following telegram from Mr. Flickinger:

Sheriff Parr, of Paulding County, will be in Columbus with convict to-night; will call on you to-morrow. He will hesitate to ask you for assistance because of the public sentiment in his county. He has thus far made no effort to protect State property to my knowledge, although have made formal application to him to do so. Perhaps he will ask you for assistance when he meets you to-morrow. I have wired the members of the Board and the Chief Engineer to come here at once.[51]

4:35 p.m., Governor Foraker received the following telegram from ADJ GEN Axline:

Will leave via Wabash road at 5:20 with about fifty men and one gatling. Will go direct to Cecil unless directed otherwise by Flickinger, whom I have wired at Defiance for information.[52]

Appx. 4:35 p.m., COL[§] Flickinger received the following telegram from ADJ GEN Axline:

Where do you want company? Will be on Wabash train, forty-three, this evening with troops. Answer, care of conductor of that train.[53]

5:16 p.m., ADJ GEN Axline received the following telegram from COL Flickinger:

Leave troops at Cecil. Will meet them at Defiance.[54]

Although Governor Foraker might have been reluctant to act when first requested to send the Ohio National Guard by Mr. Flickinger, this latest attack signaled that lightly armed (if at all), possibly untrained, and undisciplined civilian guards would not be enough to dissuade further attacks on the canal works. Mr.

---

§ I do not know what the deal is with Mr. Flickinger suddenly being referred to as a colonel. The only thing I can suppose is being the President of the Board of Public Works, he was given the honorary title 'Colonel' by Governor Foraker.

Flickinger had his request for a military presence granted, and troops would be in Paulding County within the day.

Despite the telegrams never mentioning it, reports abounded that ADJ GEN Axline was initially going to take Company F in Napoleon, Henry County, Ohio, but decided the companies in Toledo, Ohio would do better. However, he ordered CPT Charles E. Reynolds in Napoleon, and every regiment in Northwest (and possibly all of) Ohio, to be ready to move to Paulding County upon request.[55]

As soon as he received the orders at 1:20 p.m., MAJ Bunker immediately "issued written orders" to the commanders of Co. A, C, and H to prepare their troops accordingly and report to the armory@ by 4 p.m., ready for deployment.[56] Those written orders were delivered by ADJ Isaac T. P. Merrill and SGM Carl H. Beckham.[57] At roughly 4 p.m., MAJ Bunker and ADJ GEN Axline arrived at the armory to find "more than fifty men already assembled and ready for duty."[58]

ADJ GEN Axline initially asked for "about fifty men" from Toledo's Company A, C, and H.[59] He also requested a "sufficient number of men necessary to man one Gatling section" from Light Battery D.[60] This gun detachment (or Gatling section as ADJ GEN Axline refers to it) would have "ordinarily" consisted of at least one sergeant, two corporals, and seven privates.[61] In total, fifty-seven enlisted men and eight officers [62] boarded Wabash Train No. 43 and departed for Cecil at 5:20 p.m.[63]

---

@ The armory in Toledo, which doubled as the Soldiers Memorial Hall, was located on the southwest corner of Adams Street and Ontario Street, across from the Lucas County Courthouse.
(Henry Howe, *Historical Collections of Ohio in Three Volumes*, Volume II, 414; Ancestry.com, *Toledo, OH City Directories for 1886 and 1887.*

The troop train briefly stopped in Defiance,@ where "a large concourse of people gathered to witness this novel sight." [64] Those in Defiance also reportedly greeted the soldier's presence "with cheers." [65] Mr. Flickinger reportedly boarded the train bound for Cecil to "personally oversee the work of repairing."[66] The soldiers were also allegedly informed that Paulding County was "in arms," and some of the soldiers reportedly loaded their guns in preparation for a battle upon their arrival at Cecil.[67]

The Toledo correspondent for the *Cincinnati Commercial Gazette* reported that "masked bands of men have paraded the country about Antwerp for two or three days past," with one alleged instance where "an effigy of Mr. Flickinger" was carried through Antwerp to the jubilation of those who saw it. [68] Unsurprisingly, there is no report of this from any local papers. Such rumors could have made their way to the soldiers in Defiance, who, understandably, might have become fearful that they would find no allies amongst the people of Paulding County.

The Ohio National Guard arrived in Cecil sometime around 8 p.m. with a strength of roughly "sixty officers and men."[69] They unloaded themselves and their "tents, camping utensils, and a Gatling gun." [70] At once, the soldiers marched to Cecil's town hall,@@ "where guns were stacked and a sufficient guard placed

---

@ The Wabash's depot in Defiance was located on the east side of the railroad's tracks just south of 5th Street between Harrison Street and Jackson Street.
(*Sanborn Fire Insurance Map from Defiance, Defiance County, Ohio*, August 1888.)

@@ Cecil's town hall was located just north of 1st Street on the east side of Main Street.
(Ohio Historic Preservation Office, *Ohio Historic Inventory: Pau-116-2 (Cecil Town Hall)*, Prepared in November 1979.)

over them until the men could eat their suppers."[71] The Gatling gun was placed in the front yard of the Mackinaw Hotel,@ where it was also "properly guarded."[72]¶

The infantry's guns were .45-70 Springfield Breech Loading 'Trapdoor' Rifles.[73] For those rifles, the infantry were reportedly equipped with bayonets and 2,000 rounds of ammunition.[74] Light Battery D's Gatling gun was a model 1883 with an Accles positive feed-drum.[75] This gun also used .45-70 ammunition,[76] of which Light Battery D reportedly brought 4,500 of them, likely because the gun was said to be capable of firing 1,200 rounds *per minute*.[77] Evidently, Light Battery D was not expecting to use the Gatling gun too much, as this theoretically gave them less than four minutes of sustained fire from the gun.

ADJ GEN Axline was initially joined by at least nine other officers. When including ADJ GEN Axline, that makes ten officers present initially.[78] The *Executive Documents Annual Reports for 1887 Made to the Sixty-Eighth General Assembly* reports that thirteen total officers would be present.[79] That report states that

---

@ The Mackinaw Hotel in Cecil was located on the southeast corner of 2nd Street and Main Street.
(Ohio Historic Preservation Office, *Ohio Historic Inventory: Pau-114-2 (Mackinaw House)*, Prepared in November 1979.

¶ Major Bunker's report mentions that the Gatling gun was placed in front of the "Chester House." Oscar B. Chesbrough was the proprietor of what was known as the Mackinaw House, but it had also been referred to as the Chesbrough House. It is not much of a stretch to infer that Major Bunker misremembered the name as Chester rather than Chesbrough.
(State of Ohio, *Executive Documents: Annual Reports for 1887 Made to the Sixty-Eighth General Assembly*, Part II, 695; *Paulding Democrat*, January 6, 1887, 5; "Local Brevities," *Paulding County Gazette*, January 6, 1887, 1.)

ADJ Merrill, SGM Beckham, and COMSY SERG Charles G. DeShon were present, thus making thirteen.[80]

By Wednesday evening, eighty soldiers[81] from Ohio National Guard Companies A (Walbridge Light Guards), C (Toledo Grays), and H (Milburn Guards) of the 16th Infantry Regiment, as well as Light Battery D (Toledo Light Artillery) of the 1st Regiment Light Artillery would be in Paulding County.[82] By the end of the conflict, the total number of troops in Paulding County would max out at 118 soldiers (105 enlisted men, thirteen officers).[83¶] However, the average strength for the entire duration was seventy-seven total men, of which ten were officers and sixty-seven were enlisted men.[84]

| Organization | Officers | Enlisted Men | Total |
|---|---|---|---|
| Field Staff | 3 | 2 | 5 |
| Company A | 3 | 32 | 35 |
| Company C | 2 | 26 | 28 |
| Company H | 2 | 32 | 34 |
| Light Battery D | 3 | 13 | 16 |
| Total | 13 | 105 | 118 |

Source: State of Ohio, *Executive Documents: Annual Reports for 1887 Made to the Sixty-Eighth General Assembly*, Part II, 697.

When the troops arrived in Cecil and found no enemy or active rebellion in that town, the troops not actively guarding laid down their arms and began to "mingle" with the locals and

¶ For a roster of soldiers who could have been present in Paulding County, see Appendix B.

"engaged in friendly chat over the affair." [85] ¶ However, the people of Cecil were not entirely thrilled with the military display in their town, reportedly complaining about their presence and inquiring why they had not set up headquarters in Antwerp instead. [86] The Toledo correspondent for the *Cincinnati Commercial Gazette* noted, "the inhabitants wished to have nothing to do with the invaders." [87] In contrast, the same correspondent remarked that the people in Antwerp were "greatly excited over the arrival of the troops."[88] However, many citizens also reportedly considered the deployment of the soldiers to Paulding County as a "flagrant outrage"[89] and even "child's play."[90]

A guard from the reservoir, who had been captured and released the night prior, was quick to inform the authorities arriving in Cecil that "four heavy explosions" had taken place since the initial attack.[91] The correspondent for the *Cincinnati Weekly Enquirer* further stated "the Dynamiters are only seeking to destroy the banks," indicating that the Dynamiters had no intentions of fighting the Ohio National Guard directly.[92] The Toledo correspondent for the *Cincinnati Commercial Gazette* echoed this report that the Dynamiters would not fight the

---

¶ There was a report that "drunkenness" became prevalent amongst the Guardsmen after their arrival in Cecil. One saloon owner reportedly claimed he was able to sell "twenty-five kegs of beer to the boys, which is more than his total sales for the past six weeks." ADJ GEN Axline denied such allegations, stating he was "present with the troops" and "no body of men ever conducted themselves in a more becoming manner or observed better discipline than those Toledo soldiers, for every man is a gentleman and acted as such."
("War on the Wabash," *Cincinnati Commercial Gazette*, April 28, 1887, 1; "The Reservoir Row," *Cincinnati Commercial Gazette*, April 30, 1887, 5.)

troops directly. [93] The *Maysville Daily Evening Bulletin* of Maysville, Kentucky, through the correspondent for the United Press present in Antwerp, reported that eight individuals had detonated eight dynamite charges before the arrival of the Ohio National Guard. They also reported that the Dynamiters were only interested in destroying the reservoir and "will not fight the militia."[94]

After receiving more reports of Dynamiters attacking the reservoir from COL Flickinger,[95] ADJ GEN Axline immediately led a platoon of twenty[96] to twenty-six[97] enlists alongside MAJ Bunker, CPT Weir, 1LT William H. Moore, ADJ Merrill, and SGM Beckham[98] to "'the extreme front.'"[99] The march to the reservoir began around 9 p.m.[100] It was an arduous march for the soldiers, as recent "inclement weather"[101] had left the towpath "fearfully muddy."[102] The night was described as "dark as Erebus,"[103] and was reportedly so silent that there was "not a sound to break the silence that brooded over swamp and forest."[104] Except, of course, the sounds of what were possibly "signal guns" which were "fired afar on the other side of the canal" to warn the Dynamiters of the approaching troops. Though these were likely small dynamite explosions.[105]

Upon their arrival at the reservoir around midnight, the platoon encountered no resistance and fired no shots; the Dynamiters had dispersed before their arrival, and the troops never saw a soul.[106] All that was found was the blown-up and burned canal lock, the lock keeper's house burned to ashes, and a "wide cut in the levee of the reservoir which the water was rushing with great force and noise into the canal."[107] The gap in one of the reservoir banks having been widened to about thirty feet and was ten feet deep.[108]

ADJ GEN Axline, "finding nothing at the reservoir requiring our immediate attention," ordered the platoon to return to Cecil.[109] Upon arriving in Cecil at roughly 2:30 a.m., MAJ Bunker observed that the platoon had "within about twelve hours... travelled sixty-four miles by rail and marched a distance of fourteen miles over very rough roads and in intense darkness."[110] MAJ Bunker then ordered ACT QM 2LT Edward W. Rydman to have prepared a "good substantial supper" for the returning men, who, understandably, were described as being "tired," and having "sore" feet. After taking in the food "with a keen relish," the soldiers called it a night.[111] Two soldiers would "be overcome by the march to the reservoir and back, and were sent home" on the morning of April 27, 1887.[112]

Sometime after the arrival of the troops at 8 p.m., but before 11 p.m.,§ a shot rang out in downtown Cecil near town hall, where the troops were quartering for the evening.¶@ What could have only been a moment of panic as the soldiers checked their surroundings and determined if they had come under fire. It was

---

§ MAJ Bunker's report in *Executive Documents Annual Reports for 1887 Made to the Sixty-Eighth General Assembly* seems to imply it happened around arrival at 8 p.m., but most reports by area newspapers and historians put it between 9 p.m. and 11 p.m.

¶@ Troops also reportedly quartered in the passenger room of the Wabash's depot in Cecil. The depot was on the north side of the Wabash's tracks and west of where the CJ&M tracks were to be laid starting in the summer of 1887.
("War on the Wabash," *Cincinnati Commercial Gazette*, April 28, 1887, 1; "Paulding County," *Ohio Railroad Stations Past & Present*, https://www.west2k.com/ohpix/cecil.jpg; "Mackinaw Notes," *Paulding County Gazette*, May 26, 1887, 5; "Local Gossip," *Paulding Democrat*, June 30, 1887, 5.)

discovered that eighteen-year-old PVT Frederick L. Reeves, a soldier in Company H who was as green as they come, having just turned eighteen on April 8, 1887,[113]¶ and had only just enrolled and mustered into Company H five days earlier, on April 21, 1887,[114] had been shot dead.[115]

What exactly happened to PVT Reeves is purely conjecture. The least probable possibility is that PVT Reeves was shot by a comrade fooling around with their weapon. This is an unlikely scenario not only because the only newspapers that claim this were not local,[116] but the only evidence for this claim came from a likely misprinted quote from a telegram sent by ADJ GEN Axline to Governor Foraker. The quote in the *Cincinnati Commercial Gazette* stated he messaged, "Soldiers accidentally killed a guard last night."[117] While the official transcript in the *Annual Reports for 1887* reports that the telegram stated, "Soldier accidentally killed on guard last night."[118]

Those non-local papers further insinuated that PVT Reeves was shot by someone else by also claiming that a post-mortem report stated that the bullet entered his neck "four inches below the left ear and emerged in the right side an inch below the entrance point." [119] A downward trajectory would have only reasonably occurred from somebody standing and pointing the gun slightly above PVT Reeves, almost requiring the shooter to

---

¶ It was unanimously reported that PVT Reeves was nineteen at the time of his death, likely based on his death record reporting he died at 19 years 1 month and 18 days, thus making his birthday March 8, 1868. However, based on his actual birth record, his birthday was April 8, 1869, thus he had only just turned eighteen in 1887.
("Ohio, County Death Records, 1840-2001," *FamilySearch*, accessed
      August 29, 2022, Lucas, Death records, 1868-1888, Image 472
      of 546; "Michigan, County Births, 1867-1917," *FamilySearch*,
      accessed August 29, 2022, Births 1869-1871, Image 12 of 157.)

be standing on stairs, or PVT Reeves had stooped down for a moment before the weapon discharged. The *Cincinnati Commercial Gazette* also acknowledged this claim but believed it was "difficult to account for the bullet ranging downward if Reeves shot himself." Asserting that the doctors were probably mistaken in their observation, as "the verbal testimony of those who were present was that Reeves' gun was empty and still smoking when it was picked up."[120]

Whatever the case may be, the bullet most likely entered the left side§ of his neck below the ear (one report says it first entered the collarbone on the same side[121]) and exited at the base of his brain, severing his jugular vein on the way and causing mortal damage otherwise.[122] The overwhelming majority of reports indicate he was killed instantly.[123] Only the *Antwerp Argus* and *Cincinnati Commercial Gazette* indicate that he may have suffered a short time.[124]

MAJ Bunker's report and the Toledo correspondent to the *Cincinnati Commercial Gazette*'s reported that, while leaning on his weapon during guard duty, the weapon was accidentally discharged.[125] The Toledo correspondent to the *Cincinnati Commercial Gazette* further specified that PVT Reeves "accidentally struck the hammer, causing the discharge."[126] This is an implausible explanation, for the most part. Based on the reports of prematurely loaded weapons and one report where he may have loaded the weapon himself "against orders."[127] It is

---

§ It is possible that the reverse is true, and the shot entered the right side and exited the left. However, most of the reports indicate the shot entered the left side and exited the right side.
("The Only Victim of the War," *Cincinnati Commercial Gazette*, April 30, 1887, 5.)

reasonable to assume that the gun's hammer may have been in the full-cock position sufficient to fire the weapon rather than the half-cocked position required to load the weapon. Whatever the case, it would typically require a great deal of force from bumping the weapon into something or dropping it to move the sear enough to accidentally discharge the weapon. This would be unlikely from a standing position while leaning on the gun allegedly "laughing and talking."[128]

What is more likely the case is that PVT Reeves, upon returning from supper with other soldiers at the Mackinaw Hotel to begin guard duty,[129] "clumsily" picked up a gun "he did not know was loaded" and accidentally shot himself.[130] This explanation is entirely plausible given the reports of preemptively loaded weapons which made it possible that he unwittingly grabbed a loaded and cocked weapon. When PVT Reeves went to pull the gun toward him (assuming the barrel was facing the sky), the trigger possibly caught on another gun's hammer or some other fixed object. Because he was newly enlisted and possibly inadequately trained, PVT Reeves could have unwittingly applied sufficient force to the trigger to discharge the weapon while clumsily attempting to dislodge the weapon from being stuck.

In a similar vein, another report states while on guard duty, PVT Reeves, "while mischievously fooling with his musket in careless sport," shot himself.[131] This could also be plausible because he was a new recruit who may not have been adequately trained and possibly lacked discipline. That said, this scenario does still require the assumption that PVT Reeves either dropped or bumped the weapon with enough force to jar the sear, which has already been established as possible but unlikely; or caught the weapon's trigger on something which applied sufficient pressure to fire the weapon. Both assumptions also require that the weapon needed to be pointed upwards to account for the reported trajectory of the bullet wound.

However it happened, the Reservoir War had its first, and ultimately only fatality. The *Paulding County Gazette* lamented that "cruel war, however small its magnitude, ever has its victims."[132] CPT Alpheus R. Rogers, PVT Reeves' superior officer, "telegraphed for a casket," and on the morning of April 27, 1887, PVT Reeves' body, guarded by an unnamed corporal and two other soldiers (likely those two who were reportedly overcome by the march the night prior), was taken to his family in Toledo for burial sometime before 7:36 a.m.[133] In his debriefing report after the Reservoir War, MAJ Bunker would later inform ADJ GEN Axline that PVT Reeves' mother was "a widow in poor circumstances financially, and was largely dependent upon her son for support." [134] He humbly requested that the next legislative session "make suitable appropriation for her relief."[135]¶

At noon on April 27, 1887, ADJ GEN Axline and MAJ Bunker began to march the troops to Six Mile Reservoir, where they were to set up camp for the foreseeable future.[136] A "small guard under the command of Captain Rogers" was kept in Cecil to protect the

---

¶ Though it would not happen in 1888, PVT Reeves' mother, Adelia S. Kelsey, would receive $200 (~$6,274 in 2023) in January 1889 to compensate for her lost son.

("House in Detail," *Cincinnati Enquirer*, January 16, 1889, 2; State of Ohio, *General and Local Acts Passed and Joint Resolutions Adopted by the Sixty-Eighth General Assembly*, Volume LXXXVI, 99.)

National Guard's supplies.[137] Once at the reservoir, the National Guard began to set up their tents "in an open field just north of the reservoir lock"[138] and positioned their Gatling gun, which was reportedly placed in such a way as to be able to "rake the north bank and east bank."[139]

Everett A. Budd posited that such positioning of the Gatling gun could have also made attacks by "gunboat" harder, as the Gatling gun could also be fired down on the canal.[140] As expected, guards were posted "at all proper places along the banks of the reservoir and in rear of our camp." A "countersign was given out at night," and "picket posts" were also established to give advance warning of any approaching Dynamiters.[141]

While the "Army life in all its romantic grandeur" was taking place with the soldiers eating "fresh bread and other rations" and "jollity abounded in the camp;"[142] It became apparent that they did not have enough coats and blankets at the camp. At about 9:50 a.m. on April 27, 1887,[143] ADJ GEN Axline telegraphed 1LT Henry A. Guitner, Superintendent of the State Arsenal, asking for "forty overcoats and fifty blankets." At 10:21 a.m., ADJ GEN Axline was informed that his requested overcoats and blankets were on a train that had left Toledo at 10:20 a.m.[144]

SURG MAJ Dr. Thomas J. Cronise would later state that the weather was "cold, rainy, and very windy" for the first week, thus necessitating "good fire... be kept burning day and night." [145] It did warm up during the last few days, and "occasional rains" had fallen, but in general, the campgrounds remained in "good condition" during the National Guard's deployment.[146] Regarding the health of the camp, aside from one soldier who was "excused from duty for one day," the troops were healthy. [147] Dr. Cronise attributed this to having a "good cook" on staff during the deployment, as well as having "good" water and "excellent" rations. However, he did inform MAJ Bunker that every soldier ought to be "furnished with a blanket, poncho, knapsack, canteen, and in fact, all the appurtenances of a soldier."[148] Despite the request for more coats and blankets, Dr. Cronise reported that "a number of soldiers, not having blankets, suffered from cold." Never mind that some soldiers did not have their own canteen to drink from.[149]

Unsurprisingly, the presence of the National Guard in the county attracted many area citizens to the camp, gathering near the lock while the troops were in the process of setting up "taking in the sights and discussing the situation." [150] While these citizens were nearby, Sheriff David W. Parr read Governor Foraker's proclamation either on his own accord or at the request of MAJ Bunker, the latter of which told the gathered citizens to leave immediately. [151] The following is the proclamation that was recited:

> Whereas, it has been reported to me that on the night of the 25th inst an armed mob of lawless and rioting men drove away from the public works of the State in Paulding County the guards who were in possession of the same and with dynamite blew up certain locks of the canal, and with powder and fire destroyed others and otherwise by cutting the banks of the canal and reservoir, did great damage and injury thereto and,
>
> Whereas, this armed and lawless mob are reported to be still banded together for the purpose of preventing the State authorities from again taking possession and control of the property so wrongfully wrestled from them and threaten by violence to prohibit the repair of the damage so as aforesaid inflicted by them

And, whereas, the civil authorities of Paulding County appear to be either unable or unwilling to suppress said rioters and protect the authorities of the State in resuming control of the property of the State and making repairs thereof, and appear to be either unable or unwilling to disperse said mob and preserve the public peace

Now, therefore, I, Joseph B. Foraker, Governor of the State of Ohio, do hereby call upon said rioters and evil disposed persons to desist at once from their unlawful actions and to disperse immediately to their homes, and I hereby warn them, failing to do so they will be immediately compelled to such a course so far as the protection, repair, and preservation of the public property of the State is concerned. All persons failing to observe and comply with the commands hereof will do so at their peril.

In testimony whereof I have herein subscribed my name and caused to be affixed the great seal of the State, at Columbus this 26th day of April, in the year of our Lord, 1887.[152]

Having finished the speech in an "ordinary tone of voice," Sheriff Parr attracted the scrutiny of MAJ Bunker, who was dissatisfied with the lack of volume in Sheriff Parr's voice, calling it "rather poor."[153] MAJ Bunker then proceeded to loudly recite the proclamation "in a tone which he no doubt thought would strike terror to the hearts of the natives, bull frogs, and all." [154] After this, any citizens who had not already started walking to their homes did so, as MAJ Bunker described his order being followed with "alacrity."[155]

While Mr. Flickinger had initially gone to Paulding County on April 26, 1887, his venturing to the area might have been premature. Having spoken to a correspondent for the *Cincinnati*

*Weekly Enquirer*, he noted that he had made an "attempt to estimate the damage" that night, but "nothing definite could be had until the engineer had gone over the work." Nevertheless, he would do as the Governor ordered him and prepare to rebuild the damaged structures.[156] On the morning of April 27, 1887, Chief Engineer Samuel Bachtell and Canal Division Superintendent Homer Meacham met with Mr. Flickinger and William H. Hahn in Defiance. They proceeded to Six Mile Reservoir at noon the same day, taking "printed copies of the Governor's proclamation to post up."[157]

When the group arrived in Paulding County, Thomas Thompson and Charles Decker, the two guards captured in Junction two nights prior, reported to Mr. Hahn (and presumably the others) that Henry W. Sperry had been one of the men who had captured them. Upon this revelation, Sheriff Parr was promptly ordered, by Mr. Hahn, to place Mr. Sperry under arrest immediately.[158] Sheriff Parr had been posting notices of a "$200 (~$6,274 in 2023) reward for the arrest and conviction" (Mr. Flickinger had reportedly offered $250 (~$7,842 in 2023) for the same[159]) of any Dynamiter.[160] Upon getting word of the order, he successfully arrested Mr. Sperry in Antwerp that afternoon.[161]

Mr. Hahn then instructed Sheriff Parr to bring Mr. Sperry before Justice of the Peace Hubert Naveau, Jr. in Junction,[162] the Justice of the Peace for Auglaize Township. The *Antwerp Argus* believed this was done specifically to have Mr. Sperry appear before a "Defiance sympathetic Justice."[163] Realistically, taking Mr. Sperry to Junction was likely necessary as he probably needed to stand before the Justice of the Peace of the township where the crime was allegedly committed. Nevertheless, Sheriff Parr "objected" to this order,[164] as he may have believed the proper action was to first take Mr. Sperry before the Justice of the Peace of the township where he was arrested, which would have been Charles S. Carpenter in Antwerp.[165] Sheriff Parr was then informed by Mr. Hahn that if Mr. Sperry was not taken to Junction by Sheriff Parr, the State authorities would do it for him.[166] With that threat, Sheriff Parr acquiesced and escorted Mr. Sperry to Junction.[167]

At the preliminary hearing, Kidder V. Haymaker of Defiance was the prosecuting attorney for the State of Ohio, and Mr. Sperry's defense attorney was Charles A. Seiders of Paulding.[168] Mr. Thompson and Mr. Decker testified that "Sperry was one of the men who stood guard over them at Junction while the lock was being destroyed." When pressed on how they could be sure it was Mr. Sperry, they both responded by noting they recognized him by not only his clothing, but when Mr. Sperry got careless and failed to wear his mask properly,[169] a distinctive piece of dental prosthesis became visible, a gold tooth.[170]

Mr. Sperry was charged with "disarming a guard,"[171] and his bail was set at $500 (~$14,797 in 2023).[172] Sheriff Parr was to take him to the Paulding Jail@ immediately.[173] However, on the way to Paulding, Sheriff Parr encountered a group of Antwerp citizens who "accompanied the Sheriff to Paulding;" where the group of men promptly posted bail for Mr. Sperry upon being

---

@ The Paulding Jail is still standing in 2023. It is located just south of Courthouse Square on the northwest corner of Williams Street and Harrison Street. As of 2023, it is a paranormal activity attraction.
(*Sanborn Fire Insurance Map from Paulding, Paulding County, Ohio,* June 1895.)

booked into the jail, and he was dutifully released from custody.[174] As legend has it, so many people chipped in to post bail that the "bond was insufficient in size to hold all the names of the citizens from [Antwerp]" who wanted to "place their names on the bond for his release."[175]

On April 28, 1887, while the news was just breaking in weekly local and state newspapers, the news of the Reservoir War had already reached locations as far east as Maine,[176] as far west as Los Angeles,[177] and just about everywhere in-between.§ Back in Paulding County, a team ranging from fifteen to fifty men, supervised by Mr. Meacham, began repairing the banks of Six Mile Reservoir that afternoon.[178] Later that evening, ADJ GEN Axline left for Columbus to "report particulars" directly to Governor Foraker,[179] and MAJ Bunker and CPT Owen J. Hopkins left for Toledo.[180] Despite what seemed like significant officers leaving, if only temporarily, Camp Dynamite/Reservoir still had at least six officers present. ADJ GEN Axline also informed Governor Foraker by telegram, "everything quiet; property well guarded,"[181] implying that his presence in Paulding County was not necessarily needed at the time.

ADJ GEN Axline informed Governor Foraker that he would arrive in Columbus sometime around 2 p.m. on April 29, 1887.[182] By that same evening, water was no longer escaping from the reservoir. COL Flickinger telegraphed Governor Foraker, "cut closed," and he expected to have the repairs completed in another twenty days after giving it his "personal attention."[183]

---

§ I encourage readers to look at their local newspaper archives and see if any mention the Reservoir either in detail or in passing. Just from a cursory look, about every state seems to have at least one newspaper that ran an article talking about it.

The reservoir had "lowered about ten inches" but was not completely drained. The damage was estimated at $10,000 (~$313,695 in 2023) [184] but could have reached upwards of $20,000 (~$627,389 in 2023).[185]

COL Flickinger also informed Governor Foraker that same evening that "everything [is] quiet and working well." ADJ GEN Axline informed COL Flickinger that the National Guard "cannot be retained here unless matters are pressed vigorously," informing COL Flickinger that the "Governor directs that your board act promptly." [186] Despite being asked to respond "immediately," COL Flickinger seemingly did not respond until May 2, 1887, assuring ADJ GEN Axline that the "matters are pushed with vigor," and that he should "come down on [the] first train." [187] This request was apparently ignored, as COL Flickinger sent a more desperate sounding telegram a little less than two hours later stating "I wish you to come down. Please answer."[188] That telegram was also seemingly ignored.

PVT Reeves was also interred on April 29, 1887, at Forest Cemetery in Toledo, Ohio. While BG Patrick S. Slevin, chaplain of the 16th Infantry Regiment, delivered the sermon, CPT William V. McMaken and fifty-five other soldiers served as honor guards. A twenty-one-gun salute was performed by "a squad of cadets," and the music was "furnished by The Great Western Band."[189]

Nothing of significance occurred on April 30, 1887, beyond the sentinels of the Ohio National Guard turning away a Mr. Delong from Harrison Township. Not having been aware of the military presence in the county and having a gun shouldered, he wandered onto the banks of Six Mile Reservoir. After being stopped by the National Guard, and possibly "imagined himself in rebeldom," Mr. Delong proceeded to leave the area immediately, without incident.[190]

Many citizens from throughout Paulding County again set off to visit Camp Dynamite/Reservoir on Sunday May 1, 1887.[191] Except, this time, they were not turned away. Some "gaily conversed and cracked jokes" with the troops stationed there.[192] The *Paulding County Gazette* described the first Sunday for the soldiers as having a morning filled with distant thunder, but the storms relented by the afternoon and "all the 'pomp and splendor of glorious war' was ushered in and became visible to the timid civilians" that had travelled to the camp.[193] Some took to admiring the Gatling gun mounted on the reservoir bank,[194] and "some Antwerp young ladies furnished music."[195]

Among those who went to the camp on Sunday was the Antwerp Presbyterian Church's The Reverend James W. McClusky. The Rev. McClusky "conducted religious services" for the soldiers[196] and reportedly "delivered a short address."[197] That address was not reported in the newspapers, but Everett A. Budd would later claim that the Rev. McClusky said the following: "The sword of Foraker be upon us, and the roaring of mighty water is heard throughout the land, and groans and lamentations riseth up from the city of Defiance; but the reservoir must go."[198] The *Paulding County Gazette* reported that the command and officers were "perfect gentlemen" and the enlisted soldiers were "mostly young and this was the first 'service' they had seen."[199] ADJ GEN Axline returned from Columbus to Camp Dynamite/Reservoir around 4 p.m. on May 1, 1887.[200]

The statement about the Reservoir War being most of the soldiers' first active service is not an exaggeration. While the Reservoir War was not the first time Company A, C, H, and Light Battery D were deployed against citizens in Ohio, the most recent deployment for Company A, C, and H was to help quell the Cincinnati Riots of 1884.[201] Light Battery D itself had not been deployed for any notable reason since the Great Railroad Strike of 1877, which Company A and C were also present for.[202] Only about 42 of the roughly 187[§] possible soldiers (excluding officers) present at the Reservoir War could have participated in the events at Cincinnati in 1884, and all of them came from Company A, C, and H. No enlisted soldiers (excluding officers) present at the Reservoir War had enlisted prior to 1880 and therefore could not have been present for the Great Railroad Strike of 1877 mission.[203]

The most experienced unit was Company C, which had also been deployed to Bowling Green, Ohio in 1883 to "aid civil authorities" in keeping the peace at the public execution of murderer Carl Bach. [204][§§] Even still, only about half of those enlisted in Company C in 1887 could have been present at Bowling Green.[205] Company H was the least experienced unit, having only seen action at the Cincinnati Riots in 1884, to which only about one quarter of those enlisted were possibly present for that mission.[206]

---

§ Only 105 of those roughly 187 men were present in Paulding County for the Reservoir War.

§§ If you wish to learn more about Carl Bach and his murdering of his wife Mary, you can visit the Wood County Museum in Bowling Green, Ohio to see their exhibit *The Mary & Carl Bach Story*.

Despite the weather and issues with lack of certain supplies mentioned earlier, life in the camp was reported to be hospitable. When CPT James R. Wade went to Toledo on May 3, 1887, he reported that "he had such a jolly good time at the camp, which is well located and healthy... All the boys are having a good time and nothing to do except guard the reservoir, which is not trying to get away."[207] The *Paulding County Gazette* also reported that the "boys seemed to enjoy it hugely... and jollity abounded in the camp." Food and other necessities were also never in short supply, as they were amply supplied by towns in the vicinity of the camp.[208]

CPT Wade also reported that "the citizens of Antwerp are anxious to give the boys in blue a banquet."[209] Indeed, as the *Paulding County Gazette* reported, "the boys have been invited to come and pitch their tents near [Antwerp], which they have decided to do, providing their stay is prolonged any great time."[210] Two individuals from the Ohio National Guard had even visited Antwerp. The first was SURG MAJ Dr. Cronise, who reportedly had "many old comrades in town."[211] It can be presumed that these 'comrades' were, at least, Charles W. Boland, Joseph S. Champion, Sr., John B. Zuber, and Antwerp Mayor William F. Fleck, as they all served together in the 14th Ohio Volunteer Infantry during the Civil War, though in different companies.[212]

It is possible, but unlikely, that SURG MAJ Dr. Cronise could have also made the acquaintance of individuals such as Franz J. Zuber, Oliver S. Applegate, William E. Osborn, Henry Harris, and Jesse H. Bond during the Atlanta Campaign of the Civil War.[213] The second individual to visit Antwerp was 2LT George U. Roulet of Light Battery D, who visited Antwerp to "make the acquaintance of [Antwerp's] citizens" on May 2, 1887.[214]

However, life was not nearly as swell for some of the locals. Already mentioned was the case of Mr. Delong, who would "doubtless give [Antwerp] a wide berth until all differences are settled" after encountering the Ohio National Guard.[215] Judge Alexander S. Latty reportedly had much to say about the military presence in Paulding County, mainly because they were stationed on some of his lands. He had inadvertently found himself "ruthlessly ground between the evils of lawlessness on one hand and the almost equally disastrous evils of the means taken by the authorities to repair the damages and protect the public property on the other."[216]

Judge Latty even went so far as to suggest that the Dynamiters "did him less injury than the State is doing for it is occupying and crossing his fields, has let water upon his land by tearing away the aqueduct, etc."[217] His only redress for damages would be in petitioning the Ohio Legislature.[218] William H. Robertson, to solve his dilemma, sent a telegram to Mr. Flickinger stating, "Gatling gun directed on my building supposed to contain arnica." Mr. Robertson humbly requested that Mr. Flickinger "please direct captain commanding to change front" so that the Gatling gun was no longer pointed his way.[219]

A few citizens, who would much later in life be implicated as Dynamiters in interviews with Otto E. Ehrhart, also left the area after the Ohio National Guard showed up, Mr. Sperry had been arrested, and more arrests were threatened.[220] Frank L. Saylor left for Fort Wayne on May 1, 1887. Henry Harris and David Zuber left for Fort Wayne on April 29, 1887. John R. McCabe left for

Kingsland, Indiana, on May 2, 1887. Dr. Thomas H. Cave[¶] and his daughter left for St. Louis to visit family on May 2, 1887. John H. Chester returned to Antwerp on April 30, 1887, from a stay in Fostoria, Ohio, during the week. Lewis S. Gordon and his family left for Greenville, Ohio, on May 2, 1887.[221]

Their leaving the area may have also come from a report on April 29, 1887 in the *Fort Wayne Sentinel* that three of their comrades had turned scab and met with Mr. Flickinger, Mr. Hahn, and ADJ GEN Axline and "agreed for $100 apiece, to turn state's evidence and give the names of the entire organization."[222] ADJ GEN Axline reportedly had the names of "seven or eight of the leaders, whom he will have arrested and punished by law."[223] The *Evening Review* of East Liverpool, Ohio even reported that a "card was picked up yesterday bearing the names of a dozen men who were probably assigned to a certain piece of work. The names are those of well known people."[224]

On May 4, 1887, Detective John T. Norris, a private and special detective from Springfield, Ohio,[225] had arrived in Antwerp to uncover the Dynamiters. After only "a few hours observations," he had reportedly overstayed his welcome. Upon fearing the detective "might in his thirst for notoriety court bodily harm," Mayor Fleck telegraphed Governor Foraker to determine if he had been the one who sent him to Antwerp or had the detective come on his own volition. Governor Foraker responded that he had been the one who sent the detective to Antwerp.[226]

---

¶ Antwerp's mayor between May 1880 and February 1881.
(Dale L. Ehrhart, "Municipal History of Antwerp," in *A Century of Progress: Antwerp, Ohio*, 32.)

Mayor Fleck promptly responded to the Governor that he should recall the detective immediately, as he was unwelcome in the community.[227] Whether the Governor recalled Mr. Norris was not said, and it is unlikely considering the Governor was in the interest of maintaining law and order in the locality. Having a mayor brazenly request a detective be removed because he was unwelcome was a laughable request.

That said, Mr. Norris was so unwelcome in Antwerp that he was allegedly approached by a "reception committee of Dynamiters."[228] There were five men who approached Detective Norris, among them were Oliver S. Applegate and Warner D. Ryel, the latter of the two carrying a noose with him to meet the detective. After being told to leave town immediately, and seeing the Dynamiter's "grim and determined faces," Detective Norris reportedly said, "'Alright gentlemen, if that's the way you feel about it, I'll bid you good day.'"[229] Detective Norris promptly left town for Hicksville around 11 p.m., either by walking or horse and buggy.[230]

On May 3rd and May 4, 1887, ADJ GEN Axline and Governor Foraker had the following conversation by telegram:

9:46 a.m., May 3, 1887, Governor Foraker received the following telegram from ADJ GEN Axline:

> Have been with the troops at the reservoir since Sunday morning. Everything quiet and in good condition. Had interview here with Flickinger and Haymaker this morning. Haymaker visits Antwerp to-day. Nothing new to report. Address Defiance to-day.[231]

11:46 a.m., May 3, 1887, ADJ GEN Axline received the following telegram from Governor Foraker:

> Remain at or about Defiance, and keep me advised as to where I can communicate with you until I hear from Haymaker.[232]

9:35 a.m., May 4, 1887, Governor Foraker received the following telegram from ADJ GEN Axline:

> Haymaker's dispatch to-day explains situation. Will retain about fifty men on duty until further action is taken, unless otherwise directed. Further arrests will probably be made to-morrow. Will go to camp at reservoir at noon to-day. Address Cecil.[233]

As mentioned in one of ADJ GEN Axline's telegrams to Governor Foraker on May 4, 1887, "about fifty" soldiers were retained at Camp Dynamite/Reservoir, the balance presumably being recalled to Toledo.[234] Unfortunately for the soldiers stationed at Camp Dynamite/Reservoir, their stay in Paulding County would not be prolonged enough to move camp closer to Antwerp. CPT Wade correctly predicted that "they will probably be relieved this week."[235]

The following are two telegrams sent on the morning of May 5, 1887, indicating a shift in plans.

8:28 a.m., while riding Wabash Train No. 42 back to Toledo, ADJ GEN Axline received the following telegram from Mr. Haymaker:

> Governor telegraphs. Fleck goes to Columbus. I stop proceedings until further instructed.[236]

8:37 a.m., Governor Foraker received the following telegram from ADJ GEN Axline:

> All quiet this morning. Will report in person this afternoon on arrival of Hocking Valley train.[237]

Sometime earlier in the week, "a committee of Antwerp citizens," including Alonzo B. Holcombe, Mayor Fleck, and Wilson H. Snook, Paulding County's Prosecuting Attorney, were requested to appear before Governor Foraker regarding the whole muddle.[238] This meeting presumably occurred on or about May 5, 1887. After some conversing about the 'truth' of the matter, the result of the meeting was that Governor Foraker would recall the troops from Paulding County immediately.[239] Governor Foraker was reportedly "anxious for some excuse to get his army out of the county" as the cost alone of keeping the soldiers present was reportedly $300 to $400 (~$9411 to $12,548 in 2023) per day. That cost was reportedly a "heavy draft on the almost depleted State Treasury."[240]

However, the troops would only be recalled on the condition that Mayor Fleck and Mr. Snook give him "satisfactory assurance that if he did so, the property of the State would not be again molested" [241] by "exerting their influence upon the Dynamiters and endeavor to dissuade them from any further lawless demonstrations."[242] The Governor then promised a "full and complete amnesty will be granted" so long as the Dynamiters would "concede to the 'terms of the capitulation,' and lay down their dynamite."[243]

Governor Foraker promised mercy from the law and possible gubernatorial influence to abandon the canal works at the price of the Dynamiters surrendering. The *Paulding County Gazette* stated that there "never were terms of peace more equitable than those which end the 'Reservoir War.'" [244] A significant, yet practically unreported agreement was also brokered by citizens of Paulding County, wherein they were reportedly "resolved to protect the public works from further vandalism." [245]

Governor Foraker also promised to visit Paulding County at some time in the future. [246] If upon his visit it became clear to him that the reservoir was indeed a nuisance as claimed, he would recommend that it be abandoned at the next Legislative session. [247] If he "could not conscientiously do that he would at least recommend something for our relief." [248]

At 8 p.m. on May 5, 1887, ADJ GEN Axline telegraphed MAJ Bunker "the official recall" [249] of the remaining troops, which is as follows:

> The troops on duty at the Paulding Reservoir are hereby relieved, and the commanding officer is directed to break camp as early as practicable and to proceed with his command to Toledo and there dismiss the same. He will arrange for transportation of men and baggage. Telegraph receipt of these orders. By command of the Governor. [250]

This message apparently reached Camp Dynamite/Reservoir around 10:30 p.m., [251] but CPT Rogers, on behalf of MAJ Bunker, did not respond until the next morning; the telegraph ADJ GEN Axline received at 8:40 a.m. is as follows:

> Dispatch received. Will leave for Toledo May 6, 3 P.M. [252]

The "Reservoir Army" broke camp on May 6, 1887, at 9 a.m.[253] Simultaneously, work on repairing the reservoir and canal structures was temporarily suspended. [254] Attorney General Jacob A. Kohler, who "had the papers all ready for filing" to prosecute "men known to have been implicated in the riot," also ceased prosecution of their cases in accordance with the surrender agreement.[255] The Ohio National Guard then marched to Knox Station and boarded a train back home to Toledo.[256] A week prior, the *Paulding County Gazette* stated, "we are confident our soldier 'feller' have not seen a genuine Dynamiter since coming here as they all took to the woods or left on the first train for Chicago."[257]§

MAJ Bunker informed ADJ GEN Axline in a telegram received by the latter at 7:46 p.m.:

> Troops returned this evening from the Reservoir, and all in good health. The conduct of officers and men has been soldiery and credible in every respect. Will report fully in writing at earliest possible moment.[258]

The *Paulding County Gazette*, again, put it best; The "citizens breathe easier, the canal war is over." [259] The *Delphos Weekly Herald* dryly stated in their May 12, 1887, issue: "Who will mourn for Paulding County now? The Paulding County dynamiters have surrendered, and the canal still lives." [260] A reminder that, although the Reservoir War had ended, the entire next year would have to, again, be spent trying to get the canal and reservoir formally abandoned.

---

§ Another subtle reference to the Haymarket Affair.

## Chapter 6 Notes

1 "Wrecked Wabash!," *Paulding Democrat*, April 28, 1887, 1.

2 Otto E. Ehrhart, "Wabash-Erie Canal," in *A Century of Progress: Antwerp, Ohio*, 18, 21.

3 Otto E. Ehrhart, "Wabash-Erie Canal," in *A Century of Progress: Antwerp, Ohio*, 18.

4 "Blown Up," *Cincinnati Weekly Enquirer*, May 4, 1887, 5; "Exciting Times in Ohio," *Defiance Democrat*, May 5, 1887, 1; "Damnable Dynamite Deeds," *Defiance Democrat*, April 28, 1887, 3; "Wrecked Wabash!," *Paulding Democrat*, April 28, 1887, 1; Otto E. Ehrhart, "Wabash-Erie Canal," in *A Century of Progress: Antwerp, Ohio*, 19; Everett A. Budd, "Brief History of Paulding County, Ohio," in *Historical Atlas of Paulding County, Ohio, 1892*, 26; "Mob Outrages in Ohio," *Biddeford Daily Journal*, April 27, 1887, 1.

5 "Blown Up," *Cincinnati Weekly Enquirer*, May 4, 1887, 5; "Deadly Dynamiters!!" *Paulding County Gazette*, April 28, 1887, 8; "H-ll On The Wabash!" *Antwerp Argus*, April 28, 1887, 2; "Damnable Dynamite Deeds," *Defiance Democrat*, April 28, 1887, 3; "Ohio State News," *Defiance County Express*, May 5, 1887, 12; "Ohio State News," *Paulding County Gazette*, May 5, 1887, 2.

6 "Blown Up," *Cincinnati Weekly Enquirer*, May 4, 1887, 5.

7 "War in Paulding County," *Defiance County Express*, April 28, 1887, 10; "Ohio State News," *Defiance County Express*, May 5, 1887, 12; "Ohio State News," *Paulding County Gazette*, May 5, 1887, 2; "Deadly Dynamiters!!" *Paulding County Gazette*, April 28, 1887, 8; "Wrecked Wabash!," *Paulding Democrat*, April 28, 1887, 1; Everett A. Budd, "Brief History of Paulding County, Ohio," in *Historical Atlas of Paulding County, Ohio, 1892*, 26.

8 Otto E. Ehrhart, "Wabash-Erie Canal," in *A Century of Progress: Antwerp, Ohio*, 18-19.

9 "War in Paulding County," *Defiance County Express*, April 28, 1887, 10; "Ohio State News," *Defiance County Express*, May 5, 1887, 12; "Ohio State News," *Paulding County Gazette*, May 5, 1887, 2; "Damnable Dynamite Deeds," *Defiance Democrat*, April 28, 1887, 3; "Blown Up," *The Cincinnati Weekly Enquirer*, May 4, 1887, 5; "Deadly Dynamiters!!" *Paulding County Gazette*, April 28, 1887, 8; "Wrecked Wabash!," *Paulding Democrat*, April 28, 1887, 1.

10 "Reminiscence of Pioneer Days," *Payne Reflector and Press Review*, July 13, 1916, 1.

11 "Deadly Dynamiters!!" *Paulding County Gazette*, April 28, 1887, 8; "Wrecked Wabash!," *Paulding Democrat*, April 28, 1887, 1; "H-ll On The Wabash!" *Antwerp Argus*, April 28, 1887, 2.

12 Otto E. Ehrhart, "Wabash-Erie Canal," in *A Century of Progress: Antwerp, Ohio*, 18.

13 "Reminiscence of Pioneer Days," *Payne Reflector and Press Review*, July 13, 1916, 1.

14 "Reminiscence of Pioneer Days," *Payne Reflector and Press Review*, July 13, 1916, 1.

15 Otto E. Ehrhart, "Wabash-Erie Canal," in *A Century of Progress: Antwerp, Ohio*, 19.

16 "The Old Home Town," *Paulding County Republican*, August 8, 1935, 5.

17 "Reminiscence of Pioneer Days," *Payne Reflector and Press Review*, July 13, 1916, 1.

18 Otto E. Ehrhart, "Wabash-Erie Canal," in *A Century of Progress: Antwerp, Ohio*, 19.

19 "Rioters Realizing Their Mistake," *New York Tribune*, April 28, 1887, 1; "The Reservoir Trouble," *Quincy Daily Journal*, April 30, 1887, 1.

20 "The Reservoir Trouble," *Quincy Daily Journal*, April 30, 1887, 1; "The Reservoir Trouble," *Decatur Daily Review*, April 30, 1887, 1.

21 "Rioters Realizing Their Mistake," *New York Tribune*, April 28, 1887, 1.

22 "Reminiscence of Pioneer Days," *Payne Reflector and Press Review*, July 13, 1916, 1.

23 "Blown Up," *Cincinnati Weekly Enquirer*, May 4, 1887, 5; "Deadly Dynamiters!!" *Paulding County Gazette*, April 28, 1887, 8; "Wrecked Wabash!," *Paulding Democrat*, April 28, 1887, 1; "H-ll On The Wabash!" *Antwerp Argus*, April 28, 1887, 2; Everett A. Budd, "The Reservoir War," in *Historical Atlas of Paulding County, Ohio, 1892*, 26; Otto E. Ehrhart, "Wabash-Erie Canal," in *A Century of Progress: Antwerp, Ohio*, 18.

24 "Wrecked Wabash!," *Paulding Democrat*, April 28, 1887, 1.

25 State of Ohio, *Executive Documents: Annual Reports for 1887, Made to the Sixty-Eighth General Assembly*, Part I, 1240.

26 "Deadly Dynamiters!!" *Paulding County Gazette*, April 28, 1887, 8; "Wrecked Wabash!," *Paulding Democrat*, April 28, 1887, 1.

27 "Deadly Dynamiters!!" *Paulding County Gazette*, April 28, 1887, 8; "Wrecked Wabash!," *Paulding Democrat*, April 28, 1887, 1.

28 "Wrecked Wabash!," *Paulding Democrat*, April 28, 1887, 1; "Deadly Dynamiters!!" *Paulding County Gazette*, April 28, 1887, 8.

29 "Blown Up," *Cincinnati Weekly Enquirer*, May 4, 1887, 5.

30 "Deadly Dynamiters!!" *Paulding County Gazette*, April 28, 1887, 8; "Wrecked Wabash!," *Paulding Democrat*, April 28, 1887, 1; "H-ll On The Wabash!" *Antwerp Argus*, April 28, 1887, 2; Everett A. Budd, "Brief History of Paulding County, Ohio," in *Historical Atlas of Paulding County, Ohio, 1892*, 26.

31 Otto E. Ehrhart, "Wabash-Erie Canal," in *A Century of Progress: Antwerp, Ohio*, 18.

32 "Blown Up," *Cincinnati Weekly Enquirer*, May 4, 1887, 5; "Mob Outrages in Ohio," *Biddeford Daily Journal*, April 27, 1887, 1.

33 "Damnable Dynamite Deeds," *Defiance Democrat*, April 28, 1887, 3; "Wrecked Wabash!," *Paulding Democrat*, April 28, 1887, 1; "Blown Up," *Cincinnati Weekly Enquirer*, May 4, 1887, 5.

34 "Wrecked Wabash!," *Paulding Democrat*, April 28, 1887, 1; "Antwerp Items," *Paulding Democrat*, April 28, 1887, 5; Exciting Times in Ohio," *Defiance Democrat*, May 5, 1887, 1; "Blown Up," *Cincinnati Weekly Enquirer*, May 4, 1887, 5.

35 "Antwerp Items," *Paulding Democrat*, April 28, 1887, 5.

36 "Antwerp Items," *Paulding Democrat*, April 28, 1887, 5.

37 "Blown Up," *Cincinnati Weekly Enquirer*, May 4, 1887, 5.

38 State of Ohio, *Executive Documents: Annual Reports for 1887 Made to the Sixty-Eighth General Assembly*, Part II, 689.

39 State of Ohio, *Executive Documents: Annual Reports for 1887 Made to the Sixty-Eighth General Assembly*, Part II, 689.

40 State of Ohio, *Executive Documents: Annual Reports for 1887 Made to the Sixty-Eighth General Assembly*, Part II, 689.

41 State of Ohio, *Executive Documents: Annual Reports for 1887 Made to the Sixty-Eighth General Assembly*, Part II, 690.

42 State of Ohio, *Executive Documents: Annual Reports for 1887 Made to the Sixty-Eighth General Assembly*, Part II, 690.

43 State of Ohio, *Executive Documents: Annual Reports for 1887 Made to the Sixty-Eighth General Assembly*, Part II, 690.

44 State of Ohio, *Executive Documents: Annual Reports for 1887 Made to the Sixty-Eighth General Assembly*, Part II, 690.

45 State of Ohio, *Executive Documents: Annual Reports for 1887 Made to the Sixty-Eighth General Assembly*, Part II, 690.

46 State of Ohio, *Executive Documents: Annual Reports for 1887 Made to the Sixty-Eighth General Assembly*, Part II, 690.

47 State of Ohio, *Executive Documents: Annual Reports for 1887 Made to the Sixty-Eighth General Assembly*, Part II, 691.

48 "H-ll On The Wabash!" *Antwerp Argus*, April 28, 1887, 2.

49 "H-ll On The Wabash!" *Antwerp Argus*, April 28, 1887, 2.

50 State of Ohio, *Executive Documents: Annual Reports for 1887 Made to the Sixty-Eighth General Assembly*, Part II, 691.

51 State of Ohio, *Executive Documents: Annual Reports for 1887 Made to the Sixty-Eighth General Assembly*, Part II, 691.

52 State of Ohio, *Executive Documents: Annual Reports for 1887 Made to the Sixty-Eighth General Assembly*, Part II, 691.

53 State of Ohio, *Executive Documents: Annual Reports for 1887 Made to the Sixty-Eighth General Assembly*, Part II, 691.

54 State of Ohio, *Executive Documents: Annual Reports for 1887 Made to the Sixty-Eighth General Assembly*, Part II, 692.

55 The News at Columbus," *Cincinnati Weekly Enquirer*, May 4, 1887, 5; "A Canal War," *Fort Wayne Gazette*, April 28, 1887, 4; "Work of an Ohio Mob," *New York Tribune*, April 27, 1887, 1.

56 State of Ohio, *Executive Documents: Annual Reports for 1887 Made to the Sixty-Eighth General Assembly*, Part II, 695; Everett A. Budd, "Brief History of Paulding County, Ohio," in *Historical Atlas of Paulding County, Ohio, 1892*, 29.

57 State of Ohio, *Executive Documents: Annual Reports for 1887 Made to the Sixty-Eighth General Assembly*, Part II, 695.

58 State of Ohio, *Executive Documents: Annual Reports for 1887 Made to the Sixty-Eighth General Assembly*, Part II, 695.

59 State of Ohio, *Executive Documents: Annual Reports for 1887 Made to the Sixty-Eighth General Assembly*, Part II, 688, 695.

60 State of Ohio, *Executive Documents: Annual Reports for 1887 Made to the Sixty-Eighth General Assembly*, Part II, 688, 695.

61 Owen J. Hopkins, *Gatling Gun Tactics – Revised Edition*, 1888, 1.

62 State of Ohio, *Executive Documents: Annual Reports for 1887 Made to the Sixty-Eighth General Assembly*, Part II, 695.

63 State of Ohio, *Executive Documents: Annual Reports for 1887 Made to the Sixty-Eighth General Assembly*, Part II, 688, 691-692, 695; "Blown Up," *Cincinnati Weekly Enquirer*, May 4, 1887, 5.

64 "Damnable Dynamite Deeds," *Defiance Democrat*, April 28, 1887, 3.

65 "War on the Wabash," *Cincinnati Commercial Gazette*, April 28, 1887, 1.

66 "Damnable Dynamite Deeds," *Defiance Democrat*, April 28, 1887, 3; "War on the Wabash," *Cincinnati Commercial Gazette*, April 28, 1887, 1.

67 "Deadly Dynamiters!!," *Paulding County Gazette*, April 28, 1887, 8.

68 "War on the Wabash," *Cincinnati Commercial Gazette*, April 28, 1887, 1.

69 State of Ohio, *Executive Documents: Annual Reports for 1887 Made to the Sixty-Eighth General Assembly*, Part II, 692, 695; Everett A. Budd, "Brief History of Paulding County, Ohio," in *Historical Atlas of Paulding County, Ohio, 1892*, 29; "Wrecked Wabash!," *Paulding Democrat*, April 28, 1887, 1; "Deadly Dynamiters!!" *Paulding County Gazette*, April 28, 1887, 8.

70 "Blown Up," *Cincinnati Weekly Enquirer*, May 4, 1887, 5; "Wrecked Wabash!," *Paulding Democrat*, April 28, 1887, 1.

71 State of Ohio, *Executive Documents: Annual Reports for 1887 Made to the Sixty-Eighth General Assembly*, Part II, 695.

72 State of Ohio, *Executive Documents: Annual Reports for 1887 Made to the Sixty-Eighth General Assembly*, Part II, 695.

73 Information courtesy of Ohio National Guard Historian SFC Joshua D. Mann, contained within the Ohio National Guard's *Quartermaster General Report for the Year Ending November 15, 1887*, and *The Report of the Regular Army Advisor*'s inspection of the 16th Regiment in August 1887.

74 Everett A. Budd, "Brief History of Paulding County, Ohio," in *Historical Atlas of Paulding County, Ohio, 1892*, 29.

75 State of Ohio, *Executive Documents: Annual Reports for 1887 Made to the Sixty-Eighth General Assembly*, Part II, 674.

76 State of Ohio, *Executive Documents: Annual Reports for 1887 Made to the Sixty-Eighth General Assembly*, Part II, 674.

77 Everett A. Budd, "Brief History of Paulding County, Ohio," in *Historical Atlas of Paulding County, Ohio, 1892*, 29; "H-ll On The Wabash!" *Antwerp Argus*, April 28, 1887, 2.

78 "Deadly Dynamiters!!" *Paulding County Gazette*, April 28, 1887, 8; Everett A. Budd, "Brief History of Paulding County, Ohio," in *Historical Atlas of Paulding County, Ohio, 1892*, 29.

79 State of Ohio, *Executive Documents: Annual Reports for 1887 Made to the Sixty-Eighth General Assembly*, Part II, 697.

80 State of Ohio, *Executive Documents: Annual Reports for 1887 Made to the Sixty-Eighth General Assembly*, Part II, 695.

81 "Exciting Times in Ohio," *Defiance Democrat*, May 5, 1887, 1.

82 Ohio National Guard, *History of the Ohio National Guard and Ohio Volunteers*, 30, 32, 34–35, 38, 138.

83 State of Ohio, *Executive Documents: Annual Reports for 1887 Made to the Sixty-Eighth General Assembly*, Part II, 697.

84 State of Ohio, *Executive Documents: Annual Reports for 1887 Made to the Sixty-Eighth General Assembly*, Part II, 698.

85 "Deadly Dynamiters!!" *Paulding County Gazette*, April 28, 1887, 8.

86 "War on the Wabash," *Cincinnati Commercial Gazette*, April 28, 1887, 1.

87 "War on the Wabash," *Cincinnati Commercial Gazette*, April 28, 1887, 1.

88 "War on the Wabash," *Cincinnati Commercial Gazette*, April 28, 1887, 1.

89 "Deadly Dynamiters!!" *Paulding County Gazette*, April 28, 1887, 8.

90 "The Reservoir Muddle," *Paulding Democrat*, May 5, 1887, 4.

91 "Blown Up," *Cincinnati Weekly Enquirer*, May 4, 1887, 5; "Exciting Times in Ohio," *Defiance Democrat*, May 5, 1887, 1; "From the War in Ohio," *Maysville Daily Evening Bulletin* (Maysville, Kentucky), April 28, 1887, 1.

92 "Blown Up," *Cincinnati Weekly Enquirer*, May 4, 1887, 5.

93 "War on the Wabash," *Cincinnati Commercial Gazette*, April 28, 1887, 1.

94 "From Cecil," *Maysville Daily Evening Bulletin* (Maysville, Kentucky), April 28, 1887, 1.

95 "War on the Wabash," *Cincinnati Commercial Gazette*, April 28, 1887, 1.

96 State of Ohio, *Executive Documents: Annual Reports for 1887 Made to the Sixty-Eighth General Assembly*, Part II, 692.

97 State of Ohio, *Executive Documents: Annual Reports for 1887 Made to the Sixty-Eighth General Assembly*, Part II, 695; "War on the Wabash," *Cincinnati Commercial Gazette*, April 28, 1887, 1.

98 State of Ohio, *Executive Documents: Annual Reports for 1887 Made to the Sixty-Eighth General Assembly*, Part II, 695.

99 "Deadly Dynamiters!!" *Paulding County Gazette*, April 28, 1887, 8.

100 State of Ohio, *Executive Documents: Annual Reports for 1887 Made to the Sixty-Eighth General Assembly*, Part II, 695.

101 Ohio National Guard, *History of the Ohio National Guard and Ohio Volunteers*, 30, 32, 34-35, 38, 138.

102 "War on the Wabash," *Cincinnati Commercial Gazette*, April 28, 1887, 1.

103 "War on the Wabash," *Cincinnati Commercial Gazette*, April 28, 1887, 1.

104 "War on the Wabash," *Cincinnati Commercial Gazette*, April 28, 1887, 1.

105 "War on the Wabash," *Cincinnati Commercial Gazette*, April 28, 1887, 1; State of Ohio, *Executive Documents: Annual Reports for 1887 Made to the Sixty-Eighth General Assembly*, Part II, 696.

106 Everett A. Budd, "Brief History of Paulding County, Ohio," in *Historical Atlas of Paulding County, Ohio, 1892*, 29; "War on the Wabash," *Cincinnati Commercial Gazette*, April 28, 1887, 1; State of Ohio, *Executive Documents: Annual Reports for 1887 Made to the Sixty-Eighth General Assembly*, Part II, 695-696.

107 State of Ohio, *Executive Documents: Annual Reports for 1887 Made to the Sixty-Eighth General Assembly*, Part II, 695-696; "War on the Wabash," *Cincinnati Commercial Gazette*, April 28, 1887, 1.

108 "War on the Wabash," *Cincinnati Commercial Gazette*, April 28, 1887, 1; "Paulding Rioters," *The Daily Reflector* (Norwalk, Ohio), April 28, 1887, 1.

109 State of Ohio, *Executive Documents: Annual Reports for 1887 Made to the Sixty-Eighth General Assembly*, Part II, 696.

110 State of Ohio, *Executive Documents: Annual Reports for 1887 Made to the Sixty-Eighth General Assembly*, Part II, 696.

111 State of Ohio, *Executive Documents: Annual Reports for 1887 Made to the Sixty-Eighth General Assembly*, Part II, 696.

112 State of Ohio, *Executive Documents: Annual Reports for 1887 Made to the Sixty-Eighth General Assembly*, Part II, 697; "War on the Wabash," *Cincinnati Commercial Gazette*, April 28, 1887, 1.

113 "Michigan, County Births, 1867-1917," *FamilySearch*, accessed August 29, 2022, Births 1869-1871, Image 12 of 157.

114 Ohio Adjutant General's Office, *Roster of Soldiers of the Ohio National Guard, 1847-1917; 16th & 6th Regiments Books 1-3 1880-1904*, Columbus: Ohio Adjutant General's Office, 61.

115 "A Soldier Killed," *Defiance County Express*, April 28, 1887, 10; "Accidental Death," *Defiance Democrat*, April 28, 1887, 3; "Exciting Times in Ohio," *Defiance Democrat*, May 5, 1887, 1; "Troops Sent Forward," *Cincinnati Weekly Enquirer*, May 4, 1887, 5; "Deadly Dynamiters!!" *Paulding County Gazette*, April 28, 1887, 8; "Wrecked Wabash!," *Paulding Democrat*, April 28, 1887, 1; Everett A. Budd, "Brief History of Paulding County, Ohio," in *Historical Atlas of Paulding County, Ohio, 1892*, 29; State of Ohio, *Executive Documents: Annual Reports for 1887 Made to the Sixty-Eighth General Assembly*, Part II, 695.

116 "The Paulding Riot," *The Daily Reflector* (Norwalk, Ohio), April 29, 1887, 1; "Not Killed by Accident," *Logansport Pharos Tribune*, April 29, 1887, 1; "Not Killed by Accident," *Dixon Evening Telegraph*, April 29, 1887, 2.

117 "War on the Wabash," *Cincinnati Commercial Gazette*, April 28, 1887, 1.

118 State of Ohio, *Executive Documents: Annual Reports for 1887 Made to the Sixty-Eighth General Assembly*, Part II, 692.

119 "The Paulding Riot," *The Daily Reflector* (Norwalk, Ohio), April 29, 1887, 1; "Not Killed by Accident," *Logansport Pharos Tribune*, April 29, 1887, 1; "Not Killed by Accident," *Dixon Evening Telegraph*, April 29, 1887, 2; "The Only Victim of the War," *Cincinnati Commercial Gazette*, April 30, 1887, 5.

120 "The Only Victim of the War," *Cincinnati Commercial Gazette*, April 30, 1887, 5.

121 "H-ll On The Wabash!" *Antwerp Argus*, April 28, 1887, 2.

122 "The Antwerp Side of the Matter," *Fort Wayne Sentinel*, April 28, 1887, 1; "Accidental Death," *Defiance Democrat*, April 28, 1887, 3; "Troops Sent Forward," *Cincinnati Weekly Enquirer*, May 4, 1887, 5; "Deadly Dynamiters!!" *Paulding County Gazette*, April 28, 1887, 8; "War on the Wabash," *Cincinnati Commercial Gazette*, April 28, 1887, 1; "H-ll On The Wabash!" *Antwerp Argus*, April 28, 1887, 2.

123 "A Soldier Killed," *Defiance County Express*, April 28, 1887, 10; "Accidental Death," *Defiance Democrat*, April 28, 1887, 3; "Exciting Times in Ohio," *Defiance Democrat*, May 5, 1887, 1; "Troops Sent Forward," *Cincinnati Weekly Enquirer*, May 4, 1887, 5; "Deadly Dynamiters!!" *Paulding County Gazette*, April 28, 1887, 8; "Wrecked Wabash!," *Paulding Democrat*, April 28, 1887, 1; Everett A. Budd, "Brief History of Paulding County, Ohio," in *Historical Atlas of Paulding County, Ohio, 1892*, 29; State of Ohio, *Executive Documents: Annual Reports for 1887 Made to the Sixty-Eighth General Assembly*, Part II, 695.

124 "H-ll On The Wabash!" *Antwerp Argus*, April 28, 1887, 2; "War on the Wabash," *Cincinnati Commercial Gazette*, April 28, 1887, 1.

125 State of Ohio, *Executive Documents: Annual Reports for 1887 Made to the Sixty-Eighth General Assembly*, Part II, 695; "War on the Wabash," *Cincinnati Commercial Gazette*, April 28, 1887, 1.

126 "War on the Wabash," *Cincinnati Commercial Gazette*, April 28, 1887, 1.

127 "Guard Accidentally Shot," *Cincinnati Commercial Gazette*, April 27, 1887, 1.

128 "War on the Wabash," *Cincinnati Commercial Gazette*, April 28, 1887, 1.

129 "Accidental Death," *Defiance Democrat*, April 28, 1887, 3.

130 "Accidental Death," *Defiance Democrat*, April 28, 1887, 3; "A
	Soldier Killed," *Defiance County Express*, April 28, 1887, 10;
	"The Antwerp Side of the Matter," *Fort Wayne Sentinel*, April
	28, 1887, 1.
131 "Deadly Dynamiters!!" *Paulding County Gazette*, April 28, 1887, 8.
132 "Deadly Dynamiters!!" *Paulding County Gazette*, April 28, 1887, 8.
133 "Deadly Dynamiters!!" *Paulding County Gazette*, April 28, 1887, 8;
	"War on the Wabash," *Cincinnati Commercial Gazette*, April 28,
	1887, 1; State of Ohio, *Executive Documents: Annual Reports for
	1887 Made to the Sixty-Eighth General Assembly*, Part II, 692.
134 State of Ohio, *Executive Documents: Annual Reports for 1887 Made to
	the Sixty-Eighth General Assembly*, Part II, 695.
135 State of Ohio, *Executive Documents: Annual Reports for 1887 Made to
	the Sixty-Eighth General Assembly*, Part II, 695.
136 State of Ohio, *Executive Documents: Annual Reports for 1887 Made to
	the Sixty-Eighth General Assembly*, Part II, 696.
137 State of Ohio, *Executive Documents: Annual Reports for 1887 Made to
	the Sixty-Eighth General Assembly*, Part II, 696.
138 "Camp Reservoir," *Paulding County Gazette*, May 5, 1887, 8; "H-ll
	On The Wabash!" *Antwerp Argus*, April 28, 1887, 2.
139 Everett A. Budd, "Brief History of Paulding County, Ohio," in
	*Historical Atlas of Paulding County, Ohio, 1892*, 29.
140 Everett A. Budd, "Brief History of Paulding County, Ohio," in
	*Historical Atlas of Paulding County, Ohio, 1892*, 29.
141 Everett A. Budd, "Brief History of Paulding County, Ohio," in
	*Historical Atlas of Paulding County, Ohio, 1892*, 29; State of Ohio,
	*Executive Documents: Annual Reports for 1887 Made to the Sixty-
	Eighth General Assembly*, Part II, 696.
142 "Camp Reservoir," *Paulding County Gazette*, May 5, 1887, 8.
143 State of Ohio, *Executive Documents: Annual Reports for 1887 Made to
	the Sixty-Eighth General Assembly*, Part II, 692.
144 State of Ohio, *Executive Documents: Annual Reports for 1887 Made to
	the Sixty-Eighth General Assembly*, Part II, 692.
145 State of Ohio, *Executive Documents: Annual Reports for 1887 Made to
	the Sixty-Eighth General Assembly*, Part II, 697.
146 State of Ohio, *Executive Documents: Annual Reports for 1887 Made to
	the Sixty-Eighth General Assembly*, Part II, 697.
147 State of Ohio, *Executive Documents: Annual Reports for 1887 Made to
	the Sixty-Eighth General Assembly*, Part II, 697.
148 State of Ohio, *Executive Documents: Annual Reports for 1887 Made to
	the Sixty-Eighth General Assembly*, Part II, 697.
149 State of Ohio, *Executive Documents: Annual Reports for 1887 Made to
	the Sixty-Eighth General Assembly*, Part II, 697.
150 "Wrecked Wabash!," *Paulding Democrat*, April 28, 1887, 1; "Deadly
	Dynamiters!!" *Paulding County Gazette*, April 28, 1887, 8; State
	of Ohio, *Executive Documents: Annual Reports for 1887 Made to
	the Sixty-Eighth General Assembly*, Part II, 696.

151 "Deadly Dynamiters!!" *Paulding County Gazette*, April 28, 1887, 8; "Wrecked Wabash!," *Paulding Democrat*, April 28, 1887, 1; State of Ohio, *Executive Documents: Annual Reports for 1887 Made to the Sixty-Eighth General Assembly*, Part II, 696.

152 "Deadly Dynamiters!!" *Paulding County Gazette*, April 28, 1887, 8.

153 "Wrecked Wabash!," *Paulding Democrat*, April 28, 1887, 1.

154 "Wrecked Wabash!," *Paulding Democrat*, April 28, 1887, 1; State of Ohio, *Executive Documents: Annual Reports for 1887 Made to the Sixty-Eighth General Assembly*, Part II, 696.

155 "Deadly Dynamiters!!" *Paulding County Gazette*, April 28, 1887, 8; State of Ohio, *Executive Documents: Annual Reports for 1887 Made to the Sixty-Eighth General Assembly*, Part II, 696.

156 "Blown Up," *Cincinnati Weekly Enquirer*, May 4, 1887, 5.

157 "Exciting Times in Ohio," *Defiance Democrat*, May 5, 1887, 1; "War on the Wabash," *Cincinnati Commercial Gazette*, April 28, 1887, 1.

158 "Deadly Dynamiters!!" *Paulding County Gazette*, April 28, 1887, 8.

159 "States Evidence," *Fort Wayne Sentinel*, April 29, 1887, 2.

160 "Wrecked Wabash!," *Paulding Democrat*, April 28, 1887, 1.

161 "Wrecked Wabash!," *Paulding Democrat*, April 28, 1887, 1; "Deadly Dynamiters!!" *Paulding County Gazette*, April 28, 1887, 8; "Exciting Times in Ohio," *Defiance Democrat*, May 5, 1887, 1; "Local and Personal," *Defiance County Express*, May 5, 1887, 9; "War on the Wabash," *Cincinnati Commercial Gazette*, April 28, 1887, 1.

162 "Deadly Dynamiters!!" *Paulding County Gazette*, April 28, 1887, 8; "Wrecked Wabash!," *Paulding Democrat*, April 28, 1887, 1; "H-ll On The Wabash!" *Antwerp Argus*, April 28, 1887, 2.

163 "H-ll On The Wabash!" *Antwerp Argus*, April 28, 1887, 2.

164 "Deadly Dynamiters!!" *Paulding County Gazette*, April 28, 1887, 8.

165 "Attachment Notice," *Antwerp Argus*, March 31, 1887, 2.

166 "Deadly Dynamiters!!" *Paulding County Gazette*, April 28, 1887, 8.

167 "Deadly Dynamiters!!" *Paulding County Gazette*, April 28, 1887, 8.

168 "Deadly Dynamiters!!" *Paulding County Gazette*, April 28, 1887, 8.

169 "The Canal War," *Cincinnati Commercial Gazette*, April 29, 1887, 2; Otto E. Ehrhart, "Wabash-Erie Canal," in *A Century of Progress: Antwerp, Ohio*, 21.

170 "Deadly Dynamiters!!" *Paulding County Gazette*, April 28, 1887, 8.

171 "Exciting Times in Ohio," *Defiance Democrat*, May 5, 1887, 1; "War on the Wabash," *Cincinnati Commercial Gazette*, April 28, 1887, 1.

172 "H-ll On The Wabash!" *Antwerp Argus*, April 28, 1887, 2; "Deadly Dynamiters!!" *Paulding County Gazette*, April 28, 1887, 8.

173 "Deadly Dynamiters!!" *Paulding County Gazette*, April 28, 1887, 8.

174 "Deadly Dynamiters!!" *Paulding County Gazette*, April 28, 1887, 8; "Wrecked Wabash!," *Paulding Democrat*, April 28, 1887, 1; "H-ll On The Wabash!" *Antwerp Argus*, April 28, 1887, 2.

175 Otto E. Ehrhart, "Wabash-Erie Canal," in *A Century of Progress: Antwerp, Ohio*, 21.

176 "The Week," *Bar Harbor Record*, May 5, 1887, 2; "Lawlessness in Ohio," *Portland Daily Press*, April 27, 1887, 1; "Mob Outrages in Ohio," *Biddeford Daily Journal*, April 27, 1887, 1.

177 "Troops Ordered Out," *Los Angeles Daily Herald*, April 27, 1887, 1.

178 "Camp Reservoir," *Paulding County Gazette*, May 5, 1887, 8; "States Evidence," *Fort Wayne Sentinel*, April 29, 1887, 2.

179 State of Ohio, *Executive Documents: Annual Reports for 1887 Made to the Sixty-Eighth General Assembly*, Part II, 692; "Camp Reservoir," *Paulding County Gazette*, May 5, 1887, 8.

180 "Camp Reservoir," *Paulding County Gazette*, May 5, 1887, 8.

181 State of Ohio, *Executive Documents: Annual Reports for 1887 Made to the Sixty-Eighth General Assembly*, Part II, 692.

182 State of Ohio, *Executive Documents: Annual Reports for 1887 Made to the Sixty-Eighth General Assembly*, Part II, 692.

183 State of Ohio, *Executive Documents: Annual Reports for 1887 Made to the Sixty-Eighth General Assembly*, Part II, 693.

184 "Ohio State News," *Defiance County Express*, May 5, 1887, 12; "Ohio State News," *Paulding County Gazette*, May 5, 1887, 2; "War on the Wabash," *Cincinnati Commercial Gazette*, April 28, 1887, 1.

185 "War on the Wabash," *Cincinnati Commercial Gazette*, April 28, 1887, 1; "Rioters Realizing Their Mistake," *New York Tribune*, April 28, 1887, 1.

186 State of Ohio, *Executive Documents: Annual Reports for 1887 Made to the Sixty-Eighth General Assembly*, Part II, 693.

187 State of Ohio, *Executive Documents: Annual Reports for 1887 Made to the Sixty-Eighth General Assembly*, Part II, 693.

188 State of Ohio, *Executive Documents: Annual Reports for 1887 Made to the Sixty-Eighth General Assembly*, Part II, 693.

189 "Additional Local," *Paulding County Gazette*, May 12, 1887, 5; "Fred Reeves," Find a Grave, Accessed March 13, 2022; Ohio Adjutant General's Office, *Annual Report of the Adjutant General to the Governor of the State of Ohio for the Year 1888*, 120, 197; State of Ohio, *Executive Documents Annual Reports for 1886 Made to the 67th General Assembly*, Part II, 582.

190 "He Went Back," *Antwerp Argus*, May 5, 1887, 3.

191 "Our Home Corner," *Antwerp Argus*, May 5, 1887, 3; "Round About—Antwerp," *Paulding County Gazette*, May 5, 1887, 5; Everett A. Budd, "Brief History of Paulding County, Ohio," in *Historical Atlas of Paulding County, Ohio, 1892*, 29.

192 Everett A. Budd, "Brief History of Paulding County, Ohio," in *Historical Atlas of Paulding County, Ohio, 1892*, 29.

193 "Camp Reservoir," *Paulding County Gazette*, May 5, 1887, 8.

194 Everett A. Budd, "Brief History of Paulding County, Ohio," in *Historical Atlas of Paulding County, Ohio, 1892*, 29; "Our Home Corner," *Antwerp Argus*, May 5, 1887, 3.

195 "Local Gossip," *Paulding Democrat*, May 5, 1887, 5.

196 "Local Gossip," *Paulding Democrat*, May 5, 1887, 5; Everett A. Budd, "Brief History of Paulding County, Ohio," in *Historical Atlas of Paulding County, Ohio, 1892*, 29; "Camp Reservoir," *Paulding County Gazette*, May 5, 1887, 8.

197 "Round About—Antwerp," *Paulding County* Gazette, May 5, 1887, 5; Everett A. Budd, "Brief History of Paulding County, Ohio," in *Historical Atlas of Paulding County, Ohio, 1892*, 29; "Camp Reservoir," *Paulding County Gazette*, May 5, 1887, 8.

198 Everett A. Budd, "Brief History of Paulding County, Ohio," in *Historical Atlas of Paulding County, Ohio, 1892*, 29.

199 "Camp Reservoir," *Paulding County Gazette*, May 5, 1887, 8.

200 "Camp Reservoir," *Paulding County Gazette*, May 5, 1887, 8.

201 Ohio National Guard, *History of the Ohio National Guard and Ohio Volunteers*, 34-35, 38, 138.

202 Ohio National Guard, *History of the Ohio National Guard and Ohio Volunteers*, 34-35, 138.

203 State of Ohio, *Executive Documents Annual Reports for 1886 Made to the 67th General Assembly*, Part II, 582-84, 587, 599.

204 Ohio National Guard, *History of the Ohio National Guard and Ohio Volunteers*, 35.

205 State of Ohio, *Executive Documents Annual Reports for 1886 Made to the 67th General Assembly*, Part II, 584.

206 State of Ohio, *Executive Documents Annual Reports for 1886 Made to the 67th General Assembly*, Part II, 587.

207 "Returned from Camp," *Paulding Democrat*, May 5, 1887, 5.

208 "Camp Reservoir," *Paulding County Gazette*, May 5, 1887, 8.

209 "Returned from Camp," *Paulding Democrat*, May 5, 1887, 5.

210 "Round About—Antwerp," *Paulding County* Gazette, May 5, 1887, 5; "H-ll On The Wabash!" *Antwerp Argus*, April 28, 1887, 2.

211 "Personal Mention," *Antwerp Argus*, May 5, 1887, 3.

212 Harvey Scribner, *Memoirs of Lucas County and the City of Toledo*, Volume II, 496; "Charles W Boland," Find a Grave, Accessed March 29, 2023; "Joseph S. Champion Dead," *Paulding Democrat*, April 27, 1922, 5; "Civil War Veteran Dies at Antwerp," *Fort Wayne Journal Gazette*, June 23, 1922, 2; "Pvt William F Fleck," Find a Grave, Accessed March 29, 2023.

213 Harvey Scribner, *Memoirs of Lucas County and the City of Toledo*, Volume II, 497; Everett A. Budd, "Personal Sketches," in *Historical Atlas of Paulding County, Ohio, 1892*, 54; "Obituary," *Paulding Democrat*, December 22, 1910, 1; William S. Hardesty, *Representative Citizens of Paulding County*, 276; "Franz Joseph 'Frank' Zuber," Find a Grave, Accessed March 31, 2023; "Jesse Hinkle Bond," Find A Grave, Accessed March 31, 2023; Frederick H. Dyer, *A Compendium of the War of the Rebellion*, 1502, 1511, 1523, 1540-1542, 1547.

214 "Personal Mention," *Antwerp Argus*, May 5, 1887, 3.

215 "He Went Back," *Antwerp Argus*, May 5, 1887, 3.

216 "Notes About Town," *Defiance County Express*, May 5, 1887, 9.

217 "Notes About Town," *Defiance County Express*, May 5, 1887, 9.

218 "Notes About Town," *Defiance County Express*, May 5, 1887, 9.

219 "The Reservoir Muddle," *Paulding Democrat*, May 5, 1887, 4.

220 "States Evidence," *Fort Wayne Sentinel*, April 29, 1887, 2.

221 "Personal Mention," *Antwerp Argus*, May 5, 1887, 3.

222 "States Evidence," *Fort Wayne Sentinel*, April 29, 1887, 2.

223 "Paulding Rioters," *The Daily Reflector* (Norwalk, Ohio), April 28, 1887, 1.

224 "The Reservoir Riot," *The Evening Review* (East Liverpool, Ohio), April 30, 1887, 6.

225 "Detective Who Out-Rivaled Sherlock Holmes," *Joplin Morning Tribune*, December 17, 1911, 17; "Doubts Sanity of John T. Norris," *Xenia Daily Gazette*, November 4, 1911, 3.

226 "Had No Use for Him," *Paulding Democrat*, May 12, 1887, 5.

227 "Had No Use for Him," *Paulding Democrat*, May 12, 1887, 5.

228 Otto E. Ehrhart, "Wabash-Erie Canal," in *A Century of Progress: Antwerp, Ohio*, 21.

229 "Reminiscence of Pioneer Days," *Payne Reflector and Press Review*, July 13, 1916, 1; Otto E. Ehrhart, "Wabash-Erie Canal," in *A Century of Progress: Antwerp, Ohio*, 21.

230 Otto E. Ehrhart, "Wabash-Erie Canal," in *A Century of Progress: Antwerp, Ohio*, 21; "Had No Use for Him," *Paulding Democrat*, May 12, 1887, 5; "Reminiscence of Pioneer Days," *Payne Reflector and Press Review*, July 13, 1916, 1.

231 State of Ohio, *Executive Documents: Annual Reports for 1887 Made to the Sixty-Eighth General Assembly*, Part II, 694.

232 State of Ohio, *Executive Documents: Annual Reports for 1887 Made to the Sixty-Eighth General Assembly*, Part II, 694.

233 State of Ohio, *Executive Documents: Annual Reports for 1887 Made to the Sixty-Eighth General Assembly*, Part II, 694.

234 State of Ohio, *Executive Documents: Annual Reports for 1887 Made to the Sixty-Eighth General Assembly*, Part II, 694.

235 "Returned from Camp," *Paulding Democrat*, May 5, 1887, 5.

236 State of Ohio, *Executive Documents: Annual Reports for 1887 Made to the Sixty-Eighth General Assembly*, Part II, 694.

237 State of Ohio, *Executive Documents: Annual Reports for 1887 Made to the Sixty-Eighth General Assembly*, Part II, 694.

238 "The War is Over," *Fort Wayne Gazette*, May 7, 1887, 1; "The Cruel War is Over!" *Paulding County Gazette*, May 12, 1887, 1; "Soldiers Gone Home," *Paulding Democrat*, May 12, 1887, 5.

239 "The War is Over," *Fort Wayne Gazette*, May 7, 1887, 1; "The Cruel War is Over!" *Paulding County Gazette*, May 12, 1887, 1.

240 "Soldiers Gone Home," *Paulding Democrat*, May 12, 1887, 5.

241 "The War is Over," *Fort Wayne Gazette*, May 7, 1887, 1; "How They See It Now," *Paulding County Gazette*, May 19, 1887, 7.

242 "The Cruel War is Over!" *Paulding County Gazette*, May 12, 1887, 1.

243 "The Cruel War is Over!" *Paulding County Gazette*, May 12, 1887, 1; "Soldiers Gone Home," *Paulding Democrat*, May 12, 1887, 5.

244 "The Cruel War is Over!" *Paulding County Gazette*, May 12, 1887, 1.

245 "How They See It Now," *Paulding County Gazette*, May 19, 1887, 7.

246 "The Cruel War is Over!" *Paulding County Gazette*, May 12, 1887, 1; "Local and Personal," *Defiance County Express*, May 12, 1887, 11; "Soldiers Gone Home," *Paulding Democrat*, May 12, 1887, 5; "The War is Over," *Fort Wayne Gazette*, May 7, 1887, 1; "How They See It Now," *Paulding County Gazette*, May 19, 1887, 7.

247 "Soldiers Gone Home," *Paulding Democrat*, May 12, 1887, 5; "The Cruel War is Over!" *Paulding County Gazette*, May 12, 1887, 1.

248 "Soldiers Gone Home," *Paulding Democrat*, May 12, 1887, 5.

249 "How They See It Now," *Paulding County Gazette*, May 19, 1887, 7.

250 State of Ohio, *Executive Documents: Annual Reports for 1887 Made to the Sixty-Eighth General Assembly*, Part II, 694.

251 State of Ohio, *Executive Documents: Annual Reports for 1887 Made to the Sixty-Eighth General Assembly*, Part II, 697.

252 State of Ohio, *Executive Documents: Annual Reports for 1887 Made to the Sixty-Eighth General Assembly*, Part II, 694.

253 State of Ohio, *Executive Documents: Annual Reports for 1887 Made to the Sixty-Eighth General Assembly*, Part II, 697; Cruel War is Over!" *Paulding County Gazette*, May 12, 1887, 1.

254 Local and Personal," *Defiance County Express*, May 12, 1887, 11.

255 "How They See It Now," *Paulding County Gazette*, May 19, 1887, 7.

256 Cruel War is Over!" *Paulding County Gazette*, May 12, 1887, 1.

257 "Round About—Antwerp," *Paulding County Gazette*, May 5, 1887, 5.

258 State of Ohio, *Executive Documents: Annual Reports for 1887 Made to the Sixty-Eighth General Assembly*, Part II, 694.

259 "Round About—Antwerp," *Paulding County Gazette*, May 12, 1887, 7.

260 *Delphos Weekly Herald*, May 12, 1887, 2.

# -7-

# Making an Auspicious Case

(May 1887)

After the Reservoir War had ended, people were left to figure out what had just happened, and what caused the fiercest discontent in Paulding County's history. Such discontent which apparently necessitated the appearance of the Ohio National Guard to preserve the peace, and "doubly increased the interest which had been taken, causing the press of the country as far away as New York to discuss the merits of the case."[1] Of the many newspapers that commented on the matter, the *Cincinnati Telegram* noted the sentiments already pointed out in the years prior:

> Here is a community almost a unit in desiring the annihilation of a pest-breeding spot which not only emits disease but renders useless tens of thousands of acres of valuable land, while at the same time the same community is a unit in favor of maintenance of the integrity of the canal system of Ohio.[2]

Again, the *Antwerp Argus* made it clear to its readers that they did not support violent acts and mob violence to get rid of the public works.[3] The *Cincinnati Commercial Gazette* noted that "there are many citizens who, while earnestly desiring to get rid of the reservoir, deeply deplore the use of lawless violence."[4] Those citizens showed concern that all the lawless depredations would bring "Paulding County into disrepute all over the State, and it is better to do with the nuisance than lose the reputation of being a law and order loving people."[5]

Contradictorily, the *Antwerp Argus* tried to downplay the entire situation, declaring that "Governor Foraker has been greatly deceived, and matters have been grossly misrepresented to him."[6] The *Antwerp Argus* declared that it was:

> The dispatches sent to the Governor, and those published in the daily papers, regarding damage done are greatly exaggerated. Also the reports that mob violence existed here, and that the guards heretofore placed at the reservoir, were overpowered, is untrue in every particular, as no disturbance of any kind have taken place, and everything done was conducted in a most orderly manner; in fact so much so, that the movements of those engaged in the work of destruction was wholly unknown outside of those immediately connected... no armed mob has existed in this section; no personal property has been injured, or the life of any person placed in jeopardy.[7]

The *Paulding County Gazette* shared a similar sentiment, asserting that, "we firmly believe that had not Gov. Foraker been imposed upon and deceived by the flaming, blood-red dispatches from Defiance he would have sent no troops to [Paulding County.]"[8]

The *Antwerp Argus* also believed that, while some structures had been "badly damaged," the destruction was "greatly exaggerated," and it would not cost more than "eight hundred or a thousand dollars" to repair them.[9] The State of Ohio would later report that the total cost to "restore the works and guard them from further violence" totaled $3,475.26 (~$109,017 in 2023).[10]§

The *Antwerp Argus* even asserted that mob violence never existed to begin with, and if mob violence had been present in Paulding County, a request would have been made for military support through Sheriff Parr, not from Charles A. Flickinger.[11] The *Antwerp Argus* believed that the latter had misrepresented the entire situation to "secure a military display in our county."[12] However, there is plenty of evidence that Sheriff Parr was requested to formally request the military presence,[13] which he possibly ignored because he found no riot he considered worthy of requesting the Ohio National Guard to handle.[14] The *Cincinnati Commercial Gazette* insinuated that Sheriff Parr was sympathetic to the Dynamiters' cause, and therefore willfully ignorant of the matter.[15]

As mentioned in the previous chapter, Sheriff David W. Parr had posted wanted posters around Paulding County and arrested Henry W. Sperry, indicating that he was looking into the issue to some extent, but likely did not consider it an issue he could not handle, and therefore did not call upon Governor Joseph B. Foraker to send the Ohio National Guard. Despite Sheriff Parr's actions to the contrary of the negative press he received, one local businessman, Joseph A. Boyd, known at one time as the "'timber king' of Melrose,"[16] reportedly removed his name from Sheriff Parr's "official bond" due to his "dissatisfaction with Sheriff Parr's official action in regard to the recent reservoir

---

§ It's not exactly clear if this number included the cost of deploying the National Guard (noted on page 203), but I doubt it. This number is more likely the cost of just the repairs and civilian guards.

war." [17] The circumstances of what this 'official bond' might have been is not known, but eight "responsible citizens" from Antwerp and Paulding reportedly "voluntarily furnished a new bond for Mr. Parr which the Commissioners accepted" on May 18, 1887.[18]

The *Paulding Democrat* asserted that, while Mr. Flickinger and others in Defiance were "robbing us of our forest wealth," they had created a "sentiment throughout the State against our petition for the abandonment of the nuisance."[19] The *Paulding Democrat* also asserted that Mr. Flickinger and company had slandered Sheriff Parr and "circulated reports as to the lawlessness of our people, which are not only maliciously false but absolutely ridiculous."[20] The *Paulding Democrat* believed that Sheriff Parr could have handled the mess himself, and that "there has been no cause for sending the State militia here. They will have no body of men to fight. Our people are a peaceful, sensible community. They don't court a conflict with the State military."[21] That last bit was true; the Dynamiters were not openly hostile toward the Ohio National Guard, just the reservoir.

The *Toledo Bee, Defiance Democrat*, and the *Delphos Herald* "either through ignorance or a spirit of vindictiveness," reportedly claimed that the citizens of Paulding County would have to bear the expenses of the military presence in their county.[22] This matter would have been especially troublesome considering that no expenses would reportedly be spared in suppressing the civil unrest,[23] and that was not far from the truth as the total cost of the Ohio National Guard's deployment was $3,070.25 (~$96,312 in 2023).[24][¶] The *Paulding Democrat* asserted that this claim was "the sheerest nonsense and without the slightest foundation of truth."[25] The *Van Wert Times*, including Judge Latty,[26] also refuted the claim that Paulding County would have to pay. Their biggest argument was "the troops were not called for by any of the Paulding County authorities but at the solicitation of outside parties."[27]

The *Toledo Commercial* also asserted that the citizens of Paulding County would not have to pay for the military presence,[28] stating that such claims were made from a misinterpretation by the *Toledo Bee*, which allegedly cited a Pennsylvania "special statute" (not an Ohio one) used against railroad rioters in Pittsburgh. Such a statute did not apply in the State of Ohio.[29] Some in Paulding County even believed that the Governor had only sent the troops "partly to satisfy the demands of Defiance parties but principally for the purpose of making political capital by pandering to the sickly sentiment by some people entertained that the abandonment of this nuisance would affect the whole public works."[30]

The *Paulding County Gazette* printed the most level-headed and factual summary of the background of the fierce discontent, asserting that, while the canal and reservoir were once held in high regard, "the hand of decay began to settle upon the canal" after the advent of the railroad removed freight and passenger patronage from the canal.[31] The *Paulding County Gazette* declared "the canals had out-lived their days of usefulness and were left in a neglected and uncared for condition."[32]

---

[¶] See Appendix G for an itemized list of expenses.

Due to the neglect, not only had the reservoir's backwater "rendered worthless many thousand acres," the banks of the canal would often fail, and the "adjacent lands and farms overflowed, fences washed away, and growing crops destroyed."[33] Furthermore, the *Paulding County Gazette* blamed the State of Indiana for having "violated her contract and abandoned her portion of the canal," making the Wabash & Erie Canal in Ohio "useless."[34]

When the citizens had had enough of their plight, they petitioned to abandon the canal and reservoir. Unfortunately for the citizens, despite their best efforts, "their petitions have been slighted and their supplications unheeded or treated with indifference and insult."[35] For this action, the *Paulding County Gazette* blamed the timber interests of Defiance and its "most influential and wealthy citizens," having gone to lobby in Columbus for their interests. [36] The *Paulding County Gazette* printed the following:

> Had it not been for the petty selfishness of a few Defiance manufacturers, this matter would have all been peacefully and legally settled last winter, and Paulding County would not have gained the unenviable notoriety which has lately been forced upon her. Had it not been for the selfish hungering after a few saw logs by a few Defiance men, the 'measured tread' of State troops would not be heard within our peaceful confines. Let the people of the State know the truth in the matter, and then the condemnation will fall where it should—upon the selfish Defiance lobby who went to Columbus last winter and defeated the Geyer Canal bill... For all this great hub bub... Let the blame fall where it should fall—upon a few greedy manufacturers of Defiance who hunger for the saw logs around the reservoir, and thirst for the water there of to float them away.[37]

With the failure to have the canal and reservoir abandoned, Paulding County was left with "its most blighting and detestable curse—the stagnant, disease-breeding reservoir and the black, unsightly and muddy ditch that leads from it to the Junction."[38] Not willing to accept this, the locals used "force and have blown out with dynamite a damnable nuisance which the lawmakers of the State have repeatedly refused to remove." [39] The *Paulding County Gazette* clarified that they did not "favor the methods which have been resorted to in trying to get rid of the despicable frog pond."[40] However, the *Paulding County Gazette* also believed "'forbearance' in this case 'had almost ceased to be a virtue' and it seemed that force was the only remedy to apply."[41]

Objections to the abandonment came from arguments that had dated back to Dr. Solomon S. Stambaugh's lawsuit in 1874 and 1877-1878. The first argument was that the attempt to abandon Six Mile Reservoir was only brought forth "in the interest of persons who desired to get hold of the reservoir lands."[42] The Toledo correspondent to the *Cincinnati Commercial Gazette* implied that a "central ring of influential men" had influenced the locals into committing the depredations so they could make their claims to the land.[43]

When taking into consideration the broken promises to fix the canal and reservoir,[44] of which their dilapidated condition often made the land adjacent to the canal "unfit for tillage."[45] The general unprofitability and lack of money the canal made compared to repair expenditures.[46] The reservoir being viewed as a "vast miasma-breeding expanse of stagnant water, spreading disease and death over the country."[47] As well as the canal and reservoir's sources of water having been cut off and diverted in Indiana.[48] The correspondent did not find it too far-fetched to see why the citizens of Paulding County had allegedly come under the influence of those seeking to profit from the land.[49]

The second argument was that the canal and Six Mile Reservoir were feeders for the Miami & Erie Canal's water supply.[50] This was arguably the most enduring argument against abandonment, primarily because the Miami & Erie Canal and Six Mile Reservoir were deemed "an absolute necessity" by the *Defiance Call.*[51] Part of this argument, however, did not hold much water (no pun intended). As mentioned earlier, the reservoir was often low or even dry during some parts of the year because of poor or nonexistent water supply from its principal feeders.

The *Paulding Democrat* asserted that "during the dry autumn months, at the time when water is most sadly needed, and when the Six Mile Reservoir is as dry as a bake oven that the Miami and Erie is kept supplied to its utmost capacity."[52] The *Paulding Democrat* then asked for the individual at the *Defiance Call* who printed such claims to visit Six Mile Reservoir during the dry months, wherein they wagered "he would fail to speak of its feeding capacity in such glowing terms."[53]

Not to be left out of making an argument on this topic, the *Antwerp Argus* refuted the claim by asserting that, because of the actions in Indiana, "the reservoir cannot be relied upon to furnish water for canal boat navigation beyond the first or the middle of July, and from that time on, during the heated months of August, September, and a portion of October."[54] That said, this issue had remained practically unchanged since the reservoir's inception, but the canal was historically furnished with water from Fort Wayne to pick up the slack in those dry months, something that was no longer capable of happening. Moreover, the *Antwerp Argus* asserted that no "competent civil engineer in the state" would believe for a second that the Mercer County Reservoir was incapable of furnishing water to Defiance.[55] The *Antwerp Argus* stated that the amount of water held in that reservoir was "for all purposes of navigation... more than adequate between Mercer County Reservoir and Defiance."[56]

Interestingly, one argument for the preservation of Six Mile Reservoir, in an attempt to assert it as the dominant feeder of the Miami & Erie Canal, claimed that "'the southern end of the Miami canal is fed by the St. Mary's reservoir'" not the northern end of the canal to Defiance.[57] The *Antwerp Argus* was quick to point out the following:

> The summit level of the canal passing New Bremen and Minster is twenty or more miles in length, and is twenty feet or more above the maximum level of the St. Mary's Reservoir; and we are obliged to ask 'K' in what manner he forces the water from the St. Mary's Reservoir over an elevation of twenty feet to supply the summit level and thus feed the southern end of the Miami canal? For his information, we will say that this twenty-mile summit level is supplied from the Loramie Reservoir (Lake Loramie), containing but a thousand acres, and then if that thousand acre reservoir can supply this twenty mile summit level, cannot the St. Mary's Reservoir, with its 17,000 acres, furnish more than all needs of water for navigation purposes between St. Mary's and Defiance, a distance of sixty miles?[58]

The *Antwerp Argus* could readily claim that "there is no earthly necessity for an additional water supply to be introduced at Junction."[59] The *Antwerp Argus* was correct in assessing how the canal's waters worked, as a gradient profile of the Miami & Erie Canal clearly shows that water from the Mercer County Reservoir was below the canal's summit on the north side. Without a massive pump, that water was not getting over the summit to the south side as claimed.[60]

Never mind that an individual, going by the pseudonym *K*, also asserted the mills between St. Mary's and Defiance use the canal water and "discharges it after use into other channels, so that it does not find its way into the canal again."[61] The *Antwerp Argus* called this "not justified by fact," and even if it was, "all leases of water between these points stipulate that it shall be taken from the upper and discharged into the lower level."[62] Granted, based on previous assertions by area newspapers of businesses not paying for things properly, it might be no surprise if this was actually occurring. Nevertheless, the *Antwerp Argus* asserted that "the authorities should do their duty" and stop that practice if it was happening.[63]

The third argument, particularly in Defiance (and supported by outside publications like *The Dayton Journal*), is still a tried-and-true argument in the twenty-first century nationwide. "The people who reside and own property in the vicinity of the nuisance knew that it was here when they came and if they didn't like it, they should have kept away from it."[64] In certain situations, this is a fair argument; the problem of invoking this argument for this issue is one salient detail.

When the people living in the vicinity of the canal works moved to the region, the works were still useful and satisfactory. However, over time, the works were allowed to fall into disrepair for one reason or another and to such an extent that they effectively became useless. The *Paulding Democrat* proposed the following scenario to those living in Defiance:

> We will suppose that the council of the village of Defiance should see fit to locate an institution in the center of that corporation which in the days of its usefulness would be satisfactory to all of its inhabitants, but in course of time would degrade to not only a nuisance but a menace to the health of the populace. Would the citizens who located there after the institution had been established console themselves by reflecting that they were unfortunate in coming in after it had been created and consent to let it remain for that reason?"[65]

The *Tiffin Advertiser* agreed with this assessment but took it one step further (against the opinion of Paulding County) when directly arguing with *The Dayton Journal*. The *Tiffin Advertiser* asserted that "all the complaints of the people of Paulding County can be obviated and avoided in the future by the abandonment of the entire canal system of the State, which has become a grievous burden and public nuisance."[66]

The remaining argument, and possibly the most significant argument against abandonment, was claimed by Defiance timber manufacturing interests. They claimed that "without their market for [Paulding County's] timber," Paulding County would "be left in the wilderness with no chance to dispose of... surplus wood."[67] The *Paulding Democrat* refuted this assertion for a multitude of reasons. Namely, Defiance timber manufacturers allegedly had a habit of scamming Paulding

County citizens out of money due for the timber removed from their land. This was allegedly achieved by coming to the county to "roll the logs in the canal when the owners are not present, afterward compelling them to settle on the purchaser's terms," or "culling the measurements before taking possession," effectively short-changing the owner on their timber.[68]

The *Paulding Democrat* even claimed that a citizen of Emerald Township had not been paid for the timber removed from his land six to eight years prior; and that the Paulding County Court of Common Pleas was "teeming with such cases."[69] Though the *Paulding Democrat* could not object that the people of Paulding County were benefitted by selling timber to "Defiance buyers," Defiance's timber manufacturers could have just as easily set up their factories in Paulding County.[70] This would have directly benefitted Paulding County's economy because "the money spent for labor would circulate in our midst and the valuation of our tax duplicate would be largely increased."[71] Thus echoing earlier sentiments that the Defiance industries ought to move their operations to Paulding County and directly benefit its economy while using the canal and reservoir.

The citizens of Paulding County's arguments in favor of abandonment also remained the same as they had been for years up to this point in 1887. As the Toledo correspondent for the *Cincinnati Commercial Gazette* noted:

> In conversation with the people owning land in the immediate vicinity, it is found that they are as much exasperated at the do-nothing policy of the State in neither putting the reservoir and canal in good repair, nor in abandoning them definitely, as at the real drawback this bast swamp (for the reservoir is nothing

else) is to the health and development of that part of the county.

The Toledo correspondent for the *Cincinnati Commercial Gazette* also stated, "the Board of Public Works has often promised that the necessary repairs shall be made, and as often have disappointed the people."[72] The money spent to fix the works did not benefit the people of Antwerp, as "the locks were put in as agreed, but when it came to cleaning out the canals as had been promised... work stopped... the matter was left in no better shape than it had previously been and has remained since."[73] Making matters worse was that more money in the last six to eight years had been pumped into fixing the Wabash & Erie Canal and Six Mile Reservoir than the State had taken in from the waterway, thus rendering it unprofitable.[74]

The Board of Public Works disagreed that the canal was unprofitable, later reporting that "the revenue from this remaining part of the Wabash and Erie Canal has more than paid its expenses up to the time of the raids on it last fall, and would probably continue to do so until the lumbering on it had ceased, provided the water supply could be maintained intact."[75] The primary issue long-term was going to be keeping the water supply intact, as it had already become "insufficient" over the previous decade.[76]

Unfortunately, as soon as everybody could recover and figure everything out, fears abounded that the Reservoir War was not actually over. Rumors persisted that another canal-related attack was imminent to "cut the canal bank and open the dams in the old canal bed leading through [Antwerp]."[77] This indicated that those dams in the canal created by the local factories were still present in 1887. Nevertheless, the *Antwerp Argus* condemned this threat regardless of its validity, declaring that "the parties are known, and any attempt of that kind would be dangerous," mainly because the locals had resolved to protect the works after the April incident.[78]

Nevertheless, sometime around May 16, 1887, Six Mile Reservoir's southern bank (on the lower end) was cut.[79] The *Fort Wayne Sentinel* reported that the cut was "not a very serious one." [80] Local papers such as the *Antwerp Argus, Paulding Democrat,* and the *Paulding County Gazette* quickly condemned the depredation, and all agreed that it was likely the work of Defiance's "timber sharks."[81] They all more or less reported that the attack was made to get water from the reservoir into the county ditch to float logs into the canal.[82]

The *Paulding Democrat* snapped at the hypocrisy, pointing out that "when the water was being allowed to pass out of its banks and flow peaceably away through the canal in a manner which was damaging to no one they raised a terrific howl and immediately implored the Governor to send in soldiers to stop the terrible results of such proceedings." [83] Now, the same parties and "their intense interest in the welfare of the State institutions has relapsed." [84] They had allegedly damaged Six Mile Reservoir, all for what the *Paulding Democrat* called "their greed for securing [Paulding] county's timber."[85]

Antwerp Mayor William F. Fleck[¶] notified Governor Foraker of the depredations by telegram[86] with the following message:

> Yesterday afternoon reservoir cut again. Water flooding the country. Fifty men on their way to close the cut. What protection may we expect?[87]

Governor Foraker responded to Mayor Fleck's telegram with:

> Stop the cut and preserve the property. You shall have any protection you may need. I will go to Antwerp this afternoon.[88]

The *Cincinnati Weekly Enquirer* reported that Governor Foraker "is of the opinion that the cutting was not done maliciously" and that he did indeed leave for Antwerp that afternoon as promised.[89] In keeping with the pledge to protect the public works, and despite the mayor saying fifty people were on the way to fix it, the *Antwerp Argus* reported that only "some twenty [Antwerp] citizens left Wednesday morning [the 18th], armed with picks and shovels, for the purpose of closing the break and stopping the flow of water."[90] After the break was repaired, a guard was reportedly placed at the reservoir "until the next morning in order to prevent further depredations."[91]

---

¶ The *Cincinnati Weekly Enquirer* stated that Oliver S. Applegate was the one who sent the telegram, but the *Antwerp Argus* states that Mr. Applegate was apparently just the recipient of Governor Foraker's response to the message. The rest of the newspapers that reported on this in Paulding County state that Mayor Fleck sent the initial telegram. ("Six-Mile Reservoir," *Cincinnati Weekly Enquirer*, May 25, 1887, 3;

"The Reservoir Question," *Antwerp Argus*, May 26, 1887, 2; "Vice Versa," *Paulding Democrat*, May 19, 1887, 5; "Second Reservoir War!," *Paulding County Gazette*, May 19, 1887, 10.)

Loring Marshall and Lyman Trowbridge of Defiance County were quick to catch flak for this depredation by the *Antwerp Argus*, who insinuated that they had been the ones who had told the timbermen to open the reservoir bank. [92] However, Mr. Flickinger was the one who caught the most press from the attacks outside of the immediate area. The *Cincinnati Weekly Enquirer* reported that he "has been accused of winking at the transgression of his fellow townsmen." [93]

This was likely due to a report by the *Defiance Call* that the men who had cut the reservoir were doing so with the "authority of the Board of Public Works" and were justified in doing so because "that is the only means available for getting water out of the reservoir into the canal." [94] The *Defiance County Express* reported that Chief Engineer Samuel Bachtell discovered when visiting with the Governor that "it was not timbermen at all that cut the banks, but the state boat crew, to get water into the canal. The only way it could be done was to deepen the waste weir on the south bank. This was done, hence the alleged trouble." [95] The *Defiance County Express* asserted that "permission was granted to timbermen to take advantage of the water in the State ditch to get their logs into the canal." [96]

The *Paulding County Gazette* reported that "the superintendent in charge had given some men the privilege of cutting the bank for the purpose of letting water into a large ditch leading around the reservoir into the canal. In this ditch they had cut and rolled many logs which they desired to float into the canal, thence to Defiance." [97] Because Governor Foraker was also reportedly informed that the cut was made by "State authority," [98] the *Cincinnati Commercial Gazette* reported that

Governor Foraker was also "of the opinion that there was nothing wrong about cutting the reservoir banks in order to float the logs into the canal. Permission had been secured from the Superintendent, and the cut has been repaired."[99]

The sticking point, however, was that regardless of what the case actually was, the locals had not been properly informed of this alleged agreement, which is why they took the action they did to repair and guard the reservoir. [100] Furthermore, the *Paulding Democrat* asserted that this entire argument made no sense, and if they wanted to get water into the canal, they would have had far better results if they had cut the northern bank instead, where the canal was.[101] The *Paulding Democrat* was also unhappy that the ditch was being used for such purposes, and asserted that the "people of this county will not submit to being assessed for an improvement of that kind only to have it destroyed by a few timber thieves of Defiance."[102] The *Paulding Democrat* also stated that the Paulding County Commissioners would have "all obstructions removed from the county ditch on the south side of the reservoir and prosecute every person who is guilty of impairing its usefulness in any way."[103]

When Mr. Flickinger was pressed on the issue by a correspondent for the *Cincinnati Weekly Enquirer*, he said:

> I have sent an inspector to examine the cut without delay. I want to say to you and the people of Paulding County that no one has ever received permission from the Board of Public Works to cut the bank. I am for the preservation of the canals, and timbermen and dynamiters alike must recognize that the reservoir is the State's property. If any of the agents or the employees of the Board of Public Works have granted permission to cut the banks, we want to know it at once.[104]

When the *Fort Wayne Sentinel* called upon Mayor Fleck to discuss what had happened, Mayor Fleck reportedly "laughed and exhibited a letter from 'Arnica Flick.'" That letter from Mr. Flickinger informed Lewis S. Gordon that he had learned that "some parties" had cut a hole in the bank of the reservoir to "get water to float logs." Mr. Flickinger denied that he had anything to do with the recent depredation, stating it had "'been done entirely without my knowledge or consent.'"[105]

Meanwhile, with the news that Governor Foraker was coming to Antwerp, and fast, Zachariah A. Graves, Mayor Fleck, Harry Saylor, and Henry George Jr. were sent to Paulding "for the purpose of inviting [Paulding's] people to be present at the reception of the Governor" when he came to Paulding County.[106] "A number" of Paulding's citizens were said to have accepted Antwerp's invitation.[107] Among those individuals from Paulding were Representative John L. Geyer of Defiance and Paulding County, Alonzo B. Holcombe, Sheriff David W. Parr, Deputy Sheriff Edward C. Swain, Everett A. Budd, and Francis B. DeWitt.[108]

Governor Foraker first arrived, via the Baltimore & Ohio Railroad,[109]@ in Defiance on the night of May 18, 1887; staying at the Crosby Hotel for the night.[110] Governor Foraker was accompanied to Defiance by Mr. Bachtell and his son Joseph B. Foraker, Jr.[111] After "personally inquiring into the canal trouble"

---

@ The B&O's depot in Defiance, at that time, was located on the east side of Deatrick Street between the Wabash and B&O tracks, but a bit closer to the north side of the B&O tracks.
("Defiance County," *Ohio Railroad Stations Past & Present*,
    https://www.west2k.com/ohpix/defiancebandoold.jpg.)

around Defiance during the morning,[112] Governor Foraker, his son, Mr. Bachtell, and Mr. Flickinger left for Antwerp on the first Wabash Railroad train on the afternoon of May 19, 1887.[113] Kidder V. Haymaker also reportedly travelled from Defiance to Antwerp to be in the company of the governor.[114] Governor Foraker reportedly stated that "he proposed to make a most thorough investigation of this matter, not accepting statements, but to personally inspect the ground and make recommendations upon his observations."[115] This time, no aide-de-camp or lobbyist would inform him about the matter; he would see it himself.

Governor Foraker and company arrived in Antwerp, via the Wabash Railroad, sometime between 12 p.m. and 1 p.m.[116] and "were met by a large number of [Paulding County's] citizens."[117] Even with short notice of the Governor coming to the area, "carriages were in waiting," ready to take the Governor and others to Six Mile Reservoir.[118] Governor Foraker was reported to have "seemed anxious to see every point and thoroughly post himself on all sides of the question."[119] Joining in the Governor's carriage were Mayor Fleck, Prosecutor Wilson H. Snook, and editor of the *Antwerp Argus,* William E. Osborn.[120] Not counting the Governor's carriage, the procession heading to the reservoir consisted of "twenty-seven other carriages filled with citizens of [Paulding] county,"[121] all reportedly "anxious" to see the Governor and "get, if possible, a word of encouragement from him" regarding the reservoir question.[122]

The procession more or less followed the route of modern-day State Route 49 south from the railroad tracks, across the canal, and to the west end of Six Mile Reservoir, roughly where the State Route 49 overpass crosses U.S. 24.[123] When crossing the canal, it was reported by the *Antwerp Argus* as the "'first view' of a portion of the pestilent breeding cesspool in controversy."[124] When the procession arrived at the reservoir's inlet, the *Antwerp Argus* reported that "here the Governor got a pretty fair sample of a portion of the lands that are made worthless by this reservoir. At this point are thousands of acres of valuable lands... extending back... to the Indiana State line, a distance of four miles."[125]

The procession then attempted what "few old residents of the county have ever attempted—a drive around the reservoir—a distance of twelve miles."[126]§ Roughly two miles into the trip on the south bank of the reservoir, the procession made it to the most recent cut made in the reservoir's bank, where the *Antwerp Argus* described the repair as "a good job."[127] The procession then worked its way toward the lock and feeder gate at the northeast corner of the reservoir; In doing so, the crowd traveled past the county ditch along the reservoir's south and east bank, which was "lined with saw logs" awaiting shipment to Defiance.[128]

At the time of Governor Foraker's visit, no "drop of water now finds its way through this feeder into the old canal, which at present is [illegible] dry."[129] This dry condition reportedly caused "the atmosphere for miles around" to be "saturated with malaria, endangering the health of all the settlers within its reach."[130] Governor Foraker "stood and gazed the landscape over,"[131] a landscape described as only "rivaled by the far-famed

---

§ Measurements this old are always a little off without precision tools. A measurement using Google Earth tells us that circumnavigating the reservoir was a journey just shy of ten miles.

'Dismal Swamp' of Virginia." [132] Everybody who was there wondered what was going through Governor Foraker's mind seeing the situation of things.[133] The Governor's "thoughts on this occasion... remained unspoken." [134] However, his expressions were said to have articulated his thoughts anyway.[135]

From the northeast corner, the procession continued to Antwerp along the towpath of the canal, the whole excursion taking roughly three hours.[136] Not content with just seeing the reservoir, Governor Foraker "expressed a wish to visit the big ditch above the State Line, nearly five miles distant."[137] Nothing of note is said of the visit to Indiana's ditch, however, it is interesting that the Ohio Governor paid a visit to Indiana without telling the Indiana Governor about it. After viewing the ditch in Indiana, the procession returned to Antwerp, where everybody took to "a sumptuous repast at the Kauffman Hotel."[138@]

After receiving "a serenade from the Antwerp Cornet Band," and with some encouragement from "many leading citizens," Governor Foraker "appeared on the veranda of the hotel." The crowd still outside greeted Governor Foraker with cheers, whereafter he made a "brief... and to the point" speech.[139] In that speech, Governor Foraker is reported to have stated to the effect that

> He was convinced that the people of [Paulding] County had grievances and that he should recommend their careful consideration, and felt confident that all difficulties pertaining to the Reservoir would be settled to

@ I am not entirely certain where the Kauffman Hotel was in Antwerp, based on an advertisement, it was likely on the northeast corner of Cleveland Street and River Street.
(*Antwerp Argus*, December 8, 1887, 2; *Sanborn Fire Insurance Map from Antwerp, Paulding County, Ohio*, August 1893.)

the perfect satisfaction of the State and to the people of Paulding County.[140]

With that, the Governor thanked the band for "their delightful music"[141] and ended a speech that was so well received that when the Governor left the veranda and went back into the Kauffman Hotel, "three rousing cheers were given."[142] When the 7 p.m. Wabash train arrived in Antwerp, Governor Foraker and his entourage bid the locals farewell, and received "the warmest wishes" from the local citizenry when he left.[143] He would only take the train to Cecil, where he was taken to Bertha Furnace (formerly Paulding Furnace) and would be in the company of Stephen F. Eagle for the night.[144] The next morning, Governor Foraker returned to Columbus.[145]

Mr. Eagle was wholly against abandonment of the canal and reservoir. To this point in May 1887, Mr. Eagle had traveled to Columbus with the Defiance delegation in opposition of the Geyer Bill, reported the depredations to Governor Foraker the morning after the Reservoir War took place, and had helped place a bounty on those responsible for one of the attacks that preceded the Reservoir War. Mr. Eagle was the Superintendent of the Bertha Furnace and had, since March 1887, been looking into restarting the furnace by June due to the "present high price of iron."[146] However, this attempt to operate the furnace did not start well. The elevated section of track used to get wood into the kilns collapsed sometime between April 7, 1887, and April 14, 1887, though work was well underway to remedy the damage.[147]

After the Reservoir War, operations at the Bertha Furnace were temporarily suspended until repairs could be made to the locks at Junction and Tate's Landing.[148] Boats with a "large lot of cord wood" from "the vicinity of Charloe" were already prepared to make the trip by canal to the Bertha Furnace when the repairs were made.[149] The good news was that this work was already underway by May 12, 1887. [150] By June 2, 1887, the *Paulding County Gazette* reported that the Bertha Furnace would "begin operations about the 8th of June."[151]

The actual day they began melting the ore was not until July 5, 1887, [152] or July 6, 1887! [153] Mr. Eagle was not able to start sooner, reportedly due to an insufficient amount of timber being acquired.[154] However, by June, there was already "about 60,000 bushels of coal on hand" at the Bertha Furnace, and enough "cord wood" was "being received by canal boats" from "the vicinity of Charloe"[155] that Mr. Eagle felt confident they could start operations. Reportedly, they wanted to produce "four casts per day and the capacity per day will be 40 or 50 tons" until October. [156] However, at the start of operations in July, only "about 20 tons of pig iron" was produced each day.[157]

Given that Bertha Furnace needed the canal to bring in raw material for their processes, it was no surprise that Mr. Eagle did not favor the abandonment of the reservoir and canal. However, a boat loaded with wood for the furnace (likely the *Tariff* on account that it had been running wood to the Bertha Furnace and the *Blockade* was in dry dock in Junction being dismantled, its engine having been removed in May.[158]) reportedly became stuck "eight times in a mile on logs which have been allowed to water soak and remain in the bottom... an illustration of the advantages to be gained by allowing Defiance timbermen the free use of it for timber rafting."[159]

## Chapter 7 Notes

1 "The Reservoir Muddle," *Paulding Democrat*, May 5, 1887, 4; "Work of an Ohio Mob," *New York Tribune*, April 27, 1887, 1; "Rioters Realizing Their Mistake," *New York Tribune*, April 28, 1887, 1.

2 *Paulding Democrat*, May 12, 1887, 4.

3 "H-ll On The Wabash!" *Antwerp Argus*, April 28, 1887, 2.

4 "War on the Wabash," *Cincinnati Commercial Gazette*, April 28, 1887, 1.

5 "War on the Wabash," *Cincinnati Commercial Gazette*, April 28, 1887, 1.

6 "H-ll On The Wabash!" *Antwerp Argus*, April 28, 1887, 2.

7 "H-ll On The Wabash!" *Antwerp Argus*, April 28, 1887, 2.

8 "The Facts in the Case," *Paulding County Gazette*, May 5, 1887, 4.

9 "H-ll On The Wabash!" *Antwerp Argus*, April 28, 1887, 2.

10 State of Ohio, *Executive Documents: Annual Reports for 1887, Made to the Sixty-Eighth General Assembly*, Part I, 1294.

11 "H-ll On The Wabash!" *Antwerp Argus*, April 28, 1887, 2.

12 "H-ll On The Wabash!" *Antwerp Argus*, April 28, 1887, 2.

13 State of Ohio, *Executive Documents: Annual Reports for 1887 Made to the Sixty-Eighth General Assembly*, Part II, 691.

14 "War on the Wabash," *Cincinnati Commercial Gazette*, April 28, 1887, 1.

15 "War on the Wabash," *Cincinnati Commercial Gazette*, April 28, 1887, 1.

16 "Local Brevities," *Paulding County Gazette*, May 26, 1887, 8.

17 "Local Gossip," *Paulding Democrat*, May 19, 1887, 5.

18 "Local Gossip," *Paulding Democrat*, May 19, 1887, 5.

19 "The Reservoir Muddle," *Paulding Democrat*, May 5, 1887, 4.

20 "The Reservoir Muddle," *Paulding Democrat*, May 5, 1887, 4.

21 "The Reservoir Muddle," *Paulding Democrat*, May 5, 1887, 4.

22 "The Reservoir Muddle," *Paulding Democrat*, May 5, 1887, 4; *Paulding Democrat*, May 12, 1887, 4.

23 "Damnable Dynamite Deeds," *Defiance Democrat*, April 28, 1887, 3.

24 State of Ohio, *Executive Documents Annual Reports for 1887 Made to the Sixty-Eighth General Assembly*, Part II, 698.

25 "The Reservoir Muddle," *Paulding Democrat*, May 5, 1887, 4.

26 "Notes About Town," *Defiance County Express*, May 5, 1887, 9.

27 *Paulding Democrat*, May 12, 1887, 4.

28 "The Reservoir Muddle," *Paulding Democrat*, May 5, 1887, 4.

29 "The Reservoir Muddle," *Paulding Democrat*, May 5, 1887, 4.

30 "The Reservoir Muddle," *Paulding Democrat*, May 5, 1887, 4.

31 "The Facts in the Case," *Paulding County Gazette*, May 5, 1887, 4.

32 "The Facts in the Case," *Paulding County Gazette*, May 5, 1887, 4.

33 "The Facts in the Case," *Paulding County Gazette*, May 5, 1887, 4.

34 "The Facts in the Case," *Paulding County Gazette*, May 5, 1887, 4.

35 "The Facts in the Case," *Paulding County Gazette*, May 5, 1887, 4.

36 "The Facts in the Case," *Paulding County Gazette*, May 5, 1887, 4.

37 "The Facts in the Case," *Paulding County Gazette*, May 5, 1887, 4.

38 "The Facts in the Case," *Paulding County Gazette*, May 5, 1887, 4.

39 "The Facts in the Case," *Paulding County Gazette*, May 5, 1887, 4.

40 "The Facts in the Case," *Paulding County Gazette*, May 5, 1887, 4.

41 "The Facts in the Case," *Paulding County Gazette*, May 5, 1887, 4.

42 "The News at Columbus," *The Cincinnati Weekly Enquirer*, May 4, 1887, 5; "War on the Wabash," *Cincinnati Commercial Gazette*, April 28, 1887, 1.

43 "War on the Wabash," *Cincinnati Commercial Gazette*, April 28, 1887, 1.

44 "The Reservoir Muddle," *Paulding Democrat*, May 5, 1887, 4; "War on the Wabash," *Cincinnati Commercial Gazette*, April 28, 1887, 1.

45 "War on the Wabash," *Cincinnati Commercial Gazette*, April 28, 1887, 1.

46 "The Reservoir Muddle," *Paulding Democrat*, May 5, 1887, 4; "War on the Wabash," *Cincinnati Commercial Gazette*, April 28, 1887, 1.

47 "War on the Wabash," *Cincinnati Commercial Gazette*, April 28, 1887, 1; "The Reservoir Muddle," *Paulding Democrat*, May 5, 1887, 4.

48 "War on the Wabash," *Cincinnati Commercial Gazette*, April 28, 1887, 1; "The Reservoir Muddle," *Paulding Democrat*, May 5, 1887, 4.

49 "War on the Wabash," *Cincinnati Commercial Gazette*, April 28, 1887, 1.

50 "Exciting Times in Ohio," *Defiance Democrat*, May 5, 1887, 1.

51 "Local Gossip," Paulding Democrat, May 19, 1887, 5.

52 "Local Gossip," Paulding Democrat, May 19, 1887, 5.

53 "Local Gossip," Paulding Democrat, May 19, 1887, 5.

54 "The Wabash And Erie Canal The Antwerp Reservoir," *Antwerp Argus*, May 26, 1887, 2.

55 "The Wabash And Erie Canal The Antwerp Reservoir," *Antwerp Argus*, May 26, 1887, 2.

56 "The Wabash And Erie Canal The Antwerp Reservoir," *Antwerp Argus*, May 26, 1887, 2.

57 "The Wabash And Erie Canal The Antwerp Reservoir," *Antwerp Argus*, May 26, 1887, 2.

58 "The Wabash And Erie Canal The Antwerp Reservoir," *Antwerp Argus*, May 26, 1887, 2.

59 "The Wabash And Erie Canal The Antwerp Reservoir," *Antwerp Argus*, May 26, 1887, 2.

60 *Profile and Map of the Miami & Erie Canal Showing Progress and Cost of Improvements*, Drafted by A. H. Sawyer and Compiled under the direction of Charles E. Perkins; Bill Oeters et. al., *Taming the Swamp*, 30-33; Carillon Historical Park, *The Miami & Erie Canal: Symbol of an Era*, 6-7.

61 "The Wabash And Erie Canal The Antwerp Reservoir," *Antwerp Argus*, May 26, 1887, 2.
62 "The Wabash And Erie Canal The Antwerp Reservoir," *Antwerp Argus*, May 26, 1887, 2.
63 "The Wabash And Erie Canal The Antwerp Reservoir," *Antwerp Argus*, May 26, 1887, 2.
64 "The Reservoir Muddle," *Paulding Democrat*, May 5, 1887, 4.
65 "The Reservoir Muddle," *Paulding Democrat*, May 5, 1887, 4.
66 *Paulding Democrat*, May 12, 1887, 4.
67 "The Reservoir Muddle," *Paulding Democrat*, May 5, 1887, 4.
68 "The Reservoir Muddle," *Paulding Democrat*, May 5, 1887, 4.
69 "The Reservoir Muddle," *Paulding Democrat*, May 5, 1887, 4.
70 "The Reservoir Muddle," *Paulding Democrat*, May 5, 1887, 4.
71 "The Reservoir Muddle," *Paulding Democrat*, May 5, 1887, 4.
72 "War on the Wabash," *Cincinnati Commercial Gazette*, April 28, 1887, 1.
73 "The Reservoir Muddle," *Paulding Democrat*, May 5, 1887, 4.
74 "The Reservoir Muddle," *Paulding Democrat*, May 5, 1887, 4; "War on the Wabash," *Cincinnati Commercial Gazette*, April 28, 1887, 1.
75 State of Ohio, *Executive Documents: Annual Reports for 1887, Made to the Sixty-Eighth General Assembly*, Part I, 1294.
76 State of Ohio, *Executive Documents: Annual Reports for 1887, Made to the Sixty-Eighth General Assembly*, Part I, 1294.
77 "Would Be Dangerous," *Antwerp Argus*, May 19, 1887, 3.
78 "Would Be Dangerous," *Antwerp Argus*, May 19, 1887, 3.
79 "Should Be Stopped," *Antwerp Argus*, May 19, 1887, 3; "Trouble Renewed," *Antwerp Argus*, May 19, 1887, 3; "Vice Versa," *Paulding Democrat*, May 19, 1887, 5; "The Reservoir Question," *Antwerp Argus*, May 26, 1887, 2; "Second Reservoir War!," *Paulding County Gazette*, May 19, 1887, 10.
80 "The Paulding Reservoir," *Fort Wayne Sentinel*, May 20, 1887, 1.
81 "Should Be Stopped," *Antwerp Argus*, May 19, 1887, 3; "Trouble Renewed," *Antwerp Argus*, May 19, 1887, 3; "Vice Versa," *Paulding Democrat*, May 19, 1887, 5; "Second Reservoir War!," *Paulding County Gazette*, May 19, 1887, 10; "Additional Antwerp," *Paulding County Gazette*, May 19, 1887, 10; "The Reservoir Question," *Antwerp Argus*, May 26, 1887, 2.
82 "Should Be Stopped," *Antwerp Argus*, May 19, 1887, 3; "Trouble Renewed," *Antwerp Argus*, May 19, 1887, 3; "Vice Versa," *Paulding Democrat*, May 19, 1887, 5; "Second Reservoir War!," *Paulding County Gazette*, May 19, 1887, 10; "Additional Antwerp," *Paulding County Gazette*, May 19, 1887, 10; "The Reservoir Question," *Antwerp Argus*, May 26, 1887, 2.
83 "Vice Versa," *Paulding Democrat*, May 19, 1887, 5.
84 "Vice Versa," *Paulding Democrat*, May 19, 1887, 5.
85 "Vice Versa," *Paulding Democrat*, May 19, 1887, 5.

86 "Vice Versa," *Paulding Democrat*, May 19, 1887, 5; "Second Reservoir War!," *Paulding County Gazette*, May 19, 1887, 10.

87 "Six-Mile Reservoir," *Cincinnati Weekly Enquirer*, May 25, 1887, 3.

88 "Six-Mile Reservoir," *Cincinnati Weekly Enquirer*, May 25, 1887, 3; "The Reservoir Question," *Antwerp Argus*, May 26, 1887, 2.

89 "Six-Mile Reservoir," *Cincinnati Weekly Enquirer*, May 25, 1887, 3.

90 "Trouble Renewed," *Antwerp Argus*, May 19, 1887, 3; "The Reservoir Question," *Antwerp Argus*, May 26, 1887, 2.

91 "The Reservoir Question," *Antwerp Argus*, May 26, 1887, 2.

92 "Trouble Renewed," *Antwerp Argus*, May 19, 1887, 3.

93 "Six-Mile Reservoir," *Cincinnati Weekly Enquirer*, May 25, 1887, 3.

94 "Poor Excuse," *Paulding Democrat*, May 26, 1887, 5.

95 "Local," *Defiance County Express*, May 26, 1887, 9.

96 "Local," *Defiance County Express*, May 26, 1887, 9.

97 "Foraker At Antwerp!" *Paulding County Gazette*, May 26, 1887, 1.

98 "Foraker At Antwerp!" *Paulding County Gazette*, May 26, 1887, 1.

99 "Local," *Defiance County Express*, May 26, 1887, 9; "State Capital Notes," *Cincinnati Commercial Gazette*, May 21, 1887, 7.

100 "Foraker At Antwerp!" *Paulding County Gazette*, May 26, 1887, 1.

101 "Poor Excuse," *Paulding Democrat*, May 26, 1887, 5.

102 "Poor Excuse," *Paulding Democrat*, May 26, 1887, 5.

103 "Poor Excuse," *Paulding Democrat*, May 26, 1887, 5.

104 "Six-Mile Reservoir," *Cincinnati Weekly Enquirer*, May 25, 1887, 3.

105 "The Paulding Reservoir," *Fort Wayne Sentinel*, May 20, 1887, 1; "The Reservoir Question," *Antwerp Argus*, May 26, 1887, 2.

106 "Vice Versa," *Paulding Democrat*, May 19, 1887, 5.

107 "Vice Versa," *Paulding Democrat*, May 19, 1887, 5.

108 "Antwerp Items," *Paulding Democrat*, May 26, 1887, 1; "Local Brevities," *Paulding County Gazette*, May 26, 1887, 8.

109 "Local," *Defiance County Express*, May 26, 1887, 9.

110 "Personals," *Defiance County Express*, May 26, 1887, 9.

111 "Six-Mile Reservoir," *Cincinnati Weekly Enquirer*, May 25, 1887, 3; "The Reservoir Question," *Antwerp Argus*, May 26, 1887, 2; "Personals," *Defiance County Express*, May 26, 1887, 9.

112 "Six-Mile Reservoir," *Cincinnati Weekly Enquirer*, May 25, 1887, 3.

113 "Local," *Defiance County Express*, May 26, 1887, 9; "Six-Mile Reservoir," *Cincinnati Weekly Enquirer*, May 25, 1887, 3; "Foraker At Antwerp!" *Paulding County Gazette*, May 26, 1887, 1.

114 "Antwerp Items," *Paulding Democrat*, May 26, 1887, 1.

115 "Six-Mile Reservoir," *Cincinnati Weekly Enquirer*, May 25, 1887, 3.

116 "The Reservoir Question," *Antwerp Argus*, May 26, 1887, 2; "Foraker At Antwerp!" *Paulding County Gazette*, May 26, 1887, 1.

117 "The Reservoir Question," *Antwerp Argus*, May 26, 1887, 2; "Foraker At Antwerp!" *Paulding County Gazette*, May 26, 1887, 1.

118 "The Reservoir Question," *Antwerp Argus*, May 26, 1887, 2.

119 "The Reservoir Question," *Antwerp Argus*, May 26, 1887, 2.

120 "Foraker At Antwerp!" *Paulding County Gazette*, May 26, 1887, 1.

121 "Foraker At Antwerp!" *Paulding County Gazette*, May 26, 1887, 1.

122 "The Reservoir Question," *Antwerp Argus*, May 26, 1887, 2.

123 "The Reservoir Question," *Antwerp Argus*, May 26, 1887, 2.

124 "The Reservoir Question," *Antwerp Argus*, May 26, 1887, 2.

125 "The Reservoir Question," *Antwerp Argus*, May 26, 1887, 2.

126 "The Reservoir Question," *Antwerp Argus*, May 26, 1887, 2.

127 "The Reservoir Question," *Antwerp Argus*, May 26, 1887, 2.

128 "The Reservoir Question," *Antwerp Argus*, May 26, 1887, 2.

129 "The Reservoir Question," *Antwerp Argus*, May 26, 1887, 2.

130 "The Wabash And Erie Canal The Antwerp Reservoir," *Antwerp Argus*, May 26, 1887, 2.

131 "The Reservoir Question," *Antwerp Argus*, May 26, 1887, 2.

132 "Foraker At Antwerp!" *Paulding County Gazette*, May 26, 1887, 1.

133 "Foraker At Antwerp!" *Paulding County Gazette*, May 26, 1887, 1; "The Reservoir Question," *Antwerp Argus*, May 26, 1887, 2.

134 "The Reservoir Question," *Antwerp Argus*, May 26, 1887, 2.

135 "Foraker At Antwerp!" *Paulding County Gazette*, May 26, 1887, 1; "The Governor Came," *Paulding Democrat*, May 26, 1887, 5.

136 "Foraker At Antwerp!" *Paulding County Gazette*, May 26, 1887, 1; "The Reservoir Question," *Antwerp Argus*, May 26, 1887, 2.

137 "The Reservoir Question," *Antwerp Argus*, May 26, 1887, 2; "Foraker At Antwerp!" *Paulding County Gazette*, May 26, 1887, 1.

138 "The Reservoir Question," *Antwerp Argus*, May 26, 1887, 2; "Round About—Antwerp, *Paulding County Gazette*, May 26, 1887, 5; "Foraker At Antwerp!" *Paulding County Gazette*, May 26, 1887, 1.

139 "The Reservoir Question," *Antwerp Argus*, May 26, 1887, 2; "Round About—Antwerp, *Paulding County Gazette*, May 26, 1887, 5; "Foraker At Antwerp!" *Paulding County Gazette*, May 26, 1887, 1.

140 "Foraker At Antwerp!" *Paulding County Gazette*, May 26, 1887, 1.

141 "Foraker At Antwerp!" *Paulding County Gazette*, May 26, 1887, 1.

142 "The Reservoir Question," *Antwerp Argus*, May 26, 1887, 2; "Foraker At Antwerp!" *Paulding County Gazette*, May 26, 1887, 1.

143 "The Reservoir Question," *Antwerp Argus*, May 26, 1887, 2; "Foraker At Antwerp!" *Paulding County Gazette*, May 26, 1887, 1.

144 "The Reservoir Question," *Antwerp Argus*, May 26, 1887, 2; "The Governor Came," *Paulding Democrat*, May 26, 1887, 5; "Foraker At Antwerp!" *Paulding County Gazette*, May 26, 1887, 1.

145 "The Governor Came," *Paulding Democrat*, May 26, 1887, 5; "Foraker At Antwerp!" *Paulding County Gazette*, May 26, 1887, 1.

146 "What 'Our Neighbors' Have To Say—Defiance Call," *Antwerp Argus*, February 17, 1887, 3; "Local Brevities," *Paulding County Gazette*, March 10, 1887, 8; "Local Brevities," *Paulding County Gazette*, March 17, 1887, 8.

147 "Local Gossip," *Paulding Democrat*, April 14, 1887, 5.

148 "Round About—East End Echoes," *Paulding County Gazette*, May 12, 1887, 7.

149 "Round About—East End Echoes," *Paulding County Gazette*, May 12, 1887, 7.

150 "Round About—Junction," *Paulding County Gazette*, May 12, 1887, 7.

151 "Bertha Furnace," *Paulding County Gazette*, June 2, 1887, 1.

152 "Local Brevities," *Paulding County Gazette*, July 7, 1887, 8.

153 "Local Gossip," *Paulding Democrat*, July 7, 1887, 5.

154 "Bertha Furnace," *Paulding County Gazette*, June 2, 1887, 1.

155 "Local Brevities," *Paulding County Gazette*, June 2, 1887, 8; "Bertha Furnace," *Paulding County Gazette*, June 2, 1887, 1.

156 "Bertha Furnace," *Paulding County Gazette*, June 2, 1887, 1.

157 "Bertha Furnace," *Paulding County Gazette*, July 14, 1887, 7.

158 "Local Brevities" *Paulding County Gazette*, July 14, 1887, 8; "Paulding Furnace," *Paulding County Gazette*, May 5, 1887, 5.

159 "Local Gossip," *Paulding Democrat*, June 2, 1887, 5.

# -8-

# Turnabout after Further Depredations

## (June 1887 – October 1887)

On the night of June 6, 1887, yet another attack occurred at Six Mile Reservoir.[1] This time dynamiters blew out the "new feeder at the lower end of the reservoir."[2] Governor Joseph B. Foraker was informed about the depredations, but this time, from "Defiance parties."[3] Governor Foraker was informed so soon after the attack that the *Antwerp Argus* reported that the citizens of Antwerp were unaware that anything had happened.[4]

Because of this, the *Antwerp Argus* asserted, "the matter has rather a suspicious look, and too close an investigation on the part of Hon. Charles A. Flickinger, might implicate his Defiance neighbors."[5] The *Paulding Democrat* believed Mr. Flickinger, "and other State authorities," to be the one who gave the instructions to dynamite the feeder.[6] However, the *Antwerp Argus* seemed to believe that the Defiance timber interests had, perhaps, taken the previous suggestion of getting water from the northern side of the reservoir to float their logs a bit too literally.[7]

Blame was quickly placed on the local citizenry for the depredation, but the *Antwerp Argus* quickly rebuked that argument by quoting the locals' agreement to protect the reservoir to the best of their ability.[8] The *Antwerp Argus,* of course, reiterated that the blame being thrust upon Paulding County citizens was unwarranted and that "by this last attempt, the perpetrators hope to injure our cause, and place us in bad odor throughout the State."[9] The *Paulding County Gazette* concurred with this assessment to some extent, further stating that the depredation was done to create "an antipathy against those who are in favor of abandoning the accused nuisance, hoping thereby to secure its permanency."[10]

The *Paulding County Gazette* declared that if this were true, it would be "the most damnable device ever invented by man to fasten a disease-breeding and unsightly curse upon Paulding County to hinder and impede its development."[11] The *Paulding Democrat* also believed much of the same,[12] however, it asserted that Mr. Flickinger had done it to galvanize the people outside of Paulding County to renominate him for the Board of Public Works. Not just that, the *Paulding Democrat* believed the scheme was to get somebody other than John L. Geyer nominated and elected. Somebody who would be more favorable to opposing abandonment.[13]

Canal Division Superintendent Homer Meacham and his team of workers were back at the reservoir to repair the damage the next day,[14] having been telegraphed by Mr. Flickinger to do so.[15] Peculiarly, according to the *Defiance County Express,* the rebuilding of the feeder bulkhead that had just been destroyed was only just finished the morning of the day of the attack.[16]¶ The

---

¶ The *Paulding County Gazette* refers to it as a "new bulkhead" but does not specify when it was rebuilt.
("Reservoir Racket Renewed," *Paulding County Gazette,* June 9, 1887, 10.)

new feeder bulkhead that had just been built was reportedly just a "temporary feeder constructed of plank... built just west of the old iron feeder."[17] By June 9, 1887, the water was stopped from escaping.[18] The overall damage done was described as "not extensive,"[19] so repairs did not take long to complete.

Unfortunately for Mr. Meacham, on the night of June 13, 1887,[20] June 14, 1887,[21] or June 15, 1887,[22] the "tumble to the reservoir lock" and the "cofferdam erected to shut off the water while repairs were being made on the main dam of the Paulding County reservoir" were blown up.[23] Mr. Flickinger again telegraphed the necessary parties and even called for "a guard of one hundred men with guns over it if necessary."[24] The reason for such a sharp response from Mr. Flickinger was reportedly due to a rumor of an impending attack on locks along the Miami & Erie Canal with the goal of "compelling the State to abandon the Paulding County reservoir."[25]

In response to these recent depredations, and likely having grown tired of getting blamed for their occurrence, a "large crowd" of Antwerp citizens (some were also from the rest of the county) held "an indignation meeting" on the evening of June 16, 1887.[26] Those attending the meeting resolved the following:

> By the citizens of Antwerp here assembled that we denounce and condemn the late attempts to destroy the feeder at the reservoir as pure maliciousness and done for the purpose of creating a feeling against the people of this locality, ad do pledge ourselves as law-abiding citizens to faithfully assist in carrying the pledges made to Governor Foraker for the prevention of damage and protection of the public property of the State then located.[27]

Prior to the meeting, Antwerp's mayor, William F. Fleck, was informed by William H. Hahn of the Board of Public Works that he would be coming to Antwerp to look at the reservoir.[28] Surprisingly, Mr. Hahn also went to Indiana to see the ditch there.[29] While at the meeting, Mr. Hahn made "some very practical and well-chosen remarks" to the attendees.[30] Mr. Hahn proved to be a popular member of the Board of Public Works among those at the meeting, and he reportedly "propounded the following conundrum at the meeting: How do our citizens navigate this canal where every line fence was continued on across as though there was no canal?" Unfortunately for him, nobody at the meeting could answer that question.[31]

The result of this meeting was another set of civilian guards, appointed by Mr. Hahn as a member of the Board of Public Works, consisting of the following individuals to be placed at four locations. Guarding One-Mile Lock west of Junction were Warren Jacobs and Leonard Wilson. At Tate's Lock in Tate's Landing were Emmet E. Pocock and Henry M. Ankney. Stationed at the aqueduct near the Paulding & Cecil Improved Road were Caleb J. Schneider and George N. Munson. At the reservoir was Charles W. Boland, Isreal R. Ream, and, most interesting of them all, Henry W. Sperry.[32] These individuals were given the "power to arrest any person or persons found meddling with [State property] contrary to law," and told to "proceed immediately to guard and protect" the public works.[33] Allegedly, whenever he could do so, Mr. Sperry would open the feeder gates to permit what little water there was to leave the reservoir.[34]

The first night for the civilian guard could only be described as "diligently killing time and mosquitoes, mostly the latter."[35]

So much so that the *Antwerp Argus* jokingly reported that the guards encountered a force of mosquitoes that "appeared to have full possession of the grounds and leveled their weapons on them immediately."[36] The result of this "terrible bloody contest on the first night of their war experience" was the ground being "covered with dead 'skeeters.'"[37]

So abundant were mosquitoes that the guards hyperbolized that there were millions of them.[38] Otto E. Ehrhart was later told that the mosquitoes were so abundant that "when they saw a man walking on the banks of the reservoir they would come in swarms large enough to carry the man off."[39] In one instance, the *Paulding Democrat* jokingly reported that "one of the guards at the reservoir thought he saw the Sheriff coming, but close investigation proved it to be a mosquito."[40] Helping the guards tend to their wounds was "a free use of 'Arnica' [sic]."[41] Frank Lamb, Frank O. Perry, and William H. Durbin traveled to the reservoir on June 28, 1887, and "took 'tea' with the guards," which likely helped the guard's resolve in some way.[42]

Within two weeks, two guards would need to be replaced. The first was Caleb J. Schneider, who resigned for unknown reasons on June 23, 1887, and was replaced by Richard S. Banks, Jr.[43] A few days later, on June 28, 1887, Emmet E. Pocock would also resign his post to begin a new job as a day operator for the Wabash Railroad in Whitehouse, Ohio.[44] Mr. Pocock had recently been let go from his position as a night operator for the Wabash Railroad in Antwerp around May 5, 1887, when that position was abolished. [45] ¶ Mr. Pocock left Antwerp for his new job, and Samuel O. Lewis was his replacement. [46]

At some point, presumably, nine guards were stationed at four points around Six Mile Reservoir, [47] while the previous reports only indicated three there, leaving six unaccounted for. The reason to suspect there were six others at the reservoir was due to the presence of Dr. Hiram M. Ayres, previously not mentioned as being appointed as a guard, who was reportedly stationed at a "camp No. 3." [48] Meanwhile, Richard S. Banks, Jr. and Samuel O. Lewis were still reported to have been posted at the aqueduct and Tate's Lock on July 28, 1887. [49]

It was also announced that Senator Robert Mehaffey from Allen County would be in Antwerp on June 29, 1887, to view the canal, reservoir, and ditch in Indiana. [50] The senator arrived in Paulding and was shuttled to the reservoir, accompanied by Representative John L. Geyer of Defiance and Paulding County, Kenton E. Shuster, Thomas B. Holland, and Antwerp Mayor William F. Fleck. [51] Despite his opposition to the Geyer Bill to abandon the canal and reservoir, upon seeing the decrepit condition of affairs in Paulding County, Senator Mehaffey talked "as though he was convinced of the righteousness of our claim." [52]

However, he did not calm any concerns about his support. He insinuated that, despite the evidence, voting in favor of abandonment would "antagonize public sentiment among people of the State who know nothing about [the] case," [53] and he

---

¶ This arrangement in Whitehouse did not last long. By September 22, 1887, Mr. Pocock was "given his old job as night operator" at Antwerp. ("Round About—Antwerp," *Paulding County Gazette*, September 22, 1887, 5.)

had opposed abandonment because it would possibly hurt his chances of being reelected.[54] After viewing the matters, the group returned to Paulding, where the senator left on a southbound CJ&M train that evening.[55]

Within a week after Senator Mehaffey left, Oliver S. Applegate, William D. Wilson, and the editor of the *Paulding County Gazette* traveled to Six Mile Reservoir to deliver supplies to the guards.[56] These three delivered "tents, guns, and other supplies... W. D. Wilson had made them a filter."[57] That filter was for a good reason, as the nearby water was described by the editor of the *Paulding County Gazette* as the worst water he had seen "for a good while."[58] Never mind that some of those at "Point No. 1" had to travel a mile to get decent water, if any water at all.[59] The men stationed at the reservoir were killing time by fishing for food, as Charles W. Boland was seen "taking the jackets off of about a dozen 'bull-heads,'" and the men had butter to fry the fish they caught.[60]

Fishing was something that ADJ GEN Henry A. Axline was alleged to have done as well, reportedly catching a bullhead in the vicinity of seven pounds.[61] Though the *Paulding County Gazette* joked that they probably "swelled to the enormous size of seven pounds" after seeing the Gatling gun, as they typically weighed less than a pound.[62] When the civilian guards were given their first pay for their services, Oliver S. Applegate was the one who handed out their pay in the form of "a voucher issued by the State."[63] Each guard was paid $21 (~$659 in 2023) for their two weeks of service between June 17, 1887 and July 1, 1887.[64] This amounted to the $1.50 (~$47 in 2023) per night that Otto E. Ehrhart was told for his history of the event.[65]

Bertha Furnace would encounter a string of misfortunes starting about this time in July, the first being when the bell of the furnace "fell in."[66] The furnace would remain idle until a new "bell and hopper" was received from Lebanon, Pennsylvania.[67] The furnace had reportedly produced "one hundred and ninety tons of iron" before the failure occurred.[68] That damage was fixed by the end of August, and the prospects were looking high with the furnace "turning out more iron per week... than it has ever done before."[69]

Representative Geyer was renominated for his position in the Ohio House of Representatives with little to no opposition.[70] The renomination of Mr. Flickinger,[71] however, would prove to be a contentious decision, so much so that the decision was referred to as "worse than a red rag in the face of a Jersey bull."[72] No fewer than three "influential Republicans of Defiance County" (L. E. Griffin, William Dilworth, and Joseph O. Kerr[73]) protested the nomination of Mr. Flickinger.[74]

> It is a notorious fact to [the Republican] convention that Defiance County, with the exception of half a dozen manufacturers at Defiance, is unalterably opposed to keeping up of the Paulding County canal and reservoir. Mr. Flickinger is in favor of this, and by his actions in the past has thrown about him the opposition of the two counties.[75]

Therefore, it was believed that Mr. Flickinger "could not carry 500 votes in the counties," and he would inevitably fail to be re-elected.[76]

By the beginning of August 1887, Six Mile Reservoir was nearly dry. Franz J. Zuber had reported that "at least there is not more than three hundred acres of this vast body of land now covered by water."[77] The civilian guards reportedly complained "bitterly of the stench arising from decayed matter, making it at times difficult to breathe freely." [78] The canal's water had become so low that, by September 1, 1887, "all of [Antwerp's] factories are obliged to have water hauled from the river in order to enable them to run as their water supply-the canal-is dry,"[79] an occurrence not heard of since the failure of the St. Joseph Feeder Dam a decade prior.

By mid-August, the *Antwerp Argus* reported that "everybody is now complaining of dull times."[80] Subsequently, the civilian guard's services were no longer necessary, and they were "discharged" on August 12, 1887.[81] Peculiarly, the decision by the Board of Public Works would have left the reservoir guarded by a single person.[82] The Antwerp citizens that had formed the committee to protect the reservoir decided that was ridiculous as "they considered one guard as good as none" and elected to remove all the guards.[83] The committee also requested that they "be relieved from further responsibility" to protect the reservoir.[84] Following their dismissal, the Board of Public Works announced they would tour the reservoir and canal on September 8, 1887.[85]

On August 29, 1887, before the Board of Public Works arrived, and conveniently after the guards had been dismissed, "lumber belonging to the State" that was in the vicinity of the reservoir along the canal was burned.[86] As promised, the Board of Public Works traveled to Paulding County.[87] Those from the Board were Charles A. Flickinger, William H. Hahn, and W. S. Jones.[88] They were also accompanied by Chief Engineer Samuel Bachtell, Canal Division Superintendent Homer Meacham, and Antwerp Mayor

William F. Fleck, among other Antwerp citizens.[89] Their goal was to make an inspection tour and "see what is needed in the way of protection."[90]

Upon their arrival, the committee was greeted with a canal and reservoir that was completely dry.[91] While Mr. Flickinger "looked on in silent contemplation," somebody allegedly suggested the possibility of feeding the canal with water from the Maumee River.[92] The only responses to such an idea were W. S. Jones smiling to himself at the very idea of it and somebody else, probably Mayor Fleck, informing them that the Maumee River was forty feet below the level of the canal,[93] and that such an idea was "preposterous in the extreme."[94]

While the Democrats of the area had renominated Representative Geyer for the Ohio House of Representatives, the Republicans nominated John Crowe of Defiance for the same.[95] With their nomination of Mr. Crowe, the Republican Representative Convention asserted that, contrary to the beliefs of Representative Geyer and others, the Wabash & Erie Canal in Paulding County was not "practically abandoned." [96] The Republican convention acknowledged that the Board of Public Works was incompetent in completing the work appropriated for in 1883 as prescribed.[97] However, as the *Defiance County Express* put it, "with the Antwerp reservoir full of water, and the Wabash canal thoroughly dredged, we will have good service from the canal. As it is it is badly crippled."[98]

The Republican Party nominated Mr. Crowe because of his favor for introducing legislation to "reappropriate the money that was left unexpended, and finish the improvement of the canal that was ordered by the legislature at that time,"[99] a fairly reasonable position to take. However, the original appropriations bill was the locals' compromise. Whether by intention or incompetence, the Board of Public Works did not fulfill the promise. For almost three years, the locals tried to make the State finish the repairs or abandon the canal works. When the pleas were ignored, the locals took matters into their own hands. When Mr. Flickinger and company had tried to offer the same compromise; the locals declared the time for compromise was over, and the reservoir and canal had to go. The *Defiance Democrat* was not sold on Mr. Crowe's ability to beat Representative Geyer in the election, noting that the Democratic vote outweighed Republicans by as much as 2,500 votes.[100]

The Republican convention explained their logic of why Six Mile Reservoir was allegedly a necessary feeder to the Miami & Erie Canal. They explained that the water from Six Mile Reservoir allowed the Miami & Erie Canal water to be easily regulated:[101]

> At this time there is no water in the Paulding reservoir, and the canal is being fed only by the Celina or St. Mary's reservoir. As a result, the supply cannot be regulated when fed from so great a distance, and while there are days when the waste-ways are running over, there are other frequent intervals when loaded boats lie for days in the mud, with not sufficient water to float them.[102]

The reason they asserted the water could not be regulated by the Mercer County Reservoir alone was due to repairs being made so that "the head gates are out and the water for weeks has been backed by a temporary dam, and the result is that a great amount of surplus water is escaping and cannot be controlled."[103] Still, they believed that the Mercer County Reservoir could not amply supply water between Junction and Defiance at all times.[104] It should not come as a surprise that the *Defiance County Express*' next argument was that Six Mile Reservoir and the Wabash & Erie Canal ought to be maintained; just in case there was a break between the Mercer County Reservoir and Junction to provide water to Defiance from the Junction level.[105]

This last sentiment was shared by the Board of Public Works, though it did concede that "during the past seasons, one of great drought, the Grand Reservoir alone supplied the M. and E. Canal from St. Marys to Defiance."[106] Nevertheless, the Board of Public Works believed the Wabash & Erie Canal and Six Mile Reservoir could be useful as a sort of backup to the Mercer County Reservoir, as it had "heretofore afforded a good supply along with the Grand Reservoir water."[107] The *Defiance County Express* asserted that Defiance manufacturers were "compelled to pay 5 cents more per cord for hauling bolts on account of low water at times."[108] Due to this claimed issue with water regulation, "on ordinary occasions it takes three days to make a trip, but without the Antwerp reservoir it takes four to five days" because the canal boats have to reportedly "wait for water."[109]

Furthermore, the *Defiance County Express* asserted that the Wabash & Erie Canal was still a productive section of the canal system. Their major proof for this was that 3,140,000 feet of timber, of which generated $1,300 (~$41,304 in 2023) worth of tolls, had already reportedly been rafted to Defiance from Paulding County via the Wabash & Erie Canal in 1887, and plenty more were still on the way.[110] The *Defiance County Express* also asserted that "stave bolts, railroad ties, cord wood, hoop-poles, and other materials" were still being shipped via the canal, thus generating revenue from tolls, and it "would seem to be a shortsighted policy to abandon a piece of property which does the amount of business shown."[111]

The *Defiance County Express*, still clinging to the idea that the abandonment of the Wabash & Erie Canal and Six Mile Reservoir would be the start of the death knell for Ohio canals, ran a nearly full-page article about the benefits the canals are to its manufacturers in that city. The *Defiance County Express* talked about how manufacturers like the Defiance Machine Works, Jarvis Woolen Mills, and the Turnbull Wagon Works used the Miami & Erie Canal to ship their goods out and receive raw materials, directly and indirectly power their facilities, and use the water in the manufacturing process.[112]

These businesses asserted that their companies would suffer immensely without the canal, and as many as 1,000 to 1,500 jobs could be jeopardized.[113] Asserting that not only were the canals, "equally true of the Wabash branch," a benefit to local farmers and woodsmen, if the canals were to abandoned in the area, those people who rely on the canal would have to pay "twice or three times as high" a rate to ship by the railroad.[114]

The *Antwerp Argus* responded to this article, and others like it by the *Defiance County Express*, calling them "all buncombe" and nothing but trying to "work on the sympathies of their citizens." [115] The *Antwerp Argus* asserted that there was "no effort... being made to abandon their canal, or shut off their supply of water."[116] The *Antwerp Argus* also reiterated that the Mercer County Reservoir fed the Miami & Erie Canal and that no water came from Six Mile Reservoir as they thought it did in Defiance.[117] The logic was that the Wabash & Erie Canal and Six Mile Reservoir had been dry for some time, nevertheless, the manufacturers in Defiance were still able to operate just fine with the waters coming entirely from the Mercer County Reservoir.[118] The *Antwerp Argus* lastly asserted that the only thing the Defiance manufacturers actually feared losing was "their supply of cheap timber from [Paulding County's] big woods."[119]

In a surprise twist, the *Defiance Democrat* spoke against the *Defiance County Express'* recent rally cry about the manufacturing interest. They had seemingly given up the ghost on saving the Wabash & Erie Canal and Six Mile Reservoir, given that they reported, "the Republican Board of Public Works have virtually abandoned the Antwerp Reservoir."[120] The *Defiance Democrat* admitted that:

> Nobody doubts the importance of maintaining the canal. The Antwerp reservoir, which has been dry as a bone for three months, is already abandoned, practically. The canal is as well supplied with water now as it ever was, and not a drop of it comes from the Antwerp Reservoir, nor ever will again, in all probability... Defiance does not depend for its continued prosperity on the Antwerp reservoir. Our city is built on a more solid foundation than that. No friend of Defiance will claim for a moment that our existence depends on a dry mud hole twenty miles away. If that reservoir is our dependence may the Lord help us. The Lima railroad will do us more good than forty such reservoirs. Go to work and get the railroad, and let the stench pot at Antwerp go, for it has already gone, practically.[121]

The *Defiance Democrat* also argued that, despite the claims that Representative Geyer's re-election would be the death knell for the Ohio canals, it was clear that this could not be further from the truth.[122] Representative Geyer was reportedly favorable to improving the Miami & Erie Canal and other Ohio canals; the most specific example was the proposed building of "stone locks through Defiance and this end of the canal."[123]

The *Defiance Democrat* further argued that Representative Geyer had "devoted his time and attention toward improvements that will make the Miami and Erie Canal a permanent fixture." Namely, his favorability to the idea of expanding the Miami & Erie Canal into a ship canal connecting Toledo and Cincinnati that could accommodate the larger Great Lakes vessels.[124] Making the Miami & Erie Canal "one of the permanent institutions of the State," the *Defiance Democrat* asserted, would "be of great importance to Defiance as it would result in doubling and thribling [*sic*] the business on the canal, and pout city would receive its share of the benefit derived from this increased business."[125]

The *Defiance Democrat* affirmed that the Miami & Erie Canal had the potential of being a very profitable part of the Ohio canal system but was being held back by "dead branches."[126] This lack of money-making ability was why there was a growing sentiment amongst legislators that the canals were worthless and needed to be abolished, as they seemingly generated "no revenue" for the State.[127] The *Defiance Democrat* stated that Representative Geyer wished to "do away with the *dead* [*sic*] branches and appropriate the money derived from that source to improving the main line."[128]

The *Defiance Democrat* asserted that every year since 1883, "every dollar earned by the canals have been appropriated for their maintenance and from $80,000 (~$2,541,777 in 2023) to $175,000 (~$5,560,137 in 2023) in addition to that, to repair and keep them in order."[129][¶] If these unprofitable branches could be abolished and money diverted from their maintenance to the main lines, the *Defiance Democrat* believed that the main lines could be made sustainable.[130] But this was only possible if they could "cut off the dead branches just as the farmer does the dead branches from his tree."[131]

The *Defiance County Express*, however, objected to the assertion that Representative Geyer had "devoted his time and attention" to improving the Miami & Erie Canal.[132] Pointing to the Geyer Bill to abandon the Wabash & Erie Canal and Six Mile Reservoir as the basis for their objection.[133] The *Defiance County Express* even went as far as to assert that Representative Geyer had, himself, "sowed the seed of discontent among dynamiters" and "incited a riot by his ultra legislation."[134] This, of course, referred to the Reservoir War, and the *Defiance County Express* called upon voters to "rebuke John L. Geyer for the work in blowing up the State's property. It must not be passed by with impunity."[135]

The *Defiance County Express* then argued against the *Defiance Democrat*'s point about cutting off branches to save the whole, stating that "if a man were to cut your head off and say it was for the good of your body that it might live and grow healthy, what would you think of such a man?"[136] The *Defiance County Express*

---

¶ Specifically, the year of 1883 saw a total appropriation and revenue of $137,921; 1884 saw a total appropriation and revenue of $163,820; 1885 saw a total appropriation and revenue of $176.014; 1886 saw a total appropriation and revenue of $98,382; 1887 saw a total appropriation and revenue of $82,769. The article provides the following sources for these numbers, *Acts of the State of Ohio*: 1883, Ohio Laws, Volume 80, pg. 35, 72, 63, 116, 122; 1884, Ohio Laws, Volume 81, pg. 11, 36, 113, 158, 176, 213; 1885, Ohio Laws, Volume 82, pg. 77, 191; 1886, Ohio Laws, Volume 83, pg. 18, 123, 150; 1887, Ohio Laws, Volume 84, pg. 178, 202.

further asserted that Representative Geyer would be better off supporting the position to "dredge the Wabash canal and deepen the reservoir than talk of destroying it."[137]

The *Defiance County Express* further argued with the *Defiance Democrat*, pointing out, with example articles,¶ that up until this election season, they had no issue calling out Representative Geyer's stance on the abandonment in a similar way that they were now denouncing.[138] The *Defiance County Express* asserted that "John L. Geyer this year is the same John L. Geyer that he was last year... He will begin his work on the canal again for their speedy abandonment."[139] The *Defiance County Express* further lamented that the *Defiance Democrat* "has witnessed a change of heart – or head."[140]

The *Defiance County Express* also asserted that the Board of Public Works had not abandoned the reservoir, and saying as much was a lie.[141] While everything the *Defiance County Express* had pointed out was true, it does not negate that what the *Defiance Democrat* was saying was accurate. The *Paulding Democrat* chimed in that,

> people who support John Crowe in his position of continuing and improving the Antwerp reservoir and piece of the Wabash canal do so to advance their personal interests to the detriment of not only the valuable portions of the public works of the State but also the vital interests and development of Paulding County... The people who favor the maintenance of the Antwerp reservoir and relic of the Wabash canal, instead of being friendly to the public works of the State are opposing

---

¶ The articles the *Defiance County Express* pulled are all from 1887, and from articles in the 1/13, 2/3, 2/10, 2/17, and 2/24 issues of the *Defiance Democrat*; With the exception of the articles from 2/3 and 5/5, they are all cited in this book.

such institutions by advocating expenditure of money on worthless and useless branches which should be used to maintain those which are serviceable and beneficial.[142]

This assertion by the *Paulding Democrat* further shows that the citizens of Paulding County were not against the canal system, just their part of the canal, which they had deemed useless for many reasons. When John Crowe came to Paulding to drum up support for his bid for election, he, unsurprisingly, "failed to find" support in that community.[143]

Throughout 1887, Mr. Flickinger had found himself mired in controversy for one reason or another. In October 1887, it came out that he had devised an ill-advised effort to "encourage navigation on the canals" and "squeeze the railroads."[144] The discovery of this scheme occurred in August 1887 when Ohio State Auditor Emil Kiesewetter was auditing the collection reports of Rollin C. Fisher, the canal collector in Defiance, Ohio, for the weeks between June 25, 1887, and July 30, 1887. Mr. Kiesewetter inquired as to why Mr. Fisher's reports showed deductions "applied on a 'new boat,'" and wished to know "upon what authority and under what provision of the law this was done."[145] Mr. Fisher responded with the following telegram:

Yours of the 9th inst. At hand. In regard to the reports of the 25th of June, July 9, 16, 23, and 30, showing the reduction of tolls was made by order of the acting commissioner of the B. of P. works for this division of the public works. Mr. Flickinger made the order giving new boats $300 (~$9,500 in 2023) in tolls, and these amounts have not been in but account has been kept of them and entered on the reports as tolls applied on new boats. This has been done since May 3rd both at this office and Toledo, the two points between which the boat plies. As to the provisions of law I refer you to Mr. Flickinger, as it is under his order that I, as collector, acted in this case.[146]

Seeing as the collector in question was apparently following the directions of Mr. Flickinger, Mr. Kiesewetter sent the following telegram to Mr. Flickinger:

> For some weeks past R. C. Fisher, collector at Defiance, in making his weekly report of collections has been deducting from certain collectors money which he states was to be applied upon the payment of a new boat. We could not understand how it was possible for him to do this and so wrote to him asking his authority. He replies it was done upon order of Mr. Flickinger, acting commissioner of the northern division of the Miami and Erie canal. We wish more definite information before accepting his reports, therefore will you please oblige us by giving the authority which based your action. We cannot see ow money required by law o be turned into the state treasury can be lawfully diverted from the same and money not appropriated used for special purposes.[147]

Mr. Flickinger, however, dodged the question and referred to Chief Engineer Bachtell as a person who could readily explain the "rebate on tolls to new boats" and informed Mr. Kiesewetter that Mr. Bachtell would meet with him to do exactly that.[148] When Mr. Bachtell failed to do so after two weeks, Mr. Kiesewetter threatened Mr. Flickinger with legal action if he did not "furnish... the desired explanation at once." [149] Mr. Flickinger then informed Mr. Kiesewetter that he could meet with him himself after the next meeting of the Board of Public Works on September 13, 1887. [150] Mr. Flickinger would have preferred meeting on September 5th, but he was to inspect the Wabash & Erie Canal and Six Mile Reservoir on September 8th.[151]

Mr. Kiesewetter was reportedly able to speak with Chief Engineer Bachtell, eventually, and Mr. Bachtell was seemingly not in on the scheme, as he allegedly stated such "bounties" were "undoubtedly illegal," and he too would bring it up at the upcoming board meeting.[152] Nothing of the board meeting could be found, and Mr. Kiesewetter was allegedly out of town that day. Mr. Flickinger allegedly asked "the clerk in charge of the public works department" to "tell Mr. Kiesewetter that matter will be all right. I will see that he loses nothing by it."[153] The Board of Public Works also reportedly took no action against Mr. Flickinger, apparently due to their only method of punishment being to "censure Mr. Flickinger and compel him to return the money to the state treasury," which is what Mr. Kiesewetter was trying to do anyway.[154]

Mr. Flickinger would apparently be given one more warning to comply with the law by returning the money himself, as the scheme was his idea. If he failed to comply, Mr. Kiesewetter would be compelled to "begin legal proceedings to recover [the money] from the collectors who have been made victims by Flickinger." [155] While Mr. Flickinger was dubiously safe from prosecution over the matter, collectors such as Mr. Fisher possibly faced misdemeanor charges that carried fines that were "double the amount of that so used or loaned," in this case, $600 (~$19,000 in 2023) for every rebate given for a new boat, and up to ninety days in the county jail.[156] As far as punishments actually occurring, nothing indicates that Mr. Flickinger or Mr. Fisher were ever punished for the scheme, and it appears that Mr. Fisher retained his position as canal collector until he seemingly resigned in July of 1889.[157]

While all of that was happening, the reservoir remained dry. It had become so dry for so long that grass had begun to grow on the reservoir bottoms by October 1887.[158] The *Antwerp Argus* reported that it would "never again be filled with water," and cattle would "soon be grazing on its green covered surface."[159] A contributor going by the pseudonym *'Muskrat Mike'* even wrote a poem titled *Reservoir Requiem* published in the *Antwerp Argus* and *Paulding Democrat.*[160]¶

---

¶ See Appendix F for the entire poem.

## Chapter 8 Notes

1 "The Dynamiters," *Antwerp Argus*, June 9, 1887, 2; "Local," *Defiance County Express*, June 9, 1887, 10; "Reservoir Racket Renewed," *Paulding County Gazette*, June 9, 1887, 10; State of Ohio, *Executive Documents: Annual Reports for 1887, Made to the Sixty-Eighth General Assembly*, Part I, 1294.

2 "The Dynamiters," *Antwerp Argus*, June 9, 1887, 2; State of Ohio, *Executive Documents: Annual Reports for 1887, Made to the Sixty-Eighth General Assembly*, Part I, 1294.

3 "The Dynamiters," *Antwerp Argus*, June 9, 1887, 2;

4 "The Dynamiters," *Antwerp Argus*, June 9, 1887, 2.

5 "The Dynamiters," *Antwerp Argus*, June 9, 1887, 2.

6 "Flick's Folly," *Paulding Democrat*, June 9, 1887, 1.

7 "The Dynamiters," *Antwerp Argus*, June 9, 1887, 2.

8 "The Dynamiters," *Antwerp Argus*, June 9, 1887, 2.

9 "The Dynamiters," *Antwerp Argus*, June 9, 1887, 2.

10 "Reservoir Racket Renewed," *Paulding County Gazette*, June 9, 1887, 10.

11 "Reservoir Racket Renewed," *Paulding County Gazette*, June 9, 1887, 10.

12 "Flick's Folly," *Paulding Democrat*, June 9, 1887, 1.

13 "Flick's Folly," *Paulding Democrat*, June 9, 1887, 1.

14 "Reservoir Racket Renewed," *Paulding County Gazette*, June 9, 1887, 10; "Local," *Defiance County Express*, June 9, 1887, 10; "Flick's Folly," *Paulding Democrat*, June 9, 1887, 1.

15 "Flick's Folly," *Paulding Democrat*, June 9, 1887, 1.

16 "Local," *Defiance County Express*, June 9, 1887, 10.

17 "Flick's Folly," *Paulding Democrat*, June 9, 1887, 1.

18 "Reservoir Racket Renewed," *Paulding County Gazette*, June 9, 1887, 10.

19 "Reservoir Racket Renewed," *Paulding County Gazette*, June 9, 1887, 10.

20 "Antwerp Locals," *Paulding County Gazette*, June 23, 1887, 1.

21 State of Ohio, *Executive Documents: Annual Reports for 1887, Made to the Sixty-Eighth General Assembly*, Part I, 1294.

22 "Dynamiters," *Antwerp Argus*, June 23, 1887, 3.

23 "Another Raid," *Cincinnati Enquirer*, June 22, 1887, 1; "Ohio State News," *Antwerp Argus*, June 23, 1887, 1; "Antwerp Locals," *Paulding County Gazette*, June 23, 1887, 1; "Dynamiters," *Antwerp Argus*, June 23, 1887, 3; State of Ohio, *Executive Documents: Annual Reports for 1887, Made to the Sixty-Eighth General Assembly*, Part I, 1294.

24 "Another Raid," *Cincinnati Enquirer*, June 22, 1887, 1.

25 "Another Raid," *Cincinnati Enquirer*, June 22, 1887, 1.

26 "Antwerp Locals," *Paulding County Gazette*, June 23, 1887, 1; "Dynamiters," *Antwerp Argus*, June 23, 1887, 3.

27 "Antwerp Locals," *Paulding County Gazette*, June 23, 1887, 1; "Dynamiters," *Antwerp Argus*, June 23, 1887, 3.

28 "Antwerp Locals," *Paulding County Gazette*, June 23, 1887, 1; "Dynamiters," *Antwerp Argus*, June 23, 1887, 3.

29 "Antwerp Locals," *Paulding County Gazette*, June 23, 1887, 1.

30 "Antwerp Locals," *Paulding County Gazette*, June 23, 1887, 1.

31 "Antwerp Locals," *Paulding County Gazette*, June 23, 1887, 1.

32 "Antwerp Locals," *Paulding County Gazette*, June 23, 1887, 1; "Local Gossip," *Paulding Democrat*, June 23, 1887, 5.

33 "Antwerp Locals," *Paulding County Gazette*, June 23, 1887, 1.

34 Otto E. Ehrhart, "Wabash-Erie Canal," in *A Century of Progress: Antwerp, Ohio*, 18.

35 "Antwerp Locals," *Paulding County Gazette*, June 23, 1887, 1.

36 "Our Home Corner," *Antwerp Argus*, June 23, 1887, 3.

37 "Our Home Corner," *Antwerp Argus*, June 23, 1887, 3.

38 "Our Home Corner," *Antwerp Argus*, June 30, 1887, 3.

39 Otto E. Ehrhart, "Wabash-Erie Canal," in *A Century of Progress: Antwerp, Ohio*, 17.

40 "From Knox," *Paulding Democrat*, August 11, 1887, 4.

41 "Our Home Corner," *Antwerp Argus*, June 23, 1887, 3.

42 "Antwerp Items," *Paulding County Gazette*, June 30, 1887, 10.

43 "Antwerp Items," *Paulding County Gazette*, June 30, 1887, 10.

44 "Place Filled," *Antwerp Argus*, June 30, 1887, 3.

45 "Abolished," *Antwerp Argus*, May 5, 1887, 3; "Round About—Antwerp," *Paulding County* Gazette, May 5, 1887, 5.

46 "Place Filled," *Antwerp Argus*, June 30, 1887, 3.

47 "A Visit to the Reservoir," *Paulding County Gazette*, July 7, 1887, 1; "Local Gossip," *Paulding Democrat*, June 30, 1887, 5; "Dynamiters," *Antwerp Argus*, June 23, 1887, 3.

48 "A Visit to the Reservoir," *Paulding County Gazette*, July 7, 1887, 1;

49 "Round About—Antwerp," *Paulding County Gazette*, July 28, 1887, 5.

50 "Viewing the Remains," *Antwerp Argus*, July 7, 1887, 2.

51 "Local Gossip," *Paulding Democrat*, June 30, 1887, 5; "Viewing the Remains," *Antwerp Argus*, July 7, 1887, 2.

52 "Local Gossip," *Paulding Democrat*, June 30, 1887, 5; "Viewing the Remains," *Antwerp Argus*, July 7, 1887, 2.

53 "Local Gossip," *Paulding Democrat*, June 30, 1887, 5; "Viewing the Remains," *Antwerp Argus*, July 7, 1887, 2.

54 "Viewing the Remains," *Antwerp Argus*, July 7, 1887, 2.

55 "Local Gossip," *Paulding Democrat*, June 30, 1887, 5.

56 "A Visit to the Reservoir," *Paulding County Gazette*, July 7, 1887, 1; "Our Home Corner," *Antwerp Argus*, July 7, 1887, 3; "Personals," *Defiance County Express*, July 9, 1887, 9.

57 "A Visit to the Reservoir," *Paulding County Gazette*, July 7, 1887, 1.

58 "A Visit to the Reservoir," *Paulding County Gazette*, July 7, 1887, 1.

59 "A Visit to the Reservoir," *Paulding County Gazette*, July 7, 1887, 1.

60 "A Visit to the Reservoir," *Paulding County Gazette*, July 7, 1887, 1.

61 "A Visit to the Reservoir," *Paulding County Gazette*, July 7, 1887, 1.

62 "A Visit to the Reservoir," *Paulding County Gazette*, July 7, 1887, 1.

63 *Antwerp Argus*, July 21, 1887, 3.

64 *Antwerp Argus*, July 21, 1887, 3.

65 Otto E. Ehrhart, "Wabash-Erie Canal," in *A Century of Progress: Antwerp, Ohio*, 18.

66 "Local Brevities," *Paulding County Gazette*, July 21, 1887, 5.

67 "Local Brevities," *Paulding County Gazette*, July 21, 1887, 5.

68 "Bertha Furnace," *Paulding County Gazette*, July 28, 1887, 1.

69 "Local Gossip," *Paulding Democrat*, August 25, 1887, 5.

70 "Local," *Defiance County Express*, August 6, 1887, 9; *Paulding County Gazette*, August 11, 1887, 4; *Paulding Democrat*, August 11, 1887, 4; "Nominated by Acclamation," *Paulding County Gazette*, August 11, 1887, 7; "Representative Named!," *Paulding Democrat*, August 11, 1887, 1.

71 "Round About—Antwerp," *Paulding County Gazette*, August 4, 1887, 5; *Antwerp Argus*, August 4, 1887, 2.

72 "Down on Flickinger," *Paulding Democrat*, August 4, 1887, 4.

73 "Down on Flickinger," *Paulding Democrat*, August 4, 1887, 4; "Our Home Corner," *Antwerp Argus*, August 11, 1887, 3.

74 "Down on Flickinger," *Paulding Democrat*, August 4, 1887, 4; "Our Home Corner," *Antwerp Argus*, August 11, 1887, 3.

75 "Down on Flickinger," *Paulding Democrat*, August 4, 1887, 4; "Our Home Corner," *Antwerp Argus*, August 11, 1887, 3.

76 "Down on Flickinger," *Paulding Democrat*, August 4, 1887, 4; "Our Home Corner," *Antwerp Argus*, August 11, 1887, 3.

77 "Nearly Dry," *Antwerp Argus*, August 11, 1887, 3.

78 "Nearly Dry," *Antwerp Argus*, August 11, 1887, 3.

79 "Round About—Antwerp," *Paulding County Gazette*, September 8, 1887, 1; "Antwerp," *Paulding County Gazette*, September 1, 1887, 1.

80 "Our Home Corner," *Antwerp Argus*, August 18, 1887, 3.

81 "Guards Relieved," *Antwerp Argus*, August 18, 1887, 3; "Round About—Antwerp," *Paulding County Gazette*, August 18, 1887, 5; "Antwerp Items," *Paulding Democrat*, August 18, 1887, 1.

82 "Guards Relieved," *Antwerp Argus*, August 18, 1887, 3.

83 "Guards Relieved," *Antwerp Argus*, August 18, 1887, 3.

84 "Guards Relieved," *Antwerp Argus*, August 18, 1887, 3.

85 "Guards Relieved," *Antwerp Argus*, August 18, 1887, 3; "Round About—Antwerp," *Paulding County Gazette*, August 18, 1887, 5.

86 State of Ohio, *Executive Documents: Annual Reports for 1887, Made to the Sixty-Eighth General Assembly*, Part I, 1294; "Local Gossip," *Paulding Democrat*, September 22, 1887, 5.

87 "Reservoir Empty," *Antwerp Argus*, September 15, 1887, 3; "Local," *Defiance County Express*, September 10, 1887, 9; *Defiance Democrat*, September 15, 1887, 2; "Local Gossip," *Paulding Democrat*, September 15, 1887, 5.

88 "Reservoir Empty," *Antwerp Argus*, September 15, 1887, 3.

89 *Antwerp Argus*, September 15, 1887, 2; "Reservoir Empty," *Antwerp Argus*, September 15, 1887, 3.

90 *Antwerp Argus*, September 15, 1887, 2; "Local," *Defiance County Express*, September 10, 1887, 9.

91 *Antwerp Argus*, September 15, 1887, 2; "Reservoir Empty," *Antwerp Argus*, September 15, 1887, 3; "Local Gossip," *Paulding Democrat*, September 15, 1887, 5.

92 *Antwerp Argus*, September 15, 1887, 2; "All Buncomb," *Antwerp Argus*, September 29, 1887, 2.

93 *Antwerp Argus*, September 15, 1887, 2; "All Buncomb," *Antwerp Argus*, September 29, 1887, 2.

94 "All Buncomb," *Antwerp Argus*, September 29, 1887, 2.

95 "Representative Ticket," *Defiance County Express*, September 15, 1887, 7; "Representative Convention," *Defiance County Express*, September 15, 1887, 7; "Some Extracts," *Paulding Democrat*, September 22, 1887, 4.

96 *Defiance County Express*, September 15, 1887, 7.

97 *Defiance County Express*, September 15, 1887, 7.

98 *Defiance County Express*, October 15, 1887, 7.

99 *Defiance County Express*, September 15, 1887, 7.

100 *Defiance Democrat*, September 15, 1887, 2.

101 *Defiance County Express*, September 15, 1887, 7.

102 *Defiance County Express*, September 15, 1887, 7.

103 *Defiance County Express*, October 15, 1887, 7; *Defiance County Express*, October 20, 1887, 8.

104 *Defiance County Express*, September 15, 1887, 7; *Defiance County Express*, October 15, 1887, 7.

105 *Defiance County Express*, October 15, 1887, 7; *Defiance County Express*, October 20, 1887, 8; *Defiance County Express*, October 8, 1887, 8.

106 State of Ohio, *Executive Documents: Annual Reports for 1887, Made to the Sixty-Eighth General Assembly*, Part I, 1294.

107 State of Ohio, *Executive Documents: Annual Reports for 1887, Made to the Sixty-Eighth General Assembly*, Part I, 1294.

108 *Defiance County Express*, October 8, 1887, 8.

109 *Defiance County Express*, October 8, 1887, 8.

110 *Defiance County Express*, September 15, 1887, 7.

111 *Defiance County Express*, September 15, 1887, 7.

112 "Our Manufactories," *Defiance County Express*, September 24, 1887, 8.

113 "Our Manufactories," *Defiance County Express*, September 24, 1887, 8.

114 "Our Manufactories," *Defiance County Express*, September 24, 1887, 8.

115 "All Buncomb," *Antwerp Argus*, September 29, 1887, 2.

116 "All Buncomb," *Antwerp Argus*, September 29, 1887, 2.

117 "All Buncomb," *Antwerp Argus*, September 29, 1887, 2.

118 "All Buncomb," *Antwerp Argus*, September 29, 1887, 2.

119 "All Buncomb," *Antwerp Argus*, September 29, 1887, 2.

120 *Defiance Democrat*, September 29, 1887, 2.

121 "The Canal," *Defiance Democrat*, September 29, 1887, 2.

122 *Defiance Democrat*, September 29, 1887, 2.

123 *Defiance Democrat*, September 29, 1887, 2.

124 *Defiance Democrat*, October 6, 1887, 2.

125 *Defiance Democrat*, October 6, 1887, 2.

126 "The Importance," *Defiance Democrat*, October 13, 1887, 2.

127 "The Importance," *Defiance Democrat*, October 13, 1887, 2.

128 *Defiance Democrat*, October 6, 1887, 2.

129 "Canal Appropriations," *Defiance Democrat*, October 13, 1887, 2.

130 "The Importance," *Defiance Democrat*, October 13, 1887, 2.

131 "The Importance," *Defiance Democrat*, October 13, 1887, 2.

132 *Defiance County Express*, October 8, 1887, 8.

133 *Defiance County Express*, October 8, 1887, 8.

134 *Defiance County Express*, October 8, 1887, 8.

135 *Defiance County Express*, October 8, 1887, 8.

136 *Defiance County Express*, October 13, 1887, 7.

137 *Defiance County Express*, October 13, 1887, 7.

138 "They Read Well," *Defiance County Express*, September 29, 1887, 8; *Defiance County Express*, October 6, 1887, 8; *Defiance County Express*, October 8, 1887, 8; *Defiance County Express*, October 15, 1887, 7.

139 "They Read Well," *Defiance County Express*, September 29, 1887, 8.

140 "They Read Well," *Defiance County Express*, September 29, 1887, 8.

141 *Defiance County Express*, October 6, 1887, 8.

142 *Paulding Democrat*, September 29, 1887, 4.

143 "Personal Points," *Paulding Democrat*, September 29, 1887, 5.

144 "Canal Corruption," *Paulding Democrat*, October 6, 1887, 4; "'Arnica,'" *Defiance Democrat*, October 6, 1887, 2.

145 "Canal Corruption," *Paulding Democrat*, October 6, 1887, 4; "'Arnica,'" *Defiance Democrat*, October 6, 1887, 2.

146 "Canal Corruption," *Paulding Democrat*, October 6, 1887, 4; "'Arnica,'" *Defiance Democrat*, October 6, 1887, 2.

147 "Canal Corruption," *Paulding Democrat*, October 6, 1887, 4; "'Arnica,'" *Defiance Democrat*, October 6, 1887, 2.

148 "Canal Corruption," *Paulding Democrat*, October 6, 1887, 4; "'Arnica,'" *Defiance Democrat*, October 6, 1887, 2.

149 "Canal Corruption," *Paulding Democrat*, October 6, 1887, 4; "'Arnica,'" *Defiance Democrat*, October 6, 1887, 2.

150 "Canal Corruption," *Paulding Democrat*, October 6, 1887, 4; "'Arnica,'" *Defiance Democrat*, October 6, 1887, 2.

151 "Canal Corruption," *Paulding Democrat*, October 6, 1887, 4; "'Arnica,'" *Defiance Democrat*, October 6, 1887, 2; "Guards Relieved," *Antwerp Argus*, August 18, 1887, 3.

152 "Canal Corruption," *Paulding Democrat*, October 6, 1887, 4; "'Arnica,'" *Defiance Democrat*, October 6, 1887, 2.

153 "Canal Corruption," *Paulding Democrat*, October 6, 1887, 4;
     "'Arnica,'" *Defiance Democrat*, October 6, 1887, 2.
154 "Canal Corruption," *Paulding Democrat*, October 6, 1887, 4;
     "'Arnica,'" *Defiance Democrat*, October 6, 1887, 2.
155 "Canal Corruption," *Paulding Democrat*, October 6, 1887, 4;
     "'Arnica,'" *Defiance Democrat*, October 6, 1887, 2.
156 "Canal Corruption," *Paulding Democrat*, October 6, 1887, 4;
     "'Arnica,'" *Defiance Democrat*, October 6, 1887, 2.
157 "Chat," *Defiance Democrat*, July 18, 1889, 3.
158 "Empty is the Hole," *Antwerp Argus*, October 6, 1887, 3; "Local
     Gossip," *Paulding Democrat*, October 13, 1887, 5.
159 "Empty is the Hole," *Antwerp Argus*, October 6, 1887, 3.
160 "Reservoir Requiem," *Antwerp Argus*, October 13, 1887, 3;
     "Reservoir Requiem," *Paulding Democrat*, October 20, 1887, 7.

# -9-

## A Second Chance

### (October 1887 – February 1888)

On the evening of October 11, 1887,[1] Representative John L. Geyer of Defiance and Paulding County and Timothy E. Tarsney of Michigan spoke to the people of Defiance at the Myers Opera House.[2]@ Despite apparent efforts by John Crowe and the Republican Party to persuade people not to attend,[3] the Myers Opera House was reportedly "filled to its utmost capacity, even the aisles, doorways, and gallery being crowded."[4] The *Defiance County Express* claimed that only "250 Democrats" were present at the meeting, the rest, claimed to at be at least half of the audience, were "Republicans and Union Labor men." [5] The *Defiance Democrat* does acknowledge that opponents of the speakers were present.[6]

The first to speak was Representative Geyer, who elaborated on his platform regarding the canal issues he sought to be reelected upon. Representative Geyer explained that his introduction of the Geyer Bill in the previous legislative session

---

@ The Myers Opera House was located on the southeast corner of Fort Street and Clinton Street in Defiance.
(*Sanborn Fire Insurance Map from Defiance, Defiance County, Ohio*, August 1888; *Sanborn Fire Insurance Map from Defiance, Defiance County, Ohio*, December 1899.)

was "the result of deliberate, conscientious, thoughtful investigation."[7] Representative Geyer argued that because the State of Indiana had abandoned their part of the canal and the source of water for the canal and reservoir was subsequently cut off, the canal was no longer viable commercially due to frequent occasions of no (or minimal) water during the dry summer.[8]

Because of the lack of water during a portion of the year, he also asserted that there was no way Six Mile Reservoir could be a feeder reservoir for the Miami & Erie Canal. That canal's feeder for the northern division through Paulding County to Defiance was the Mercer County Reservoir.[9] Representative Geyer further pointed out that Six Mile Reservoir could only possibly feed as far as a mile south of Junction to Viall's Lock, while the Mercer County Reservoir would have to supply the rest of the canal that distance to St. Mary's.[10] Therefore, Representative Geyer asked what prevented that same water that had flowed down the canal all the way from the Mercer County Reservoir from getting to the Maumee River in Defiance?[11]

Representative Geyer then stated that the Board of Public Works tried to explain to him that the waters from Six Mile Reservoir were necessary from Viall's Lock to Defiance because "the canal above Junction was forty feet wide and below Junction, fifty, and would therefore require more water."[12] While this argument could have made some sense, Representative Geyer pointed out the obvious. Their argument still ignored the primary issue that Six Mile Reservoir and the Wabash & Erie Canal were practically empty at the times of the year that the Miami & Erie Canal would have needed it most.[13]

Representative Geyer then reportedly stated, "There could only remain but one possible use to which the Wabash canal could be applied, and that is for the local purpose of conveying timber during the spring of the year to the manufactories in [Defiance]." [14] § Representative Geyer, however, argued that despite there being a want to raft timber down the canal, very little timber actually remained in the vicinity of the Wabash & Erie Canal, and what did was "in the immediate vicinity of the Six Mile Reservoir." [15] Furthermore, the distance to the river from where they had already stopped at the canal was, in his opinion, negligible,[16] enough so that the timber manufacturers could send timber down the river from the vicinity of Antwerp.[17] Some had already done so before.[18]

The *Defiance County Express* argued against this claim because it believed the river still had the same issue of being unusable when low on water and was much too dangerous when there was too much water.[19] The *Defiance County Express* also argued that the cost of shipping the timber to the river would be comparable to the railroad rates, which would have the effect of "reducing the price the timber owners would receive for their timber."[20]

Representative Geyer acknowledged the idea that abandoning the canal and reservoir would open "over twenty thousand acres" of land for cultivation, [21] continuing to echo the sentiments of Dr. Solomon S. Stambaugh a decade prior. However, Representative Geyer made it abundantly clear, with

---

§ This quote is from the *Defiance County Express* version of the speech, but the other sources say the same exact thing but just phrases it a little different.

proof, that he never shied away from taking the opportunity to appropriate money to Ohio's canal system.[22]

The *Defiance Democrat* also ran an article detailing every recent appropriations bill Representative Geyer supported, whether it was the Hocking Canal, the Walholding Canal, the Ohio & Erie Canal, or the Miami & Erie Canal, he had voted yes to appropriate money to all of them.[23] Representative Geyer then asserted his position on how to make the Ohio canal system profitable. Declaring that "the worthless end, decayed branches of the Public Works... should be abandoned and sold and that the proceeds should be used in placing the Miami & Erie and Ohio canal in permanent condition."[24]

The *Defiance Democrat* asked voters to "please take a look at the old canal bridge across the Maumee in this city" in determining who they believed should be voted for. That bridge had reportedly been a "eye-sore for fifteen years," had been "condemned and dangerous for more than twelve years," and two of its spans had fallen into the river.[25] Such condition of canal infrastructure was blamed on the policies of the "Crowe party," implying the Republican party, whom the *Defiance Democrat* asserted were "the pretended friends of the public works."[26] The *Defiance County Express*, however, claimed that the bridge had only failed because "teams," of which their weight the bridge was possibly never designed to handle, were crossing the aging structure after the nearby Clinton Street bridge had been torn down.[27]

The *Defiance Democrat* reported that "boatmen refuse to invest money in new boats; manufacturers hesitate about making permanent investments along the main line because of the unsafe policy" that had allowed Ohio's canal system to fall into disrepair, as "everything seems to be going to decay." [28] Representative Geyer proposed fixing the main lines by replacing the timber locks and aqueducts with ones constructed of stone, and to dredge the canal to a deeper depth. Such actions he believed would attract "capitalists" into using the canal. [29]

Despite appropriating upwards of one million dollars to the canal system in the previous ten years, the condition of Ohio's canal system would not give such an impression of abundant expenditure compared to its condition a decade prior. In Representative Geyer's mind, this was "particularly so because of this very fact that the money appropriated to them has been spent on such old and decayed portions that the expenditure brought in no reasonable return;" not because the canals had "outgrown their usefulness, but that the management has been bad." [30]

Representative Geyer closed his speech with the following opinion on the whole matter:

> So that since the abandonment of [the Wabash & Erie Canal] would leave the Miami and Erie intact, with all the timber tributary to it just in the same condition of access as at this time; and since the small amount of timber along the Wabash canal could be brought by the Maumee river to the factories [in Defiance], I fail to see wherein it could injuriously affect the manufacturing interests of [Defiance]. The person who claims that the Wabash canal is necessary to the success of the manufacturing interests of Defiance is either ignorant of the condition of that canal and the timber supply along it, together with the other means of conveying it to [Defiance], or he exhibits a wonderfully limited idea of what is necessary to support a manufacturing center. Defiance, by her two lines of important railroads, her rivers, and her line of canal

stretching from the lake at the north to the river at the south, has advantages of which she may justly feel proud. But when any of her citizens claim that her future prosperity depends upon the existence of ten or twelve miles of a worthless canal, located wholly within another county, and without a commercial point they belittle her and make themselves ridiculous.[31]

Lastly, Representative Geyer gave a flurry of questions for Charles A. Flickinger and Mr. Crowe.[32] Mr. Flickinger never seemed to answer those questions. However, Mr. Crowe did answer the questions pertaining to him (then asked a few of his own) when the Republican Party met at the Myers Opera House on October 15, 1887, to hear from, among other prominent Defiance Republicans, Robert S. Robertson, the Lieutenant Governor of Indiana.[33]

The details of what Mr. Robertson said are non-existent; the *Defiance County Express* only reported that the speech by Mr. Tarsney "was nothing compared to the able and convincing manner in which Mr. Robertson dealt out the 'law and gospel' to his audience."[34] The focus of the article was Kidder V. Haymaker's opening speech for the evening, wherein Mr. Haymaker spoke of the "propriety and advisability of retaining the water ways of the State intact, Antwerp reservoir, Wabash canal and all."[35] The *Defiance County Express* described Mr. Haymaker's assertions as "invincible, and put to naught the arguments John L. Geyer attempted to make."[36] Mr. Haymaker reportedly

showed by demonstration that the water in the reservoir is always under restraint when the banks are not meddled with, and that the spread of water over the flat country is not due to the reservoir no more than that body of water is to blame for the wet land in the south part of Farmer, in Mark and the east side of Hicksville townships in [Defiance] county.[37]

Mr. Haymaker also reportedly showed the audience that the fault rested on the "utter inability of the landowners to drain into the Maumee River" for why that part of Paulding County remained frequently inundated, as well as the "failure of Alfred P. Edgerton to effect the desired drainage with his big Indiana ditch."¶[38] Lastly, Mr. Haymaker asserted that Representative Geyer's position was the "result of a deliberate intention to let the land sharks gobble up a lot of territory to the sacrifice of all other interests along the canals."[39]

It then came out that Mr. Flickinger had reportedly attempted to stifle the passing of any appropriations to the Miami & Erie Canal in the 1886 legislative session, asserting that the Miami & Erie Canal could operate using its own earnings; however, $10,000 ($321,102 in 2023) of those earnings could be reallocated for use on other canals throughout the state, and no additional appropriations were needed.[40] Representative Geyer was taken aback by this assertion, seeing as he believed most if not every "lock, culvert, or aqueduct on its line in the northern part of the State... needs either to be replaced or repaired."[41]

---

¶ Mr. Haymaker may have meant to attack Alfred's brother, Joseph K. Edgerton. Joseph owned a significant amount of land in Maumee Township (among other townships) in Allen County, Indiana, and he would have presumably benefitted from the accursed ditch in that area. (Maumee Township Plat Map, 1880s, Allen Co., https://www.acgsi.org/maps/maumee.1878.pdf; *History of Allen County, Indiana, 1880*, 1972, 126; *Woodburn Centennial*, 1965, 5, 13; Beatty, John D. and Delia C. Bourne, "Maumee Township & Woodburn," In *History of Fort Wayne & Allen County, Indiana*, Volume I, 530.)

After debating with the Speaker of the House, $10,000 (~$321,102 in 2023) and all of its earnings were eventually appropriated to the Miami & Erie Canal for 1886.[42] A year later, in the 1887 legislative session, this scheme was apparently tried again, but this time Mr. Flickinger claimed that $20,000 (~$635,444 in 2023) of earnings from the Miami & Erie Canal were "not needed this year" and so the money could be used on other canals throughout the State of Ohio. After another "hard struggle," another $10,000 (~$317,722 in 2023) appropriation was secured for the Miami & Erie Canal on top of keeping those earnings from the canal.[43]

Further causing issues for the canal question was the topic of tolls and whether the Defiance timber industry was paying its fair share for using the canals. The *Defiance County Express* asserted that 9,500,000 feet of timber were rafted on the canal to Defiance.[44] The Board of Public Works also reported that the amount of timber was "between nine and ten million feet."[45] The *Defiance Democrat*, attempting to refute this, pointed to the *Report of the Board of Public Works* for 1886, which reportedly indicated that a mere 58,838 feet of timber that made it to Defiance had tolls paid on it.[46] While it might be a bit disingenuous to point to the previous year's numbers to make their point, the *Defiance Democrat* nevertheless asserted that if the *Defiance County Express*' number were correct, and if the tolls collected had remained unchanged, "the State had received toll on about one log out of every 161, while the other 160 have been allowed to go scot free."[47]

John Crowe, the Republican Party nominee for the Ohio House of Representatives, was reported to have shipped upward of

2,000,000 feet of timber on the canal annually, yet he apparently only paid enough in tolls amounting to having shipped a mere 10,000 feet of timber.[48] How Mr. Crowe accomplished this was something the *Defiance Democrat* wanted him to explain, and asked why would the people who say they support the canals send a guy to the Ohio Legislature that was "defrauding the State out of hundreds of dollars in the way of tolls every year" so that he may defend the canals from abandonment?[49]

The *Defiance County Express* again showed concern that abandoning Six Mile Reservoir would lead to the abandonment of the Mercer County Reservoir, then the rest of the Miami & Erie Canal. Both the *Defiance Democrat* and the *Defiance County Express* ran letters from the vicinity of Mercer County Reservoir, but neither shared the same tone, as acknowledged by the *Defiance County Express*.[50] The letter in the *Defiance County Express* came from an 'H. L. L.,' who remarked that "Mercer and Auglaize counties... are watching your fight with a good deal of interest."[51] According to the letter-writer, this interest was that some in and around Celina, Ohio wanted the same thing Antwerp wanted; the abandonment of their reservoir.[52] The *Defiance County Express* asserted that those in Mercer County wanted the land to "cultivate and turn money into their county treasury."[53]

Their logic was that "If Paulding County lays claim to that part of the State's property for tax purposes, have we not the same right to ask that St. Mary's Reservoir be drained and the land improved and taxed?"[54] The letter-writer also called their reservoir an "objectional stink hole,"[55] but their focus seemed more on the taxable land angle of the reservoir fight. They claimed that there could be as much as $250,000 (~$8,029,184 in 2023) in taxable land if only the reservoir was drained and the land sold off for farming purposes.[56] Worth noting is that the letter also reportedly complained that sportsmen were coming to the reservoir for wild game and fish and "impose themselves upon us," and "the lowest and most vulgar ruffians" came to the area for a drunken "big tare."[57]§

While much of this political drama unfolded leading up to the election, the last argument for there being a significant manufacturer on the Wabash & Erie Canal closed its doors.[58] On October 13, 1887, Stephen F. Eagle's Bertha Furnace "shut down indefinitely."[59] Mr. Eagle was having issues getting iron ore shipped to the Bertha Furnace due to the canal being next to useless at this date and the railroad rates were not conducive to making a profit.[60] This was the same issue that doomed the Antwerp Furnace a few years prior around 1880.[61] The final nail in the proverbial coffin was an explosion at the furnace that "severely injured a workman about the head," which possibly induced temporary blindness.[62]

While the area papers seemingly talk about two separate incidents in quick succession, they were likely referring to the same incident in late September 1887, when a foreman named William Treece was injured while inspecting the furnace's fire. The "inner wall of the stack... fell in" and caused a gas explosion, thus burning the man's face.[63] The initial rumors were that the furnace would move to Melrose, Ohio on the Miami & Erie Canal and the Nickel Plate Road.[64] However, that would not come to

---

§ I feel like this sentiment probably has not changed much from a tourism perspective. Though Grand Lake St. Mary's has probably brought in more than enough in tourism dollars to offset taxable land values.

pass, and Mr. Eagle "resigned his position as Superintendent" at the Bertha Furnace and took on the role of Superintendent at two iron furnaces somewhere east of Cleveland, Ohio, likely Leetonia, Ohio.[65] The *Paulding County Gazette* lamented losing "a citizen like Mr. Eagle."[66]

John Crowe went to Antwerp on November 1, 1887, the eve of the election, hoping to bolster his vote in the area. Unfortunately for him, because of the "reservoir muddle," the *Antwerp Argus* reported that "he was positive of carrying Defiance County, by a good majority, but he seemed to have grave hopes about Paulding." [67] A few weeks earlier, a poem from an unknown Melrose citizen was published in the *Antwerp Argus*:

> Caw! Caw! I'd vote for Crowe,
> But I want the Reservoir to go;
> Both candidates I may admire,
> But I guess I'll vote for Geyer.[68]

Representative Geyer won the election in Paulding and Defiance County by 1,840 votes,[69] securing a 1,220 vote majority over John Crowe in Paulding County alone. [70] Surprisingly, Governor Joseph B. Foraker did not get a majority of votes in Paulding County, losing by 98 votes; however, he won by almost one hundred votes in Carryall Township, the township that had the most votes for him in the county.[71] Governor Foraker won the statewide election against Thomas E. Powell[¶] by 23,329 votes.[72]

---

¶ Dr. Solomon S. Stambaugh's wife was Cornelia A. Powell, the sister of Thomas E. Powell.

(Ancestry.com, *1870 United States Federal Census*; Ancestry.com. *Ohio, U.S., County Marriage Records, 1774-1993*; Ancestry.com, 1880 United States Federal Census.)

Senator Robert Mehaffey from Allen County ran practically unopposed.[73]

Mr. Flickinger, who had secured nomination for a second term,[74] lost in Paulding County by only 261 votes; only losing by 10 votes in Carryall Township with 281 votes. [75] Carryall Township had the highest number of voters for Mr. Flickinger with 5 more votes than the Briceton Precinct of Paulding, but he still lost by 35 votes there.[76] Mr. Flickinger was most popular in Washington Township, winning by 21 votes, and in Oakwood Township, winning by 20 votes in both Melrose and Oakwood Precincts; but was least popular in Benton Township, losing by 69 votes. [77] Nevertheless, Mr. Flickinger defeated Democrat Orsamus E. Niles by 31,113 votes and won the statewide election.[78] John Crowe lost handily in Carryall Township, losing by 361 votes, the most significant deficit of any other precinct.[79] Mr. Crowe was most popular in Emerald Township, winning by 40 votes. He did not win any other precinct, only tying with Representative Geyer in the Oakwood Precinct of Brown Township.[80]

Despite the win for Paulding County, the *Defiance County Express* still expressed doubt that the abandonment bill would be well received in the Ohio Legislature.[81] Nevertheless, the *Antwerp Argus* urged their readers to support the measure, warning that "those interested in the timber interests at Defiance are already at work, and every effort will be made to defeat any movement set on foot by those of Paulding County."[82] The *Antwerp Argus* further asserted that:

> The past season has proven beyond all question that the reservoir is needless as a feeder to the Miami Canal at

Junction, which virtually substantiates all previous statements, that the ditch through this county is only needed for a few timber sharks to float logs on, to the doors of their factories in Defiance.[83]

The *Defiance County Express* responded, "You may beat us in voting, but we'll be even in the legislature, mark our words."[84] The *Paulding Democrat* responded, "It also said it would beat Mr. Geyer at the polls."[85] The *Antwerp Argus* inferred from the *Defiance County Express'* remark that the timber magnates of Defiance would "attempt a bribe of the members" and that "their nefarious work has already commenced."[86]

The Wabash & Erie Canal, which had been "entirely dry" through most of the rest of the year, was now "nearly full of water" by December 1, 1887, and the local children readied their ice skates in preparation for its freezing.[87] Meanwhile, an "immense amount of stave bolts and other timber" had begun to line the banks of the Miami & Erie Canal, still waiting to be shipped to the factories.[88] Shippers worked to move the material "as fast as possible," likely because there was not much time until the end of the shipping season.[89] However, Defiance timbermen had already started to "back out of their contracts for delivering logs on the canal" by December 1st.[90] The *Antwerp Argus* posited that they "doubtless imagine the reservoir and canal abandoned."[91]

Whatever the reason might have been, the Miami & Erie Canal was still open for navigation into mid-December, at least between Delphos, Ohio, and Defiance, and boats were still making the journey at that point in the year.[92] Despite the report of some Defiance timbermen backing out of their contracts, one

Defiance timber magnate, Loring Marshall, was still seen "making great preparations for moving logs out of the big woods south of the reservoir."[93]

Interestingly, Charles W. Boland was seen removing stumps with dynamite during a ditching job; the *Antwerp Argus* commented that "Charley seems to understand how to use the stuff." [94] ¶ The Hicksville Debate Society even got in on the reservoir question; having debated the topic, they decided that the reservoir should be abandoned.[95]

Francis B. DeWitt and Representative Geyer paid Antwerp a visit for matters related to the canal and reservoir on November 30, 1887,[96] one last time before Representative Geyer left for Columbus at the end of December.[97] The two were there for a meeting held that evening wherein "the best method of bringing the question before the legislature were discussed by those present."[98] It was decided that Representative Geyer should do it "as soon as practicable."[99]

Those attending the meeting also decided that the same language from the previous year would be applied, wherein the land would be sold in "forty and eighty-acre tracts... and to actual settlers only, in order that those who have been long sufferers from the nuisance may derive some benefits, and reap a little reward for their patient endurance."[100] To further benefit the county, it was suggested to include language that ensured the land would be transferred to the county, and the proceeds from the sale of the land went to roads and ditches in the county.[101] Those attending the meeting also wished to include

---

¶ Charles W. Boland was reportedly a Dynamiter; see Appendix A.

language that ensured the landowners had to "cultivate and improve" the land within a certain amount of time after gaining ownership of it and that no one person could buy more than "forty, or to the outside, eighty acres, and hold same in his own right."[102]

The 1888 Ohio General Assembly began on the first Monday of January as it typically did, which got the Ohio Legislature off to a very early start on January 2, 1888.[103] Governor Foraker would again address the Ohio Legislature before it began, and this was when he was expected to make his thoughts on the canal and reservoir abandonment known. As promised, he did make comments on it, and they are as follows:

> The citizens of the locality in which it is situated have become greatly dissatisfied with the presence there of the Six Mile or Paulding County Reservoir. They regard it as a nuisance, dangerous to health and calculated to retard and prevent the development of their section of the State. They have been striving for some time to secure its abandonment. They made an earnest but vain appeal to the last General Assembly.
>
> In Paulding County there is practically but one sentiment on this subject, and that is so intense that during the summer on several occasions, it took the form of an unlawful endeavor, by the use of dynamite and otherwise, to destroy this portion of the State's property. Another appeal will no doubt be made to you, to take action in regard to this matter. The people who will make it are entitled to a hearing and a thorough investigation at your hands of the grievance about which they complain.
>
> By reason of the abandonment by the State of Indiana of the Wabash and Erie Canal, and the interception of its natural water supply by drainage on the Indiana side of the state line, this reservoir has been rendered of less importance than formerly. It never was intended to be a part of our present system of canals, or to have any

relation to the same, except as a part of the Wabash & Erie Canal. There have been two or three instances, however, in the past, when it has been used to increase the supply of water in the Miami and Erie Canal.

But it is not likely there will be any great need for it of this character in the future, and should there be, it could not be reliably depended upon, because of its own limited and uncertain supply of water... There will be but little business to be done hereafter on the eleven miles between this reservoir and Junction City, on account of the fact that timber for which it has been of late years almost exclusively used, will soon be exhausted. The time will, therefore, shortly come, if it is not already here, when all interests involved, both of the State and its citizens, can be protected and the cause of complaint, which now exists, be removed.[104]

While acknowledging the argument made by Defiance Republicans and the timber industry, Governor Foraker threw his support behind abandonment, mainly because he believed it was an inevitability based on the trend of timber extraction from Paulding County. Governor Foraker also believed it was better to do it now than have to let the discontent fester a few more years.

On January 4, 1888, two days after the legislative session began, Representative Geyer introduced House Bill No. 48 (henceforth also referred to as the Geyer Bill) to abandon the canal and reservoir,[105] holding to the demands made at the meeting in December to introduce it promptly. Representative Geyer reportedly believed the bill was a sure thing to pass as it was "virtually approved in the Governor's message."[106] As a result of his bill and stances on the canals, Representative Geyer was "appointed on the house committee on Public Works."[107] Representative Geyer was also "honored with [the Democrat] caucus nomination for speaker *pro tem* of the House of

Representatives." [108] However, because the Democrats were in the minority, the nomination was only honorary. The gesture, nevertheless, reflected great credit upon Representative Geyer, and showed that his party held him in high regard. [109]

After briefly returning to Paulding on January 13, 1888, Representative Geyer informed his constituents that his reservoir bill had already been read twice in the Committee on Public Works, and "so far very little opposition to the bill has developed." [110] Although he could not be sure how much opposition the bill would get when voted upon in the House, [111] he remained optimistic it would breeze through the Ohio Legislature's two chambers on the first attempt. [112]

The House Committee on Public Works viewed Six Mile Reservoir on January 25, 1888. [113] They arrived by train on the CJ&M at Cecil, where citizens furnished transportation to the scenes they would be viewing. [114] The eleven legislators¶ would do what the Governor and others had done the summer prior, touring Six Mile Reservoir, the canal, and the ditch in Indiana. [115] "Few if any [Antwerp] citizens" joined them due to the suddenness of their arrival; those who did join the committee were "timber sharks of Defiance," who had seemingly been tipped off to the committee's arrival. [116] The *Defiance County Express*¶¶ reported that the men were sent to "see that there was fair play in enlightening the committee." [117] Seven men from

---

¶ See Appendix D for lists of those who were part of these committees that visited Paulding County.

¶¶ It was at this time that the *Defiance County Express* rebranded itself as the *Defiance County Republican and Express*.
("Change of Name," *Defiance County Republican and Express*, February 9, 1888, 8.)

Defiance were reportedly present; among these men were John Crowe and Frank J. Shead.[118]

These Defiance men reportedly appeared "in force,"[119] but perhaps were a bit too overzealous when they "strongly urged [the reservoir and canal's] retention" to the committee.[120] They reportedly followed the committee "so closely as to make their presence very disagreeable."[121] It was so bad that they did not "feel their littleness" until Noah H. Albaugh, the committee chairman, (and Speaker *pro tem* of the House of Representatives[122]) "severely criticized their actions."[123] Upon returning to Antwerp, the committee was "courteously received" by the citizens of Antwerp at the Kauffman Hotel.[124] Once the committee was finished, they left the same evening, returning to Columbus.[125] All reports in Paulding County newspapers indicated that the committee would favor the canal and reservoir's abandonment.[126]

The committee might have been convinced, but there was still a concern among some members of the Ohio House of Representatives regarding the "question of land title."[127] The *Antwerp Argus* urged Representative Geyer not to let the bill be voted on until "all points regarding the State's title to the land are made clear, and all points regarding 'land grabbers' fully settled."[128] Not that the *Antwerp Argus* believed this was a possibility, but any questions like those could jeopardize the bill again. Representative Geyer sent an inquiry to the United States General Land Office, and he reportedly would "call his reservoir bill up for final action" just as soon as they got back to him about "the grants of land to the State."[129]

That said, Wilson H. Snook reportedly sent a letter to Governor Foraker explaining that "'three-eighths of the land in the reservoir is owned by the State, and the balance belongs to private persons.'"[130] The *Delphos Herald* misreported the letter as the State of Ohio owning but one-eighth of the land and the balance belonging to "a lot of land sharks who are the loudest in their demands for abandonment."[131] Unsurprisingly, the *Paulding Democrat* refuted that report by the *Delphos Herald*, calling it "a malicious lie,"[132] asserting that Mr. Snook informed Representative Geyer that "2,000 acres of the reservoir land belonged to the State and only 800 to private parties."[133] Their math also does not match Mr. Snook's letter, which only muddles the actual situation.

Even a decade later, there were still those who were asserting that the 'land sharks' were behind the abandonment scheme.[134] The *Defiance News* reported that "the bill will pass, and then the parties who have been so long engaged in engineering the scheme will be able to realize on their efforts. A list of beneficiaries would be mighty interesting reading and would surprise many persons."[135] The *Paulding Democrat* refuted this and only mentioned that the "list won't include any of the Defiance factories or sawmills or, the news office either. But it will include every tax-payer in Paulding County."[136]

The *Columbus Dispatch* referred to the whole canal and reservoir question as an "elephant of immense proportions on the State's hands."[137] Their reasons were that the Committee on Public Works had still not issued any report on their findings, and the Governor reportedly demanded "a satisfactory abstract."[138] Timbermen in the area were also reportedly fighting over the matter, which allegedly required that it "must be settled before a final disposition of the reservoir can be made, which bids fair not to be settled for a year or two."[139]

The condition of the reservoir was also questionable, requiring it "either be sold or repaired and at some considerable expense."[140] The reservoir was also reportedly "so covered with land warrants that one of the members of the House has expressed the opinion that the State, even if it should sell it, would not realize over a thousand dollars on it."[141] Never mind "lawyers of repute" believed the land would "revert to the general government the moment its use for canal purposes is abandoned."[142] This raised fears of 'land sharks' buying the land cheap and reselling it at a profit. [143] Others believed that abandoning the work would "be but a wedge to split open the way to a final wreck of the public works."[144]

Meanwhile, there was reportedly an attempt to amend the Geyer Bill, the language being "'that the abandonment shall not take place for two years.'"[145] This would have amended Section 7 of his bill, which would have otherwise enforced the reservoir bill "from and after its passage." [146] The *Hicksville News* had another proposal, their argument being a bill that would have allowed Paulding County to acquire the lands in the reservoir "for the purpose of converting it into a park and pleasure resort."[147]§ Much later, the *Antwerp Argus* proposed that some of the reservoir lands should be turned into a "State Reform Farm." [148] This was proposed under the belief that the ones already in Ohio were at their capacity.[149]

---

§ Not unlike what happened to create Buckeye Lake, Indian Lake, Lake Loramie, and Grand Lake St. Mary's.

Acknowledging the concern that the United States Federal Government owned the land in the canal reservoir; Representative Levi Meredith of Van Wert County (formerly Senator Levi Meredith) offered the following resolution to be amended to the Geyer Bill:

> Reciting the necessity of abandoning the Wabash and Erie Canal and Six Mile Reservoir in Paulding County, and resolving that permission be and the same is hereby asked of the general government of the United States through Congress to abandon so much of the Wabash and Erie Canal and the Paulding County Reservoir as lies between the east line of Indiana and the first lock on said canal above the town of Junction.[150]

This resolution made some sense, considering if the State petitioned the United States Federal Government to abandon the works, there were but two things that could happen. The first being the Congress could say it had no authority over the land, therefore quashing the objections that the land would revert to the United States Federal Government. The second is that Congress could assert its authority over the land; should the State abandon the land and revert to the United States Federal Government, they would probably abandon it, maybe under similar terms.

## Chapter 9 Notes

1 "The First Gun!," *Defiance Democrat*, October 13, 1887, 2; *Defiance County Express*, October 8, 1887, 8; "Democratic Meeting!," *Defiance Democrat*, October 6, 1887, 2.

2 "The First Gun!," *Defiance Democrat*, October 13, 1887, 2.

3 "The First Gun!," *Defiance Democrat*, October 13, 1887, 2.

4 "The First Gun!," *Defiance Democrat*, October 13, 1887, 2.

5 *Defiance County Express*, October 15, 1887, 7;

6 "The First Gun!," *Defiance Democrat*, October 13, 1887, 2.

7 "The First Gun!," *Defiance Democrat*, October 13, 1887, 2; "Geyer Talks," *Paulding Democrat*, October 20, 1887, 1.

8 "The First Gun!," *Defiance Democrat*, October 13, 1887, 2; "Geyer's Speech," *Defiance County Express*, October 22, 1887, 18; "Geyer Talks," *Paulding Democrat*, October 20, 1887, 1.

9 "The First Gun!," *Defiance Democrat*, October 13, 1887, 2; "Geyer's Speech," *Defiance County Express*, October 22, 1887, 18; "Geyer Talks," *Paulding Democrat*, October 20, 1887, 1.

10 "The First Gun!," *Defiance Democrat*, October 13, 1887, 2; "Geyer's Speech," *Defiance County Express*, October 22, 1887, 18; "Geyer Talks," *Paulding Democrat*, October 20, 1887, 1.

11 "The First Gun!," *Defiance Democrat*, October 13, 1887, 2; "Geyer Talks," *Paulding Democrat*, October 20, 1887, 1.

12 "The First Gun!," *Defiance Democrat*, October 13, 1887, 2; "Geyer Talks," *Paulding Democrat*, October 20, 1887, 1.

13 "The First Gun!," *Defiance Democrat*, October 13, 1887, 2; "Geyer Talks," *Paulding Democrat*, October 20, 1887, 1.

14 "Geyer's Speech," *Defiance County Express*, October 22, 1887, 18; "Geyer Talks," *Paulding Democrat*, October 20, 1887, 1. "The First Gun!," *Defiance Democrat*, October 13, 1887, 2.

15 "Geyer's Speech," *Defiance County Express*, October 22, 1887, 18; "Geyer Talks," *Paulding Democrat*, October 20, 1887, 1. "The First Gun!," *Defiance Democrat*, October 13, 1887, 2.

16 "Geyer's Speech," *Defiance County Express*, October 22, 1887, 18; "Geyer Talks," *Paulding Democrat*, October 20, 1887, 1. "The First Gun!," *Defiance Democrat*, October 13, 1887, 2.

17 "Geyer's Speech," *Defiance County Express*, October 22, 1887, 18; "Geyer Talks," *Paulding Democrat*, October 20, 1887, 1. "The First Gun!," *Defiance Democrat*, October 13, 1887, 2.

18 "The First Gun!," *Defiance Democrat*, October 13, 1887, 2; "Geyer Talks," *Paulding Democrat*, October 20, 1887, 1.

19 *Defiance County Express*, October 15, 1887, 7; *Defiance County Express*, October 20, 1887, 8; *Defiance County Express*, October 27, 1887, 8.

20 *Defiance County Express*, October 15, 1887, 7; *Defiance County Express*, October 20, 1887, 8.

21 "The First Gun!," *Defiance Democrat*, October 13, 1887, 2; "Geyer's Speech," *Defiance County Express*, October 22, 1887, 18; "Geyer Talks," *Paulding Democrat*, October 20, 1887, 1.

22 "The First Gun!," *Defiance Democrat*, October 13, 1887, 2; "Geyer's Speech," *Defiance County Express*, October 22, 1887, 18; "Geyer Talks," *Paulding Democrat*, October 20, 1887, 1.

23 "John L. Geyer's Record," *Defiance Democrat*, November 3, 1887, 2.

24 "The First Gun!," *Defiance Democrat*, October 13, 1887, 2; "Geyer's Speech," *Defiance County Express*, October 22, 1887, 18; "Geyer Talks," *Paulding Democrat*, October 20, 1887, 1.

25 *Defiance Democrat*, October 20, 1887, 2.

26 *Defiance Democrat*, October 20, 1887, 2.

27 *Defiance County Express*, October 22, 1887, 8.

28 *Defiance Democrat*, October 20, 1887, 2.

29 "The First Gun!," *Defiance Democrat*, October 13, 1887, 2; "Geyer's Speech," *Defiance County Express*, October 22, 1887, 18; "Geyer Talks," *Paulding Democrat*, October 20, 1887, 1.

30 "The First Gun!," *Defiance Democrat*, October 13, 1887, 2; "Geyer Talks," *Paulding Democrat*, October 20, 1887, 1.

31 "The First Gun!," *Defiance Democrat*, October 13, 1887, 2; "Geyer Talks," *Paulding Democrat*, October 20, 1887, 1.

32 "The First Gun!," *Defiance Democrat*, October 13, 1887, 2; "Geyer's Speech," *Defiance County Express*, October 22, 1887, 18; "Geyer Talks," *Paulding Democrat*, October 20, 1887, 1.

33 *Defiance County Express*, October 22, 1887, 18.

34 *Defiance County Express*, October 22, 1887, 18.

35 *Defiance County Express*, October 22, 1887, 18

36 *Defiance County Express*, October 22, 1887, 18.

37 *Defiance County Express*, October 22, 1887, 18.

38 *Defiance County Express*, October 22, 1887, 18.

39 *Defiance County Express*, October 22, 1887, 18.

40 "Still Another!," *Defiance Democrat*, November 3, 1887 2; "The First Gun!," *Defiance Democrat*, October 13, 1887, 2; "Geyer's Speech," *Defiance County Express*, October 22, 1887, 18; "Geyer Talks," *Paulding Democrat*, October 20, 1887, 1; "Hon. John L. Geyer," *Defiance Democrat*, October 27, 1887, 2.

41 "The First Gun!," *Defiance Democrat*, October 13, 1887, 2; "Geyer's Speech," *Defiance County Express*, October 22, 1887, 18; "Geyer Talks," *Paulding Democrat*, October 20, 1887, 1; "Hon. John L. Geyer," *Defiance Democrat*, October 27, 1887, 2; "Still Another!," *Defiance Democrat*, November 3, 1887 2.

42 "Still Another!," *Defiance Democrat*, November 3, 1887 2; "The First Gun!," *Defiance Democrat*, October 13, 1887, 2; "Geyer's Speech," *Defiance County Express*, October 22, 1887, 18; "Geyer Talks," *Paulding Democrat*, October 20, 1887, 1;

43 "Still Another!," *Defiance Democrat*, November 3, 1887 2; "The First Gun!," *Defiance Democrat*, October 13, 1887, 2; "Geyer's Speech," *Defiance County Express*, October 22, 1887, 18; "Geyer Talks," *Paulding Democrat*, October 20, 1887, 1; "Hon. John L. Geyer," *Defiance Democrat*, October 27, 1887, 2.

44 *Defiance Democrat*, November 3, 1887, 2.

45 State of Ohio, *Executive Documents: Annual Reports for 1887, Made to the Sixty-Eighth General Assembly*, Part I, 1294.

46 *Defiance Democrat*, November 3, 1887, 2.

47 *Defiance Democrat*, November 3, 1887, 2.

48 *Defiance Democrat*, November 3, 1887, 2.

49 *Defiance Democrat*, November 3, 1887, 2.

50 *Defiance County Express*, November 3, 1887, 7; *Defiance County Express*, October 29, 1887, 8.

51 "Celina Talks," *Defiance County Express*, October 22, 1887, 8; "Celina Talks," *Defiance County Express*, October 27, 1887, 8.

52 "Celina Talks," *Defiance County Express*, October 22, 1887, 8; "Celina Talks," *Defiance County Express*, October 27, 1887, 8.

53 *Defiance County Express*, October 15, 1887, 7; *Defiance County Express*, October 20, 1887, 8.

54 "Celina Talks," *Defiance County Express*, October 22, 1887, 8; "Celina Talks," *Defiance County Express*, October 27, 1887, 8.

55 "Celina Talks," *Defiance County Express*, October 22, 1887, 8; "Celina Talks," *Defiance County Express*, October 27, 1887, 8.

56 "Celina Talks," *Defiance County Express*, October 22, 1887, 8; "Celina Talks," *Defiance County Express*, October 27, 1887, 8.

57 "Celina Talks," *Defiance County Express*, October 22, 1887, 8; "Celina Talks," *Defiance County Express*, October 27, 1887, 8.

58 "Local Gossip," *Paulding Democrat*, October 13, 1887, 5; "Our Home Corner," *Antwerp Argus*, October 13, 1887, 3; "Local Brevities," *Paulding County Gazette*, October 13, 1887, 1.

59 "Our Home Corner," *Antwerp Argus*, October 13, 1887, 3; "Local Gossip," *Paulding Democrat*, October 13, 1887, 5.

60 *History of Crane Township Paulding County*, unknown publisher, 1941.

61 "Will Go Elsewhere," *Antwerp Argus*, July 8, 1886, 3.

62 "Local Gossip," *Paulding Democrat*, October 13, 1887, 5.

63 "Painful Accident," *Paulding County Gazette*, September 29, 1887, 1.

64 "Our Home Corner," *Antwerp Argus*, October 13, 1887, 3.

65 "Local Brevities," *Paulding County Gazette*, October 13, 1887, 1; "Local Gossip," *Paulding Democrat*, October 20, 1887, 7.

66 "Local Brevities," *Paulding County Gazette*, October 13, 1887, 1.

67 "Personal Mention," *Antwerp Argus*, November 3, 1887, 5.

68 "East End Items by Tom," *Antwerp Argus*, October 13, 1887, 2.

69 "Victory!," *Paulding Democrat*, November 10, 1887, 1; *Defiance County Express*, December 3, 1887, 8.

70 "Official Vote of Paulding County," *Paulding County Gazette*, November 10, 1887, 1; "Official Vote," *Paulding Democrat*, November 17, 1887, 1.

71 "Official Vote of Paulding County," *Paulding County Gazette*, November 10, 1887, 1; "Official Vote," *Paulding Democrat*, November 17, 1887, 1.

72 Joseph P. Smith, *History of the Republican Party in Ohio*, Volume I, 541.

73 "Official Vote of Paulding County," *Paulding County Gazette*, November 10, 1887, 1; "Official Vote," *Paulding Democrat*, November 17, 1887, 1.

74 Joseph P. Smith, *History of the Republican Party in Ohio*, Volume I, 538.

75 "Official Vote of Paulding County," *Paulding County Gazette*, November 10, 1887, 1.

76 "Official Vote of Paulding County," *Paulding County Gazette*, November 10, 1887, 1.

77 "Official Vote of Paulding County," *Paulding County Gazette*, November 10, 1887, 1.

78 Joseph P. Smith, *History of the Republican Party in Ohio*, Volume I, 541.

79 "Official Vote of Paulding County," *Paulding County Gazette*, November 10, 1887, 1; "Official Vote," *Paulding Democrat*, November 17, 1887, 1.

80 "Official Vote of Paulding County," *Paulding County Gazette*, November 10, 1887, 1; "Official Vote," *Paulding Democrat*, November 17, 1887, 1.

81 *Defiance County Express*, December 3, 1887, 8.

82 "The Canal Question," *Antwerp Argus*, December 1, 1887, 3; "The Canal Question," *Defiance County Express*, December 8, 1887, 7.

83 "The Canal Question," *Antwerp Argus*, December 1, 1887, 3; "The Canal Question," *Defiance County Express*, December 8, 1887, 7.

84 "The Canal Question," *Defiance County Express*, December 8, 1887, 7.

85 "Local Gossip," *Paulding Democrat*, December 15, 1887, 9.

86 "The Reservoir Question," *Antwerp Argus*, December 22, 1887, 5.

87 "Our Home Corner," *Antwerp Argus*, December 1, 1887, 3.

88 *Paulding Democrat*, November 17, 1887, 1.

89 *Paulding Democrat*, November 17, 1887, 1.

90 "From Hazlett's Crossing," *Antwerp Argus*, December 1, 1887, 2.

91 "From Hazlett's Crossing," *Antwerp Argus*, December 1, 1887, 2.

92 "Melrose Musings," *Paulding Democrat*, December 22, 1887, 1.

93 "From Hazlett's Crossing," *Antwerp Argus*, December 15, 1887, 2.

94 "From Hazlett's Crossing," *Antwerp Argus*, December 15, 1887, 2.

95 "Our Home Corner," *Antwerp Argus*, December 15, 1887, 3.

96 "Personal Mention," *Antwerp Argus*, December 8, 1887, 3.

97 "Personal Points," *Paulding Democrat*, December 22, 1887, 5; "Local Brevities," *Paulding County Gazette*, January 5, 1888, 1.

98 "The Canal Question," *Antwerp Argus*, December 8, 1887, 2.

99 "The Canal Question," *Antwerp Argus*, December 8, 1887, 2.

100 "The Canal Question," *Antwerp Argus*, December 8, 1887, 2.

101 "The Canal Question," *Antwerp Argus*, December 8, 1887, 2.

102 "The Canal Question," *Antwerp Argus*, December 8, 1887, 2.

103 "Personal Points," *Paulding Democrat*, December 22, 1887, 5.

104 "The Governor Speaks," *Antwerp Argus*, January 5, 1888, 2; "Paulding County Reservoir," *Paulding County Gazette*, January 5, 1888, 4; "Foraker's Message," *Defiance County Express*, January 12, 1888, 4; "Governor's Message," *Paulding Democrat*, January 12, 1888, 3.

105 *Cincinnati Enquirer*, January 5, 1888, 4; "The House," *Cincinnati Enquirer*, January 5, 1888, 2; "Local," *Defiance County Express*, January 26, 1888, 10; "The Reservoir Bill," *Paulding Democrat*, February 16, 1888, 4.

106 *Cincinnati Enquirer*, January 5, 1888, 2.

107 "Local Gossip," *Paulding Democrat*, January 5, 1888, 1; "Ohio Legislature," *Defiance County* Express, January 19, 1888, 19.

108 "Local Gossip," *Paulding Democrat*, January 5, 1888, 1.

109 "Local Gossip," *Paulding Democrat*, January 5, 1888, 1.

110 "Personal Points," *Paulding Democrat*, January 19, 1888, 5.

111 "Personal Points," *Paulding Democrat*, January 19, 1888, 5.

112 "Personal Points," *Paulding Democrat*, January 19, 1888, 5.

113 "The Legislative Committee," *Antwerp Argus*, February 2, 1888, 2; "Reservoir Committee," *Paulding Democrat*, January 26, 1888, 5; *Paulding County Gazette*, January 26, 1888, 4.

114 "The Legislative Committee," *Antwerp Argus*, February 2, 1888, 2.

115 "The Legislative Committee," *Antwerp Argus*, February 2, 1888, 2.

116 "The Legislative Committee," *Antwerp Argus*, February 2, 1888, 2; *Defiance County Express*, February 4, 1888, 8.

117 *Defiance County Express*, February 4, 1888, 8.

118 "Personal Mention," *Antwerp Argus*, February 2, 1888, 3.

119 "The Legislative Committee," *Antwerp Argus*, February 2, 1888, 2.

120 *Paulding County Gazette*, January 26, 1888, 4.

121 "The Legislative Committee," *Antwerp Argus*, February 2, 1888, 2.

122 Joseph P. Smith, *History of the Republican Party in Ohio*, Volume I, 542.

123 "The Legislative Committee," *Antwerp Argus*, February 2, 1888, 2.

124 "The Legislative Committee," *Antwerp Argus*, February 2, 1888, 2; "Reservoir Committee," *Paulding Democrat*, January 26, 1888, 5.

125 "Reservoir Committee," *Paulding Democrat*, January 26, 1888, 5.

126 *Paulding County Gazette*, January 26, 1888, 4; "Reservoir Committee," *Paulding Democrat*, January 26, 1888, 5; "The Legislative Committee," *Antwerp Argus*, February 2, 1888, 2.

127 "The Legislative Committee," *Antwerp Argus*, February 2, 1888, 2.

128 "The Legislative Committee," *Antwerp Argus*, February 2, 1888, 2.

129 *Paulding Democrat*, February 9, 1888, 4.

130 "Our Home Corner," *Antwerp Argus*, February 2, 1888, 3.

131 *Paulding Democrat*, February 9, 1888, 4.

132 *Paulding Democrat*, February 9, 1888, 4.

133 *Paulding Democrat*, February 9, 1888, 4.

134 *Paulding Democrat*, February 9, 1888, 4; "Paulding Reservoir,"
  *Paulding Democrat*, February 2, 1888, 6.

135 "Paulding Reservoir," *Paulding Democrat*, February 2, 1888, 6.

136 "Paulding Reservoir," *Paulding Democrat*, February 2, 1888, 6.

137 "An Elephant," *Antwerp Argus*, February 9, 1888, 2.

138 "An Elephant," *Antwerp Argus*, February 9, 1888, 2.

139 "An Elephant," *Antwerp Argus*, February 9, 1888, 2.

140 "An Elephant," *Antwerp Argus*, February 9, 1888, 2.

141 "An Elephant," *Antwerp Argus*, February 9, 1888, 2.

142 "An Elephant," *Antwerp Argus*, February 9, 1888, 2.

143 "An Elephant," *Antwerp Argus*, February 9, 1888, 2.

144 "An Elephant," *Antwerp Argus*, February 9, 1888, 2.

145 "Our Home Corner," *Antwerp Argus*, February 2, 1888, 3.

146 "The Reservoir Bill," *Paulding Democrat*, February 16, 1888, 4.

147 "From Our Neighbors," *Antwerp Argus*, February 16, 1888, 3.

148 "Reform Farm," *Antwerp Argus*, May 10, 1888, 3; "Local Gossip,"
  *Paulding Democrat*, May 17, 1888, 5; "Chat," *Defiance Democrat*,
  May 17, 1888, 3.

149 "Local Gossip," *Paulding Democrat*, May 17, 1888, 5.

150 "Local Gossip," *Paulding Democrat*, February 23, 1888, 5; *Defiance
  County Republican and Express*, March 3, 1888, 8; "Local,"
  *Defiance County Republican and Express*, March 8, 1888, 10;
  "Local," *Defiance County Republican and Express*, March 8,
  1888, 9.

# -10-

# The Agony Ends

## (February 1888 – May 1888)

On February 22, 1888, the House Committee on Public Works finally reported the Geyer Bill back to the Ohio House of Representatives, "signed by six members."[1] The members who did not sign the bill were Noah H. Albaugh of Miami County, Benjamin F. Kitchen of Jackson County, and John W. Barger of Pike County.[2] Representatives Albaugh and Kitchen were both present at the reservoir when the committee visited; Representative Barger was not.[3] The *Antwerp Argus* asserted that their support (as well as that of Representative Levi Meredith of Van Wert County) had been interrupted by "our Defiance neighbors."[4] The Geyer Bill would come up for a vote in the Ohio House of Representatives on March 1, 1888, and Representative John L. Geyer of Defiance and Paulding County reported that "the prospects of the bill's success are very favorable."[5] It came up for debate as a special order, and the debate was described as "lengthy."[6] Francis B. DeWitt and Alonzo B. Holcombe were reportedly in attendance when the Geyer Bill came up for consideration.[7]

At 11:30 a.m.,[8] Representative Geyer "opened the argument for the advocates of the bill, making a strong argument in favor of its passage."[9] Representative Geyer then "produced copies of the weekly reports of the canal collector, showing that the receipts did not exceed $400 (~$12,709 in 2023) per annum,"[10] further stating that "the total amount collected at Defiance did not much exceed $2,000 (~$63,544 in 2023)."[11] Representative Geyer then pointed out that the two lock keepers on the Wabash & Erie Canal, needing to be paid for their services, each received $180 annually. [12] Doing that math, Representative Geyer rightfully acknowledged that just paying those two employees ate up "almost as much as the entire receipts" that was paid on the Wabash & Erie Canal.[13]

The *Antwerp Argus*, however, asserted that the $2000 in tolls collected was a ploy to "make a good showing" in the House,[14] claiming that the "amounts charged up for years past, were all put together and paid up at the last end of the year... This sum would doubtless never have been paid, had not the question of abandonment been agitated,"[15] further calling the payment of the tolls late in the year an act showing that the "'timber sharks'... were forced to the wall, and in order to save their pet scheme and make a good showing on the collector's books, have virtually donated the amount claimed."[16]

Representative Geyer also acknowledged the longstanding argument that the reservoir was "a public nuisance, being a cesspool in summer and overflowing in the fall and spring, preventing the proper drainage of the farms in Paulding County."[17] Representative Geyer further stated that the State of Ohio owned 2,015 acres of the 2,700 acres present in the reservoir.[18]

The *Cincinnati Commercial Gazette*, however, claimed that Representative Geyer stated the Wabash & Erie Canal's tolls would only average $150 (~$4,766 in 2023) annually. [19] Representative Geyer also reportedly claimed that "the sale of the land would aggregate to the State between $50,000 (~$1,588,611 in 2023) and $60,000 (~$1,906,333 in 2023)." [20] Most dubiously, however, the *Cincinnati Commercial Gazette* claimed that Representative Geyer asserted that the "there were 2,700 acres of land in the reservoir, 201 of which belong to the State." [21]

As noted in the previous chapter, the *Delphos Herald* claimed only one-eighth of the land belonged to the State of Ohio. [22] The *Paulding Democrat*, however, asserted that Wilson H. Snook informed Representative Geyer that "2,000 acres of the reservoir land belonged to the State and only 800 to private parties." [23] The 2,015 acres that Representative Geyer is reported to have stated seems a tad more realistic than the mere 201 acres reported by the *Cincinnati Commercial Gazette*, a figure that is not even one-eighth of the total acreage.

Representative Albaugh was next to speak. [24] He opposed the bill and asserted that those who supported the bill had done "a great deal of lying." [25] Representative Geyer reportedly "immediately jumped to his feet," calling for a "question of privilege," as he believed Representative Albaugh was "slurring his constituents and he hoped his remarks would be couched [*sic*] in respectful language." [26] After that interruption, Mr. Albaugh explained that there had also been attempts to abandon "almost every reservoir in the state." [27]

Representative Albaugh conceded that Six Mile Reservoir was not a feeder for the Miami & Erie Canal and that "if he owned land in the neighborhood he would want the reservoir abandoned." [28] However, he opposed abandonment entirely because he asserted the tolls from timber rafting amounted to about $2,000 the previous year and that the timber manufacturers had offered the Board of Public Works "$1,000 per year on a ten-year lease."[29] So long as the canal was making some money, and there was timber to be rafted, he would oppose any abandonment proposals. [30] Representative Albaugh also believed that "the time would soon come when the timber along the canal would be exhausted, and the floating of logs cease," at which point abandonment would be on the table.[31]

Representative John T. McCray of Ashland County agreed with Representative Albaugh in opposition of the legislation. [32] ¶ Representative McCray still argued that the State of Ohio "had no title in fee simple to a single acre of the lands in the Paulding County Reservoir," further asserting that nobody had offered any physical proof that the state did.[33] Representative McCray provided the "act of congress under which the canal and reservoir were granted,"[34] asserting that the "grant was made to be used forever for canal purposes."[35]

Representative William T. Clark of Cuyahoga County reportedly inquired, "if the lands do not belong to the State, who owns them?" [36] Representative McCray only responded by informing Representative Clark that should the State of Ohio

---

¶ "Although Ashland was not a canal county, he felt considerable interest in the bill because these lands belonged to the whole people." ("Passed The House," *Paulding Democrat*, March 8, 1888, 4.)

cease using the land for canal purposes, "the lands at once revert to the original owner, the Government." [37] Furthermore, Representative McCray also asserted that the Ohio Supreme Court had decided that the State of Ohio did not own the lands, and that an 1887 act of legislation to "abandon[] a portion of the Hocking Canal" did not have provisions to sell the land because "the land reverted back to the United States."[38]

Representative McCray also provided the legislation from the Ohio General Assembly that indicated the State of Ohio accepted those terms,[39] calling the whole abandonment bill "one of the most gigantic and unmitigated land swindles ever attempted to be perpetrated on the people of the State." [40] Two entities Representative McCray claimed would benefit as much as $200,000 (~$6,354,442 in 2023) from the abandonment scheme, was, of course, Dr. Solomon S. Stambaugh, and oddly enough the Antwerp Furnace Company.[41] Representative McCray reportedly believed the latter was the entity behind the bill's existence. [42] Lastly, he asserted that the works should not be abandoned because they still generated some revenue for the state.[43]

The problems with Representative McCray's assessment were twofold. As already noted, Dr. Stambaugh had long since moved away from Ohio and presumably had no interest in the property anymore, as he was running a medical practice in San Francisco, California, by this time in 1888.[44] Further proving this point is that Dr. Stambaugh likely had already lost, if not all of the land, a portion of it by 1887 due to unpaid taxes.[45] The second issue was that the Antwerp Furnace Company did not exist by this time in 1888. The furnace was in the process of being torn down by July 8, 1886,[46] and it had not been operational for "five or six years" by that time.[47] By March 17, 1887, the Antwerp Furnace Company was in the process of divesting its land interests and had already "sold about $90,000 (~$2,823,253 in 2023) worth of land."[48]

Representative Edward J. Kennedy of Cuyahoga County motioned for a point of order, stating that Representative McCray, "being unable to bring forward any other reasons, advanced the constitutional objection." [49] Representative Kennedy then argued that, after having seen the reservoir in person as a member of the Committee on Public Works,[50] "any reasonable man who could visit the place would be convinced that the bill should pass."[51] Representative Kennedy objected to any assertion that some in the committee were "wined and dined and pestered by lobbyists" for their position, and asserted that those in the committee were "left to judge for themselves."[52]§ Representative Kennedy further argued Representative Geyer's point that a "large part" of the 2,700 acres in the reservoir could be claimed by the State of Ohio as their land, and also provided a statement from the "canal clerk of the state auditor's office" regarding the "small receipts of the canal."[53]

Representative Kennedy also pointed out that six of the nine committee members agreed that the canal and reservoir should be abandoned.[54]§§ He closed his arguments with a plea to the

---

§ That objection is debatable, as they were welcomed into the saloons of the Kauffman Hotel as mentioned earlier. They were also reportedly pestered by lobbyists, just not from Antwerp.

§§ While it is a majority, 66.6% of the committee is not as damning as he was maybe expecting that assertion to be.

House that they "listen to the just request of the farmers of Paulding; there hasn't been a drop of water in the reservoir this winter. The universal replies of the people of Paulding to the questions of the committee were that the abandoning would be a godsend to the county."[55]

Following Representative Kennedy was Representative Daniel H. Gaumer of Muskingum County, another member of the Committee of Public Works present at the reservoir viewing.[56] Representative Gaumer lamented to the chamber that "his only regret was that all the members of the House had not seen the condition of affairs in Paulding County."[57] After a brief recess on the motion of Representative Meredith, [58] Representative Gaumer then "demanded the previous question, which was carried."[59] When all was said and done, the bill passed fifty-seven to thirty-three.[60]¶

Representative Geyer "received many congratulations" for the victory.[61] It had taken three readings and a special order for it to be brought up for a vote, but the Geyer Bill had passed on the first try in 1888.[62] However, it was a somewhat hollow victory considering it passed by a single vote over the previous year. Some members of the House "were not inclined to vote," and Representative Geyer had to "skip[] about the hall nervously getting members to record their votes."[63] This further cast doubt on the legislation's prospects going forward, and the *Defiance County Republican and Express* acknowledged this fact and asserted that "[the bill] would die in the Senate."[64]

---

¶ See Appendix E for a complete list of how the representatives voted.

The *Antwerp Argus* warned its readers that the bill "stands a favorable chance of defeat, as the enemies of the bill are at work to bring about such a result."[65] The *Paulding Democrat* echoed this same conclusion.[66] On March 6, 1888, the Geyer Bill was referred to the Ohio Senate Committee on Public Works.[67] The *Antwerp Argus* alerted its readers to keep an eye out for the senate committee,[68] namely to give them "such a reception, as to convince them that we are a unit on the question of abandonment... We do not mean by a reception that they be 'wined and dined'... but that they be met by an outpouring of our citizens such as greeted Gov. Foraker when he visited us for alike purpose."[69] The *Antwerp Argus* also encouraged its readers to not only "meet this committee *en masse*," but to also travel to Columbus when the Geyer Bill was to be put up for a vote to "indicate that we are determined in our demand for right and justice."[70] The *Paulding Democrat* called for similar action from Paulding residents.[71]

When the senators arrived in Antwerp on the morning of March 27, 1888, a "good crowd of all classes of people" met the senators despite the "inclemency of the weather and bad condition of the roads."[72] Only two senators showed up in Paulding County, those honorable two were Senators Edwin Sinnett from Licking County and Walter S. Crook from Montgomery County.[73] Senator William Geyser from Fulton County was also reportedly on the way, but he failed to appear.[74]

Accompanying the two senators was Representative Geyer, who, with but a few Antwerp citizens, toured the canal works.[75] The weather was disagreeable enough to prevent many area residents from accompanying the committee on their tour.[76]

Upon their return to Antwerp, the citizens of Antwerp invited the senators into the Kauffman Hotel to "exchange views on the question" and "partaking of a sumptuous meal,"[77] after which, the committee returned to Paulding, then returned to Columbus by train on an afternoon CJ&M train.[78]

Representative Geyer joined the two senators back to Paulding,[79] however, he stayed in town with his family until the evening before returning to Columbus, accompanied by Francis B. DeWitt and Floyd Atwill.[80] The *Paulding Democrat* predicted that more citizens from the area would travel to Columbus, as the Ohio Senate was reportedly voting on the Geyer Bill as early as March 30, 1888.[81] Both the *Antwerp Argus* and *Paulding Democrat* believed that the committee was "convinced" on the idea of abandonment,[82] the *Paulding Democrat* was confident that the bill would surely pass.[83] However, March 30, 1888, came and went with no news on the bill's status.

In other news, the *Antwerp Argus* asserted that an outbreak of measles in the region was being "traced to the miasmatic influences of the Antwerp Reservoir."[84] The *Antwerp Argus* reported that the "Board of Health are looking into the matter, and should compel the abandonment of the stink-pond, and that without delay."[85] There had already been "over two thousand cases of measles... many of which have proven fatal."[86] Later in May, the *Antwerp Argus* also insinuated that the reservoir's presence also caused a local epidemic of mumps and whooping cough.[87] It goes without saying that Six Mile Reservoir, by itself, did not cause these epidemics. However, some if not most of the local citizens believed that it did at this time, and this was nevertheless part of their justification to have the canal works abandoned.

Word soon came that the Geyer Bill would be voted on sometime during the week of April 1, 1888.[88] Lewis S. Gordon, Henry George, Sr., and Oliver S. Applegate traveled to Columbus on April 2, 1888, to be in attendance at the Ohio Senate Chamber for the vote.[89] On the afternoon of April 6, 1888, the Ohio Senate debated the Geyer Bill.[90]

After Senator Edwin Sinnett from Licking County presented the report from the Senate Committee on Public Works, which recommended the Geyer Bill's passage, [91] Senator John Park Alexander from Summit County offered a resolution (S. R. J. No. 9) that amended the bill to include a Governor appointed three-person committee[92] "to plat the canal lands to the State, to make the sale under certain restrictions,"[93] and for the committee to survey and decide "if in their opinion it will be to the best interest and welfare of Paulding County and the State."[94] If their decision warranted it, the state would sell the land at the Paulding County courthouse within ninety days.[95]

This fell in line with the recommendation by the Committee on Public Works to attach the matter to S. B. No. 21's provision, which finally made good on what AG John Little had requested the state to do over a decade prior, which was to survey the canal system to "define and protect the ownership and title of the state in and to all lands belonging to and connected with said canals."[96] The proceeds from the sale would be credited to the funds for the Ohio and Miami & Erie canals.[97] After that, and many other small details were squared away, the Ohio Senate voted on the Geyer Bill. What could have only been followed by audible gasps in the Ohio Senate chamber, the vote was unanimous, "Not a senator voting against it."[98]¶ The Geyer Bill had successfully passed the Senate.[99]

The amended bill (which can be read in full in the April 19, 1888 edition of the *Antwerp Argus* on page two) greatly differed from the original Geyer Bill. First, the amended bill stated that "the commissioners of Paulding County are hereby authorized to deepen and widen, under the drainage laws of the state, any portion of said canal so abandoned."[100] Second, the amended bill did not call for the entire Wabash & Erie Canal in Paulding County to be abandoned with the bill's passing and recommendation of the commission.

The only part of the canal that would be abandoned was "from the place of its intersection with the Indiana and Ohio state line to the first lock below the Six Mile Reservoir, all in Paulding County, Ohio, together with the Six Mile Reservoir."[101] This likely was intended to be Hutchins Lock, as the *Annual Report for 1888* stated that "about ten miles of this canal remain, and is of no possible advantage to the State or citizen... it should be abandoned and sold."[102]¶¶ Furthermore, the report notes that the only remaining section of the canal extended from "Junction, on the Miami and Erie, to, and including, the lock next below the Six-mile Reservoir."[103]

---

¶ See Appendix E for a complete list of how the representatives voted.

¶¶ It is not certain when the canal was abandoned west of One-Mile Lock. The last mile of the canal would not be abandoned until House Bill No. 185 passed on March 31, 1902.
(State of Ohio, *General and Local Acts Passed and Joint Resolutions Adopted by the Seventy-Fifth General Assembly*, Volume XCV, 77-78.)

News reached Antwerp that evening by telegram, and the occasion was "celebrated by the booming of cannon and loud hurrah."[104] However, some noted that the "jollification may be a little premature."[105] The amended bill was now on its way to the House for another vote to resolve the difference in the passed bills before going to Governor Joseph B. Foraker's desk. Five days later, on April 11, 1888, at noon, Representative Geyer telegraphed to inform Antwerp that the House "concurred with the Ohio Senate amendments," and the House's vote was also unanimous.[106]¶ The Geyer Bill was formally passed on April 12, 1888. [107] The *Antwerp Argus* then told those who may have celebrated prematurely, "Now, boys, jollify."[108]

More good news was that House Bill No. 585 passed, which made "appropriations to meet deficiencies and pay liabilities." The expense of particular note is the appropriation of $3,063.74 (~$96,108 in 2023) from the state to cover the expenses of the Ohio National Guard's deployment to Paulding County.[109]¶¶ This indicated that Paulding County and its citizens would not have to pay a dime for the deployment of the Ohio National Guard.

Before any celebration could begin in earnest, Six Mile Reservoir was again dynamited on the nights of April 11, 1888,

---

¶ See Appendix E for a complete list of how the representatives voted.

¶¶ The state did not appropriate the $3,070.25 reported to the same legislature in 1888 but were close with $3,063.74. Why the full amount was not appropriated is unknown. Regardless of the reason for that discrepancy, the $3,063.74 that was appropriated was 'drafted' from the state's account in two increments. The first was a draft of $2,969.24 at an unknown date or throughout 1888, and a further $94.50 on November 15, 1888.
(State of Ohio, *Annual Report of the Auditor to the Governor of the State of Ohio for the Fiscal Year Ending November 15, 1888*, 18, 287-288.)

and April 12, 1888.[110] The attacks had created a hole in the bank of the reservoir where the Board of Public Works had already filled it in previously, and destroyed "all that part of the new feeder remaining."[111] Rather than a form of celebration, it was supposed that it was again the work of timbermen from Defiance trying to get water for timber rafting.[112] The *Defiance Local News* reported the reservoir had been "badly blown by dynamite last night. The parties who did the despicable work came from Antwerp with lanterns and torches, doing the work in a manner worthy a better cause."[113]

There was only one small problem with the reporting from Defiance that the *Antwerp Argus* picked up on. In the *Antwerp Argus*' belief, "the *News* man must have been onto 'the racket' and knew the reservoir was to be again 'dynamited' as the work could hardly have been accomplished before the *News* was printed."[114] The *Antwerp Argus* further asserted that the work was done to "influence the Commission by committing depredations, and then try to make it appear that the work was done by parties from Antwerp."[115]¶

As prescribed by the amended Geyer Bill, Governor Foraker appointed the men that would be tasked with "making an accurate survey and statement of all the canal lands and interests owned by the State." [116] This commission was also responsible for "disposing of the Six Mile Reservoir" within the

---

¶ Six Mile Reservoir was "quite full" with water at this time of year, especially so because of an alleged broken dam "above the State line, which break it is claim was made by these same timber men from Defiance."
("Our Home Corner," *Antwerp Argus*, April 19, 1888, 3; "More Scared Than Hurt," *Paulding Democrat*, April 19, 1888, 5.)

guidelines of their duties.[117] Those appointed were William H. Gibson of Tiffin, Ohio, Charles E. Baldwin of Mt. Vernon, Ohio, and a familiar name, Alexander S. Latty of Defiance.[118] The man who oversaw the construction of Six Mile Reservoir forty years prior would have a say in whether it be abandoned or preserved.

The *Paulding Democrat* questioned whether the committee was necessary, though they misunderstood the bill's language.[119] They pointed to the clause in section one stating that the part of the canal and reservoir was "hereby abandoned as hereinafter provided for."[120] The property was only abandoned as provided for "in the following part of this document," at least if it is based on the definition from Merriam-Webster.[121] The *Paulding Democrat*'s assertion was that the committee was designed to "take from the author and champion of the bill the credit for its success."[122]

On May 3, 1888, a poem appeared in the *Antwerp Argus*, written by '*Rambling Roland*,'[123]¶ who may have been the last person to use the Wabash & Erie Canal in Paulding County by floating along in his "timber shanty" that he called a "floating palace."[124] At the same time, despite the committee not officially declaring the works abandoned, the *Paulding Democrat* reported, "the old canal bed from [Antwerp] to the reservoir has been ditched and its banks are being graded down and farmed."[125]

Keep in mind the fact that the Geyer Bill had only passed about two weeks prior, and the commission had not formally chosen to abandon the reservoir just yet. The people of Paulding County were nevertheless making quick work of the canal, and

---

¶ See the full text in Appendix F.

soon, reported the *Paulding Democrat*, "this once great commercial highway will have passed out of sight."[126] That said, with the assistance of "private subscription" to pay for it, work would begin on properly "opening ditches and the bank [of the reservoir] into the canal" in July 1888.[127]

For the first two weeks of May, the commission appointed by Governor Foraker was seen "surveying and inspecting the reservoir."[128] Those nominated to the commission were only appointed for two years and paid about $1,300 (~$41,304 in 2023) plus the costs of their expenses annually for their services.[129] The commission, however, took longer than the *Antwerp Argus* would have liked, and so the paper commented that they "seem to think they have an endless job on their hands... It will doubtless take them three years to complete their labors."[130] By May 17, 1888, the commission had viewed Six Mile Reservoir, then returned to Antwerp to convene in the Kauffman Hotel to make their decision.[131]¶

Their decision was unanimous, and they believed that the "property had passed its usefulness as a branch to the Public Works system of the State,"[132] and it would

> be for the best interests and welfare of the citizens of Paulding County, and the State of Ohio,' to abandon the Wabash and Erie Canal from the place of its intersection with the Indiana and Ohio State line, to the first lock

---

¶ The *Annual Report for 1888* implies the men made the decision on May 4, 1888, but that is contrary to the local newspaper report implying they made their decision on "Thursday of last week" from the May 24, 1888, edition of the *Antwerp Argus*; which would have been May 17 at the latest. (State of Ohio, *Executive Documents: Annual Reports for 1888, Made to the Sixty-Eighth General Assembly*, Part II, 815; "The Agony Ended," *Antwerp Argus*, May 24, 1888, 2.)

below the 'Six-mile Reservoir,' together with the Six-mile Reservoir.[133]

All that was left to do was finish the surveying, which was completed by May 28, 1888,[134] appraise the land, then sell it.[135] The almost fourteen-year fight to abandon the Wabash & Erie Canal and Six Mile Reservoir was over, and the people could now rejoice, for "the agony is at last ended."[136]

It was determined that the State of Ohio "owned 932 acres in the reservoir, and will be able to sell about 1,050 acres in all, which includes the portion of the canal authorized to be sold under the Geyer law."[137] The value of the land varied "from $25 (~$784 in 2023) to $30 (~$941 in 2023) an acre."[138] In all, the State of Ohio was expected to make between $21,000 (~$667,216 in 2023) and $22,000 (~$698,989 in 2023) from the sale of the reservoir lands.[139]

After the three-person commission notified the Board of Public Works and the Sinking Fund Commissioners, the Sinking Fund Commissioners elected to make the terms of the land sale "one-fifth down and the balance in four equal payments, with six percent interest."[140] A petition was reportedly circulated in Antwerp that "asked our fellow townsmen, O. S. Applegate, be appointed as auctioneer to sell the lands in the reservoir."[141]

Two roads were also proposed by the *Paulding Democrat* to be built "through the heart of the territory heretofore made desolate by the reservoir."[142] One was an east-west road along the township line "between Carryall and Harrison and Crane and Paulding townships from the Antwerp and Payne road to the Cecil and Paulding road."[143] This proposal matches Township Road 162 between State Route 49 and U.S. 127, which skirts just south of the reservoir, not through it. The other proposed road was a north-south road "between Harrison and Paulding and Crane and Carryall from Paulding and Antwerp road to the Maumee River road." [144] This proposal matches what became Township Road 61, which does cut through the heart of the reservoir lands.

## Chapter 10 Notes

1 "The Geyer Bill," *Antwerp Argus*, March 1, 1888, 2.
2 "The Geyer Bill," *Antwerp Argus*, March 1, 1888, 2.
3 "The Legislative Committee," *Antwerp Argus*, February 2, 1888, 2.
4 "The Geyer Bill," *Antwerp Argus*, March 1, 1888, 2.
5 "Local Gossip," *Paulding Democrat*, March 1, 1888, 5.
6 "Ohio Legislature," *Paulding Democrat*, March 8, 1888, 3.
7 "Personal Points," *Paulding Democrat*, March 1, 1888, 5.
8 "Local Option Law," *Cincinnati Commercial Gazette*, March 2, 1888, 1.
9 "Passed The House," *Paulding Democrat*, March 8, 1888, 4.
10 "Passed The House," *Paulding Democrat*, March 8, 1888, 4.
11 "Passed The House," *Paulding Democrat*, March 8, 1888, 4.
12 "Passed The House," *Paulding Democrat*, March 8, 1888, 4.
13 "Passed The House," *Paulding Democrat*, March 8, 1888, 4.
14 "Time for Action," *Antwerp Argus*, March 8, 1888, 2.
15 "Time for Action," *Antwerp Argus*, March 8, 1888, 2.
16 "Time for Action," *Antwerp Argus*, March 8, 1888, 2.
17 "Passed The House," *Paulding Democrat*, March 8, 1888, 4.
18 "Passed The House," *Paulding Democrat*, March 8, 1888, 4.
19 "Local Option Law," *Cincinnati Commercial Gazette*, March 2, 1888, 1.
20 "Local Option Law," *Cincinnati Commercial Gazette*, March 2, 1888, 1.
21 "Local Option Law," *Cincinnati Commercial Gazette*, March 2, 1888, 1.
22 *Paulding Democrat*, February 9, 1888, 4.
23 *Paulding Democrat*, February 9, 1888, 4.
24 "Passed The House," *Paulding Democrat*, March 8, 1888, 4.
25 "Passed The House," *Paulding Democrat*, March 8, 1888, 4.
26 "Passed The House," *Paulding Democrat*, March 8, 1888, 4.
27 "Passed The House," *Paulding Democrat*, March 8, 1888, 4.
28 "Passed The House," *Paulding Democrat*, March 8, 1888, 4; "Local Option Law," *Cincinnati Commercial Gazette*, March 2, 1888, 1.
29 "Passed The House," *Paulding Democrat*, March 8, 1888, 4; "Local Option Law," *Cincinnati Commercial Gazette*, March 2, 1888, 1.
30 "Passed The House," *Paulding Democrat*, March 8, 1888, 4; "Local Option Law," *Cincinnati Commercial Gazette*, March 2, 1888, 1.
31 "Passed The House," *Paulding Democrat*, March 8, 1888, 4.
32 "Passed The House," *Paulding Democrat*, March 8, 1888, 4.
33 "Passed The House," *Paulding Democrat*, March 8, 1888, 4; "Local Option Law," *Cincinnati Commercial Gazette*, March 2, 1888, 1.
34 "Passed The House," *Paulding Democrat*, March 8, 1888, 4; "Local Option Law," *Cincinnati Commercial Gazette*, March 2, 1888, 1.
35 "Passed The House," *Paulding Democrat*, March 8, 1888, 4; "Local Option Law," *Cincinnati Commercial Gazette*, March 2, 1888, 1.
36 "Local Option Law," *Cincinnati Commercial Gazette*, March 2, 1888, 1.
37 "Local Option Law," *Cincinnati Commercial Gazette*, March 2, 1888, 1.

38 "Passed The House," *Paulding Democrat*, March 8, 1888, 4.

39 "Passed The House," *Paulding Democrat*, March 8, 1888, 4.

40 "Passed The House," *Paulding Democrat*, March 8, 1888, 4; "Local Option Law," *Cincinnati Commercial Gazette*, March 2, 1888, 1.

41 "Local Option Law," *Cincinnati Commercial Gazette*, March 2, 1888, 1.

42 "Local Option Law," *Cincinnati Commercial Gazette*, March 2, 1888, 1.

43 "Passed The House," *Paulding Democrat*, March 8, 1888, 4.

44 *The Bay of San Francisco: The Metropolis of the Pacific Coast and its Suburban Cities: A History*, Volume I, 656.

45 Andrew J. Stenger: Treasurer vs. Solomon S. Stambaugh, No. 3693, Doc. 7, 217, July 1, 1886.

46 "Will Go Elsewhere," *Antwerp Argus*, July 8, 1886, 3.

47 "Will Go Elsewhere," *Antwerp Argus*, July 8, 1886, 3.

48 "Personal Mention," *Antwerp Argus*, March 17, 1887, 3.

49 "Passed The House," *Paulding Democrat*, March 8, 1888, 4.

50 "The Legislative Committee," *Antwerp Argus*, February 2, 1888, 2.

51 "Passed The House," *Paulding Democrat*, March 8, 1888, 4.

52 "Passed The House," *Paulding Democrat*, March 8, 1888, 4.

53 "Passed The House," *Paulding Democrat*, March 8, 1888, 4.

54 "Passed The House," *Paulding Democrat*, March 8, 1888, 4.

55 "Passed The House," *Paulding Democrat*, March 8, 1888, 4.

56 "Passed The House," *Paulding Democrat*, March 8, 1888, 4; "The Legislative Committee," *Antwerp Argus*, February 2, 1888, 2.

57 "Passed The House," *Paulding Democrat*, March 8, 1888, 4.

58 State of Ohio, Journal of the House of Representatives of the State of Ohio, for the Regular Session of the Sixty-Eighth General Assembly, Volume LXXXIV, 391.

59 "Passed The House," *Paulding Democrat*, March 8, 1888, 4; "Local Option Law," *Cincinnati Commercial Gazette*, March 2, 1888, 1; State of Ohio, Journal of the House of Representatives of the State of Ohio, for the Regular Session of the Sixty-Eighth General Assembly, Volume LXXXIV, 392.

60 "Ohio Legislature," *Paulding Democrat*, March 8, 1888, 3; "Local," *Defiance County Republican And Express*, March 10, 1888, 9; "Local," *Defiance County Republican And Express*, March 10, 1888, 10; "Local," *Defiance County Republican and Express*, March 10, 1888, 20; "Local," *Defiance County Republican and Express*, March 15, 1888, 6; "Ohio Legislature," *Defiance County Republican and Express*, March 10, 1888, 21; "Ohio Legislature," *Defiance County Republican and Express*, March 15, 1888, 7; "Ohio Legislature," *Defiance County Republican and Express*, March 17, 1888, 3-4; "Passed The House," *Paulding Democrat*, March 8, 1888, 4; "Local Option Law," *Cincinnati Commercial Gazette*, March 2, 1888, 1; State of Ohio, Journal of the House of Representatives of the State of Ohio, for the Regular Session of the Sixty-Eighth General Assembly, Volume LXXXIV, 392-393.

61 "Passed The House," *Paulding Democrat*, March 8, 1888, 4.

62 State of Ohio, Journal of the House of Representatives of the State of Ohio, for the Regular Session of the Sixty-Eighth General Assembly, Volume LXXXIV, 391.

63 "Local," *Defiance County Republican and Express*, March 10, 1888, 9-10, 20; "Local," *Defiance County Republican and Express*, March 15, 1888, 6; "Passed the House," *Paulding Democrat*, March 8, 1888, 4.

64 "Local," *Defiance County Republican and Express*, March 10, 1888, 9-10, 20; "Local," *Defiance County Republican and Express*, March 15, 1888, 6.

65 "Time for Action," *Antwerp Argus*, March 8, 1888, 2.

66 "Our People Should Assist," *Paulding Democrat*, March 15, 1888, 4.

67 *Antwerp Argus*, March 8, 1888, 3.

68 "Time for Action," *Antwerp Argus*, March 8, 1888, 2.

69 "Time for Action," *Antwerp Argus*, March 8, 1888, 2.

70 "Time for Action," *Antwerp Argus*, March 8, 1888, 2.

71 *Paulding Democrat*, March 22, 1888, 4.

72 "Senatorial Committee," *Antwerp Argus*, March 29, 1888, 3; "Senate Committee," *Paulding Democrat*, March 29, 1888, 5.

73 "Senate Committee," *Paulding Democrat*, March 29, 1888, 5.

74 "Senate Committee," *Paulding Democrat*, March 29, 1888, 5.

75 "Senate Committee," *Paulding Democrat*, March 29, 1888, 5; "Senatorial Committee," *Antwerp Argus*, March 29, 1888, 3.

76 "Senatorial Committee," *Antwerp Argus*, March 29, 1888, 3; "Senate Committee," *Paulding Democrat*, March 29, 1888, 5.

77 "Senatorial Committee," *Antwerp Argus*, March 29, 1888, 3.

78 "Senatorial Committee," *Antwerp Argus*, March 29, 1888, 3; "Senate Committee," *Paulding Democrat*, March 29, 1888, 5.

79 "Senate Committee," *Paulding Democrat*, March 29, 1888, 5.

80 "Senate Committee," *Paulding Democrat*, March 29, 1888, 5.

81 "Senate Committee," *Paulding Democrat*, March 29, 1888, 5.

82 "Senatorial Committee," *Antwerp Argus*, March 29, 1888, 3; "Senate Committee," *Paulding Democrat*, March 29, 1888, 5.

83 "Senate Committee," *Paulding Democrat*, March 29, 1888, 5.

84 "State Board of Health," *Antwerp Argus*, April 5, 1888, 4.

85 "State Board of Health," *Antwerp Argus*, April 5, 1888, 4.

86 "State Board of Health," *Antwerp Argus*, April 5, 1888, 4.

87 "Our Home Corner," *Antwerp Argus*, May 3, 1888, 3.

88 "Personal Mention," *Antwerp Argus*, April 5, 1888, 4.

89 "Personal Mention," *Antwerp Argus*, April 5, 1888, 4.

90 State of Ohio, *Journal of the Senate of the State of Ohio, for the Regular Session of the Sixty-Eighth General Assembly*, Volume LXXXIV, 762-763.

91 State of Ohio, *Journal of the Senate of the State of Ohio, for the Regular Session of the Sixty-Eighth General Assembly*, Volume LXXXIV, 762-763.

92 "The Canals," *Cincinnati Enquirer*, April 7, 1888, 4; "Antwerp Happenings," *Paulding Democrat*, April 12, 1888, 5; State of Ohio, *Journal of the Senate of the State of Ohio, for the Regular Session of the Sixty-Eighth General Assembly*, Volume LXXXIV, 27–28; State of Ohio, *General and Local Acts Passed, and Joint Resolutions Adopted by the Sixty-Eighth General Assembly*, Volume LXXXV, 127.

93 "The Canals," *Cincinnati Enquirer*, April 7, 1888, 4; State of Ohio, *General and Local Acts Passed, and Joint Resolutions Adopted by the Sixty-Eighth General Assembly*, Volume LXXXV, 127–129.

94 *Defiance County Republican and Express*, April 14, 1888, 9–10; "Local," *Defiance County Republican and Express*, April 19, 1888, 9–10; "The 'Old Stink Pond,'" *Antwerp Argus*, April 12, 1888, 3; State of Ohio, *Journal of the Senate of the State of Ohio, for the Regular Session of the Sixty-Eighth General Assembly*, Volume LXXXIV, 763; State of Ohio, *General and Local Acts Passed, and Joint Resolutions Adopted by the Sixty-Eighth General Assembly*, Volume LXXXV, 208.

95 "Antwerp Happenings," *Paulding Democrat*, April 12, 1888, 5; "The 'Old Stink Pond,'" *Antwerp Argus*, April 12, 1888, 3; State of Ohio, *Journal of the Senate of the State of Ohio, for the Regular Session of the Sixty-Eighth General Assembly*, Volume LXXXIV, 763; State of Ohio, *General and Local Acts Passed, and Joint Resolutions Adopted by the Sixty-Eighth General Assembly*, Volume LXXXV, 208.

96 State of Ohio, *Journal of the Senate of the State of Ohio, for the Regular Session of the Sixty-Eighth General Assembly*, Volume LXXXIV, 27–28, 70, 762–763; State of Ohio, *General and Local Acts Passed, and Joint Resolutions Adopted by the Sixty-Eighth General Assembly*, Volume LXXXV, 127.

97 "As Amended," *Antwerp Argus*, April 19, 1888, 2; State of Ohio, *General and Local Acts Passed, and Joint Resolutions Adopted by the Sixty-Eighth General Assembly*, Volume LXXXV, 209.

98 "Antwerp Happenings," *Paulding Democrat*, April 12, 1888, 5; "The 'Old Stink Pond,'" *Antwerp Argus*, April 12, 1888, 3; "As Amended," *Antwerp Argus*, April 19, 1888, 2; State of Ohio, *Journal of the Senate of the State of Ohio, for the Regular Session of the Sixty-Eighth General Assembly*, Volume LXXXIV, 763.

99 *Defiance County Republican and Express*, April 14, 1888, 9–10; "The Canals," *Cincinnati Enquirer*, April 7, 1888, 4; "Antwerp Happenings," *Paulding Democrat*, April 12, 1888, 5; "Local," *Defiance County Republican and Express*, April 19, 1888, 9–10; "The 'Old Stink Pond,'" *Antwerp Argus*, April 12, 1888, 3; "As Amended," *Antwerp Argus*, April 19, 1888, 2.

100 State of Ohio, *Journal of the Senate of the State of Ohio, for the Regular Session of the Sixty-Eighth General Assembly*, Volume LXXXIV, 762–763; "As Amended," *Antwerp Argus*, April 19, 1888, 2; *Paulding Democrat*, April 26, 1888, 4; "Local," *Defiance County Republican and Express*, April 19, 1888, 9–10; "The 'Old Stink Pond,'" *Antwerp Argus*, April 12, 1888, 3; State of Ohio, *General and Local Acts Passed, and Joint Resolutions Adopted by the Sixty-Eighth General Assembly*, Volume LXXXV, 207.

101 "As Amended," *Antwerp Argus*, April 19, 1888, 2; *Defiance County Republican and Express*, April 14, 1888, 9–10; State of Ohio, *Journal of the Senate of the State of Ohio, for the Regular Session of the Sixty-Eighth General Assembly*, Volume LXXXIV, 762; State of Ohio, *General and Local Acts Passed, and Joint Resolutions Adopted by the Sixty-Eighth General Assembly*, Volume LXXXV, 207.

102 State of Ohio, *Executive Documents: Annual Reports for 1888, Made to the Sixty-Eighth General Assembly*, Part II, 816.

103 State of Ohio, *Executive Documents: Annual Reports for 1888, Made to the Sixty-Eighth General Assembly*, Part II, 1091.

104 "The 'Old Stink Pond,'" *Antwerp Argus*, April 12, 1888, 3.

105 "The 'Old Stink Pond,'" *Antwerp Argus*, April 12, 1888, 3.

106 "The 'Old Stink Pond,'" *Antwerp Argus*, April 12, 1888, 3; "As Amended," *Antwerp Argus*, April 19, 1888, 2; State of Ohio, Journal of the House of Representatives of the State of Ohio, for the Regular Session of the Sixty-Eighth General Assembly, Volume LXXXIV, 825.

107 State of Ohio, *General and Local Acts Passed, and Joint Resolutions Adopted by the Sixty-Eighth General Assembly*, Volume LXXXV, 209.

108 "The 'Old Stink Pond,'" *Antwerp Argus*, April 12, 1888, 3.

109 State of Ohio, *General and Local Acts Passed, and Joint Resolutions Adopted by the Sixty-Eighth General Assembly*, Volume LXXXV, 342–343.

110 "From Hazlett's Crossing," *Antwerp Argus*, April 19, 1888, 2; "More Scared Than Hurt," *Paulding Democrat*, April 19, 1888, 5.

111 "More Scared Than Hurt," *Paulding Democrat*, April 19, 1888, 5.

112 "From Hazlett's Crossing," *Antwerp Argus*, April 19, 1888, 2; "More Scared Than Hurt," *Paulding Democrat*, April 19, 1888, 5.

113 "Our Home Corner," *Antwerp Argus*, April 19, 1888, 3.

114 "Our Home Corner," *Antwerp Argus*, April 19, 1888, 3.

115 "Our Home Corner," *Antwerp Argus*, April 19, 1888, 3; "More Scared Than Hurt," *Paulding Democrat*, April 19, 1888, 5.

116 "The Canal Commission," *Paulding Democrat*, April 19, 1888, 4; *Defiance Democrat*, April 26, 1888, 2.

117 "The Canal Commission," *Paulding Democrat*, April 19, 1888, 4; *Defiance Democrat*, April 26, 1888, 2.

118 "The Canal Commission," *Paulding Democrat*, April 19, 1888, 4; "Canal Commission," *Antwerp Argus*, April 19, 1888, 3; *Defiance Democrat*, April 26, 1888, 2.

119 *Paulding Democrat*, April 26, 1888, 4.

120 "As Amended," *Antwerp Argus*, April 19, 1888, 2; *Paulding Democrat*, April 26, 1888, 4; State of Ohio, *General and Local Acts Passed, and Joint Resolutions Adopted by the Sixty-Eighth General Assembly*, Volume LXXXV, 207.

121 Merriam-Webster, "hereinafter," accessed March 17, 2022, https://www.merriam-webster.com/dictionary/hereinafter.

122 *Paulding Democrat*, April 26, 1888, 4.

123 "The Reservoir-Present and Future," *Antwerp Argus*, May 3, 1888, 2.

124 "Our Home Corner," *Antwerp Argus*, May 3, 1888, 3.

125 "Antwerp Happenings," *Paulding Democrat*, April 26, 1888, 5.

126 "Antwerp Happenings," *Paulding Democrat*, April 26, 1888, 5.

127 "Our Home Corner," *Antwerp Argus*, July 19, 1888, 3.

128 "Local Gossip," *Paulding Democrat*, May 17, 1888, 5.

129 "The Canal Commission," *Paulding Democrat*, April 19, 1888, 4; *Defiance Democrat*, April 26, 1888, 2; State of Ohio, *Journal of the Senate of the State of Ohio, for the Regular Session of the Sixty-Eighth General Assembly*, Volume LXXXIV, 28; State of Ohio, *General and Local Acts Passed, and Joint Resolutions Adopted by the Sixty-Eighth General Assembly*, Volume LXXXV, 127.

130 "Our Home Corner," *Antwerp Argus*, May 10, 1888, 3.

131 "The Agony Ended," *Antwerp Argus*, May 24, 1888, 2.

132 "The Agony Ended," *Antwerp Argus*, May 24, 1888, 2; "Unanimously in Favor of It," *Paulding Democrat*, May 24, 1888, 5.

133 State of Ohio, *Executive Documents: Annual Reports for 1888, Made to the Sixty-Eighth General Assembly*, Part II, 815.

134 "Finished Up," *Antwerp Argus*, May 31, 1888, 3.

135 "The Agony Ended," *Antwerp Argus*, May 24, 1888, 2.

136 "The Agony Ended," *Antwerp Argus*, May 24, 1888, 2.

137 "The Canal Commissioners," *Paulding Democrat*, May 31, 1888, 5; "The Canal Commissioners," *Cincinnati Enquirer*, May 25, 1888, 1; "The Paulding Reservoir," *Defiance Democrat*, May 31, 1888, 3.

138 "The Canal Commissioners," *Paulding Democrat*, May 31, 1888, 5; "The Canal Commissioners," *Cincinnati Enquirer*, May 25, 1888, 1; "The Paulding Reservoir," *Defiance Democrat*, May 31, 1888, 3.

139 "The Canal Commissioners," *Paulding Democrat*, May 31, 1888, 5; "The Canal Commissioners," *Cincinnati Enquirer*, May 25, 1888, 1; "The Paulding Reservoir," *Defiance Democrat*, May 31, 1888, 3.

140 "The Canal Commissioners," *Paulding Democrat*, May 31, 1888, 5;
    "The Paulding Reservoir to be Sold," *Fort Wayne Sentinel*," May
    24, 1888, 1; "Canal Lands," *Cincinnati Enquirer*, May 24, 1888,
    1; "Sale of the Paulding County Reservoir Lands," *Defiance
    Democrat*, May 31, 1888, 3.
141 "Personal Mention," *Antwerp Argus*, May 31, 1888, 2.
142 "Improved Roads Needed," *Paulding Democrat,* May 24, 1888, 5.
143 "Improved Roads Needed," *Paulding Democrat,* May 24, 1888, 5.
144 "Improved Roads Needed," *Paulding Democrat,* May 24, 1888, 5.

# -Epilogue-

## Now, Boys, Jollify!
### (May 1888 – December 1888)

With the matter concluded, Antwerp and its people were going to rejoice, planning an entire celebration to "jollify over the reservoir abandonment... and a grand and glorious time is anticipated."[1] While the *Antwerp Argus* was not initially ready to say when the event would occur, the *Paulding Democrat* first reported it would be "about the first of June" and that it would be "a grand picnic on the banks of the reservoir.... Eloquent orations will be made, banners will wave, bands will discourse sweet music, an ox will be roasted, and glad songs will be sung."[2]

However, the next week, the *Paulding Democrat* informed its readers that "the date has not yet been fixed upon,"[3] and the event was to be a "grand celebration and barbecue" rather than a simple picnic.[4] On May 28, 1888, citizens of Antwerp met at the Band Hall@ to make "preliminary arrangements for a Grand Jollification in the village of Antwerp, on Wednesday, July 4,

---

@ The Band Hall being referred to is likely the Antwerp Cornet Band's Opera House, built in 1888, that was located on Daggett Street about halfway between Cleveland Street and Monroe Street in Antwerp.
(Otto E. Ehrhart, "Business History of Antwerp," in *A Century of Progress: Antwerp, Ohio*, 51; *Sanborn Fire Insurance Map from Antwerp, Paulding County, Ohio*, August 1893.)

1888." [5] This preliminary meeting mostly just set up various committees to plan various aspects of the event.¶ The May 28, 1888 meeting then adjourned until May 31, 1888, [6] when another meeting at the Antwerp Band Hall would take place "for the purpose of making necessary arrangements for a grand jollification in this place, July 4, 1888." [7]

With the announcement of a date, the Antwerp correspondent to the *Paulding Democrat* said, "the 'Dynamiters' will have a great Fourth of July celebration." [8] By June 14, 1888, arrangements were made with the Wabash Railroad "for half rates on all trains to Antwerp," for the celebration on July 4, 1888. [9] It was also announced that "handsome" [10] badges made of "red, white and blue satin ribbon" with "gold and mahogany bronze" print [11] for the occasion would be available for purchase, for five cents (~$1.57 in 2023), [12] at the Smith newsstand and Osborn bookstore starting on June 22, 1888. [13] The purpose of which was to be a "memento of the occasion, and to assist in defraying expenses of celebration." [14] The following announcement was made about the "Grand Jollification" in the *Paulding Democrat*:

> The Reservoir War is ended, and therefore know ye that the Dynamiters will disband after holding a Grand Jollification and olden time barbecue at Riverside Park, Antwerp, Ohio, Wednesday, July 4th, 1888. Gov. Foraker, Gen. Gibson, Hon. Alfred P. Edgerton, Judge Boersox, and Hon. J. L. Geyer have been invited to address the masses of this occasion. Justice prevails and Paulding County celebrates the victory. Let all the Northwest join with us in celebrating our emancipation from reservoir rule. [15]

---

¶ For full lists of committees and their members, see Appendix C.

Thousands were expected to attend the celebration in Antwerp, and final preparations were still being made well into June.[16] At another meeting in the Band Hall on June 14, 1888, a motion was made to purchase fireworks for the event, but that decision was left to the arrangements committee.[17] Burton B. Banks was appointed to "make all necessary arrangements for shooting tournament," and determine the cost of acquiring "pigeons."[18] John Yeager was appointed to "arrange for a match game of baseball."[19] The grounds committee was instructed to "advertise and sell right to locate restaurant stands in the park."[20] Maroni P. Jacobs, at his request, was relieved of his reception committee duties and replaced by John H. Oswalt on the reception committee.[21]

Two weeks later, it was announced that the 16th Regiment of the Ohio National Guard, the same regiment that made their appearance at the Reservoir War, was reportedly contemplating joining the locals at their celebration on July 4, 1888.[22] One week before the celebration, it was confirmed to the populace that a portion of the soldiery that was at the Reservoir War would be in attendance. Particularly CPT Owen J. Hopkin's Light Battery D and CPT Alpheus R. Rogers' Company H.[23] CPT Rogers would also bring the regiment's brass band at the cost of $15 (~$471 in 2023).[24] Light Battery D was not initially invited to participate in the celebration; CPT Hopkins telegraphed the Committee of Arrangements to ask if he could bring Light Battery D to the celebration. His reasoning being:

> Having taken part in the invasion of Paulding county during the late 'reservoir unpleasantness' and feeling that we should shake hands over the bloody chasm, it

would give the battery boys great pleasure to revisit the scene of their bloodless campaign, and with a patriotism born of the fathers, mingle in friendly reunion with their late enemies—the 'dynamiters' of Antwerp, and do all in their power to reunite our once distracted country.[25]

CPT Hopkins congratulated Antwerp and Paulding County for its recent success in abandoning the "death breeding pond in your midst—the prime cause of your recent rebellion." [26] Furthermore, for a small price, he could also bring a Gatling gun or other piece of artillery and "give an exhibition drill."[27]

On one of those summer days when "the days are bright and sunny, and the skies have donned the cerulean blue, and the trees have put on their garb of green," [28] banners reportedly stretched across Antwerp's streets that bore "appropriate inscriptions." [29] Antwerp's businesses were also decorated for the occasion, "and the stars and stripes waved everywhere."[30] The *Paulding Democrat* stated Antwerp was "draped in the gayest holiday attire and presented a most beautiful appearance." [31] While an early morning storm threatened the day, the weather cleared before the ceremonies began. [32] "Everything, even the weather, surrendered to the 'Dynamiters.'"[33]

Light Battery D arrived the evening of July 3, 1888, with a Gatling gun and one 3-inch ordnance rifle.[34] Light Battery D would fire a "national salute" in the early daylight hours of July 4, 1888.[35] Soon after, the whistles from the factories and the bells of the churches began to sound, ushering in the day's festivities.[36] By 9 a.m., Antwerp was already becoming quite full with "happy people, all anxious to witness the subsequent events of the day."[37] An estimated five to ten thousand people made their appearance in Antwerp on that summer day.[38] The

*Antwerp Argus* quipped that "our neighboring towns were well represented, which shows that all our sympathizers do not live in Chicago."[39]§

The parade began at 10 a.m.,[40] and the procession lined up on River Street between Monroe Street and Main Street; the order of procession was as follows. 1st, Antwerp Cornet Band; 2nd, Mayor and City Council; 3rd, Clergy and Speakers; 4th, Committee of Ladies;¶ 5th, Melvertseds Band, of Toledo, Ohio; 6th, Company H of the 16th Infantry Regiment, Ohio National Guard;¶¶ 7th, Light Battery D of the 1st Regiment Light Artillery, Ohio National Guard; 8th, Drum Corps; 9th, Jubilee Singers; 10th, Sunday Schools; 11th, Other Visiting Organizations; 12th, Roasted 'Ox,' decorated; 13th, Fantastics.[41] The Fantastics were a wagon full of "products of the reservoir."[42]

Those items on the wagon reportedly included a stump from the reservoir bottoms with a "black flag" planted in it.[43] This flag bore the inscription "'No Compromise—The Reservoir Must Go!'" and was allegedly hoisted at the reservoir on the night of the attack in April 1887.[44] Also on the wagon were "splintered timbers blown from the locks," [45] "blue racers, thunder pumpers, wild ducks,"[46] "turtles, a frog, several bunches of wild flag, and the hangman's rope prepared for detectives and opposers of the 'Dynamiters.'" [47] Everything was reportedly

---

§ Another reference to the Haymarket Affair.

¶ See the Appendix C for a full list of those ladies in the committee.

¶¶ Company H did not make it in time for the parade but was still listed as part of the procession.
("The Grand Jollification!," *Antwerp Argus*, July 5, 1888, 3.)

"artistically arranged and made a fine display."[48] The roasted ox was towed on a wagon "drawn by Munger's steam engine."[49]

At precisely 10 a.m., Marshall Jesse H. Bond marched the parade west on River Street to Monroe Street; turned south on Monroe Street to Washington Street; turned east on Washington Street to Main Street; turned north on Main Street back to River Street; and east on River Street to Riverside Park.[50] Once settled at Riverside Park, some citizens sat on a "handsomely decorated" grandstand erected in the park.[51] Wilson H. Snook, "acting as master of ceremonies called the assemblage to order by ringing the bell,"[52] followed by some music from the Antwerp Cornet Band[53] and the Jubilee Singers.[54]

Following the music, the Reverend James W. McCluskey said a prayer, which was followed by more music and a reading of the Declaration of Independence by John W. Pyfer.[55] After a brief interlude of more music from the Antwerp Cornet Band, Mr. Snook introduced Antwerp's 'new' mayor, Charles S. Carpenter.[56]¶ In Mayor Carpenter's speech, he welcomed those gathered to Antwerp, and:

> wished to speak of another 'Revolutionary War,' called the 'Reservoir war' but that war is now over and the participants meet today, not in war paint, but to 'shake hands across the bloody chasm,' In peace, and to celebrate the victory of freedom and of the 'Reservoir War.'[57]

---

¶ Mr. Carpenter was not completely new to the role of mayor as he was previously Antwerp's mayor in 1883 for a single month before resigning the position. He would only be Antwerp's mayor in 1888 for a little under eight months from early April until late November before resigning again, this time due to "ill health."
(Dale L. Ehrhart, "Municipal History of Antwerp," in *A Century of Progress: Antwerp, Ohio*, 32-33.)

Another interlude of music bridged the gap in the itinerary until Representative John L. Geyer of Defiance and Paulding County was called upon to speak.[58] After being introduced to the crowd by Mr. Snook, Representative Geyer remarked that the reservoir had been built "nearly 50 years ago" and "at that time it was necessary, and the people perhaps jollified over its construction."[59] However, the time had now come to jollify over its abandonment as it had become a "detriment, and the people were compelled to rid the county of the curse."[60] He informed the crowd that "he was proud of the people he represents."[61] Representative Geyer asserted that the reservoir lands would soon be occupied, not by the water and wildlife indicative of the reservoir, but by "beautiful farms, cultivated fields, and handsome residences."[62]

The Reverend H. A. Brown took the opportunity to express appreciation on behalf of the people for the efforts of Representative Geyer.[63] Three "loud[]" cheers "with the addition of a 'tiger' were given with hearty enthusiasm."[64] Another musical interlude occurred before Mr. Snook closed with remarks on the Dynamiters. They were preparing for a parade "down near the reservoir."[65] He assured the crowd that none of the Dynamiters were from Antwerp, but were from Chicago,§ Hicksville, Paulding, and Payne.[66] The Dynamiters would appear before the crowd in the afternoon, where they would ceremoniously disband.[67] After those remarks, the crowd was dismissed to eat.[68] The day's meal was the aforementioned

§ Another reference to the Haymarket Affair.

roasted ox, prepared by Oilyer Brehm and some assistants.[69] The tables throughout the park were amply supplied for the Ohio National Guard soldiers, who were served by "the fair dynamite daughters of Antwerp."[70] The citizenry took to eating "in the customary picnic style."[71]

There was only one problem: some soldiers had not arrived yet. Unfortunately, Company H would not arrive in town until 12:52 p.m. on the 4th, having missed their morning train to Antwerp.[72] Coincidentally, the soldiers likely arrived in Riverside Park about the same time the Dynamiters did, the latter having begun their parade at 1 p.m.[73] When the Dynamiters arrived from their meeting place at the Harrmann Tile Factory,[74] they "halted around the speakers' stand."[75] Some mounted on horseback, the Dynamiters were "disguised and armed with weapons and implements used in the 'Reservoir War.'"[76] Warner D. Ryel later stated that many of the Dynamiters were "wearing the same masks they wore on the night of the blowout at the reservoir."[77] The Dynamiters were also apparently the ones who had towed the wagon filled with "products of the reservoir."[78]

At 2 p.m., Mr. Snook called to order the next set of affairs for the day.[79] Mr. Snook remarked that the Dynamiters would ceremoniously disband and introduced Leona D. Applegate, the daughter of Oliver S. Applegate, who "represented the 'Captain of the 'Dynamiters.'"[80] The Captain had asked Ms. Applegate to deliver the speech on his behalf, as he feared "his voice might betray his identity."[81]

The speech explained why the Dynamiters took arms against the state, particularly for the same reasons that have already been stated before, that the reservoir was a nuisance to the area, the reservoir covered potentially bountiful farmland, and the pleas through peaceful means had been ignored.[82] The speech also retells the events of the April attacks, but in an idealized sort of way, never getting into many details about the night, but just enough to be somewhat accurate to the actual history.[83] The one exception is that the speech claimed the Dynamiters returned so much fire in the firefight at Tate's Landing that a wagon bed toward the enemy "had the resemblance of a pepper box" and they had sent their ambushers running,[84] while the reports from that night only suggest a few shots were fired.

The speech also lamented the death of PVT Frederick L. Reeves, and noted that his death "caused many a tear to fall from the eyes of those, who, at the time, were regarded as outlaws."[85] Furthermore, the Dynamiters believed PVT Reeves "died like a man, in the discharge of his duty, and we believe that today he is a soldier in that army above whose ranks will never be broken."[86] What followed this statement was the extension of a proverbial olive branch to Company H. The villagers of Antwerp and the Dynamiters presented to Company H a "beautiful floral wreath of paper flowers, the handiwork of Mrs. Mary Swank of Huntertown, Indiana, in a handsome case" to honor their fallen comrade.[87]

Before concluding the speech, Leona thanked Representative Geyer for everything he had done to make the reservoir's abandonment a reality, and Governor Joseph B. Foraker for siding with the citizens "after viewing circumstances through the telescope of truth." [88] To conclude the speech, the following was stated:

And now in conclusion, let me say to the boys who fought under the black flag, that your manly courage and heroic bravery, has won for you the admiration of all good citizens. But now the war is over. The foundation of our county which was made to tremble by the shots fired by your hands, is now at rest. The heavens which were illuminated by the lurid flames of war, is now refulgent with the bright light of peace, and today we bury forever the black flag. You fought for a just cause and you fought well. And in this as in all other just war, right has prevailed. Now let no man disgrace his fair record by any act of Gorillaism [*sic*]. Should any man of you from this time forth, be found applying dynamite to any part of the reservoir or canal, he shall be regarded as a traitor and shall not be protected. But I do not fear that for I know you are all too manly for such acts.

The war is over, and in a few years hence, when, where once arose a loathsome vapor of pestilence and disease, the atmosphere is freighted with the sweet perfume of the golden harvest field; when, where once the fishes, snakes, toads and turtles roamed, is seen droves of cattle, sheep, horses and hogs; when, where once was heard the music of the screech owl and blackbird, is head the songs of happy children; in short when that wild sickly waste, known as the reservoir, is changed into happy homes and the products of the rich soil begin to pour into surrounding warehouses, then our work will be appreciated and it will be said, what a noble set of Philanthropists those Dynamiters were. Preserve your fair and honorable record.[89]

Following the speech by Ms. Applegate was the singing of the *Reservoir Song*, and a song written by Naomi H. Osborn, *Dedicated to the Dynamiters*.[90]¶ Addie Halleck had the honors of singing the solo (and playing the organ[91]) while the "Glee Club sang the chorus of the song."[92] Mr. Snook then thanked everyone for coming and closed the ceremonies with more music from the

---

¶ See Appendix F for the full songs.

Antwerp Cornet Band.[93] The rest of the afternoon was dotted with various events, such as a baseball game between the Antwerp and Cecil clubs,[94] and other races and games.[95] At 3 p.m., the Clay Pigeon Tournament proposed by Burton B. Banks was to begin,[96] but the real attention came afterward with demonstrations by the Ohio National Guard.[97]

The most exciting demonstration was that of the Gatling gun, which was "fired across the river at a barrel, as a target. In the words of a witness, the barrel was 'literally riddled.'"[98] Such a display reportedly reminded some of the "'old boys'" of the Civil War, and a time when the "'bloody chasm' was wider and deeper than in the 'later unpleasantness.'"[99] Others, particularly some Dynamiters, reportedly saw the spectacle and were caused to "shiver to think what that gun might have done to them."[100] Company H also gave an exhibition drill at about 5 p.m.[101]

After that, whoever was left partook in "varied amusements."[102] In the evening, the men of Light Battery D were invited to an ice cream social put on by the "young ladies of the reception committee" on the lawn of the William E. Osborn family on North Main Street,[103] to which seventy-five people attended.[104] In the evening, the fireworks began. It was such a spectacle that the men of Light Battery D reportedly stated, "the display surpassed any exhibition of fireworks they had ever witnessed in the city of Toledo, or any other city."[105] After the fireworks, those who enjoyed "'poetry of motion'" attended the "bowery dances until the sleepy 5th was ushered in."[106]

The following day, all was quiet again, and the citizens had an "'I was out last night' expression."[107] The *Antwerp Argus* noted that there was "no drunkenness nor fights. The Dynamiters are peaceable, law-abiding citizens." [108] The *Paulding Democrat* phrased it a bit differently, stating that there was "not an intoxicated man on the grounds at any time during the day and not an arrest was made."[109] A few men from Light Battery D were still in town, having missed their morning train back to Toledo.[110] The reason given for missing their train was due to the soldiers becoming "mashed on [Antwerp's] pretty girls."[111]

About a week later, the area just south and west of Antwerp was suddenly submerged in about one or two feet of water.[112] The reservoir was "nearly dry" at this time,[113] so that was not the culprit for the flooding. The *Paulding Democrat* reported that the sudden flooding was caused by unknown individuals having "cut a hole in the dam in Six Mile Creek" near the State Line. The *Antwerp Argus*, however, reported that the likely cause of the sudden flooding was due to the waterways that once fed Six Mile Reservoir having become almost entirely blocked by the excessive growth of weeds, flag, dead timber, and grass.[114]

On Friday, August 31st, 1888, the first auction to sell former canal and reservoir lands took place at 10 a.m.[115] The auction would take place as prescribed, on the doorstep of the courthouse in Paulding.[116] Francis B. DeWitt had already prepared to erect a fence around the reservoir land he was interested in buying in late July.[117] He reportedly intended to plant corn in his newfound fields and hoped to "raise from 60 to 75 bushels to the acre."[118] Paulding County also got a new post office in the vicinity of Six Mile Reservoir in August 1888. Knox Station was the location of this new office, which would be renamed Knoxdale. Francis S. Shaw was Knoxdale's first postmaster.[119]

When the auction day came, "quite a number of [Antwerp's] citizens invested in reservoir land."[120] Wilson H. Snook purchased 80 acres. George N. Munson also purchased 80 acres. Peter Munson bought 40 acres. William F. Fleck also bought 40 acres. Lastly, Oliver S. Applegate bought 35 acres.[121] The State sold eight hundred acres of land on the 31st, averaging $17.50 (~$549 in 2023) an acre, or roughly $14,000 (~$439,173 in 2023) in revenue for the State of Ohio.[122] The price paid for the land reportedly "exceeded the appraisement in every case."[123] That said, not all of the land was sold, and as of August 31, 1888, there remained 237 acres of unsold land.[124] Not available for sale in the auction was "the iron, the square stone in the waste weir and bulkhead, and the rip-rap stone" at various locations along the canal lands.[125]

The last reported parcels of land would not be sold until November 23, 1888, the last buyers being Fred Inselman, 54 acres; S. M. Thompson, 56 acres; and John L. DeWitt, 94 acres.[126] However, the *Annual Report for 1888* reported that "three tracts remain unsold, aggregating one hundred and thirty-seven and one-half acres, besides five thousand and two hundred lineal feet of canal bed."[127] When the remaining land was finally sold is not certain.

In total, $16,284.57 (~$510,838 in 2023) plus interest was made from the sale of the reservoir lands.[128] One-fifth of the purchase price had to be paid in cash, while the rest could be paid in "four equal annual payments" with a six percent interest rate.[129] By 1889, $3,362 (~$108,903 in 2023) had been paid to the State Treasury.[130] Beyond the money the state was making, the new farmland and the improved drainage of the land once occupied by the canal and reservoir would invariably support the growing county population for decades. A population that had nearly doubled to 25,932 residents between 1880 and 1890.[131]

Oliver S. Applegate and his wife Emily were reportedly the first to traverse the reservoir bottoms unimpeded by water.[132] Francis B. DeWitt did get the land he was preparing for and was seen erecting that fence around the property in mid-September.[133] By the middle of October, Mr. DeWitt would have a "large two story home" built on the property, and his property was shaping up to be an admirable farm.[134] By January 1889, Mr. DeWitt was not alone in the reservoir lands, as the *Annual Report for 1888* reported:

> The wisdom of abandoning this portion of the public works is illustrated by the extensive improvements and tasty cottages now seen within the area of land covered with water nine months since, as well as in the improved health of the surrounding country, and the rapid settlement and improvement of a full township of land outside of the reservoir, that could not be occupied or brought into cultivation, so long as the reservoir was maintained. The water supply of the Miami and Erie Canal has not been affected. The cause of the irritation and unfortunate lawlessness has been removed, and a large body of the most fertile land has been made available for cultivation, that will furnish homes for more than two thousand people.[135]

When all was said and done, the bulk of the land in the reservoir that was once owned by Dr. Solomon S. Stambaugh, was now owned by Francis B. DeWitt.[136] The same man who circulated the first known petition to abandon the reservoir a decade prior, and in doing so used rhetoric similar to that of Dr. Stambaugh. A man whose third-born son (born in 1885) was named Clayton Everett DeWitt,[137] the same name as one of the lawyers that represented and employed Dr. Stambaugh. There may just be an important fact about Mr. DeWitt's involvement in abandoning Six Mile Reservoir that remains hidden.

## Epilogue Notes

1 "Will Celebrate," *Antwerp Argus*, April 26, 1888, 3.

2 "Antwerp Happenings," *Paulding Democrat*, April 26, 1888, 5.

3 "County and Vicinity," *Paulding Democrat*, May 3, 1888, 8.

4 "Will Celebrate," *Antwerp Argus*, April 26, 1888, 3; "County and Vicinity," *Paulding Democrat*, May 3, 1888, 8.

5 "Avaunt—Reservoir!," *Antwerp Argus*, May 31, 1888, 2.

6 "Avaunt—Reservoir!," *Antwerp Argus*, May 31, 1888, 2.

7 "Avaunt Reservoir," *Antwerp Argus*, May 31, 1888, 3.

8 "From Antwerp," *Paulding Democrat*, May 31, 1888, 5.

9 "Our Home Corner," *Antwerp Argus*, June 14, 1888, 3.

10 "Our Home Corner," *Antwerp Argus*, June 14, 1888, 3; "Our Home Corner," *Antwerp Argus*, June 21, 1888, 3.

11 "Our Home Corner," *Antwerp Argus*, June 21, 1888, 3.

12 "Our Home Corner," *Antwerp Argus*, July 12, 1888, 3.

13 "Our Home Corner," *Antwerp Argus*, June 14, 1888, 3.

14 "Our Home Corner," *Antwerp Argus*, June 21, 1888, 3.

15 "County and Vicinity," *Paulding Democrat*, June 14, 1888, 1.

16 "The Grand Jollification," *Antwerp Argus*, June 21, 1888, 2.

17 "The Grand Jollification," *Antwerp Argus*, June 21, 1888, 2.

18 "The Grand Jollification," *Antwerp Argus*, June 21, 1888, 2.

19 "The Grand Jollification," *Antwerp Argus*, June 21, 1888, 2.

20 "The Grand Jollification," *Antwerp Argus*, June 21, 1888, 2.

21 "The Grand Jollification," *Antwerp Argus*, June 21, 1888, 2.

22 "Local Gossip," *Paulding Democrat*, June 28, 1888, 5.

23 "The 4th in Antwerp," *Antwerp Argus*, June 28, 1888, 2; "Coming!," *Antwerp Argus*, June 21, 1888, 3.

24 "The 4th in Antwerp," *Antwerp Argus*, June 28, 1888, 2.

25 "The 4th in Antwerp," *Antwerp Argus*, June 28, 1888, 2.

26 "The 4th in Antwerp," *Antwerp Argus*, June 28, 1888, 2.

27 "The 4th in Antwerp," *Antwerp Argus*, June 28, 1888, 2.

28 "Antwerp Happenings," *Paulding Democrat*, April 26, 1888, 5.

29 "The Grand Jollification!," *Antwerp Argus*, July 5, 1888, 3; "The Fourth At Antwerp." *Paulding Democrat*, July 12, 1888, 1.

30 "The Grand Jollification!," *Antwerp Argus*, July 5, 1888, 3.

31 "The Fourth At Antwerp." *Paulding Democrat*, July 12, 1888, 1.

32 "The Grand Jollification!," *Antwerp Argus*, July 5, 1888, 3.

33 "The Grand Jollification!," *Antwerp Argus*, July 5, 1888, 3.

34 "The Fourth At Antwerp." *Paulding Democrat*, July 12, 1888, 1; State of Ohio, *Executive Documents: Annual Reports for 1887 Made to the Sixty-Eighth General Assembly*, Part II, 674.

35 "The Fourth At Antwerp." *Paulding Democrat*, July 12, 1888, 1.

36 "The Fourth At Antwerp." *Paulding Democrat*, July 12, 1888, 1.

37 "The Fourth At Antwerp." *Paulding Democrat*, July 12, 1888, 1.

38 "The Grand Jollification!," *Antwerp Argus*, July 5, 1888, 3; "The Fourth At Antwerp." *Paulding Democrat*, July 12, 1888, 1.

39 "The Grand Jollification!," *Antwerp Argus*, July 5, 1888, 3.

40 "The Grand Jollification!," *Antwerp Argus*, July 5, 1888, 3; "Program of Exercises for the 4th of July in Antwerp," *Antwerp Argus*, June 28, 1888, 3.

41 "Program of Exercises for the 4th of July in Antwerp," *Antwerp Argus*, June 28, 1888, 3.

42 "The Grand Jollification!," *Antwerp Argus*, July 5, 1888, 3; "The Fourth At Antwerp." *Paulding Democrat*, July 12, 1888, 1.

43 "The Grand Jollification!," *Antwerp Argus*, July 5, 1888, 3; "The Fourth At Antwerp." *Paulding Democrat*, July 12, 1888, 1.

44 "The Grand Jollification!," *Antwerp Argus*, July 5, 1888, 3; "The Fourth At Antwerp." *Paulding Democrat*, July 12, 1888, 1.

45 "The Fourth At Antwerp." *Paulding Democrat*, July 12, 1888, 1.

46 "Reminiscence of Pioneer Days," *Payne Reflector and Press Review*, July 13, 1916, 1.

47 "The Grand Jollification!," *Antwerp Argus*, July 5, 1888, 3; "The Fourth At Antwerp." *Paulding Democrat*, July 12, 1888, 1.

48 "Reminiscence of Pioneer Days," *Payne Reflector and Press Review*, July 13, 1916, 1.

49 "The Grand Jollification!," *Antwerp Argus*, July 5, 1888, 3.

50 "Program of Exercises for the 4th of July in Antwerp," *Antwerp Argus*, June 28, 1888, 3; "The Fourth At Antwerp." *Paulding Democrat*, July 12, 1888, 1; "The Grand Jollification!," *Antwerp Argus*, July 5, 1888, 3.

51 "The Grand Jollification!," *Antwerp Argus*, July 5, 1888, 3; "The Fourth At Antwerp." *Paulding Democrat*, July 12, 1888, 1.

52 "The Grand Jollification!," *Antwerp Argus*, July 5, 1888, 3.

53 "The Grand Jollification!," *Antwerp Argus*, July 5, 1888, 3.

54 "Program of Exercises for the 4th of July in Antwerp," *Antwerp Argus*, June 28, 1888, 3; "The Fourth At Antwerp." *Paulding Democrat*, July 12, 1888, 1.

55 "The Grand Jollification!," *Antwerp Argus*, July 5, 1888, 3; "Program of Exercises for the 4th of July in Antwerp," *Antwerp Argus*, June 28, 1888, 3; "The Fourth At Antwerp." *Paulding Democrat*, July 12, 1888, 1.

56 "The Grand Jollification!," *Antwerp Argus*, July 5, 1888, 3; "Program of Exercises for the 4th of July in Antwerp," *Antwerp Argus*, June 28, 1888, 3; "The Fourth At Antwerp." *Paulding Democrat*, July 12, 1888, 1.

57 "The Grand Jollification!," *Antwerp Argus*, July 5, 1888, 3.

58 "The Grand Jollification!," *Antwerp Argus*, July 5, 1888, 3; "Program of Exercises for the 4th of July in Antwerp," *Antwerp Argus*, June 28, 1888, 3; "The Fourth At Antwerp." *Paulding Democrat*, July 12, 1888, 1.

59 "The Grand Jollification!," *Antwerp Argus*, July 5, 1888, 3.

60 "The Grand Jollification!," *Antwerp Argus*, July 5, 1888, 3.

61 "The Grand Jollification!," *Antwerp Argus*, July 5, 1888, 3.

62 "The Grand Jollification!," *Antwerp Argus*, July 5, 1888, 3.

63 "The Grand Jollification!," *Antwerp Argus*, July 5, 1888, 3.
64 "The Grand Jollification!," *Antwerp Argus*, July 5, 1888, 3; "The Fourth At Antwerp." *Paulding Democrat*, July 12, 1888, 1.
65 "The Grand Jollification!," *Antwerp Argus*, July 5, 1888, 3.
66 "The Grand Jollification!," *Antwerp Argus*, July 5, 1888, 3.
67 "The Grand Jollification!," *Antwerp Argus*, July 5, 1888, 3.
68 "The Grand Jollification!," *Antwerp Argus*, July 5, 1888, 3; "The Fourth At Antwerp." *Paulding Democrat*, July 12, 1888, 1.
69 "The Grand Jollification!," *Antwerp Argus*, July 5, 1888, 3.
70 "The Fourth At Antwerp." *Paulding Democrat*, July 12, 1888, 1.
71 "The Grand Jollification!," *Antwerp Argus*, July 5, 1888, 3.
72 "The Grand Jollification!," *Antwerp Argus*, July 5, 1888, 3.
73 "Program of Exercises for the 4th of July in Antwerp," *Antwerp Argus*, June 28, 1888, 3; "The Fourth At Antwerp." *Paulding Democrat*, July 12, 1888, 1.
74 "Program of Exercises for the 4th of July in Antwerp," *Antwerp Argus*, June 28, 1888, 3.
75 "The Grand Jollification!," *Antwerp Argus*, July 5, 1888, 3.
76 "The Grand Jollification!," *Antwerp Argus*, July 5, 1888, 3; "The Fourth At Antwerp." *Paulding Democrat*, July 12, 1888, 1.
77 "Reminiscence of Pioneer Days," *Payne Reflector and Press Review*, July 13, 1916, 1.
78 "The Grand Jollification!," *Antwerp Argus*, July 5, 1888, 3.
79 "Program of Exercises for the 4th of July in Antwerp," *Antwerp Argus*, June 28, 1888, 3.
80 "The Grand Jollification!," *Antwerp Argus*, July 5, 1888, 3.
81 "The Captain's Address," *Antwerp Argus*, July 12, 1888, 2; "The Grand Jollification!," *Antwerp Argus*, July 5, 1888, 3.
82 "The Captain's Address," *Antwerp Argus*, July 12, 1888, 2; "The Fourth At Antwerp." *Paulding Democrat*, July 12, 1888, 1.
83 "The Captain's Address," *Antwerp Argus*, July 12, 1888, 2; "The Fourth At Antwerp." *Paulding Democrat*, July 12, 1888, 1.
84 "The Captain's Address," *Antwerp Argus*, July 12, 1888, 2; "The Fourth At Antwerp." *Paulding Democrat*, July 12, 1888, 1.
85 "The Captain's Address," *Antwerp Argus*, July 12, 1888, 2; "The Fourth At Antwerp." *Paulding Democrat*, July 12, 1888, 1.
86 "The Captain's Address," *Antwerp Argus*, July 12, 1888, 2; "The Fourth At Antwerp." *Paulding Democrat*, July 12, 1888, 1.
87 "The Grand Jollification!," *Antwerp Argus*, July 5, 1888, 3.
88 "The Captain's Address," *Antwerp Argus*, July 12, 1888, 2; "The Fourth At Antwerp." *Paulding Democrat*, July 12, 1888, 1.
89 "The Captain's Address," *Antwerp Argus*, July 12, 1888, 2; "The Fourth At Antwerp." *Paulding Democrat*, July 12, 1888, 1.
90 "The Grand Jollification!," *Antwerp Argus*, July 5, 1888, 3; "The Fourth At Antwerp." *Paulding Democrat*, July 12, 1888, 1.
91 "The Fourth At Antwerp." *Paulding Democrat*, July 12, 1888, 1.
92 "The Grand Jollification!," *Antwerp Argus*, July 5, 1888, 3.
93 "The Grand Jollification!," *Antwerp Argus*, July 5, 1888, 3.

94 "The Fourth At Antwerp." *Paulding Democrat*, July 12, 1888, 1.

95 "Program of Exercises for the 4th of July in Antwerp," *Antwerp Argus*, June 28, 1888, 3.

96 "Program of Exercises for the 4th of July in Antwerp," *Antwerp Argus*, June 28, 1888, 3.

97 "Program of Exercises for the 4th of July in Antwerp," *Antwerp Argus*, June 28, 1888, 3.

98 "The Grand Jollification!," *Antwerp Argus*, July 5, 1888, 3; "The Fourth At Antwerp." *Paulding Democrat*, July 12, 1888, 1.

99 "The Grand Jollification!," *Antwerp Argus*, July 5, 1888, 3.

100 "Reminiscence of Pioneer Days," *Payne Reflector and Press Review*, July 13, 1916, 10.

101 "The Fourth At Antwerp." *Paulding Democrat*, July 12, 1888, 1.

102 "The Grand Jollification!," *Antwerp Argus*, July 5, 1888, 3.

103 "Antwerp on the Banks of the Maumee a Wonderful Place to Live," *Paulding County Republican*, August, 8, 1935, 5; "The Grand Jollification!," *Antwerp Argus*, July 5, 1888, 3.

104 "The Grand Jollification!," *Antwerp Argus*, July 5, 1888, 3.

105 "The Grand Jollification!," *Antwerp Argus*, July 5, 1888, 3.

106 "The Grand Jollification!," *Antwerp Argus*, July 5, 1888, 3.

107 "The Grand Jollification!," *Antwerp Argus*, July 5, 1888, 3.

108 "The Grand Jollification!," *Antwerp Argus*, July 5, 1888, 3.

109 "The Fourth At Antwerp." *Paulding Democrat*, July 12, 1888, 1.

110 "The Grand Jollification!," *Antwerp Argus*, July 5, 1888, 3.

111 "The Grand Jollification!," *Antwerp Argus*, July 5, 1888, 3.

112 "Under Water," *Antwerp Argus*, July 19, 1888, 3; "Local Gossip," *Paulding Democrat*, July 19, 1888, 5.

113 "Under Water," *Antwerp Argus*, July 19, 1888, 3.

114 "Our Home Corner," *Antwerp Argus*, July 19, 1888, 3; "Under Water," *Antwerp Argus*, July 19, 1888, 3.

115 "Our Home Corner," *Antwerp Argus*, August 2, 1888, 3; "Our Home Corner," *Antwerp Argus*, August 9, 1888, 3; "Chat," *Defiance Democrat*, August 23, 1888, 3; "State Land Sale," *Antwerp Argus*, August 2, 9, 16, 23, 30, 1888, 3; "State Land Sale," *Paulding Democrat*, August 9, 1888, 8.

116 "Our Home Corner," *Antwerp Argus*, August 30, 1888, 3; "State Land Sale," *Antwerp Argus*, August 2, 9, 16, 23, 30, 1888, 3; "State Land Sale," *Paulding Democrat*, August 9, 1888, 8.

117 "Personal Mentions," *Antwerp Argus*, August 2, 1888, 3.

118 "Personal Mentions," *Antwerp Argus*, August 2, 1888, 3.

119 "Chat," *Defiance Democrat*, August 23, 1888, 3.

120 "Our Home Corner," *Antwerp Argus*, September 6, 1888, 3.

121 "Our Home Corner," *Antwerp Argus*, September 6, 1888, 3.

122 "Paulding County Reservoir Land," *Antwerp Argus*, September 13, 1888, 3; "State Lands Profitably Sold," *Cincinnati Enquirer*, September 2, 1888, 1; "Sale of Canal Lands," *Defiance Democrat*, September 6, 1888, 3.

123 "Paulding County Reservoir Land," *Antwerp Argus*, September 13, 1888, 3; "State Lands Profitably Sold," *Cincinnati Enquirer*, September 2, 1888, 1; "Sale of Canal Lands," *Defiance Democrat*, September 6, 1888, 3.

124 "Paulding County Reservoir Land," *Antwerp Argus*, September 13, 1888, 3; "State Lands Profitably Sold," *Cincinnati Enquirer*, September 2, 1888, 1; "Sale of Canal Lands," *Defiance Democrat*, September 6, 1888, 3.

125 State of Ohio, *Executive Documents: Annual Reports for 1888, Made to the Sixty-Eighth General Assembly*, Part II, 815.

126 "Local Gossip," *Paulding Democrat*, November 29, 1888, 5; "All Sold," *Antwerp Argus*, December 6, 1888, 3.

127 State of Ohio, *Executive Documents: Annual Reports for 1888, Made to the Sixty-Eighth General Assembly*, Part II, 815.

128 State of Ohio, *Executive Documents: Annual Reports for 1888, Made to the Sixty-Eighth General Assembly*, Part II, 815.

129 State of Ohio, *Executive Documents: Annual Reports for 1888, Made to the Sixty-Eighth General Assembly*, Part II, 815.

130 State of Ohio, *Executive Documents: Annual Reports for 1888, Made to the Sixty-Eighth General Assembly*, Part II, 815.

131 U.S. Census Bureau. *1890 Census: Report on Population of the United States*. Minor Civil Divisions - Table 5. Ohio. 278.

132 "Across the Bed," *Antwerp Argus*, October 4, 1888, 3.

133 "Hazlett's Crossing," *Antwerp Argus*, September 20, 1888, 2.

134 "Improvements," *Antwerp Argus*, October 18, 1888, 3; "Improvements from the Antwerp Argus," *Paulding Democrat*, October 25, 1888, 5; "Antwerp," *Paulding County Republican*, October 18, 1888, 4.

135 State of Ohio, *Executive Documents: Annual Reports for 1888, Made to the Sixty-Eighth General Assembly*, Part II, 815-16.

136 O. Morrow and F.W. Bashore, *Historical Atlas of Paulding County, Ohio, 1892*, 90.

137 Ancestry.com. *1900 United States Federal Census*; "Clayton Everett DeWit," Find a Grave, Accessed October 28, 2022.

# -Appendix A-

## Who Were the Dynamiters?

This appendix is dedicated to preserving a basic list of every known Dynamiter. As for other possible Dynamiters, or those just sympathetic to the Dynamiters' cause, I leave that as an exercise for the reader to decide based on who else appeared in the rest of the book.

Please note that care has been taken to make sure names are accurate, but there is no guarantee that the records were accurate, and the names could have been misspelled to begin with. The best assumption was made, and most names were able to be cross-referenced with local headstones and genealogical records.

## Ringleaders[1]

- Oliver Spencer Applegate, Jr.
- Henry Worden Sperry

## Handled Dynamite[2]

- Bob Perry
- Asa H. Boland, Jr.
- Charles Willard Boland
- Isreal R. Ream
- George Platter Hardy
- Warner D. Ryel

## Guard, Digger, or Other Duty[3]

- Charles Henry Graves
- Emanuel M. Sunday
- Joseph S. Champion, Sr.¶
- George N. Munson
- Francis 'Frank' S. Shaw
- Eli Maine Munson
- Henry Harris
- Franz (Francis/Frank) Joseph Zuber
- Jesse Hinkle Bond
- Nicholas O. Harrmann

---

1 Otto E. Ehrhart, "Wabash-Erie Canal," in *A Century of Progress: Antwerp, Ohio*, 22.
2 Otto E. Ehrhart, "Wabash-Erie Canal," in *A Century of Progress: Antwerp, Ohio*, 22.
3 Otto E. Ehrhart, "Wabash-Erie Canal," in *A Century of Progress: Antwerp, Ohio*, 22; "Reunion of Former Antwerp Citizens," Antwerp Bee-Argus, October 19, 1944, 1.

¶ Antwerp's mayor between May 1892 and May 1896.
(Dale L. Ehrhart, "Municipal History of Antwerp," in *A Century of Progress: Antwerp, Ohio*, 35.)

- Westley Peter Johnston
- Frank Lamb
- Harrison 'Harry' Houston Gordon
- Frank Leamon
- Lewis 'Lew' S. Gordon
- Simon Nedrow
- John Baptist Zuber
- William Albert 'Al' Marlin
- Hiram Alvestus Overmyer
- Edward L. Overmyer
- George E. Overmyer
- William H. Smith
- Andrew 'Andy' J. Smith
- Jacob Saylor
- Franklin 'Frank' Ladd Saylor
- Phaon Peter Doering
- Joseph Lorain Doering

**Additional Note:**

On several occasions, I have noticed that Otto E. Ehrhart has been assumed to be a Dynamiter or brought up as a possible candidate among the hundreds of possible names of Dynamiters lost to history. While I believe being a descendant of (or even just related to) a known Dynamiter should be recognized, the fact of the matter is that Mr. Ehrhart being a Dynamiter would have been impossible. Not only because Mr. Ehrhart was born in 1884, a mere three years before the Reservoir War, but because, according to his memoir, he and his family did not immigrate from Chemnitz, Germany, to Antwerp, Ohio, until 1893.[4]

---

4 Otto E. Ehrhart, *Memories*, Unknown Date, transcribed by Kim K. Sutton.

# -Appendix B-

## Who Were the Guardsmen?

This appendix is dedicated to preserving a basic list of every known Guardsmen at the Reservoir War. A list of soldiers who could have possibly been present in the Reservoir War is also provided. There were only 105 infantrymen present at the Reservoir War, but there were many more than that between Company A, C, and H, never mind discerning the cannoneers from Light Battery D.

Please note that care has been taken to make sure names are spelled accurately, but there is no guarantee that the records were accurate, and the names could have been misspelled to begin with, or the cursive was sloppy and hardly readable. The best assumption was made, and most names were able to be cross-referenced to a published version of the roster which was not in cursive.

**List of Soldiers Confirmed Present at the Reservoir War**

<u>Field Commanders</u>
- MG/ADJ GEN Henry Augustus Axline – O.N.G.
- MAJ Henry Silas Bunker – 16th Regiment – O.N.G.

<u>Officers of Light Battery D – 1st Regiment Light Artillery, O.N.G.</u>
- CPT Owen Johnston Hopkins
- 2LT George Upton Roulet
- SURG MAJ Dr. Thomas Jefferson Cronise

<u>Officers of Co. A – 16th Regiment, O.N.G.</u>
- CPT Jacob M. Weier
- ACT QM 2LT Edward W. Rydman

<u>Officers of Co. C – 16th Regiment, O.N.G.</u>
- CPT James R. Wade
- 1LT William H. Moore

<u>Officers of Co. H – 16th Regiment, O.N.G.</u>
- CPT Alpheus Romeyn Rogers

<u>Non-Commissioned Officers – Unknown Units, O.N.G.</u>
- ADJ Isaac Tichenor Pheatt Merrill
- SGM Carl Herbert Beckham
- COMSY SERG Charles G. DeShon

<u>Infantry of Co. H – 16th Regiment, O.N.G.</u>
- PVT Frederick 'Fred' L. Reeves †

## Possible NCO and Enlisted Infantry Present at the Reservoir War.[1]

NOTE: The gun detachment (or Gatling section as ADJ GEN Henry A. Axline referred to it) of Light Battery D that went to Paulding County would have "ordinarily" consisted of at least one sergeant, two corporals, and seven privates.[2]

**Light Battery D – 1st Regiment Light Artillery, O.N.G.**
**'Toledo Light Artillery'**

SGT William Kimmerlen

SGT Almon S. Carpenter

SGT George Fraser

SGT W. R. Hamman

SGT John D. Wiggins

QTR SGT Charles W. Waite

VET SGT Stephen Van Buren

CPL William H. Brown

CPL Oliver P. Hopkins

CPL R. C. Potter

CPL Thomas Carr

Harry B. Eley

CPL William Eubody

CPL August Gossman

CPL John A. Meissner

CPL Frank A. Taylor

PVT Edward Bernor

PVT N. Boetchl

PVT D. E. Boudrie

PVT Joseph M. Boudrie

PVT T. J. Brinker

PVT Victor Blane

PVT T. J. Carrington

PVT W. L. Cherry

PVT Edward Closson

PVT Herbert Crane

PVT C. B. Culver

---

1 State of Ohio, *Executive Documents: Annual Reports for 1886 Made to the 67th General Assembly*, Part II, 582–88, 599; State of Ohio, *Executive Documents: Annual Reports for 1887 Made to the Sixty-Eighth General Assembly*, Part II, 762–763, 837–842; Ohio Adjutant General's Office, *Roster of Soldiers of the Ohio National Guard, 1847–1917; 16th & 6th Regiments Books 1–3 1880–1904*, Columbus: Ohio Adjutant General's Office.

2 Owen J. Hopkins, *Gatling Gun Tactics – Revised Edition*, 1888, 1.

PVT J. A. Darcus

PVT William Dean

PVT Jackson Deneal

PVT Charles Dillman

PVT Peter Doyle

PVT Alfred Frid

PVT Richard Gibbons

PVT Augustus Henniger

PVT Alfred E. Hinds

PVT D. D. Jenks

PVT Frank A. Johnson

PVT Henry Kiser

PVT Archie Laird

PVT Peter LeBarge

PVT John R. Markley

PVT John Matheny

PVT Otto Meissner

PVT James Monnette

PVT Alfred Nants

PVT R. B. O'Dell

PVT Charles M. Pomeroy

PVT Frank Reagan

PVT James/Joseph Reinbold

PVT William Schreppel

PVT W. A Stamer

PVT Clarence Upham

PVT L. G. Vartu

PVT James/Joseph Vetter

PVT William Vetter

PVT Edward Vena

PVT Charles Welch

PVT L. D. Wright

## Co. A – 16th Regiment, O.N.G. 'Walbridge Light Guard'

SGT Alexander Young

SGT Wendell P. Skidmore

CPL Joseph A. Schrun

CPL Samuel J. Nieding

CPL Jacob S. Schick

CPL William H. Steele

CPL Frank C. Roshong

PVT Edward H. Ahrens

PVT Chester F. Baldwin

PVT Hugh J. Bartley

PVT Howard Byers

PVT William H. D. Bunde

PVT Fred A. Brown

PVT John D. Coonrad

PVT Taylor S. Cosgrove

PVT George C. Cramer

PVT James Eaton

PVT Charles S. Emery

PVT Edwin W. Emery

PVT John J. Gallagher

PVT Simon L. Gullerd

PVT Fred Hagen

PVT Charles F. C. Hahn

PVT Harley H. Hancock

PVT John M. Hanline

PVT George Hoehler

PVT Charles S. Laufraw

PVT Richard Lawler

PVT Henry Lutz

PVT Dominick L. McGloyne

PVT Louis L. Metzer

PVT Edmund Morris

PVT Herman Neipp

PVT Frank S. Paule

PVT Burt Prouty

PVT Charles Saco

PVT Adolph Schladdetsch

PVT Magnus Schladdetsch

PVT Joshua L. Taylor

PVT Frederick Stock

## Co. C – 16th Regiment, O.N.G.
### 'Toledo Grays'

SGT John Christen

SGT Joseph Weber

SGT Elwood B. Squire

SGT John R. Longshore

SGT Joseph Shinaver

CPL Edward Swinhart

CPL Charles O. Phelps

CPL George M. Mason

CPL John F. Gable

CPL John J. Diefenbach

CPL Arthur M. O'Dell

CPL Clayton Craley

CPL John S. Meek

PVT Frank N. Baker

PVT Louis Becker

PVT William D. Beamer

PVT Charles H. Bender

PVT Henry J. Bracht

PVT Joseph H. Braker

PVT George A. Cherry

PVT Elry S. Consaul

PVT Joseph Dallas

PVT Herman DeBall

PVT Frank Deno

PVT Charles Diefenbach

PVT Henry Ebert

PVT Charles C. Flack

PVT George O. Geisert

PVT John Gruhler

PVT Albert S. Hill

PVT August Kagle

PVT Theodore Keck

PVT Christ Kohn

PVT Edward G. Medford

PVT. Frank Pflock

PVT Thomas Rafter

PVT Frank Rector

PVT George W. Rudd

PVT Gustave Schillinger

PVT Henry Singuets

PVT Edward R. Smiley

PVT William L. Trotter

PVT Charles Vannetten

PVT William H. Wadock

PVT Louis C. Wagenknecht

PVT George Wells

## Co. H – 16th Regiment, O.N.G.
### 'Milburn Guard'

SGT Charles Marchant

SGT John W. Clark

SGT Oren McDougal

SGT William C. Bettis

CPL Henry A. Werdehoff

CPL Frederick Smith

CPL Alpheus Chapman

CPL Martin Graham

CPL Robert Newton

CPL Charles A. King

PVT George Bartlett

PVT William H. Barringer

PVT Alfred J. Becker

PVT John A. Becker

PVT Phillip E. Behmer

PVT Henry L. Birkenhauer

PVT Andrew A. Bowers

PVT Robert Brower

PVT Frank Burns

PVT Leonard Christ

PVT Louis Clipstine

PVT Nathan Cone

PVT Lawrence B. Farrow

PVT Dennis Ford

PVT John Graham

PVT Frank Huber

PVT Frank R. Kirk

PVT Frederick Kolling

PVT John Kolling

PVT Orson Litchfield

PVT Edwin O. Loeber

PVT James M. McCreary

PVT Charles Moon

PVT Thomas Nichols

PVT William E. Page

PVT Charles H. Pierce

PVT Carle A. Rogers

PVT Claude S. Rogers

PVT Scott A. Ross

PVT Warren B. Sabin

PVT John Schultz

PVT Henry J. Shatto

PVT August Silky

PVT William H. Somers

PVT Isidore Valequette

PVT Martin Waldvogle

PVT James I. Webb

PVT John Werdehoff

PVT William White

# -Appendix C-

## Jollification Committees

The lists on the following pages contain every person involved with a committee in the preparation for the Fourth of July Jollification in 1888. I hope some readers will recognize some of the names from the historical narrative, as well as possible ancestors.[1]

Please note that care has been taken to make sure names are accurate, but there is no guarantee that the records were accurate, and the names could have been misspelled to begin with. The best assumption was made, and most names were able to be cross-referenced with local headstones and genealogical records.

---

1 "Full List of Committees," *Antwerp Argus*, June 21, 1888, 3;
  "Additional Committees," *Antwerp Argus*, June 28, 1888, 2;
  "Committee of Arrangements," *Antwerp Argus*, June 28, 1888,
  2; "Avaunt—Reservoir!," *Antwerp Argus*, "May 31, 1888, 2.

**Officer of the Day**

Jesse H. Bond

**Assistants**

David W. Parr

John Radenbaugh

David McMillen

C. W. Starr

Harry Stevenson

**Subscription**

Oliver S. Applegate

Charles A. Doering

Henry George, Jr.

**Speakers**

William E. Osborn

John H. Chester

Dr. D. W. Wilson

**Printing and Program**

T. C. Banks

J. H. Scovil

John S. Snook

John H. Oswalt, Jr.

Maroni P. Jacobs

William H. Durbin

**Music**

William D. Wilson

Richard S. Banks, Jr.

Burton 'Burt' B. Banks

The Cornet Band

**Invitation**

Lewis S. Gordon

Charles A. Doering

Wilson H. Snook

William F. Fleck

Henry George, Sr.

**Decoration**

Emmet E. Pocock

William D. Wilson

William H. Durbin

Henry George, Jr.

Henry Cline

Rich S. Banks, Jr.

John Oswalt

Adam Cline

Lime Robinson

Frank O. Perry

Cory Wyer

### Ice and Water

Joel Dresser

William Brown

Simon Nedrow

Dan Rumbaugh

James Scovel

Thomas Murphy

### To Purchase Ox

John H. Chester

### To Purchase Fantastics

George N. Munson

### Reception

William F. Fleck

Dr. Daniel W. Hixson

John H. Oswalt

Harry H. Gordon

Dr. B. E. Miller

### Railroads

William F. Fleck

William E. Osborn

### Park

Dr. Thomas Cave

Henry W. Sperry

William R. Cromley

### Finance

Henry George, Jr.

Charles A. Doering

John F. Barnett

### Amusements

William D. Wilson

William H. Durbin

Thomas C. Banks

### Shooting Tournament

Burton 'Burt' B. Banks

### Baseball

John Yeager

### Arrangements – Antwerp

Oliver S. Applegate

Maroni P. Jacobs

John B. Zuber

David Zuber

Harry H. Gordon

John Barnett

Frederick 'Fred' Barchard

John H. Chester

Frank Lamb

George N. Munson

William H. Durbin

Jesse H. Bond

Westley P. Johnston

James Scovel

Emmet E. Pocock

Henry Harris

Nicholas O. Harrmann

### Arrangements – Paulding

Alonzo B. Holcombe

Joseph B. Cromley

Francis B. DeWitt

John D. Lamb

David W. Parr

Ralph D. Webster

Nelse Webster

W. A. Scarch

Levi Thompson

### Arrangements – Payne

Henry M. Lawson

Edwin O. Harris

Darius Leeth

John King

Captain Elliott

### Arrangements – Cecil

William H. Robertson

Henry Wiswell

Henry B. Ferguson

### Arrangements – Knoxdale

C. A. Bowland

Francis 'Frank' S. Shaw

### Arrangements – Oakwood

S. L. Ackley

Allen N. Wiseley

### Arrangements – Hicksville

John M. Ainsworth

C. E. Everett

S. C. Ryan

William D. Wilson

Frank Snyder

Homer G. Elliott

T. G. Dowell

## Arrangements – Defiance

Press Zeigler

T. J. Prettyman

Benjamin F. Casebeer

## Arrangements – Toledo

Abner L. Backus

R. W. Scott

## Ladies¶

Clara L. Emanuel

Lotta 'Lottie' M. Doering

Cora Z. Carpenter

Libbie Banks

Naomi H. Osborn

Caroline M. Hertel

Mary Shaffer

Callie J. Doering

Leona 'Ona' D. Applegate

Stella Applegate

[illegible] Wentworth

Minnie C. Harris

Elizabeth Sunday

Maggie A. Doering

Maggie [illegible]

Lillie Harris

Netta 'Nettie' B. Daggett

Clara [illegible]

Minnie E. Champion

Christena P. Schilb

Lizzie Cussen

Attie Zuber

Bridgie Hallman

Ona Jacobs

Ella Barchard

## Gentlemen

John S. Snook

J. C. Jones

John Yeager

Henry Cline

Tom Foster

Adam Cline

Andrew 'Andy' J. Smith

Frank Lamb

Nora Wert

Henry George, Jr.

Ab. Dunderman

Will Shaffer

Frank Graves

---

¶ Wore "bright Turkey Red Calico Aprons"

### To Supervise Tables

Louisa Goshorn

Laura 'Laurie' Straley

Mrs. Zett Doering

Roena P. Harris

Hannah M. Ream

Georgianna 'Georgia' Harris

Eliza K. Sperry

Martha E. Terwilliger

Gertrude Miller

Frances M. Barchard

Mrs. Frank Wentworth

Emlie Robinson

### Bouquet

Hattie E. Smith

Dora Schriver

Maude Hixson

Lillie E. Goshorn

Belle Stanger

Harriet 'Hattie' S. Champion

Gertrude 'Gertie' R. Barchard

### Refreshments – East River and Oswalt Streets

Lotta 'Lottie' M. Doering

### Refreshments – West of South Main Street

Harriet M. Banks

### Refreshments – East of South Main Street

Netta 'Nettie' B. Daggett

### Refreshments – North Main Street

Cora Z. Carpenter

### Refreshments – West River Street

Mrs. Emma Wesner

### Roasting

Emmet E. Pocock

William D. Wilson

Jesse H. Bond

H. Ross

### Decorate Ox and Wagon

Frederick 'Fred' Barchard

### Reader

John W. Pyfer

### Master of the Ceremonies

Wilson H. Snook

### Arrange for Factories to Blow Whistles and Churches to Ring Bells

Eli C. Munson

## Fireworks

William D. Wilson

Lime Robinson

## Dynamiters

[Redacted]
Only Instructed to be at the
Harrmann Tile Factory by 1
P.M. on July 4th

# –Appendix D–

## Legislative Committees

The following are lists of the legislative committees that travelled to Paulding County throughout the Reservoir War. The senate committee in 1887 failed to appear in Paulding County, and the senate committee in 1888 was a small enough group that they are named in Chapter 10.

**February 1887 House Committee**[1]

The *Paulding Democrat* only mentions that fifteen individuals arrived, including Representative Geyer. The *Paulding County Gazette* mentions sixteen. Whatever the case, only fourteen of them were actual legislators, one was the First Assistant Sergeant-at-Arms.

> Carl H. Buerhaus, Hocking County
>    - Secretary[2]
>
> Thomas R. Martin, Union County
>    - First Assistant Sergeant-at-Arms[3]
>
> Franklin R. Vinnedge, Butler County
>
> Leander C. Cole, Stark County
>
> Noah H. Albaugh, Miami County
>
> Oscar F. Edwards, Montgomery County
>
> James M. Williams, Coshocton County
>
> George Kreis, Morrow County
>
> William M. Farrar, Guernsey County
>
> Francis Ankeny, Tuscarawas County
>
> Leroy S. Holcomb, Morgan County
>
> John Y. Williams, Columbiana County
>
> David Stewart, Muskingum County
>
> Amos Boehmer, Putnam County
>
> John I. Roberts, Washington Court House, OH
>    - Not a Representative
>
> John L. Geyer, Paulding County[4]

---

1 "The Reservoir Inspected, *Paulding Democrat*, February 3, 1887, 4.

2 "Round About—Antwerp," *Paulding County Gazette*, February 3, 1887, 5.

3 Journal of the House of Representatives for Adjourned Session Sixty-Seventh General Assembly, vol. LXXXIII, 12-13, 756.

4 "The Reservoir Inspected, *Paulding Democrat*, February 3, 1887, 4.

## January 1888 House Committee[5]

Noah H. Albaugh, Miami County
 - Speaker *pro tem*[6]

Martin Eidemiller, Montgomery County

Henry C. Sanford, Summit County

Mark Ames, Trumbull County

John L. Geyer, Paulding County

William E. Watkins, Allen County

Edward J. Kennedy, Cuyahoga County

Daniel H. Gaumer, Muskingum County

Benjamin F. Kitchen, Jackson County

P. Burkhard, Cleveland, OH
 - Not a Representative

Franklin R. Vinnedge, Butler County

---

5 "The Legislative Committee," *Antwerp Argus*, February 2, 1888, 2; "Reservoir Committee," *Paulding Democrat*, January 26, 1888, 5.

6 Joseph P. Smith, *History of the Republican Party in Ohio*, Volume I, 542.

# -Appendix E-

## Representative Votes

The following lists are the recorded votes of the Ohio Legislature on the Geyer Bill in 1887 and 1888. Though there were multiple votes on the Geyer Bill in each chamber, I have only listed the 'final' votes that passed or failed the Geyer Bill. If you would like to see how the other votes looked, they are cited in their appropriate places throughout the book.

## Sources:

1887 House:
State of Ohio, Journal of the House of Representatives of the
State of Ohio, for the Adjourned Session of the Sixty-
Seventh General Assembly, Volume LXXXIII, 328; Joseph
P. Smith, History of the Republican Party in Ohio, Volume
I, 513–514.

1887 Senate:
State of Ohio, *Journal of the Senate of the State of Ohio, for the
Adjourned Session of the Sixty-Seventh General Assembly*,
Volume LXXXIII, 459; "Notes About Town," Defiance
County Express, March 17, 1887, 16; Joseph P. Smith,
History of the Republican Party in Ohio, Volume I, 512–
513, 542.

1888 House:
State of Ohio, Journal of the House of Representatives of the
State of Ohio, for the Regular Session of the Sixty-Eighth
General Assembly, Volume LXXXIV, 392–393; Joseph P.
Smith, History of the Republican Party in Ohio, Volume I,
542–543.

1888 Senate:
State of Ohio, Journal of the Senate of the State of Ohio, for the
Regular Session of the Sixty-Eighth General Assembly,
Volume LXXXIV, 763; Joseph P. Smith, History of the
Republican Party in Ohio, Volume I, 542–543.

1888 House Reconciliation:
State of Ohio, Journal of the House of Representatives of the
State of Ohio, for the Regular Session of the Sixty-Eighth
General Assembly, Volume LXXXIV, 825; Joseph P.
Smith, History of the Republican Party in Ohio, Volume I,
542–543.

## 1887 House Vote that Passed the Geyer Bill

### Yeas: 56

Mark Ames
- Trumbull Co.

David Baker
- Darke Co.

John W. Baughman
- Wayne Co.

William W. Beatty
- Logan Co.

Amos Boehmer
- Putnam Co.

John S. Braddock
- Knox Co.

Absalom P. Byal
- Hancock Co.

Jesse L. Cameron
- Union Co.

Hugh L. Chaney
- Franklin Co.

George W. Clements
- Geauga Co.
- Lake Co.

Leander C. Cole
- Stark Co.

William T. Cope
- Columbiana Co.

Thomas A. Cowgill
- Champaign Co.

Albert Deyo
- Fulton Co.

Alexander Dickson
- Mahoning Co.

John Eggers
- Hamilton Co.

Elijah P. Emerson
- Wood Co.

William M. Farrar
- Guernsey Co.

John H. Fimple
- Carroll Co.

James R. Francisco
- Sandusky Co.

John L. Geyer
- Defiance Co.
- Paulding Co.

Thomas W. Graydon
- Hamilton Co.

William Habbeler
- Ottawa Co.

Robert H. Higgins
- Brown Co.

Samuel Hilles
- Belmont Co.

Elisha B. Hubbard
- Seneca Co.

Watson D. Johnston
- Huron Co.

Solomon Johnson
- Williams Co.

Edward J. Kennedy
- Cuyahoga Co.

George Kreis
- Morrow Co.

Benjamin L. Linduff
- Jefferson Co.

Elijah Little
- Muskingum Co.

Henry Lyons
- Monroe Co.

John McBride
- Stark Co.

John T. McCray
- Ashland Co.

James McKeever
- Clermont Co.

Theodore F. Neiman
- Hamilton Co.

Frederick Ohlemacher
- Erie Co.

Oliver Outcalt
- Hamilton Co.

George M. Patton
- Harrison Co.

Christian L. Poorman
- Belmont Co.

John H. Puck
- Lucas Co.

George C. Rawlins
- Clark Co.

George L. Sackett
- Delaware Co.

Matthias A. Smalley
- Wyandot Co.

David Stewart
- Muskingum Co.

Thomas H. Stewart
- Trumbull Co.

Henry C. Taylor
- Franklin Co.

George G. Washburne
- Lorain Co.

Friend Whittlesey
- Portage Co.

John Y. Williams
- Columbiana Co.

James M. Williams
- Coshocton Co.

Thomas C. Williams
- Noble Co.

Wesley Work
- Pickaway Co.

David I. Worthington
- Fayette Co.

Boston G. Young
- Marion Co.

## Nays: 41

Noah H. Albaugh
- Miami Co.

Francis Ankeny
- Tuscarawas Co.

Thomas Armor
- Holmes Co.

Benjamin W. Arnett
- Greene Co.

Isaac Austill
- Pike Co.

Frederick Bader
- Hamilton Co.

James F. Bailey
- Hamilton Co.

William A. Blair
- Adams Co.

Daniel Boyd
- Madison Co.

Henry Brockman
  - Hamilton Co.

Jere A. Brown
  - Cuyahoga Co.

Seth W. Brown
  - Warren Co.

Orville S. Brumbach
  - Lucas Co.

William R. Coates
  - Cuyahoga Co.

Oscar F. Edwards
  - Montgomery Co.

Martin Eidemiller
  - Montgomery Co.

John C. Entrekin
(Speaker)
  - Ross Co.

Frank M. Green
  - Summit Co.

John P. Haley
  - Cuyahoga Co.

Robert Harlan
  - Hamilton Co.

Andrew L. Harris
  - Preble Co.

Walter Hartpence
  - Hamilton Co.

Leroy S. Holcomb
  - Morgan Co.

James E. Howard
  - Richland Co.

Joseph G. Huffman
  - Perry Co.

William C. Ingman
  - Hardin Co.

Benjamin F. Kitchen
  - Jackson Co.

Charles M. Le Blond
  - Mercer Co.

James Lisle
  - Licking Co.

Cornelius N. Lyman
  - Medina Co.

William S. Matthews
  - Gallia Co.

Walter W. Merrick
  - Meigs Co.

J. Dwight Palmer
  - Cuyahoga Co.

Daniel J. Ryan
(Speaker *pro tem*)
  - Scioto Co.

William A. Schultz
  - Fairfield Co.

Melville D. Shaw
  - Auglaize Co.

John Strecker, Jr.
  - Washington Co.

James H. Terrell
  - Clinton Co.

James Turner
  - Montgomery Co.

Franklin R. Vinnedge
  - Butler Co.

George M. Ziegler
  - Crawford Co.

**Present/Abstained/No Vote: 13**

David M. Barrett
    - Highland Co.
Carl H. Buerhaus
    - Hocking Co.

John V. Cuff
    - Henry Co.

George W. Hull
    - Allen Co.

Phanuel Hunt
    - Shelby Co.

Elias F. Johnson
    - Van Wert Co.

Elbert L. Lampson
    - Ashtabula Co.

Thomas F. McClure
    - Vinton Co.

William Shepard
    - Franklin Co.

John J. Stranahan
    - Cuyahoga Co.

William B. Tomlinson
    - Lawrence Co.

Emmitt Tompkins
    - Athens Co.

Byron S. Wydman
    - Hamilton Co.

## 1887 Senate Vote that Failed the Geyer Bill

### Yeas: 8

Thomas B. Coulter
- Jefferson Co.

George W. Crites
- Tuscarawas Co.

Duncan Dow
- Logan Co.

George H. Ford
- Geauga Co.

Solomon Hogue
- Belmont Co.

William Lawrence
- Guernsey Co.

Frank L. Lindsey
- Brown Co.

Calvin S. Welch
- Athens Co.

### Nays: 26

Alva Curtis Cable
- Miami Co.

Charles G. Codding
- Medina Co.

Silas A. Conrad
(Rep. President *pro tem*)
- Stark Co.

Ezra S. Dodd
- Lucas Co.

Ferdinand H. Eggers
- Cuyahoga Co.

William F. Eltzroth
- Warren Co.

George H. Ely
- Cuyahoga Co.

Alonzo D. Fassett
- Mahoning Co.

Abel W. Glazier
- Washington Co.

John W. Gregg
- Pike Co.

Henry C. Groschner
- Henry Co.

George W. Hardacre
- Unknown Co.

Samuel E. Kemp
- Montgomery Co.

Frank Kirchner
- Unknown Co.

Amzi McGill
- Unknown Co.

Robert Mehaffey
- Allen Co.

Levi Meredith
- Auglaize Co.

John O'Neill
(Dem. President *pro tem*)
- Muskingum Co.

Thomas J. Pringle
- Clark Co.

William J. Rannells
- Vinton Co.

James C. Richardson
- Unknown Co.

Edwin Sinnett
- Licking Co.

Jeremiah J. Sullivan
- Holmes Co.

Aaron R. Van Cleaf
- Pickaway Co.

John H. Williston
- Crawford Co.

Joseph Zimmerman
- Sandusky Co.


**Present/Abstained/No
Vote: 3**

George W. Crouse
- Summit Co.

Madison Pavey
- Fayette Co.

Jacob J. Pugsley
- Highland Co.

### 1888 House Vote that Passed the Geyer Bill

#### Yeas: 57

Mark Ames
- Trumbull Co.

John W. Baughman
- Wayne Co.

William W. Beatty
- Logan Co.

William E. Bense
- Ottawa Co.

Charles Bird
- Hamilton Co.

Samuel L. Blue
- Licking Co.

Amos Boehmer
- Putnam Co.

Daniel Boyd
- Madison Co.

Jonah Britton
- Highland Co.

Jere A. Brown
- Cuyahoga Co.

Henry Brown
- Hancock Co.

William T. Clark
- Cuyahoga Co.

William Copeland
- Hamilton Co.

Dennis D. Donovan
- Henry Co.

Charles L. Doran
- Hamilton Co.

Michael F. Eggerman
- Hardin Co.

Martin Eidemiller
- Montgomery Co.

John H. Fimple
- Carroll Co.

Daniel H. Gaumer
- Muskingum Co.

John L. Geyer
- Defiance Co.
- Paulding Co.

John S. Gill
- Delaware Co.

John P. Haley
- Cuyahoga Co.

James H. Hamilton
- Monroe Co.

John C. Hart
- Hamilton Co.

Elisha B. Hubbard
- Seneca Co.

Wilford C. Hudson
- Clinton Co.

James Hunt
- Sandusky Co.

Nial R. Hysell
- Perry Co.

Andrew Jackson
- Greene Co.

Edward J. Kennedy
- Cuyahoga Co.

Frederick Klensch
- Hamilton Co.

George Kreis
- Morrow Co.

Jasper N. Lantz
- Harrison Co.

Alexander T. McKelvey
- Belmont Co.

James C. Messer
- Lucas Co.

John E. Monnot
- Stark Co.

Robert Ogle
- Williams Co.

Lemuel C. Ohl
- Mahoning Co.

Oliver Outcalt
- Hamilton Co.

William W. Pennell
- Brown Co.

George C. Rawlins
- Clarke Co.

Andrew C. Robeson
- Darke Co.

Estell H. Rorick
- Fulton Co.

Henry C. Sanford
- Summit Co.

Philip Schuler
- Crawford Co.

Melville D. Shaw
- Auglaize Co.

John H. Shearer
- Union Co.

Matthias A. Smalley
- Wyandot Co.

George B. Spencer
- Wood Co.

Thomas H. Stewart
- Trumbull Co.

Emmitt Tompkins
- Athens Co.

Hosmer G. Tryon
- Geauga Co.
- Lake Co.

Franklin R. Vinnedge
- Butler Co.

Capell L. Weems
- Noble Co.

William T. Whitacre
- Warren Co.

Friend Whittlesey
- Portage Co.

Byron S. Wydman
- Hamilton Co.

## Nays: 33

Noah H. Albaugh
(Speaker *pro tem*)
- Miami Co.

Francis Ankeny
- Tuscarawas Co.

Thomas Armor
- Holmes Co.

John W. Barger
- Pike Co.

Wickliffe Belville
- Montgomery Co.

William E. Boden
- Guernsey Co.

William A. Braman
- Lorain Co.

Charles W. Clancey
- Jefferson Co.

Joseph P. Coates
- Scioto Co.

William T. Cope
- Columbiana Co.

Jesse B. Forbes
- Coshocton Co.

Wilson S. Harper
- Montgomery Co.

Walter Hartpence
- Hamilton Co.

Leroy S. Holcomb
- Morgan Co.

Elkany B. Holmes
- Clermont Co.

James E. Howard
- Richland Co.

Benjamin F. Kitchen
- Jackson Co.

Lewis C. Laylin
- Huron Co.

Charles M. LeBlond
- Mercer Co.

John T. McCray
- Ashland Co.

Levi Meredith
- Van Wert Co.

Walter W. Merrick
- Meigs Co.

Stephen W. Monahan
- Vinton Co.

Frank V. Owen
- Knox Co.

Thomas Palmer
- Medina Co.

Christian L. Poorman
- Belmont Co.

William H. Reed
- Ross Co.

Alfred Robinson
- Lawrence Co.

Joseph W. Shinn
- Adams Co.

John J. Stranahan
- Cuyahoga Co.

John Strecker
- Washington Co.

Samuel M. Taylor
- Champaign Co.

George W. Wilhelm
- Stark Co.

**Present/Abstained/No Vote: 18**

Carl H. Buerhaus
- Hocking Co.

Jachomyer C. Counts
- Shelby Co.

Thaddeus E. Cromley
- Pickaway Co.

Evan H. Davis
- Cuyahoga Co.

Thomas H. Dill
- Fairfield Co.

Jehu Eakins
- Gallia Co.

Charles P. Griffin
- Lucas Co.

Andrew L. Harris
- Preble Co.

Elbert L. Lampson
(Speaker)
    - Ashtabula Co.

John B. Lawlor
    - Franklin Co.

John C. McGregor
    - Muskingum Co.

Frederick Ohlemacher
    - Erie Co.

Frederick Pfeister
    - Hamilton Co.

Lot L. Smith
    - Franklin Co.

William E. Watkins
    - Allen Co.

John Y. Williams
    - Columbiana Co.

David I. Worthington
    - Fayette Co.

Boston G. Young
    - Marion Co.

## 1888 Senate Vote that Passed the Geyer Bill

### Yeas: 28

Perry M. Adams
- Seneca Co.

John Park Alexander
- Summit Co.

Isaac M. Barrett
- Greene Co.

John S. Braddock
- Knox Co.

Harmon W. Brown
- Hamilton Co.

William L. Carlin
- Hancock Co.

Amos B. Cole
- Scioto Co.

Thomas A. Cowgill
- Champaign Co.

Walter Crook
- Montgomery Co.

James Cutler
- Union Co.

Theodore F. Davis
(President *pro tem*)
- Washington Co.

George H. Ford
- Geauga Co.

William Geyser
- Fulton Co.

Joseph G. Huffman
- Perry Co.

Henry Mack
- Hamilton Co.

David Meade Massie
- Ross Co.

Robert Mehaffey
- Allen Co.

David Morison
- Cuyahoga Co.

David H. Mortley
- Coshocton Co.

James C. Richardson
- Hamilton Co.

Andrew J. Robertson
- Shelby Co.

Edwin Sinnett
- Licking Co.

Thomas C. Snyder
- Stark Co.

John M. Stull
- Trumbull Co.

Vincent A. Taylor
- Cuyahoga Co.

Charles Townsend
- Athens Co.

William T. Wallace
- Franklin Co.

Joseph Zimmerman
- Sandusky Co.

### Nays: 0

**Present/Abstained/No Vote: 8**

Thomas B. Coulter
    - Jefferson Co.

Anthony I. Dorr
    - Noble Co.

George W. Glover
    - Harrison Co.

Winfield S. Kerr
    - Richland Co.

Frank L. Lindsey
    - Brown Co.

William J. Rannells
    - Vinton Co.

Estes G. Rathbone
    - Butler Co.

Henry Steuve
    - Hamilton Co.

## 1888 House Reconciliation Vote for the Geyer Bill

### Yeas: 65

Noah H. Albaugh
(Speaker *pro tem*)
- Miami Co.

Mark Ames
- Trumbull Co.

Francis Ankeny
- Tuscarawas Co.

Thomas Armor
- Holmes Co.

John W. Baughman
- Wayne Co.

William E. Boden
- Guernsey Co.

Amos Boehmer
- Putnam Co.

William A. Braman
- Lorain Co.

Jonah Britton
- Highland Co.

Jere A. Brown
- Cuyahoga Co.

William Copeland
- Hamilton Co.

Jachomyer C. Counts
- Shelby Co.

Thaddeus E. Cromley
- Pickaway Co.

Evan H. Davis
- Cuyahoga Co.

Thomas H. Dill
- Fairfield Co.

Dennis D. Donovan
- Henry Co.

Charles L. Doran
- Hamilton Co.

Jehu Eakins
- Gallia Co.

Michael F. Eggerman
- Hardin Co.

Martin Eidemiller
- Montgomery Co.

Jesse B. Forbes
- Coshocton Co.

John L. Geyer
- Defiance Co.
- Paulding Co.

John S. Gill
- Delaware Co.

Charles P. Griffin
- Lucas Co.

Elkany B. Holmes
- Clermont Co.

James E. Howard
- Richland Co.

James Hunt
- Sandusky Co.

Nial R. Hysell
- Perry Co.

Andrew Jackson
- Greene Co.

Benjamin F. Kitchen
- Jackson Co.

George Kreis
- Morrow Co.

Jasper N. Lantz
- Harrison Co.

Lewis C. Laylin
- Huron Co.

John C. McGregor
- Muskingum Co.

Alexander T. McKelvey
- Belmont Co.

Levi Meredith
- Van Wert Co.

James C. Messer
- Lucas Co.

John E. Monnot
- Stark Co.

Lemuel C. Ohl
- Mahoning Co.

Frederick Ohlemacher
- Erie Co.

Oliver Outcalt
- Hamilton Co.

Frank V. Owen
- Knox Co.

Thomas Palmer
- Medina Co.

William W. Pennell
- Brown Co.

Frederick Pfeister
- Hamilton Co.

Christian L. Poorman
- Belmont Co.

Andrew C. Robeson
- Darke Co.

Estell H. Rorick
- Fulton Co.

Henry C. Sanford
- Summit Co.

John H. Shearer
- Union Co.

Joseph W. Shinn
- Adams Co.

Matthias A. Smalley
- Wyandot Co.

Lot L. Smith
- Franklin Co.

George B. Spencer
- Wood Co.

Thomas H. Stewart
- Trumbull Co.

John J. Stranahan
- Cuyahoga Co.

John Strecker
- Washington Co.

Samuel M. Taylor
- Champaign Co.

Emmitt Tompkins
- Athens Co.

Franklin R. Vinnedge
- Butler Co.

William E. Watkins
- Allen Co.

William T. Whitacre
- Warren Co.

George W. Wilhelm
- Stark Co.

Byron S. Wydman
- Hamilton Co.

Boston G. Young
- Marion Co.

**Nays: 0**

**Present/Abstained/No Vote: 43**

William W. Beatty
- Logan Co.

William E. Bense
- Ottawa Co.

Charles Bird
- Hamilton Co.

Samuel L. Blue
- Licking Co.

Daniel Boyd
- Madison Co.

Henry Brown
- Hancock Co.

William T. Clark
- Cuyahoga Co.

John H. Fimple
- Carroll Co.

Daniel H. Gaumer
- Muskingum Co.

John P. Haley
- Cuyahoga Co.

James H. Hamilton
- Monroe Co.

John C. Hart
- Hamilton Co.

Elisha B. Hubbard
- Seneca Co.

Wilford C. Hudson
- Clinton Co.

Edward J. Kennedy
- Cuyahoga Co.

Frederick Klensch
- Hamilton Co.

Robert Ogle
- Williams Co.

George C. Rawlins
- Clarke Co.

Philip Schuler
- Crawford Co.

Melville D. Shaw
- Auglaize Co.

Hosmer G. Tryon
- Geauga Co.
- Lake Co.

Capell L. Weems
- Noble Co.

Friend Whittlesey
- Portage Co.

John W. Barger
- Pike Co.

Wickliffe Belville
- Montgomery Co.

Charles W. Clancey
- Jefferson Co.

Joseph P. Coates
- Scioto Co.

William T. Cope
- Columbiana Co.

Wilson S. Harper
- Montgomery Co.

Walter Hartpence
- Hamilton Co.

Leroy S. Holcomb
- Morgan Co.

Charles M. LeBlond
- Mercer Co.

John T. McCray
- Ashland Co.

Walter W. Merrick
- Meigs Co.

Stephen W. Monahan
- Vinton Co.

William H. Reed
- Ross Co.

Alfred Robinson
- Lawrence Co.

Carl H. Buerhaus
- Hocking Co.

Andrew L. Harris
- Preble Co.

Elbert L. Lampson
(Speaker)
- Ashtabula Co.

John B. Lawlor
- Franklin Co.

John Y. Williams
- Columbiana Co.

David I. Worthington
- Fayette Co.

# -Appendix F-

## Poetry & Songs

I have elected to omit the use of [sic] in this appendix of the book, as I have determined it would be needlessly confusing should anybody wish to recite these songs and poems. Odd spellings and phrasing are often necessary to make these kinds of songs and poems work to maintain the rhyming scheme.

"Reservoir Requiem," *Antwerp Argus*, October 13, 1887, 3;
"Reservoir Requiem," *Paulding Democrat*, October 20,
1887, 7.

### Reservoir Requiem
### By Muskrat Mike

I stood on the Reservoir banks to day,
The cold autumn winds were sighing;
No wavelets o'er its bosom did play,
For its last drop of water was drying.

I thought if the days long agone,
When the sea gulls were o'er it flying;
But never upon my mind did it dawn,
How soon Paulding's lake'd lie dying.

I remembered, too, how from its foul slime,
The sweet pond lilies stood growing;
And also how in the lovely spring-time,
Its waters were farms o'erflowing.

I thought how oft through its scum
I had rowed—
Ever fond of frogging and boating—
And how many rafts by mule teams towed,
Adown the canal I'd seen floating.

Then my memory drifted to Dynamite Dick—
How he dropt canned h—l in the feeder;
And said "Paulding's lakelets are too thunderin' thick."
"Confound this old one, we done need 'er!"

Au revoir? Reservoir, little sadly I said.
As I saw the old pond expiring;
Let an elm tree slab be placed at its head,
With an epitaph thus: "Gone Geyering."

"The Reservoir—Present and Future," *Antwerp Argus*, May 3,
1888, 2.

### The Reservoir—Present and Future
### By "Rambling Roland"

From fair Antwerp I turned away,
And down to the reservoir banks did stray;
As I walked upon its rip-rapped shore,
I said to myself: Ah, nevermore!
Will I see thee in such a wretched plight,
Thou loathsome and soul-sickening sight;
Thy bosom's now by miry bogs,
Covered o'er with snags and allmy logs,
While lying around in massive clumps.
Are piles of huge, old shaggy stumps,
Like giant teeth the looked at me,
Extracted from the inland sea—
Emblems all of misery.
No wonder Antwerp folks did "kick"
And cut its banks in spite of "Flick;"
No wonder that much time was spent,
And lobbies to Columbus sent;
No wonder the man of dynamite,
Sallied forth at dead of night,
And freed the world from such a blight.
Then future's veil for me was raised,
And as I o'er the landscape gazed,
Fair farms arouse on every side;
Ditches were out both deep and wide;
The reservoir had been surveyed,
Good roads across it had been made,
Houses and barns did its surface dot,
And each eighty-acre lot,
Had been made a fertile spot.
All honor, then, to the midnight men,
Who have blown its banks time and again;
All honor, too, to John L. Geyer,
Who blew it up a great deal higher.
But "mary" and honor falls on "Flick"—
He's smeared with "arnica" six inches thick.

"Dedicated to the Dynamiters," *Antwerp Argus*, July 12, 1888, 3.

### Dedicated to the Dynamiters
### By Mrs. Naomi H. Osborn

Tune—"Tramp, Tramp, Tramp"

O! the day has come at last,
And we are gathered here en masse,
To celebrate our victory loud and strong,
But we'll grasp you by the hand,
And we'll whisper as we pass—
Hear the dynamiters thunder roll along!

Chorus:
Boom, boom, boom, the Dynamiters,
Let it echo o'er the way—
How we met the foe at night,
And we placed the dynamite,
While the Ohio guards came marching to the fray.

O! we'll ne'er forget the time,
When brave General Axline,
Sent the thrilling word down to our Battery D,
"Take your Gatling gun and go,
To this dreadful scene of woe,
At Antwerp, near this Paulding County sea!

Chorus:
Boom, boom, boom, the Dynamiters
Now, let all contention cease,
With our brothers on the East,
For the cause we fought and struggled for, is won,
And we'll raise our banner high,
With the olive branch of peace,
For Paulding County still keeps marching on.

Chorus:
Boom, boom, boom, the Dynamiters

"Reservoir Song," *Paulding Democrat*, July 12, 1888, 1.

## Reservoir Song
## By "Dynamite Dick"

[Air—Yankee doodle]
"The following was written to be sung at the dynamite
celebration in Antwerp on the Fourth but came too late."

Yankee doodle is the tune,
To sing on this occasion;
Then hearken while we call to mind
The Reservoir invasion.

Chorus:
O Yankee doodle, doodle doo,
It comes so nation handy;
So mind the music "Arnica,"
Whose front name is Andy.

Near Antwerp there is a pond,
Twas once a Wabash feeder;
But for many years 'tis been
Only an ague breeder.

Chorus:
O yankee doodle, darn the pond,
It raised a big commotion;
But dynamiters if they'd try,
Could drain the Arctic ocean.

The people voted Johnny Geyer,
In him they had reliance;
He passed the reservoir bill,
In spite of all Defiance.

Chorus:
O yankee doodle, Bud DeWitt,
Hurrah for John L. Geyer
He's in the Legislature now—
Some day he'll go up higher.

Ol Applegate "he lost his cow,"

And didn't know where to find her.
But barber Lamb he drove her home
With dynamite behind her.

Chorus:
O yankee doodle, praise the cow,
Let's ever idoliz'er;
And if she's ever lost again,
We'll surely advertis'er

On a dark and dreary night,
In April, eighty-seven;
A shock was heard along the line
Which shook both earth and heaven.

Chorus:
O yankee doodle, dynamite,
It made the people wonder;
But on the morrow all did hear,
"The locks are blown to thunder."

Defiance raised a hullabaloo,
And telegrapghed Foraker.
"There's riot at the Reservoir!
For God's sake don't forsake her."

Chorus:
O yankee doodle, Zachary Graves.
Hurrah for Joseph Benson
He did his duty like a man
And kept on office fencin'

Major Bunker soon did come
With a regiment of soldiers,
But all he found for them to fight
Was "skeeters" on their shoulders.

Chorus:
O yankee doodle—Gatling gun,
It killed no dynamiter.
Though Captain Hopkins, we are told,
Was a brave and gallant fighter.
John T. Norris came to town,

But didn't stay till morning.
He cut cross lots to Hicksville
Without a second warning.

Chorus:
O yankee doodle, detective,
A rope was at you pointed.
And had you raised a finger up,
Your neck would been unjointed.

In Antwerp lives a bald head man,
His name is P P Doering.
He says much timber he can use
In making staves and flooring.

Chorus:
O yankee doodle—elm logs.
No more you'll go a floating;
And on the Wabash timber sharks,
No more will go a boating.

Lewis Gay in Antwerp dwells,
He makes the pails for candy.
His song upon the Geyer bill
Was yankee doodle dandy

Chorus:
O yankee doodle—Jacob Saylor,
And also Harry Gordon:
The Wabash spur by dynamite,
Was blown 'way over Jordan.

Here's a health to Uncle Ed.,
The man who runs the paper.
All through the Reservoir War,
He "did the proper caper."

Chorus:
O yankee doodle to the press,
It is a might lever.
Which dynamiters all should praise
Forever and forever.

Let's not forget the Antwerp girls,
To-day they smile so sweetly;
Their lovers helped to blow the locks
And did the job up neatly.

Chorus:
O yankee doodle, doodle doo,
Let everybody shout it;
The old frog pond is "up a spout,"
And all can do without it.

"'Arnica Flick' to the Rescue," *Antwerp Argus*, May 5, 1887, 3.

### "Arnica Flick" to the Rescue

In Antwerp when the sun went down—
All quiet lay our little town;
When through the air came the electric tones,
That chilled our very marrow bones,
Then caused the blood to leap so quick
To hear what came from "Arnica Flick."

And thus the wires wildly rung:
*"Send armed men! A Gatling gun!*
To quell the mob near Antwerp town,
That's blown a hole in our State ground.
"We will, my boy" came the answer quick,
From Governor F to "Arnica Flick."

In Antwerp, long after the sun went down,
All quiet lay our peaceful town,
Brave troops were landing miles below
To hunt the hole the *mob* did blow
"You'd better, boys, your bayonets fix"
Came in whispered tones, from "Arnica Flick."

They fixed and loaded their guns so bright,
Preparing them well for a midnight fight.
With the *rioting mob* 'hark' that awful thud
The dynamiters heaving the mud
*To arms! To arms! Be quick! Be quick!*
In exciting tones, cried "Arnica Flick."

"The water will rush all over our town!
Our dear ones at home will surely be drowned.
Our timber 'the wolf' the awful gloom.
It strikes my heart each dynamite boom.
In the name of the Public Works, be quick!
Groaned aloud the honorable "Arnica Flick."

In the dead of night, they marched along,
To the government bank of the old 'stink pond.'
They saw not, heard not, throughout the long march—
But the basso bull fogs that witted the starch

Of a soldier boy—who muttered "I'm sick."
While the bull frogs echoed—"d—m Flick, d—am Flick."

"No Compromise!," *Antwerp Argus*, May 5, 1887, 5.


**No Compromise!**
**How the Battle-cry of the Lowlanders of Paulding County was
Drowned in "Arnica**

The shades of night were falling fast
When through the streets of Antwerp passed
A gang with banners over head
Which bore the legend dire and dread
"No Compromise."

The townsmen cry "Where do you go,"
"Ye men with measured tread and slow?"
"Can nothing turn you from your course?"
The answer came in accents hoarse.
"No Compromise."

"The reservoir must go" they cry.
"We'll drain it out and run it dry."
"We'll blow it up with dynamite."
"And all resistance put to flight."
"No Compromise."

"Our rage can never be beguiled."
"We'll raise a tempest fierce and wild."
"Whose waves shall roll in billows strong,
until the reservoir is gone."
"No Compromise."

"Fall swift the dire rumor flies
To where Defiance city lies.
Fierce lightning from a cloudless sky,
Would fright them less than that wild cry,
"No Compromise."

Her factory wheels all ease to turn;
Her engine fires all ceased to burn.
Her people crowd into the street,
With white lips whispering as they meet
"No Compromise."

To Flickinger, whose silvery tongue
In matchless speech full oft hath-rung.
The people crowd to ask him, why
The Antwerp people raise the cry,
"No Compromise."

He of the silvery tongue and hair,
This answer made the people there;
The thing which makes Antwerpers fight
The reservoir with dynamite
"Is Arnica."

"Will nothing satisfy their hate?"
"And cause their passions to abate?"
"Will naught this angry gang appease?"
"Will nothing cure that dread disease,
Called Arnica?"

"If I have learned the adage right,
The hair of dogs will cure their bite."
"Since Arnica has raised the row
The proper thing to cure it now,
Is Arnica."

Convention day comes on a pace
And Flickinger will loose the race;
And when that happens, it is said,
He'll hide away and soak his head
"In Arnica."

# -Appendix G-

## Itemized Expenses

The following is an itemized list of expenses incurred by the Ohio National Guard during the Paulding Reservoir Mission.

*Source:* State of Ohio, *Executive Documents: Annual Reports for 1887 Made to the Sixty-Eighth General Assembly*, Part II, 698.

| *Per Diem Expenses* | Amount |
|---|---|
| MAJ Henry S. Bunker, 16th Infantry, Field and Staff............ | $231.89 |
| CPT Jacob M. Weier, Co. A, 16th Infantry............................... | $530.50 |
| CPT James R. Wade, Co. C, 16th Infantry................................ | $486.67 |
| CPT Alpheus R. Rogers, Co. H, 16th Infantry......................... | $492.83 |
| CPT Owen J. Hopkins, Battery D, 1st Light Artillery............ | $301.33 |
| Total | $2,043.22 |

| *Subsistence Expenses* | Amount |
|---|---|
| Oscar B. Chesbrough........................................................ | $133.30 |
| Herman, Swalley & Hogart.............................................. | $69.95 |
| M. N. Utley....................................................................... | $190.37 |
| John White........................................................................ | $30.80 |
| Board of Public Works..................................................... | $100.00 |
| Edward W. Rydman.......................................................... | $28.88 |
| Antwerp Hub & Spoke Company.................................... | $5.50 |
| John Dallas....................................................................... | $22.00 |
| Henry Sterling.................................................................. | $14.00 |
| W. M. Cullison.................................................................. | $26.90 |
| Total | $621.70 |

| Transportation Expenses | Amount |
|---|---|
| Wabash Railway | $261.95 |
| MAJ Henry S. Bunker | $9.01 |
| Paulding Furnace and Farm | $10.50 |
| Albert Johnson | $1.50 |
| George McCormick | $3.00 |
| Henry F. Wiswell | $80.75 |
| Albert Hutchins | $28.75 |
| Toledo Transfer Company | $9.87 |
| Total | $405.33 |

| Recapitulation | Amount |
|---|---|
| *Per Diem* | $2,043.22 |
| Subsistence | $621.70 |
| Transportation | $405.33 |
| Grand Total | $3,070.25 |

# -Bibliography-

## Primary Sources:

Ancestry.com. *1870 United States Federal Census.* [database on-line]. Provo, UT, USA: Ancestry.com Operations, Inc., 2009. Images reproduced by FamilySearch.

Ancestry.com. *1880 United States Federal Census* [database on-line]. Lehi, UT, USA: Ancestry.com Operations Inc, 2010.

Ancestry.com. *1900 United States Federal Census.* [database online]. Provo, UT, USA: Ancestry.com Operations, Inc., 2004.

Ancestry.com. *Ohio, U.S., County Marriage Records, 1774-1993.* [database on-line]. Lehi, UT, USA: Ancestry.com Operations, Inc., 2016.

Ancestry.com. *Toledo, OH City Directories for 1875, 1876, 1877, 1886, and 1887.* [database online]. Lehi, UT, USA: Ancestry.com Operations, Inc., 2011.

Andrew J. Stenger: Treasurer vs. Solomon S. Stambaugh. July 1, 1886. No. 3693. Doc. 7. Page 217. Paulding County, Ohio Court of Common Pleas. Paulding County, Ohio Clerk's Office Archive.

*Antwerp Argus* (Antwerp, Ohio) Newspaper Collection. Online Newspaper Archive of the Paulding County Carnegie Library, Advantage Archives. http://paulding.advantage-preservation.com/

*Antwerp Gazette* (Antwerp, Ohio) Newspaper Collection. Online Newspaper Archive of the Paulding County Carnegie Library, Advantage Archives. http://paulding.advantage-preservation.com/

*Bar Harbor Record*, (Bar Harbor, Maine) Newspaper Collection. NewspaperARCHIVE.com. *https://newspaperarchive.com/browse/us/me/bar-harbor/bar-harbor-record/.*

Barrel Builders, Inc., *Barrel Maintenance and Repair Manual.* St. Helena: Barrel Builders, Inc., 1995. https://barrelbuilders.com/wp-content/uploads/2015/02/Barrel-Maintenance-Repair-Manual.pdf.

*Biddeford Daily Journal*, (Biddeford, Maine) Newspaper Collection. NewspaperARCHIVE.com. https://newspaperarchive.com/browse/us/me/biddeford/biddeford-daily-journal/.

Budd, Everett A. "Personal Sketches." In *Historical Atlas of Paulding County, Ohio, 1892*, compiled by O. Morrow and F.W. Bashore. Dallas: Taylor Publishing Company, 1978.

Center for Disease Control and Prevention. *Malaria.* Accessed March 17, 2022. https://www.cdc.gov/parasites/malaria/index.html.

*Cincinnati Commercial* (Cincinnati, Ohio) Newspaper Collection. NewspaperARCHIVE.com. https://newspaperarchive.com/browse/us/oh/cincinnati/cincinnati-commercial/.

*Cincinnati Commercial Gazette* (Cincinnati, Ohio) Newspaper Collection. NewspaperARCHIVE.com. https://newspaperarchive.com/browse/us/oh/cincinnati/cincinnati-commercial-gazette/.

*Cincinnati Enquirer* (Cincinnati, Ohio) Newspaper Collection. Newspapers.com. https://www.newspapers.com/paper/the-cincinnati-enquirer/844/?id=844&title=the-cincinnati-enquirer.

*Cincinnati Weekly Enquirer* (Cincinnati, Ohio) Newspaper Collection. NewspaperARCHIVE.com. https://newspaperarchive.com/browse/us/oh/cincinnati/cincinnati-weekly-enquirer/.

*Daily Exchange* (Baltimore, Maryland) Newspaper Collection. Chronicling America: Historic American Newspapers, Library of Congress. https://chroniclingamerica.loc.gov/lccn/sn83009573/.

*Daily Reflector* (Norwalk, Ohio) Newspaper Collection. NewspaperARCHIVE.com. https://newspaperarchive.com/browse/us/oh/norwalk/norwalk-daily-reflector/.

*Defiance County Express* (Defiance, Ohio) Newspaper Collection. NewspaperARCHIVE.com. https://newspaperarchive.com/browse/us/oh/defiance/defiance-county-express/.

*Defiance County Republican and Express* (Defiance, Ohio) Newspaper Collection. NewspaperARCHIVE.com. *https://newspaperarchive.com/browse/us/oh/defiance/defiance-county-republican-and-express/*.

*Defiance Democrat* (Defiance, Ohio) Newspaper Collection. NewspaperARCHIVE.com. https://newspaperarchive.com/browse/us/oh/defiance/defiance-democrat/.

*Delphos Weekly Herald* (Delphos, Ohio) Newspaper Collection. NewspaperARCHIVE.com. https://newspaperarchive.com/search/location/us/oh/delphos/delphos-weekly-herald/.

*Democratic Northwest and Henry County News* (Napoleon, Ohio) Newspaper Collection. NewspaperARCHIVE.com. https://newspaperarchive.com/browse/us/oh/napoleon/democratic-northwest-and-henry-county-news/.

*Dixon Evening Telegraph* (Dixon, Illinois) Newspaper Collection. NewspaperARCHIVE.com. https://newspaperarchive.com/browse/us/il/dixon/dixon-evening-telegraph/.

Ehrhart, Otto E. *Memories*. Unknown Date. Transcribed by Kim K. Sutton.

*Evening Review* (East Liverpool, Ohio) Newspaper Collection. NewspaperARCHIVE.com. https://newspaperarchive.com/search/location/us/oh/east-liverpool/east-liverpool-evening-review/.

*Fort Wayne Gazette* (Fort Wayne, Indiana) Newspaper Collection. NewspaperARCHIVE.com. https://newspaperarchive.com/browse/us/in/fort-wayne/fort-wayne-gazette/.

*Fort Wayne Journal Gazette* (Fort Wayne, Indiana) Newspaper Collection. NewspaperARCHIVE.com. https://newspaperarchive.com/search/location/us/in/fort-wayne/fort-wayne-journal-gazette/.

*Fort Wayne Sentinel* (Fort Wayne, Indiana) Newspaper Collection. NewspaperARCHIVE.com. https://newspaperarchive.com/browse/us/in/fort-wayne/fort-wayne-sentinel/.

*Fort Wayne Weekly Sentinel* (Fort Wayne, Indiana) Newspaper Collection. NewspaperARCHIVE.com. https://newspaperarchive.com/browse/us/in/fort-wayne/fort-wayne-weekly-sentinel/.

Hardesty, William S. *Representative Citizens of Paulding County.* Toledo: Self-published, 1902.

Hopkins, Owen J. *Gatling Gun Tactics – Revised Edition.* Self-Published, 1888.

Information courtesy of Ohio National Guard Historian SFC Joshua D. Mann. Contained within the Ohio National Guard's *Quartermaster General Report for the Year Ending November 15, 1887,* and *The Report of the Regular Army Advisor*'s inspection of the 16th Regiment in August 1887.

*Joplin Morning Tribune* (Joplin, Missouri) Newspaper Collection. NewspaperARCHIVE.com. https://newspaperarchive.com/search/location/us/mo/joplin/joplin-morning-tribune/.

Little, John. *Biennial Report of the Attorney General to the Governor of the State of Ohio, for the Years 1874-1875.* Columbus: Nevins & Myers, Book and Job Printers, 1876.

*Logansport Pharos Tribune* (Logansport, Indiana) Newspaper Collection. NewspaperARCHIVE.com. https://newspaperarchive.com/browse/us/in/logansport/logansport-pharos-tribune/.

*Los Angeles Daily Herald* (Los Angeles, California) Newspaper Collection. NewspaperARCHIVE.com. https://newspaperarchive.com/browse/us/ca/los-angeles/los-angeles-daily-herald/.

*Maysville Daily Evening Bulletin* (Maysville, Kentucky) Newspaper Collection. NewspaperARCHIVE.com. https://newspaperarchive.com/browse/us/ky/maysville/maysville-daily-evening-bulletin/.

"Michigan, County Births, 1867-1917: Fred Reeves." Database with images. *FamilySearch.* Accessed August 29, 2022. Fred Reeves, April 8, 1869. Citing Birth. Various county courts. Michigan. https://www.familysearch.org/ark:/61903/1:1:QPWQ-67VR.

*New York Tribune* (New York, New York) Newspaper Collection. NewspaperARCHIVE.com. https://newspaperarchive.com/browse/us/ny/new-york/new-york-tribune/.

Ohio Adjutant General's Office. *Annual Report of the Adjutant General to the Governor of the State of Ohio for the Year 1888.* Columbus: The Westbote Company, 1889.

Ohio Adjutant General's Office. *Roster of Soldiers of the Ohio National Guard, 1847-1917; 16th & 6th Regiments Books 1-3 1880-1904.* Columbus: Ohio Adjutant General's Office. https://www.familysearch.org/search/film/008512724?cat=327213.

"Ohio, County Death Records, 1840-2001: Fred Reeves." Database with images. *FamilySearch.* Accessed August 29, 2022. Lucas. Death records, 1868-1888. https://www.familysearch.org/ark:/61903/1:1:F62G-DZW.

Ohio National Guard. *History of the Ohio National Guard and Ohio Volunteers.* Cleveland: Plain Dealer Publishing Co., 1901. https://www.genealogycenter.info/military/spanishamerican/search_ohionationalguard.php.

*Paulding County Gazette* (Paulding, Ohio) Newspaper Collection. Online Newspaper Archive of the Paulding County Carnegie Library, Advantage Archives. http://paulding.advantage-preservation.com/

*Paulding County Republican* (Paulding, Ohio) Newspaper Collection. Online Newspaper Archive of the Paulding County Carnegie Library, Advantage Archives. http://paulding.advantage-preservation.com/

*Paulding Democrat* (Paulding, Ohio) Newspaper Collection. Online Newspaper Archive of the Paulding County Carnegie Library. Advantage Archives. http://paulding.advantage-preservation.com/

Poor, Henry Varnum. *Manual of the Railroads of the United States: 1882.* Volume 15. H. V. and H. W. Poor Co., 1882.

*Portland Daily Press* (Portland, Maine) Newspaper Collection. NewspaperARCHIVE.com. *https://newspaperarchive.com/browse/us/me/portland/portland-daily-press/.*

*Quincy Daily Journal* (Quincy, Illinois) Newspaper Collection. NewspaperARCHIVE.com. https://newspaperarchive.com/browse/us/il/quincy/quincy-daily-journal/.

Stambaugh vs. Herznig et al. Filed December 21, 1874. Case number 1050. Paulding County, Ohio Court of Common Pleas. Paulding County, Ohio Clerk's Office Archive.

Stambaugh vs. Herznig et al. Answer of the Lessees of the Public Works, filed February 4, 1875. Case number 1050. Paulding County, Ohio Court of Common Pleas. Paulding County, Ohio Clerk's Office Archive.

State of Ohio. *Acts of a General Nature, Passed by the Thirty-Seventh General Assembly of Ohio*, Volume XXXVII. Columbus: Samuel Medary, 1839.

State of Ohio. *Annual Report of the Auditor to the Governor of the State of Ohio for the Fiscal Year Ending November 15, 1888.* Columbus: The Westbote Company, 1889.

State of Ohio. *Annual Reports, Made to the Governor of the State of Ohio for the Year 1859.* Part I. Columbus: Richard Nevins, 1860.

State of Ohio. *Executive Documents: Annual Reports for 1877, Made to the Sixty-Third General Assembly of the State of Ohio.* Part II. Columbus: Nevins & Myers, 1878.

State of Ohio. *Executive Documents: Annual Reports for 1886 Made to the 67th General Assembly of the State of Ohio.* Part II. Columbus: The Westbote Company, 1887.

State of Ohio. *Executive Documents: Annual Reports for 1887 Made to the Sixty-Eighth General Assembly*, Part I, Columbus: Myers Brothers, 1888.

State of Ohio. *Executive Documents: Annual Reports for 1887 Made to the Sixty-Eighth General Assembly*, Part II, Columbus: The Westbote Co., 1888.

State of Ohio. *Executive Documents: Annual Reports for 1888, Made to the Sixty-Eighth General Assembly of the State of Ohio*, Part II. Columbus: The Westbote Company, 1889.

State of Ohio. *General and Local Laws, and Joint Resolutions, Passed by the Fifty-Ninth General Assembly.* Volume LXVII. Columbus: L. D. Myers & Bro., 1870.

State of Ohio. *General and Local Acts Passed and Joint Resolutions Adopted by the Seventy-Fifth General Assembly.* Volume XCV. Columbus: Fred J. Heer, 1902.

State of Ohio. *General and Local Acts Passed, and Joint Resolutions Adopted by the Sixty-Eighth General Assembly.* Volume LXXXV. Columbus: The Columbian Printing, Co., 1888.

State of Ohio. *General and Local Acts Passed and Joint Resolutions Adopted by the Sixty-Eighth General Assembly.* Volume LXXXVI. Columbus: The Westbote Company, 1889.

State of Ohio. *Journal of the House of Representatives of the State of Ohio, for the Adjourned Session of the Fifty-Seventh General Assembly.* Volume LXIII. Columbus: L. D. Myers & Bro., 1867.

State of Ohio. *Journal of the House of Representatives of the State of Ohio, for the Adjourned Session of the Sixty-Fifth General Assembly.* Volume LXXVIII. Sandusky: Layman Brothers, 1882.

State of Ohio. *Journal of the House of Representatives of the State of Ohio, for the Adjourned Session of the Sixty-Seventh General Assembly.* Volume LXXXIII. Columbus: Columbian Printing Company, 1887.

State of Ohio. *Journal of the House of Representatives of the State of Ohio for the Regular Session of the Fifty-Ninth General Assembly.* Volume LXVI. Columbus: Columbus Printing Company, 1870.

State of Ohio. *Journal of the House of Representatives of the State of Ohio, for the Regular Session of the Sixty-Eighth General Assembly.* Volume LXXXIV. Columbus: Columbian Printing Company, 1888.

State of Ohio. *Journal of the House of Representatives of the State of Ohio, for the Regular Session of the Sixty-Seventh General Assembly.* Volume LXXXII. Columbus: The Westbote Company, 1886.

State of Ohio. *Journal of the Senate of the State of Ohio, for the Adjourned Session of the Fifty-Seventh General Assembly.* Volume LXIII. Columbus: L. D. Myers & Bro., 1867.

State of Ohio. *Journal of the Senate of the State of Ohio, for the Adjourned Session of the Sixty-Seventh General Assembly.* Volume LXXXIII. Columbus: Columbian Printing Company, 1887.

State of Ohio. *Journal of the Senate of the State of Ohio, for the Regular Session of the Sixty-Eighth General Assembly.* Volume LXXXIV. Columbus: Columbian Printing Company, 1888.

State of Ohio. *Message and Reports Made to the General Assembly and Governor of the State of Ohio for the Year 1858.* Part II. Columbus: Richard Nevins, 1859.

State of Ohio. *Sixth Annual Report of the Board of Public Works, of the State of Ohio, to the Forty-First General Assembly.* Columbus: Samuel Medary, 1843.

State of Ohio. The *Revised Statutes of the State of Ohio.* Edited by James M. Williams. Volume III. Cincinnati: The Wrightson Printing Co., 1887.

*The Bay of San Francisco: The Metropolis of the Pacific Coast and its Suburban Cities: A History.* Volume I. Chicago: The Lewis Publishing Company. 1892.

U.S. Census Bureau. *1840 Census: Compendium of the Enumeration of the Inhabitants and Statistics of the United States.* Ohio.
https://www.census.gov/library/publications/1841/dec/1840c.html.

U.S. Census Bureau. *1880 Census: Population of Each State and Territory by Counties, in the Aggregate, at the Censuses.* Table II. Ohio.
https://www.census.gov/library/publications/1883/dec/vol-01-population.html.

U.S. Census Bureau. *1890 Census: Report on Population of the United States.* Minor Civil Divisions - Table 5. Ohio.
https://www.census.gov/library/publications/1895/dec/volume-1.html.

U.S. Department of the Interior. United States of America Bureau of Land Management. General Land Office Records: BLM Certificate 210117, 210118, and 210119. November 20, 1874.

*Xenia Daily Gazette* (Xenia, Ohio) Newspaper Collection. NewspaperARCHIVE.com.
https://newspaperarchive.com/search/location/us/oh/xenia/ohio-xenia-daily-gazette/.

## Secondary Sources:

Allen County Public Library, *Canal Celebrations in Old Fort Wayne*, Fort Wayne: Allen County Public Library, 1953.

*Antwerp Bee-Argus* (Antwerp, Ohio) Newspaper Collection. Online Newspaper Archive of the Paulding County Carnegie Library, Advantage Archives. http://paulding.advantage-preservation.com/

Beatty, John D. and Delia C. Bourne. "Maumee Township & Woodburn." In *History of Fort Wayne & Allen County, Indiana*, Volume I, edited by John D. Beatty. Evansville: M.T. Publishing Company, Inc., 2006.

Baldwin, Peter C. "How Night Air Became Good Air," in *Environmental History*. Volume 8. No. 3. July 2003. https://www.jstor.org/stable/3986202.

Budd, Everett A. "Brief History of Paulding County, Ohio." In *Historical Atlas of Paulding County, Ohio, 1892*, compiled by O. Morrow and F.W. Bashore. Dallas: Taylor Publishing Company, 1978.

Carillon Historical Park. *The Miami & Erie Canal: Symbol of an Era*. unknown date of publication, possibly 1950s or 1960s.

Castaldi, Thomas E. "The Wabash & Erie Canal." In *History of Fort Wayne & Allen County, Indiana*, Volume I, edited by John D. Beatty. Evansville: M.T. Publishing Company, Inc., 2006.

Celley, Albert F. and Daniel F. Perch. "The Junction of Two Historic Waterways in the Early History of Ohio and Indiana." In *Towpaths: A Collection of Articles from the Quarterly Publication of the Canal Society of Ohio*, edited by Boone Triplett and Bill Oeters, 257-260. Akron: Canal Society of Ohio, 2011.

City of Fort Wayne Parks & Recreation. "Swinney Park." Accessed August 11, 2022. https://www.fortwayneparks.org/parks/38-parks/park-page-links/186-swinney-park.html.

*CPI Inflation Calculator*. All inflation conversions were done using https://www.in2013dollars.com/us/inflation.

Dyer, Frederick H. *A Compendium of the War of the Rebellion*. Des Moines: The Dyer Publishing Company, 1908.

Ehrhart, Otto E. and Dale L. Ehrhart. *A Century of Progress: Antwerp, Ohio, Souvenir Edition, 1841-1941*. Antwerp: Antwerp Bee-Argus, 1941.

Faber, Don. *The Toledo War: The First Michigan-Ohio Rivalry.* Ann Arbor: The University of Michigan Press, 2008.

Fatout, Paul. *Indiana Canals.* West Lafayette: Purdue University Press, 1985.

Find a Grave. "Charles W Boland." Accessed March 29, 2023. https://www.findagrave.com/memorial/67284679/charles-w-boland.

Find a Grave. "Clayton Everett DeWit." Accessed October 28, 2022. https://www.findagrave.com/memorial/139529720/clayton-everett-dewit.

Find a Grave. "Francis Joseph 'Frank' Zuber." Accessed March 31, 2023. https://www.findagrave.com/memorial/60208532/francis-joseph-zuber.

Find a Grave. "Fred Reeves." Accessed March 13, 2022. https://www.findagrave.com/memorial/208663218/fred-reeves.

Find a Grave. "Jesse Hinkle Bond." Accessed March 31, 2023. https://www.findagrave.com/memorial/150233103/jesse-hinkle-bond.

Find a Grave. "Pvt William F Fleck." Accessed March 29, 2023. https://www.findagrave.com/memorial/37924166/william-f-fleck.

Grant, H. Roger. *"Follow the Flag": A History of the Wabash Railroad Company.* Ithaca: Northern Illinois University Press, 2019.

Hampton, Taylor. *The Nickel Plate Road: The History of a Great Railroad.* Cleveland: The World Publishing Company, 1947.

Hardesty, William S. *Representative Citizens of Paulding County.* Toledo: Self-published, 1902.

Harlow, Alvin F. *Old Towpaths: The Story of the American Canal Era.* Washington: Westphalia Press, 2014.

*History of Allen County, Indiana, 1880.* Evansville: Unigraphic, Inc., 1972.

*History of Crane Township Paulding County.* Unknown publisher. 1941. Located in the Crane Township folder at the John Paulding Historical Society, Paulding, Ohio.

*Home Community U. S. A.: Woodburn, Indiana.* Berne: Berne Witness Company, 1955.

Howe, Henry. *Historical Collections of Ohio in Three Volumes, Volume II.* Columbus: Henry Howe & Son, 1891.

Howe, Henry. *Historical Collections of Ohio in Three Volumes, Volume III.* Columbus: Henry Howe & Son, 1891.

Jordan, Stan. "O.S. Applegate 1844 to 1910." *West Bend News,* December 28, 2016.

Krick, Melinda. "Timber Era Brought Workers, Growth, Wealth." *The West Bend News* (Antwerp). July 06, 2020. https://www.westbendnews.net/autonews/2020/07/06/timber-era-brought-workers-growth-wealth/.

Merriam-Webster. "hereinafter." Accessed March 17, 2022. https://www.merriam-webster.com/dictionary/hereinafter.

Oeters, Bill and Nancy Gulick. *Images of America: Miami and Erie Canal.* Charleston: Arcadia Publishing, 2014.

Oeters, Bill, et al. *Taming the Swamp.* Canal Societies of Ohio and Indiana, 2011.

Ohio Ghost Town Exploration Co. "Tate's Landing (Reids) (Sharp's Lock) — Emerald Township, Paulding County." Accessed August 11, 2022. https://ohioghosttowns.org/paulding-county/.

Ohio Historic Preservation Office. *Ohio Historic Inventory: Pau-114-2 (Mackinaw House).* Prepared in November 1979.

Ohio Historic Preservation Office. *Ohio Historic Inventory: Pau-116-2 (Cecil Town Hall).* Prepared in November 1979.

*Ohio Railroad Stations Past & Present.* "Defiance County." https://www.west2k.com/ohpix/defiancebandoold.jpg.

*Ohio Railroad Stations Past & Present.* "Paulding County." https://www.west2k.com/ohpix/cecil.jpg.

*Payne Reflector and Press Review* Newspaper Collection. Online Newspaper Archive of the Paulding County Carnegie Library. Advantage Archives. http://paulding.advantage-preservation.com/

Poinsatte, Charles R. *Fort Wayne During the Canal Era, 1828-1855: A Study of a Western Community in the Middle Period of American History.* Indiana Historical Bureau, 1969.

Roebuck, Mary E. *Genealogy of the Chapman Family.* Fort Wayne: self-published, 1947.

Scheiber, Harry N. *Ohio Canal Era: A Case Study of Government and the Economy, 1820-1861.* Athens: Ohio University Press, 2012.

Schmidt, Carolyn I., et al. *Canalabration.* Fort Wayne: Canal Society of Indiana, 2002.

Schmidt, Carolyn I., et al. *Gateway to the East.* Fort Wayne: Canal Society of Indiana, 2006.

Scribner, Harvey. *Memoirs of Lucas County and the City of Toledo*. Volume II. Madison: Western Historical Association, 1910.

Shah, Sonia. *The Fever: How Malaria Has Ruled Humankind for 500,000 Years*. New York: Picador, 2010.

Slocum, Charles E. *The History of the Maumee River Basin from the Earliest Account to Its Organization into Counties*. Defiance: Self-published. 1905.

Smith, Joseph P. *History of the Republican Party in Ohio*. Volume I. Chicago: The Lewis Publishing Company, 1898.

Sutton, Kim. "Railroads & their forgotten towns: Cincinnati Northern." *Paulding Progress*. May 15, 2020. https://progressnewspaper.org/Content/Social/Social/Article/Railroads-their-forgotten-towns-Cincinnati-Northern/-2/-2/200728.

"Tour Directions to Old Six Mile Reservoir." Document Found Within Wabash-Erie Canal — Antwerp Folder. Folder Found within Box File 0031 / Contents: Canal History at the John Paulding Historical Society, Paulding, Ohio.

Unrau, Harlan D. *Historic Resource Study: Chesapeake & Ohio Canal*. Hagerstown: National Park Service, 2007. https://www.nps.gov/parkhistory/online_books/choh/unrau_hrs.pdf.

"The Wabash & Erie Canal." In *Towpaths: A Collection of Articles from the Quarterly Publication of the Canal Society of Ohio*, edited by Boone Triplett and Bill Oeters, 59-60. Akron: Canal Society of Ohio, 2011.

Winter, Nevin O. *A History of Northwest Ohio*. Chicago: The Lewis Publishing Company, 1917.

*Woodburn Centennial – July 7, 8, 9, 10 – Woodburn, Indiana 1865-1965*. Unknown Publisher, 1965.

Yenser, Dorothy M. and Peter Wilhelm. *The "Junction" of the Canals*, 1988. Collection of the John Paulding County Historical Society. Located in Box File 0031 / Contents: Canal History.

## Maps:

*Map of Paulding County, Ohio*. Drawn and Compiled by W. A. Strong. Paulding, Ohio. 1878. https://pauldingcountyengineer.com/wp-content/uploads/2019/03/COUNTY-MAP.pdf.

Maumee Township Ditch Map, 1870s, Allen Co. Collection of the Allen County Genealogical Society of Indiana. https://www.acgsi.org/maps/maumee.1870s.pdf.

Maumee Township Plat Map. 1880s. Allen Co. Collection of the Allen County Genealogical Society of Indiana. https://www.acgsi.org/maps/maumee.1878.pdf.

Morrow, O. and F.W. Bashore. *Historical Atlas of Paulding County, Ohio, 1892*. Dallas: Taylor Publishing Company, 1978.

*Profile and Map of the Miami & Erie Canal Showing Progress and Cost of Improvements*. Drafted by A. H. Sawyer and Compiled under the direction of Charles E. Perkins. Original restored and reproduced by the Miami & Erie Canal Corridor Association. A copy is located at the John Paulding Historical Society, Paulding, Ohio. Tube titled: *Map of Miami & Erie Canal-1907-1909 Progress of Improvements*. Catalog Number: 2015-21-4.

*Profile of the Wabash & Erie Canal*. Drawn by Thomas Meek with assistance from Julia Meek. From the collection of the author, but a copy of the map can generally be acquired from the Canal Society of Indiana upon request or after becoming a member. A copy is also located at the John Paulding Historical Society, Paulding, Ohio.

*Sanborn Fire Insurance Map from Antwerp, Paulding County, Ohio*. Sanborn Map Company, August 1893. Map. https://www.loc.gov/item/sanborn06582_001/.

*Sanborn Fire Insurance Map from Defiance, Defiance County, Ohio*. Sanborn Map Company, August 1888. Map. https://www.loc.gov/item/sanborn06673_002/.

*Sanborn Fire Insurance Map from Defiance, Defiance County, Ohio*. Sanborn Map Company, December 1899. Map. https://www.loc.gov/item/sanborn06673_004/.

*Sanborn Fire Insurance Map from Paulding, Paulding County, Ohio*. Sanborn Map Company, June 1895. Map. https://www.loc.gov/item/sanborn06853_002/.

# -Index-

Made in the USA
Columbia, SC
18 May 2024

a284ed33-de39-4446-82a3-084357bf106dR01